W9-CHI-511

# The
# Bible
# Tour Guide

## A 365 Day
## Spiritual Journey

# The Bible

## Tour Guide

### A 365 Day
### Spiritual Journey

by
Rev. Kevin C. Rudolph

## Rich Publishing Co.
10611 Creektree * Houston, Texas 77070

To my parents,
who taught me about God's unconditional love
and grace before I was old enough to say the words,
and to my children, Amanda and Daniel, whom I
hope learn the same lesson from their parents.

© Copyright 1991 by
Reverend Kevin C. Rudolph

All rights reserved. No part of this book may be reproduced in any
form or by any means without permission from the author, except for
brief quotations embodied in critical articles or reviews. For further
information write to Reverend Kevin C. Rudolph, 11914 Fawnview,
Houston, Texas 77070.

First Edition 1991
Second Printing 1994
Third Printing 1998

Library of Congress Card No. 94 - 66386
ISBN 0- 927577-01-1
Printed in the United States of America

The Scripture quotations in this publication are from the Revised
Standard Version Bible, copyright 1946, 1952, and © 1971 by the
Division of Chrisitan Education, National Council of the Churches of
Christ in the U.S.A., and used by permission.

# CONTENTS

V

# Acknowledgements

No work of this kind can come into being without the help and support of many people to whom I owe a great deal of gratitude.

Thanks to Rev. W. Jack Noble for all his support in letting me, as one of his staff members, take on this project and involve members of his congregation!

Thanks to the members of Canyon Creek Presbyterian Church, Richardson, Texas, who allowed me the grace to write this devotional. And a special thanks to those 50 brave souls who went through the Bible with me that first time, enduring all the flaws of a first manuscript which was never more than two weeks ahead of the due date!

Thanks to the congregation at Windwood Presbyterian Church, Cypress, Texas, and especially Dobby Dobson, without whose support, this book would not have been published.

Thanks to my loving wife, Robyn, who allowed me to ruin two vacations (and many nights sleep) to get this ready for print.

And finally, thanks to Vicki Olson, who prayed harder for this book to be published than anyone else, because she printed, cut, collated, and hole punched the first 150 copies herself off of a photocopy machine!

# Preface

Welcome to *The Bible Tour Guide*. This book was designed to get you through the whole Bible in one year, reading three or four chapters a day. It was my intention that you read the Scripture first before reading the *Guides*. I think it would be much better to read the passages first with an open mind. The *Guides* are not intended to be a commentary on the Bible. They will be full of comments about the Scripture readings for the day, but it will only be those things which struck me about those chapters. I will not be attempting to deal with all of the material, and much will be left out. As with all guides, there will be things upon which I focus that may not be the most important to you. One of the greatest things about the Bible is that it is so profound that it can be studied for a lifetime without exhausting its resources.

What I hope this book will provide, is some help to make the Scriptures come alive for you. The Bible is God's Word to everyone, but it is specifically, God's word to you. I hope that these guides will help you develop the sense that God is speaking to you today, not just telling us about things in the past.

With that in mind, I would recommend that you begin your time of reading with prayer. Ask God specifically, to speak to you through His Word. Don't always expect it to be earth shattering. If He shattered our "earths" every day, we would go nuts in a month! Feeding on God's word, like eating, changes us more gradually then suddenly. Ask God to give you the insight you need today - that's really what the "daily bread" is that Jesus tells us to ask for in the Lord's prayer.

One short note on versions of the Bible. I will be reading and quoting from the Revised Standard Version. It is the one I grew up with and feels most comfortable to me. When people ask me which is the best translation, I tell them, the one they will read! The Bible is the most widely sold and least read of all books in history! You are about to make that different for yourself. Choose a Bible that you like and with which you are comfortable. After you read through the whole thing, it will be the one you know best! All of the versions currently available are sincere attempts to translate properly. The differences will not be important for our task. We want to see an overview of the whole forest. We will not be noticing a handful of different leaves on one or two trees!

My hope is that this guide will be at least half as much help for you to read as it has been for me to write, and half as much fun! If so, it will have served its purpose. Enjoy your journey!

# Old Testament Structure

| 5 Books of the Law | 12 Books of History | 5 Books of Poetry |
|---|---|---|
| Genesis<br>Exodus<br>Leviticus<br>Numbers<br>Deuteronomy | Joshua<br>Judges<br>Ruth<br>I Samuel<br>II Samuel<br>I Kings<br>II Kings<br>I Chronicles<br>II Chronicles<br>Ezra<br>Nehemiah<br>Esther | Job<br>Psalms<br>Proverbs<br>Ecclesiastes<br>Song of Solomon |

## Salvation History

| The Beginnings | The Patriarchs | Israel Becomes A Nation | Israel Enters The Land |
|---|---|---|---|
| Creation<br>Fall<br>Flood<br>Tower of Babel | Abraham<br>Isaac<br>Jacob<br>Joseph | Moses<br>Exodus<br>The Law<br>The Wanderings | Joshua<br>Judges<br>Samuel |
| | 2000 | 1500 | 1400 |
| Genesis | Genesis<br>Job | Exodus<br>Leviticus<br>Numbers<br>Deuteronomy | Joshua<br>Judges<br>Ruth<br>I Samuel |

All Dates
Approximations

# Old Testament Structure

| 5<br>Major Prophets | 12<br>Minor Prophets |
|---|---|
| Isaiah<br>Jeremiah<br>Lamentations<br>Ezekiel<br>Daniel | Hosea<br>Joel<br>Amos<br>Obadiah<br>Jonah<br>Micah<br>Nahum<br>Habakkuk<br>Zephaniah<br>Haggai<br>Zechariah<br>Malachi |

## Old Testament Timeline

| The United Kingdom | The Divided Kingdom | The Exile | The Return |
|---|---|---|---|
| Saul<br>David<br>Solomon | Israel - 10 tribes<br>    of the North<br>Judah - 2 tribes<br>    of the South | Ezekiel<br>Daniel | Ezra<br>Nehemiah<br>Esther |

| 1000 | 931 | 722 | 586 | 536 | 400 |
|---|---|---|---|---|---|

| I Samuel<br>II Samuel<br>I Kings<br>I Chronicles<br>II Chronicles<br><br>Psalms<br>Proverbs<br>Ecclesiastes<br>Song of Solomon | I Kings<br>II Kings<br>II Chronicles<br><br>Israel -<br>    Jonah<br>    Amos<br>    Hosea<br><br>Judah -<br>    Obadiah<br>    Joel<br>    Isaiah<br>    Micah<br>    Jeremiah<br>    Nahum<br>    Zephaniah<br>    Habakkuk | Ezekiel<br>Daniel<br>Lamentations | Ezra<br>Nehemiah<br>Esther<br><br>Haggai<br>Zechariah<br>Malachi |

IX

# New Testament Structure

| 4<br>**Gospels** | 1<br>**History** | 13<br>**Pauline Epistles** |
|---|---|---|
| Matthew<br>Mark<br>Luke<br>John | Acts | Romans     Philemon<br>I Corinthians<br>II Corinthians<br>Galatians<br>Ephesians<br>Philippians<br>Colossians<br>I Thessalonians<br>II Thessalonians<br>I Timothy<br>II Timothy<br>Titus |

## Salvation History

| **Intertestamental<br>Period** | **First Coming of<br>the Messiah** | **The Birth of<br>the Church** |
|---|---|---|
| 400 years no prophet<br>The Maccabees<br>The Pharisees<br>    and Sadduccees | John the Baptist<br>Jesus the Christ<br>His Ministry, Death,<br>    and Resurrection | Pentecost<br>The acts of the<br>    Apostles<br>Peter and the 12 |

400 B.C. ——————— A.D. ——————— 35 ——————————▶

| * Apocrypha<br>    (Means "of<br>    doubtful origin") | Matthew<br>Mark<br>Luke<br>John | Acts |
|---|---|---|

*Not in Protestant
  Bibles

X

# New Testament Structure

| 8<br>**Other Epistles** | 1<br>**Apocalypse** |
|---|---|
| Hebrews<br>James<br>I Peter<br>II Peter<br>I John<br>II John<br>III John<br>Jude | Revelation |

# New Testament Timeline

| The Expansion<br>of the Church | | The Second Coming<br>of the Messiah | The Age<br>to Come |
|---|---|---|---|
| Stephen<br>Saul/Paul<br>The Missionary Journeys<br>The Letters | | Revelation<br>Judgement and<br>Eternity<br>The City of God | The End of the<br>Beginning and<br>the Beginning of<br>Something New! |

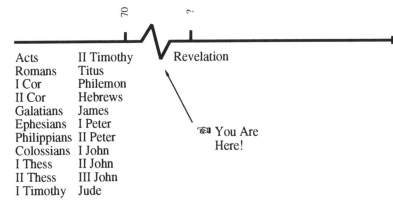

| | |
|---|---|
| Acts | II Timothy |
| Romans | Titus |
| I Cor | Philemon |
| II Cor | Hebrews |
| Galatians | James |
| Ephesians | I Peter |
| Philippians | II Peter |
| Colossians | I John |
| I Thess | II John |
| II Thess | III John |
| I Timothy | Jude |

Revelation

☞ You Are Here!

# Six Major Biblical Covenants

**Definitions - Covenant vs Contract**
**Contract** - Your performance is based on the performance of the other person in the contract. If they do not perform their end, you are not bound to perform yours.
**Covenant** - Your performance is based on your character, your ability to keep your promise, regardless of the other person's performance.

**God's Covenants always reflect His sovereign and gracious nature.**

**Six Major Covenants:**

| | |
|---|---|
| **Covenant** | Adamic - promise to send a savior |
| **By Choice** | Gen. 3:15 |
| **By Grace** | Gen. 3:15 |
| | |
| **Covenant** | Noahic - promise not to destroy the earth |
| **By Choice** | Gen. 8:21,22 |
| **By Grace** | Gen. 6:18 |
| | |
| **Covenant** | Abrahamic - promise of many descendants and to bless the world through his descendants |
| **By Choice** | Gen. 12:2,3 |
| **By Grace** | Gen. 15:1-6; Ro. 4:1-8 |
| | |
| **Covenant** | Mosaic - promise of land and nationhood |
| **By Choice** | Ex. 20:1-17 |
| **By Grace** | Ex. 20:2; Deut. 7:6-11 |
| **Definitions** | Positive definitions of the covenant - Deut. 28:1-14 Negative definitions of the covenant - Deut. 28:15-68 |
| | |
| **Covenant** | Davidic - promise of King and kingdom everlasting |
| **By Choice** | I Chron. 17:3-14 |
| **By Grace** | I Chron. 17:3-14 |
| | |
| **Covenant** | Christological - Salvation by grace / Holy Spirit |
| **By Choice** | Jn. 3:16 |
| **By Grace** | Eph. 2:8,9 |

Implications - Faith is more than intellectual assent. It is the confidence born of the personal assurance that God is sovereign. Read Ro. 11:29

# Daily Guides

# Guides

# Day 1
# Genesis 1-3

henever I read these first chapters of Genesis I am awestruck at their scope. They tell of the majesty, power and genius of a God who called our entire universe into existence, out of nothingness. Even after its fall, it is so full of examples of the beauty and majesty of an infinite God that it staggers the imagination.

But it is a sad story too. A story of the first two people, and a test to create faith. That's what the tree was all about. God told them not to do something. He gave them no good reason not to eat the fruit, except that if they did, they would die. Would they believe Him? Would they trust Him? Or would they believe the lie that He would withhold something good from them. Of course, we know the sad answer. They didn't trust Him, and faith has been hard for our race to come by ever since.

These chapters also hold the promise of redemption as God foretold the birth of the deliverer. The seed of woman would come to repair the damage done to all of creation. And so the scene is set for the whole Bible and in fact all of human history.

But this is not just the story of the creation of the universe, it is the story of my creation and yours. For God has called us into existence out of nothingness, and He has done so as purposefully as He did the sun, the moon and the stars. He knows why He brought you into being - do you? Perhaps you have not thought of it in quite this way before, but rest assured, you are *no* accident.

This is also the story of *our* fall. We have failed to trust God. We too are afraid that if we really surrender to Him we will have to do something "good" we don't want to do. But does that make sense? Will He really withhold something good from us?

And it is *our* redemption story too. For long before we knew it, He has loved us and proven it in the blood of His own Son. It is a simple story, but a profound one. And these are the questions we must all ask. Why are we here? Can God really be trusted? Who will save us?

How will we answer these questions? Helping answer them is the purpose of the Bible. May God grant that as we read through this history of salvation, we would find answers not just to our historical questions, but to the deepest questions of our own hearts.

# Day 2
# Genesis 4-6

he first murder. How quickly it happens - and between brothers. But our surprise betrays our lack of perspective. Murder is always between brothers - always a family affair. As sons and daughters of Adam and Eve, we are really all family, no matter how distantly removed.

In his book, *The Meaning of the City*, French theologian Jacques Ellul points out that Cain is credited with building the first city. He suggests that this was a further example of Cain's disbelief and disobedience to God. God had promised to mark Cain so that he would be safe even as he wandered. Cain had violated the most fundamental rule of any society: don't kill one another. His punishment, to be cut off from his family (society), was also perhaps his opportunity to learn from his mistake. To wander the land depending on the graciousness of God for his protection was what he needed to do - not just for society, but for himself. Perhaps if he had learned to trust he might have rejoined the family one day.

But Cain rejected the protection of God, and missed the lesson. And, Ellul suggests, he set the tone for all cities to come. They were to be places where people gathered to take care of their own needs. No need for God, we will take care of ourselves - our own laws, our own rulers, our own lives.

Whether or not this is the real nature of cities, it is interesting to note that at the other end of the Bible, in Revelation, it is not the Garden that returns, but the Holy City of God - a city wherein God will dwell with His people. How like God, to take even those things which we intend to use against Him and transform them into gifts that He gives to us. It is the nature of His greatness that He can work with our choices, even when we have chosen badly.

What needs transforming in your life? God wants us to trust Him with our whole lives. Not just the good parts, but also the bad. Offer Him not just your best self, but your worst. He will not be disgusted, He will heal, renew and transform. Don't be afraid to be honest with Him. He can take even our worst and transform it. Don't shut Him out. He won't change the past, but He is the master of transforming the future!

# Day 3
## Genesis 7-9

I have often wondered why God didn't put an end to Adam and Eve after they sinned and start again. It certainly seems to me that it would have been neater and cleaner. But there is a marvelous thoroughness to God's nature. He sees things through to the end. No quitting before the final buzzer. He is the ultimate long haul player. And we should be glad, or we might not exist!

But it seems that by Noah's time, even God's patience had worn thin. Some diseases are so advanced, the only cure is removal. People had become such a blight upon the earth the only cure was to do away with them and start over. I suppose that this is what the flood was all about. But the results of the surgery had an interesting side effect.

God promised never again to destroy all life on the planet. 8:21,22 This is the Noahic covenant. Most people think that the covenant is the passage later, in which God seals His promise with the sign of the rainbow, and they think that God's promise was that He would never again destroy the earth by flood. But this is much too narrow. Before God made the promise to Noah, He had already decided never to make the whole world suffer because of the sinfulness of man.

As a member of the generation raised with the fear of nuclear annihilation, this is a significant difference. For too long the church has stood by quietly while our young people faced the future with fear. We have behaved as if the future was in our hands alone and we have missed the opportunity to spread the gospel that God is in control. Whether it is through the efforts of those who want disarmament, or through deterrence, or both, God will not allow human history to end in the grip of a nuclear winter. That is not His plan. Summer and winter, springtime and harvest will continue until He comes again.

That doesn't mean that we should sit back and do nothing. What it does mean is that our work should reflect our confidence in God, not a paralyzing fear of the end of the world. We must not, and need not, panic. The world is God's and its end is in His hands, not ours. Praise God! As Martin Luther said, "I do not know what the future holds, but I know the one who holds the future!"

# Day 4
# Genesis 10-11

he genealogies of the Bible. For most they just make boring reading. Unfortunately, some have used them to argue that a race or nation of people is cursed or inferior in some way. How sad to have missed the whole point of the story: that we are really all related to one another, brothers and sisters in the truest sense.

But I think there is another message for us in these lists of begats. The Bible is telling us that what we do and who we are is of longer lasting import than we might think. We are all recipients of both the genetics and decisions of our ancestors. What they were like in body and in heart is part of the heritage we each receive. And likewise, what we are in body and in heart is what we pass on to our children and our children's children, for who knows how long.

The Chinese venerate their ancestors and even pray for their help. The Bible knows nothing of help from beyond the grave. In fact, praying to contact the dead is strictly prohibited. But it affirms that we have plenty of impact upon future generations (read Ex. 20:5,6). We are not to be revered because we have died (that takes no special talent - we all do it). But we should remember that our presence will be felt, even by some whom we will never meet. To them, we can be a blessing, or a very real curse.

In Germany, not so many years ago, a young Jewish boy grew up in a very devote family. The father was faithful about attending worship and instruction and he required the same of his family. When the boy was a teenager, the family had to move to a new town because of business reasons. The town to which they moved had no synagogue and the community leaders all belonged to the Lutheran church. The father came home one day and announced that the whole family would be abandoning their Jewish faith and joining the Lutheran church because it would be better for business.

The young man was shocked, angry, and bitter. He left Germany to study in England and eventually wrote a book in which he called religion an "opiate for the masses." Karl Marx's bitterness at his father's hypocrisy has enslaved billions of people.

What will your legacy be?

# Day 5
# Genesis 12-14

**T**he great Patriarch Abraham. Of course, at this point he is still Abram. His new name and developing identity are what this account in Genesis is all about. We will see them unfold in the days to come. But our introduction to him is somewhat less than auspicious. After receiving God's promise about the promised land, we find him traveling down to Egypt during a drought and lying about his relationship with Sarai to protect himself.

While this might seem to be a prudent thing to do, it is not the sort of thing you expect from a great man of the faith. It is more the sort of thing you might expect from us. We think of ourselves as rather common, regular people and people like Abram as spiritual giants. But that is one of the most marvelous things about our Bible. It tells things as they were. No candy coating, just the plain, unvarnished truth. Abram could have trusted that God would keep him safe, but he lacked faith, and used his own wits. Only God's gracious intervention got Sarai returned to him.

Abram would later go on to be quite a man of faith. But it is important to note that God chose him while he was still a doubting and questioning man. The important thing about Abram was not his ability to be great, but his availability to God to do great things in him and through him.

This was Abram's most important virtue. You never saw him trying to earn God's favor. Abram, from the very beginning, showed no sign of believing in a works religion. He seems to have understood without having to be told, that God's love is gracious. There is no demanding it, there is no sense in trying to earn it, one must learn to accept it and trust it. Abram accepted this grace intuitively, but as we shall see, it took him a long time to learn to trust it.

We really are much more like Abram than we might think. He did not start out being some kind of spiritual giant. You may feel that you do not measure up to God's standards for one reason or another, but when was the last time you let a member of your family be taken away in order to save your life?! If God can work through Abram, He can work through me and you if we let Him. Will we? Will you?

# Day 6
# Genesis 15-17

think I would have liked Abram if I had known him. There is something very down to earth about him that appeals to me. He comes across to me as the kind of person who had deep religious convictions without being "religious." I would very much like to have the kind of relationship with God that he had. While there is no question about Abram's respect for God, there was a sense of friendship there that impresses me.

There is an important message to us in that kind of a relationship with God. We tend to take God too seriously in areas where it doesn't matter, and too lightly in areas where it does matter. Many people are afraid to be honest with God, to admit that they wonder about just what He is doing in their lives. Abram was not. God had promised to give him a son by Sarai, and after it took so long, Abram began to doubt. So when God told him again that Sarai would conceive and bear a son when Abram was 100 years old and Sarai was 90 - Abram laughed. God wasn't offended. He picked up the joke and told Abram to name his son just that - "he laughs." It was an inside joke that would always remind them both of that moment together.

That was the important thing about Abram and God's relationship. It was not based on the unrealistic ground that Abram would prove to be perfect. Remember what it says in 15:6, "And he believed the Lord, and he reckoned it to him as righteousness." Paul points out the importance of this later in Romans 4. Abram was *not* righteous, but God graciously counted his faith as if it were righteousness. Even when Abram doubted to the point that he accepted Sarai's offer to give him a son by her handmaiden (a normal practice back then), God understood. Abram could not reasonably be expected to understand why God was waiting to fulfill His promise. But Abram kept trusting, albeit imperfectly, and God came through.

Do you think God expects too much of you? Do you think He is terribly disappointed or angry when you prove your lack of obedience? Or, can you learn to trust as Abram, that your relationship is based on His goodness not yours? He doesn't expect us to be perfect, He needs us to be honest, with ourselves and Him. Think about it!

# Day 7
# Genesis 18-19

Sodom and Gomorrah are famous for all the wrong reasons. They were the recipients of the direct judgement of God. However, most of the time God allows His indirect judgement to be sufficient. When we eat too much of the wrong foods, our arteries harden and we get heart disease. If we are promiscuous, we open ourselves to diseases that we otherwise would not get. But on special occasions, God's direct judgement is unleashed and we get a glimpse of the awesome power of the One who will have the final word.

It is interesting to note the interplay of all the characters in this drama. The angels were sent to bring the divine judgement personally. Abraham interceded for those "righteous" people who might simply be caught up in the judgement. It was a brave move. And we should not miss the point that his plea was heard.

How can it be that our prayers make a difference? I don't think I can fully answer that question, but do think that John Calvin was on the right track when he spoke of "human agency." God has chosen to work in our world, most of the time, through people. If we will not do our part, some things that God would otherwise like to do, don't get done. It is certainly a heavy burden, but it is also a tremendous gift to us. Our lives *do* count. Perhaps much more than we know.

But there were not even five righteous found in the whole city to save it. And I am not at all sure there could have been. Can we really live in a society and claim no responsibility for what its other members do? Can we really be innocent if we do nothing to stop things that we know are wrong? We may not be guilty of the acts themselves, but we are not innocent either. Bad people depend on the complacency of the good. And if we let it go long enough, we should not be surprised to find ourselves suffering some of the same judgement as those who commit the crimes.

How "just" is our city, state, and nation? How patient will God be with our society? What can we do about making a difference? Perhaps we should not underestimate the power of our own prayers. Let us pray and follow where that leads. Let us, at least, not be silent.

# Day 8
# Genesis 20-22

**S**ome scholars find it hard to believe that Abraham would have tried to pass Sarah off as his sister a second time. But I do not find it hard to believe at all. It seems like just the kind of hedging of our bets that we like to do. He had pulled this stunt before and gotten away with it. And God bailed him out again.

One wonders how this Abraham could have been the same man whose faith was so great that he would be willing to sacrifice his son Isaac?

We should take note of the impact of seeing God finally fulfill His promise. Between Abraham's lack of faith that gave Sarah away again, and his willingness to sacrifice Isaac, was a miraculous birth. God did fulfill His promise, and that helped Abraham to trust God. That may not seem so outstanding, but how often have we had our prayers answered just the way we asked, and not given God the credit after all? We can be terribly ungrateful creatures. Abraham was not.

Also, we need to consider the fact that in Abraham's time, sacrificing a child to the gods to receive favor (like more children) was a common practice, especially among the Canaanites. So it may have seemed very disappointing to Abraham to think that God was the kind of god who would have ordered a sacrifice like this, but it would not be as surprising to him as it would be to us. And herein was a large part of the purpose for having Abraham go up on the mountain. God wanted to convince Abraham that He was a very different kind of god, one that provided a substitute for our sacrifice. And it worked. Human sacrifice was always strictly forbidden among the Jews. This basic morality set the Jews apart from the very beginning.

Does God test us as He did Abraham? I do not believe that He does. I think this was a very special circumstance. He certainly does not need to test us in order to know what is in our hearts, He knows what is in them already. But we should not miss the message from up there on the mountain. We need not fear putting God first in our lives. He requires no sacrifice from us before He loves us. He has provided that sacrifice Himself already in His Son. We only need to trust Him. Praise God, He has done the rest!

# Day 9
## Genesis 23-24

**D**ivine guidance. Why is it that it seems to be so much more direct in the Bible, than it is in our lives? (I never said I had all the answers!) When I read accounts like this one, I feel envious of Abraham's servant. He simply asked, and simply received an answer. Why doesn't that happen for me?

I suppose that this was probably a more important event than most of what happens in my life. Abraham and his family had been chosen as the ones through whom salvation history would flow. His children would eventually become the nation of Israel: God's chosen priestly people. One of his descendants would finally be born who would be the King, whose Kingdom will have no end - even Jesus the Lord! So, I guess for something of that magnitude, special grace seems fair.

But, James (in the New Testament) writes that we *have* not because we *ask* not. Lord knows I don't ask as often as I should. I think it is because I am afraid of what would happen to my faith if I didn't get an answer. This really begs the question, though. I know that God always answers our prayers. I suppose I am really more worried about what I would do if He said *no*. This would then put my wants and desires in a direct conflict with God, a confrontation I would just as soon avoid. Better not to ask for help, assume that what I want is the right thing, and work on getting it myself! Or so I reason.

The human heart can be such a conniving thing, working to get what it wants, one way or another. But that element is lacking in this story. Abraham sent his servant out with confidence. He told him that if all did not happen a certain way, the servant was free to do what he thought best. No hedging his bets for Abraham. No duplicity of heart. He had prayed for God's help and he knew it would be there, one way or another. He had real faith by then, and he was able to take real risk.

But I need to stop comparing myself with Abraham. He certainly wouldn't be comparing himself with me. He did not look to himself, but to God. And God is as big for me as He was for Abraham. Perhaps that is the essence of divine guidance - the confidence to do one's own part and trust God to do His. It really is a safe bet - isn't it?

# Day 10
# Genesis 25-26

rom father to son it is passed on. From mother to daughter it goes. The good and the bad alike. It has never been easy to be the son or daughter of a great man or woman. I suppose Isaac deserves some credit for making the transition so well. He kept the family business going (if following God can be considered a business). That is not always easy to do. Ask the child of any star.

There is an important principle here for us to consider. It has been said that God has no grandchildren. We cannot inherit faith from our parents. Try as they might, they cannot give us their faith - they can only model it, and hope we notice. There comes a time in our lives, when we must decide for ourselves. Will we believe what we have been taught, or will we make a different decision. This is agonizing for parents who can only watch and pray.

Our children are greatly influenced by us though, both positively and negatively. Isaac decided he too would trust the God of his father, Abraham. He also apparently learned some of Abraham's other tricks, like passing your wife off as your sister. Some scholars have a hard time believing that Isaac would have done this too, but I think they are too hopeful about human nature. I don't find it difficult to believe it at all, because I have seen it hundreds of times myself. The children are very much like the parents.

Just how much are we a product of our genetics and how much of our environment? This is a difficult question to answer. One thing we can be sure of is that the answer cannot be 100 per cent either way. There is some part of us (who knows how much) that must finally make up our own minds. We are not locked into a deterministic world for good or for evil. The choices Abraham made still had to be made by Isaac and Esau and Jacob after him. We see most clearly the difference in these twin brothers. Jacob chose (even though he had to cheat to do it) to value the legacy of the God of his grandfather, and Esau did not. That choice made all the difference.

What then is our legacy? How much of it will we choose to keep? Mom, Dad, can we talk?

# Day 11
# Genesis 27-28

The Isaac, son of Abraham, family. Today we would refer to them as "dysfunctional." Each parent had a favorite between their twin sons. This sowed the seeds of discord very deep and very early. As they got older, the differences between the brothers was not celebrated, it was used to fuel a sick competition between the two. Then there was the inequity of the division of the inheritance. Who was better? Who was loved more? Who would get the most? These were all questions that should not and need not have come up.

God used the deception of Rebekah and Jacob to accomplish His purpose, but was this the only way it could have happened? I appreciate the honesty of the Bible because it tells the truth about the true nature of the people and events that went on. However, we must not interpret the recording of the events as necessarily being the way God intended them to come about. Did Jacob have to cheat Esau out of the birthright? Was it not possible that Isaac could have discovered for himself, that Jacob was the son God would be using to accomplish His purposes? Certainly, the Canaanite women Esau chose to marry (over the objections of his parents) would have been a clue. Is it right to do wrong to do right?

We so often limit the power of God in our lives by narrowly thinking there is only one way He can accomplish His will. The testimony of these Scriptures should be telling us just how secure His intentions are. Whether we end up being a means or a roadblock to His will, God *will* accomplish His purpose. But if we would follow His laws, we could avoid a lot of pain along the way.

God had chosen Jacob to be His "ladder" (at least one rung of it) by which the people of the earth would receive the blessings of heaven. Nothing would stop that purpose, even Jacob's questionable character. But that does not make Jacob and Rebekah right for taking matters into their own hands. God could still have accomplished His purpose, and the Isaac family could also have been "functional."

Are you "taking a shortcut" to achieving some good? Do you really have to? Will you reconsider?

# Day 12
# Genesis 29-30

One can't help but notice that dating seems to have been a lot easier in the Old Testament. Jacob saw Rachel, found out who she was, watered her sheep, and one month later, they are ready to get married. Of course, seven years is a pretty long engagement period!

It is important to remember that the Bible has to condense a lot of history into a short space or it would be even longer than it is! I am sure that there were many hours spent in private conversation with Rachel during that first month that Jacob was staying with Laban. We just aren't told about it. But we should remember that these Old Testament people were just that - people. We need to develop the ability to read between the lines lest we forget that fact.

I could not help but notice the humor in this account too. In describing Leah, the writer says of her that "Leah's eyes were weak, but Rachel was beautiful and lovely." It sounds more like he wanted to say, "It helps to have weak eyes when you look at Leah, but Rachel is worth seeing clearly!" But you can be kind even while you are being honest. And she turns out to be a good wife, even if she was not as pretty as her sister.

There is a strong sense of irony in this part of the story, too. Here was Jacob, who had prospered by cheating, having the tables turned on him by his uncle. He was also a twin who ended up marrying two sisters! If ever there were a prescription for disaster, this would seem like one. But Leah and Rachel's relationship seems to have been quite different from Jacob and Esau's. In spite of their competition for Jacob's attention, there does not appear to be the same bitterness present. Or perhaps, these details were left out.

It is hard to say if there is a cause and effect chain that creates this kind of irony, or whether we just notice it when it happens. But our sins do seem to find us out. In the end though, God's plan superseded all of that. God's blessing was with Jacob, and He would have the final word.

Nevertheless, we should perhaps heed the old proverb, "Be careful the words you say today, for tomorrow you may have to eat them."

# Day 13
## Genesis 31-32

 hat a different Jacob we see returning to the land of Canaan, from the one who left twenty years earlier. It gives one hope to see the patient work of God eventually make a difference in the human heart.

Jacob had learned his lesson at his uncle's house. He watched Laban change the agreement with him ten times, and still God was one step ahead all the way. No need for Jacob to manipulate and connive, God was going to bless him and he could trust that.

It was quite a new Jacob who went to face his brother. He had learned to follow the leading of God, and now, as he approached that meeting with Esau, he was not plotting, but praying. He was still afraid, but the events in his life, the vision of the ladder, the intervention of God with Laban, had taught him where to put his hope - where to turn in times of trouble.

We sometimes feel bad that it is only during the tough times that we seem to turn to God. Most certainly, we should not be reluctant to turn to Him at all times. But let us swallow our pride and turn to Him when we need Him. This may seem like obvious advice, yet many people, because they feel guilty about bringing only their troubles, deny themselves the help of God even in times of distress. How silly we can be!

I have two children myself, and I am learning a lot of lessons about being a parent. It has helped me see myself as a child of God in a new and different light. I want my children to grow up and be their own people. I do not want to be cutting their meat for them when they are in college. But if they are injured, and need their meat cut, I hope they will call on me. I love them. And I would love them even if they called only when they needed me.

God loves us, even when we aren't attentive. He is faithful to us, even when we neglect Him. Israel - "he who strives with God, or God strives" - the name says it all. We are all Israel in that sense. But remember, God loves Israel and He always will. He is willing to struggle with us as long as it takes. So, don't give up, even on yourself, and tell Him you love Him. He likes hearing that from His kids. I know I do.

Check Here
When Read

❏

# Day 14
# Genesis 33-35

**A**ll too often, family quarrels do not end as well as this one did. There had been a great change in both of these brothers. The bitterness and strife had been replaced with real love and concern between them. Isaac and Rebekah would have been happy to see it. We should be too. It reminds us that sometimes, things do get better.

What happened for Esau is not told to us, but the change was most miraculous. Perhaps he felt that with Jacob's leaving, he had in some sense inherited his birthright after all. Or perhaps he had just learned what was important in life as he got older. In any event, it is no small matter that he had changed. Far too many people never do.

It is nice to see the change in Jacob, too. Our families should be places where, even when we disagree, we can trust each other. The duplicity that Esau and Jacob grew up with, often causes divisions that last a lifetime. For those splits to be healed requires change on both sides. Forgiveness may be offered unilaterally, but for there to be reconciliation, both parties must participate. Esau could have been willing to forgive, but if Jacob had not changed too, another betrayal of some kind would have been inevitable.

Perhaps I focus too much on the aspect of the change of heart in these accounts. But I suppose it is because, as a pastor, I see so much need for that kind of change, and so little evidence of it. Couples come in to talk to me who have long since stopped talking to each other. Parents send their children to talk to me because their own communications with them broke down years before and they didn't see it. And no one seems to be willing to change.

So when I see the thawing of a human heart, I rejoice. It reminds me that God still works miracles in people. And I believe it is always a miracle. There is no formula for that change. There are no magic words, no special ideas to convey ("If they just understood. . .") that will work all the time. It is still a mystery to me what finally gets through. But sometimes it does and then it is all worth the waiting. Look at Esau and Jacob.

Their parents would have been proud.

# Day 15
# Genesis 36-37

nce again we find the sins of the father being passed on to the son. It is amazing to me that after the trouble that playing favorites caused for Jacob and Esau, Jacob would turn around and do the same with his own sons. But it just shows how deeply impressed we are by the way people live and not as much by what they say. In any case, Jacob could not break the cycle, and he handed down to his sons the injustice and pain that he had received.

Not that Joseph was innocent of being a "teacher's pet" sort of kid. But that is the insidious part of sin. It masquerades as some version of the good. It was right for Joseph to want to be a good and loving son, but it is such a small step from there to believing in your own "press": that you really are superior in some significant way and therefore you deserve the preferential treatment. So, quickly, the attitude changes from the humility of, "...there but by the grace of God, go I," to the proud, "God certainly knew what He was doing when He made me!" And a little of that attitude can go a long way - especially among family members.

This is, of course, no justification for plotting to murder Joseph. Reuben knew that and tried to change the final outcome with a deception of his own. To his credit, he was at least trying to do the right thing. But he learned, too late, that some evil needs to be resisted head on. He was, after all, the eldest brother, and that meant something back then. No doubt, he was haunted for years by the thought that he should have said, "No! If you kill him, you will have to kill me, too!" He was fortunate to have lived to have his guilt forgiven. Many do not.

In what ways have we played the part of Joseph? When have we taken the preferential treatment in our homes, or businesses, or schools, and then in mock surprise wondered why others feel slighted? People's sense of injustice runs deep. And they have been known to take the law into their own hands.

How often have we been guilty of the same sin as Reuben? How many times have we tried to resist evil from a safe distance? The lessons of the sons of Israel are before us. Will we learn them?

# Day 16
# Genesis 38-40

e all attend God's school. Joseph had been sent to Egypt, for a special assignment. He would not only learn some important lessons there himself, but he would become an excellent teacher in his own right. And his pupils would eventually be his own brothers.

This particular story shows why it had probably been very easy for Jacob to favor Joseph. Joseph was not only a talented and good looking young man, but it is quite evident that he had a deep faith in the God of his fathers. While there were undoubtably times he felt abandoned by God and his family, these feelings are not recorded, and his actions speak of his faith, not his doubt.

What jumps off the page at me in the account with Potiphar's wife, is Joseph's response to her advances. He told her that this would not only be a betrayal of Potiphar's trust in him, but, most importantly, "... how then can I do this great wickedness, and sin against God?" 39:9 What an amazing insight from such a young man! All our sins, in the final analysis, are against God Himself.

When we break something, it is the owner whom we have injured, and to whom we must go to seek forgiveness and make amends. God is most certainly our creator and "owner." But much more, when we injure a child, the pain is often felt much more acutely by the parents. God's love for us certainly exceeds that of our parents. In the final analysis, it is the very heart of God that we injure whenever we sin against others and even ourselves, since He loves us too.

This is why we need to ask His forgiveness when we do wrong to others or even ourselves. It is also why He can forgive us our sins, because He is the injured party. It is the heart of God that has suffered most in this life. We may not fully understand this until we can see Him face to face, but we will know it then, when we look into His eyes.

Joseph could not treat Potiphar, his wife, or himself as things to be used and discarded. That would not only hurt them, but God, who made them and loved them. It was an amazing insight from one so young. We should not miss this message. Forgive us Lord, forgive us.

# Day 17
# Genesis 41-42

Eyes that see are a great gift. We have more than one set of eyes. There are the ones we use to see the physical world around us. They get bloodshot, strained, and need glasses but they tell us so much about the world around us. And then there are the eyes of faith. It would be hard to understate the importance of either pair.

The eyes of faith allow us to see the spiritual realities that are all around us. I'm not talking about angels and devils. We live in a spiritual world all the time, we are in fact an integral part of that world, but we are strangely blind to it. The spiritual realities I'm talking about are as common as love, justice, courage, hope, and faith. But just because we think of them as common, does not make them so. They are the truly profound things in our world. They are of greater value than any wealth which can be accumulated and they are the things that will endure long after the earth and stars have faded away.

So many people ask for great faith in order to accomplish "miracles." But what kind of miracles do they want to perform? Spiritual power is not the ability to heal someone's disease. Doctors do that on a regular basis. Real spiritual power is the ability to bring hope and courage into the heart and life of someone, even as they are dying. Let us not forget that all physical healings, no matter how complete, will not last forever. Eventually we will all die. To bring comfort then, that is real spiritual power.

Joseph impressed the Pharaoh by being able to interpret his dream. The real miracle was that Joseph was not bitter toward God, but faithful. Joseph was still loyal and trustworthy even after being sold into slavery and imprisoned wrongfully. How could he do that?

Perhaps it was because he could see God at work in him and through him. Faith is the power to see that all events have meaning, even when it cannot understand all the meaning. His vision could not see what God was doing with him in the future, but he could see that day - and that was enough.

Have you seen God's purpose in your life? Too broad a vision? How about God's purpose for you today?

# Day 18
# Genesis 43-45

These chapters remind me of a soap opera. The brothers who sold Joseph into slavery appear before him seeking favor, but don't recognize him because of all the years and his new manner and position. Joseph, for his own reasons, doesn't reveal himself, and instead toys with his brothers by accusing them of being spies and holding one brother as hostage. He forces them to bring Benjamin back with them and then arranges to have him arrested on a trumped-up charge. Finally, after much begging by the brothers, Joseph reveals himself - *and they don't believe him!* All they needed were a few babies with unknown fathers and they would be ready for prime time!

One summer while I was still in seminary, I got involved watching a soap opera with my wife. I was amazed at how much of the plot was dependent on people never telling each other the truth. They didn't always lie, but they never told the whole story. Before I quit watching, frustrated at the never-ending deception, I remember shouting at my TV, "Tell her you love her, you jerk! Just tell her you love her!"

There is no clear reason given for Joseph not telling his brothers who he was from the beginning. Perhaps he wanted them to suffer a little for what they had done to him. Perhaps he wanted to see if they would ever come clean about what they had really done with the brother they said was killed. Perhaps he just wanted to see if they had changed over the years or if they were still the mob that had sold him into slavery. Whatever the case, it seems that the unvarnished truth early on would have served better. It would have at least spared Jacob the agony of worrying about Benjamin.

I'm sure this story made great telling around the fires late at night in the households of the Hebrews. But I wonder what lesson they derived from it. For me, it is an example of why I cannot afford to make up the rules about life as I go along. My vision is neither clear enough nor long enough to see all the consequences of my choices and actions. I need to stay within the protection of God's instructions, to "tell the truth in love." Anything more can lead to life in a soap opera. And most of those characters never get out!

# Day 19
## Genesis 46-47

o wonder Pharaoh liked Joseph so much. By the end of the drought, because of Joseph's shrewd handling, Pharaoh owned all the land in Egypt and had made slaves of his own people. They would work the land for Pharaoh and give him 20 per cent of all they gained. That's really making the most out of a disaster!

Accounts like this seem to be offensive to our sense of New Testament "niceness." Why should Pharaoh profit from the misfortune of the people from the drought? Wouldn't it have been better for Joseph to have opened up the storehouses to feed everyone through the drought until it started raining again?

These are difficult questions, in part because there seems to be no particular political or economic system endorsed in the Scriptures. There will be a broad based sort of plan in Exodus for the way Israel should live, but this was unique to Israel, part of God's plan to show them as a special people. Why this lack of direction from our Bible?

Mohammed made much of this "defect" in the Scriptures. In the Koran, he spelled out a very specific economic and sociological scheme to be followed rigorously. Muslims still find this to be a weakness in Christianity; too much freedom, not enough direction.

Of course, I don't agree, but they are right about one thing. God gives His people a good deal of latitude in life. The law of love, if followed, will prevent you from doing some things that are harmful, but it is wide open when it comes to the good. Freedom is not the antithesis of justice. The two can coexist quite well together.

But freedom is no guarantee of success. If we are free to succeed, we must risk failure. Pharaoh's people had the same chance to plan ahead that Joseph did during the seven years of plenty. That they failed to do so may have been unfortunate, but it was not unfair. God has granted that we may enjoy the fruits of our own labor. Those who do not labor have no claim on those who do.

To share with those in need is a constraint of love, not justice. Pharaoh was fair, but not very loving. We can be glad that the same is not true about God! What then about us?

# Day 20
# Genesis 48-50

The story of Joseph is one of the longest and most detailed in the Scriptures. Joseph is certainly one of the most outstanding of the Patriarchs, for his strength of character and depth of faith prove to be critical elements in God's plan for His people. His is certainly a life worth studying and emulating.

Even here at the end of his story, Joseph proves to have a greater understanding than his brothers. After Jacob dies, the brothers are once again fearful that Joseph would take revenge on them for what they did. His answer to them shows how well grounded his theology was. He tells them, "Fear not, for am I in the place of God? As for you, you meant evil against me; but God meant it for good..." 50:19,20 Joseph knew that it was not his prerogative to judge his brothers, it was God's.

Joseph also kept clear the nature of all the players in the drama. His brothers had indeed intended evil towards him. They were not under divine direction to sell him into slavery. God is not the author of evil. He does not do wrong to do right. Instead, God is the one who can transform bad into good. This is His power and glory. In His great genius, He can use even what is meant for evil, to serve His purpose, can transform the very character of the deed from curse into blessing. Who knows what way God would have brought about the salvation of the house of Israel during the famine if Joseph had not been sold into slavery. But if He can make good come from evil, He can certainly make good come from good. God does not manipulate people, nor is He manipulated by them. This does not mean, however, that He cannot act in history and in our lives. He does not send us evil, but He will send us the power to transform it, if we are willing to accept the gift.

Joseph knew God was with him. We need to know this too. This does not mean our lives will be clear sailing, but it does mean we have a rudder by which to control the direction it will go. God does not intend all things that happen to us, but He can use them.

Are you facing some difficulty? Take heart. It did not take God by surprise. He can transform it if you let Him. He is a most unlikely God and He does the most unlikely things. He did for Joseph. He can for you and me.

# Day 21
# Exodus 1-4

oses. What can you say about him? Volumes have been written. We shall spend quite a bit of time reading about him in the days to come. He certainly occupies an important part in salvation history. He went on to be an historic figure almost larger than life. But he was very human, and we should not miss the evidences of his humanity as they are shared with us in these accounts.

The Bible is replete with accounts of God's working His plan and His will through flawed people. Our society has created an image of what a great person should be like. When you compare that image to any person who ever was, or is, great, the image looks silly. The whitest teeth, the freshest breath, and the fragrance that drives men/women wild, do not appear to be part of the reality. Neither does near genius, unshakable courage, or overpowering charm, seem to be essential. Moses had none of these things.

Moses, by his own admission, was not eloquent. He practically ran off the mountain the first time the staff turned into a snake (I appreciated that - I can identify with him). He argued with God about being the one to go and speak to Pharaoh until even God got frustrated. And remember, he was an escaped killer hiding out in the mountains. But he was also the one God had chosen.

I think God is more than a little disquieting in that way. He doesn't require our permission to make up His mind to do something. We don't lose our ability to reject His will, but He can be pretty persuasive when He wants to be. And Moses is a prime example.

It is all there in His name: "I am." He is the only God out there. There are no others. And He is not just sitting and watching passively.

He has chosen us, too. We are no accidents. He had a purpose for us before we were born, and He wants us to find it. Oh, He probably won't be speaking to us through any burning bushes (He so seldom repeats Himself), but He will be trying to get our attention none-the-less. Maybe through these Scriptures? Maybe today? Are you listening? Do you dare not?

Check Here
When Read

❏

# Day 22
# Exodus 5-8

How do you know a miracle even when you see it? This was the dilemma facing Pharaoh. History is filled with instances of amazing feats. The great Houdini performed tricks that still haven't been repeated. In our own time, the magician, David Copperfield, has "walked" through the Great Wall of China, and made an airplane, train car and even the Statue of Liberty, disappear! How do you tell reality from illusion?

The answer is that you cannot see these things with your eyes, you must see them with your heart. Pharaoh's heart was hard and he could not see the miracles that were happening right in front of him. But before we are too hard on him, let us not miss the fact that even Moses and Aaron weren't "seeing" too well either. The first time they go to Pharaoh to tell him to let the people go and he makes things harder, it is Moses and Aaron who go running back to complain to God.

Why is it so hard for human beings to acquire faith? I think at least part of the answer lies in our inherent belief in cause and effect. We observe cause and effect chains in every aspect of our daily lives. We count on cause and effect in everything that we do. Yet in the spiritual world we cannot seem to get a handle on cause and effect. God does not always punish the sinner, reward the righteous or heal the sick. Why not? Have we done something we shouldn't, or not done something we should? What do we have to do to get this "god thing" to work?

This is the essence of all pagan religions, the attempt to control the deity. If you do the right dance, give the right sacrifice, say the right words, the gods will be "pleased" and grant your request. But the God of Abraham, Isaac, Jacob, Joseph and Moses, cannot be controlled. He has purposes of His own, not all of which are told to us. Just look at Moses and Aaron. They received their marching orders one day at a time. They received no more than their "daily bread."

God is always at work, but it is sometimes very difficult to see what He is doing, even when it's right in front of our faces. Perhaps the key is remembering that God is a person, not a set of rules. This means He can be known more readily than He can be understood. Ask Him about it!

# Day 23
# Exodus 9-11

Over the years, some scholars have sought to explain away the miracles of the plagues as being just natural disasters. It seems rather strange when you consider that this is precisely what Pharaoh must have been doing to miss the fact that he was witnessing the hand of God at work.

Even more puzzling is how these scholars could dismiss the other two elements of the story; namely, the timing of the plagues and Moses' ability to foretell their happening. The fact that some of the plagues (such as the frogs and the flies) were creatures of nature, does not make them any less extraordinary. Not to see the miraculous hand of God in these events at any level requires a hardness of heart that would have shamed even Pharaoh. Yet, we are capable of such spiritual blindness.

What constitutes a miracle? Definitions vary, but most include the idea of something out of the ordinary. Why is it that so many people are in search of miracles? Often, I think we are in search of short cuts to hard work. We lack the patience or perseverance to do what can be done. We don't want to take the time to develop the talent we have been given or practice our skills until we are proficient  We don't want to have to eat the right foods, or exercise, instead we want instant health and success from a pill or a prayer. But God is not redundant. If He has provided us some means to obtain or achieve something, He seldom grants it "miraculously." If we look closely, we will notice that miracles are done to suit His purpose, not necessarily ours.

If God had wanted Moses simply to lead the people out of Egypt there were other means at His disposal. Most governments can be toppled by less than the plagues Egypt endured. But He had a purpose in mind, an example to make and ten plagues (not five or eight) suited His purpose.

Have you been hoping for a miracle? Whose purpose would it serve? God delights in giving good gifts to His people; that He does so, is a miracle in itself. Ask yourself, before you begin praying, has He already provided a means for me to have what I am asking for? It may not be the short cut, but God never promised easy gifts, just good ones.

# Day 24
# Exodus 12-13

The Passover. This was, and still is, the central event for the Jewish faith. This celebration has been an anchor for God's people throughout the centuries. Where are the Hittites? Where are the Moabites? Where are the Edomites? Empires and civilizations have come and gone, and yet the Jews, in spite of being scattered over the whole world, have maintained their ancient identity. They are truly God's showcase people.

The rules for this ritual are set out simply and explicitly. It was to be a lamb without blemish, roasted, not raw or boiled. It was to be fully eaten that night. If any remained, it was to be burned. And when the children would ask in years to come, they were to tell the story - the story of God passing over their houses and delivering them out of the land of Egypt, out of the house of bondage.

Why? That all might know that the Lord is God. What a shame that the message of God's graciousness toward Israel (they did not deserve this treatment) was so quickly lost in racial pride. The whole understanding of the substitutionary atonement (remember the ram back with Abraham and Isaac) was lost in the mistaken idea that God favored the Jews above all other people. The message of the passover was never about the Jews, it was always about the greatness of God. He is not a god who could be placated and controlled by sacrifices as the pagans thought, He is a righteous God, before whom we all stand guilty of our sins, all of us under a death sentence. Yet He is also a God of grace - that is, unmerited favor - and through the sacrifice of another, He has provided a means of escape from the judgement we all deserve. It is a gift He offers, not one we can in any way earn.

In the New Testament, we will read of the ultimate passover lamb - Jesus, the Christ, who takes away the sins of the world. Yet, like the Jews, we need to remember that our salvation is not about our righteousness, it is about His. We are not forgiven because we are better people, we can be better people because we are forgiven. Humility, not pride, is the proper attitude for the pardoned criminal. Have you thanked God today for giving us not what we deserve, but what we need? Perhaps it is time again to remember.

# Day 25
# Exodus 14-15

The parting of the Red Sea was a brilliant military maneuver on God's part. It is natural that Pharaoh, recovering his composure after losing his son, would want to pursue the Jews. That would be easy, for after all, they were slaves, not an army, and he commanded a magnificent army. They had humiliated Pharaoh not just by leaving, but by claiming to be responsible for all the disasters that had come to Egypt. This is not to say Pharaoh wanted them back, but he most certainly would have wanted them dead.

One of the temptations of having a strong military is that when the opportunity arises to use it against an inferior force, the motivation to do so becomes almost overwhelming. That the United States has resisted as often as it has, is quite unusual historically. Pharaoh proved to be much more typical in that respect. So, God had to not only to deliver the Jews, He had to make sure that they would not be hunted down and killed.

Deliberately fleeing toward a natural barrier must have appeared to Pharaoh to be the ultimate strategic blunder. The Jews had cornered themselves and total annihilation seemed certain. But God had a different plan, one that no one else could have anticipated, and one which proved to be absolutely decisive.

The Jews would whine and complain a lot during the Exodus, but this one complaint seems very reasonable to me. To lead them out of Egypt and then to walk right into a trap would have confirmed for me that Moses may have been a great many outstanding things, but a military genius he was not. However, Moses was not in charge, God was, and that made all the difference.

Following God is not always easy to do. It means putting ourselves in positions where, without His intervention, we will be at a real loss. That is the nature of faith, though. Belief can sit comfortably on the sidelines and watch, but faith must go out and act: it must take real risk.

Where is God calling you to "excerise" your faith? It may not be as dramatic as delivering you from a persecutor, but He wants to show His power through your life. Can you trust Him? He can part your Red Sea too.

# Day 26
# Exodus 16-18

 uail and manna. This was to be the diet of the Jews in the wilderness. They were provided daily, as it turns out, for over forty years. The daily provision was to be a lesson to the Israelites, and one we should not miss ourselves. Of course, learning this lesson, like so many others, often depends on one's perspective.

We should notice that it was not originally part of God's plan to continue this particular object lesson for forty years. We have not read this far yet, but the wandering in the wilderness was because of Israel's disobedience. It appears that if they had proven faithful, God had been ready to lead them into the promised land in short order. What then was the lesson supposed to be?

We are told that God would provide daily, in order that they might know that He was God and that He was with them. God knew what He was going to be expecting of them as they "took" the land from the Canaanites. They would need to know that He was with them, all the time. What better way to teach them trust than to have them see Him deliver on His promise daily? This seems to me to be the way to see it from God's perspective.

Unfortunately, the Jews did not exactly excel at seeing things from God's perspective. One can almost hear them saying, "And just how many ways can one prepare a quail?" and "If I have to look at one more omer of manna, I'll die!" We humans can be an impossible lot. First we ask for daily evidence of God's power, then when we receive it, we still aren't satisfied. Instead of seeing this time in the wilderness as a preparation, they saw it a disagreeable interruption in their lives.

Beyond the lack of variety in their diet, I think there must have been a fear factor too. Why couldn't you preserve any of this food? What if God didn't come through one day? What if He got busy somewhere else, or had something more important to do than send manna?

God has called us to some purpose too, and He needs to prepare us for it. Are you wondering what He is doing in your life? Perhaps He is trying to build your faith, teaching you to trust Him. Look around, that may be manna at your feet.

# Day 27
# Exodus 19-21

he giving of the Ten Commandments. This is one of the most significant, and most misunderstood, passages in the whole Bible. Most of us have not only read this passage, but probably had to memorize the Ten Commandments in our Sunday School classes as children. So, why have these simple commandments been so misunderstood?

It is the tendency of all people to be idolatrous. We would like to worship (if we have to at all) a god who can be "dealt" with - one with whom our duties and responsibilities are clear. If we do our part, then the "gods" will do theirs. We leave "them" alone and "they" return the favor. But that is not the God of Abraham, Isaac, and Jacob.

The Ten Commandments are not the legalistic code that must be followed in order to earn God's favor. That favor has already been given to us. In Genesis three, God promised to send a savior. From Adam to Noah to Abraham and to Moses, the relationship was established by God's grace. The favor the Israelites received comes "unmerited." He chose them to be a priestly people: to make them an example to the world. The real beginning of the Ten Commandments is not "You shall have no other gods before me" it is, "I am the LORD, your God, who brought you out of the land of Egypt, out of the house of bondage."

The relationship being thus established, what follows are the terms of how each party agrees to act. God, for His part, promises to continue to be their God, and to keep His covenants which were made with the Patriarchs. The Jews, on their part, agree to be the "priestly" people. They are then given explicit instructions on how their role of a priestly people should be lived. They could be good priests or bad ones, but priests they had become.

The God of the Old Testament is not a legalistic one who expected people to earn their salvation. He is a gracious one, who called them to a priestly office. That call (as we shall see later) becomes the same for the Church. That makes you a priest and these covenant conditions are then descriptions of how your life ought to look. Are you being a good priest or a bad one? People are watching.

# Day 28
# Exodus 22-24

et's get specific! This might reasonably be the title of this section in Exodus. The Ten Commandments having provided the basic guidelines for ethical behavior, it becomes necessary to be explicit about how to apply those guidelines. I am struck with how eloquently Jesus is later able to sum up the law and the prophets with His "golden rule." Here in Exodus we can already see the "death by a thousand qualifications" that the law of God would suffer at the hands of those who are more interested in obeying its letter than its intent.

Moses had already established a system of judges (thanks to his father-in-law, Jethro) to try the cases that would come up. Sadly, these "courts" would have to be given more specific instructions than the Ten Commandments provided. So we see the "law" from the very beginning was a mixed blessing. On the one hand, it provided an ethical system that could make Israel a truly just nation, and on the other, it opened the door to endless arguing for those who would try to live by the letter of the law but not its intent.

I am also impressed with how well this system defines justice in its most fundamental sense: fairness. An eye for an eye, and a tooth for a tooth, is simply fair. It also has no room, and no need, for mercy. The Hindus call this "karma": ultimate justice. They believe that you will pay for *all* of your sins, if not in this life, you will be reincarnated to pay for them later. In the 1960's and 1970's, "karma" was popularized in America as some kind of mystical quality for the individual. It is, instead, the most cold and brutal application of "simple justice" ever conceived.

God's law is more than just "simple justice." It does require that justice be served: when harm is done, a price must be paid. But it allows, from the outset, that the payment may come from somewhere else. This testifies to God's character as not only just, but merciful. There is a warmth and compassion even in God's law that speaks of His love beyond the law.

God calls us to be like Him. We must not leave justice undone in our desire to be merciful, nor should we be cold in our application of fairness. He has called us to love: a far more demanding, and worthwhile endeavor. Think about it!

# Day 29
# Exodus 25-27

irections for how to make the Ark of the Covenant. This must surely seem like boring reading to us. Why should precious space in Scripture be used up for such menial details as these? I'm not sure I can answer that fully, but there were a couple of things that struck me as I read through these tiresome instructions.

First, it seems significant to me, that God tells Moses to ask for an offering from the people, from everyone whose heart makes them willing. What a wonderful thing! God, who could require anything and everything from us, wants only what we *want* to give Him! For anyone who works with people, this is perhaps not so surprising. We all know what a tremendous difference it makes when people help who want to do so. The help given that comes grudgingly, is almost not worth having. Almost any general would rather have a smaller force of willing volunteers than an army of conscripts. Willing people are truly a force to be reckoned with.

Another thing that strikes me in this account is the detail that was given and the detail that was left out. The people were told specifically how many cherubim to make, where to put them, and what direction they were to face, but how did they know what cherubim looked like? I really liked the description in 26:31 which is translated in the RSV as, "And you shall make a veil of blue and purple and scarlet *stuff* and fine twined linen; in skilled work shall it be made, with cherubim; ..." (italics mine). This seems to me to be the way God would like us to live our lives, in cooperation with Him. It is supposed to be something we are doing together. He has His contribution to make, and we have ours - a joint effort.

Finally, I think it is important to notice that the Ark was supposed to be made with the best materials and workmanship available. If the work were done by willing people, this almost doesn't have to be said. Willing people give their best. God deserves ours.

Are we willing to give God our best? Are we doing our part in making something out of our lives? We ourselves are a tabernacle of God in our world, a place where He can be found. How well-built are we?

# Day 30
# Exodus 28-29

**H**oly to the LORD. Just what is meant by that phrase? We read it over and over again in these chapters. It is a word that we are all familiar with, but it is far from understood. Yet we ourselves are called holy before the LORD. We need to understand more fully the implications of this high calling and how it applies to our lives every day.

The primary meaning of "holy" in the Old Testament is "something set aside." The implication of one hundred per cent purity had a different connotation in the Old Testament than it does today. It would be impossible to find a "perfect" lamb. Something which was to be used as a sacrifice was to be among the "best," but what made it "holy" was not something intrinsic, but that it was "set aside." Aaron and his sons (as we shall see) were not morally superior, they were just "set apart"; holy to God. Ordination is less of a mystical, metaphysical act, than it is an act of the will. God, and His people, make things holy by choosing to set them apart for a special purpose. We are more "holy" in purpose than we are in being.

This understanding becomes important when we connect our concept of holiness with its close cousin: righteousness. We have the tendency to think of righteousness as purity: being "without spot or blemish." But righteousness has less to do with lack of fault than it does with strength of integrity. The focus should not be on what is missing (any imperfections) but on the strength that comes from the "soundness" of something - its "rightness." So often we think of God as rather prim and prissy, holy and righteous in the sense that dirt and filth (sin and evil) offend His clean and proper self, like a man who wears a white suit to an outdoor barbecue.

But holiness and righteousness are not frail things that can be overcome by a slip in the mud. They are durable and tough. They set us aside with a purposefulness that will not be dissuaded. We are holy and righteous before God, not because He has bad eyesight, but because He has an unflinching and unfailing purpose for us. Let us lose this silly idea that being holy means being "other worldly." Holiness is for the here and now. Go out today and be righteous!

# Day 31
# Exodus 30-31

ou learn a lot about a person by finding out what they treat as holy. These are the things which are set apart in their lives to be treated with an extra measure of respect and seriousness. We may joke about many things, but those which we hold sacred are not a laughing matter. I think we can learn about God in the same way. What things does He set aside as being holy?

We have seen the concept of the sabbath several times already in Exodus. The formula has been repeated on several different levels. The manna came each day, and double measure on the sixth, but not at all on the seventh. The Israelites were told to rest each seventh day as part of the Ten Commandments, and to keep a sabbath of years; to let the fields rest each seventh year. Always, God promised to provide enough in the six day or year, to carry them through the seventh as they rested. This sabbath is holy to God, set apart, sacred.

Why is this so important to God? In these chapters we are told that the reason is that after God worked creating the world, even He rested on the seventh day. We are to observe a sabbath rest too. But why should we rest?

Watchman Nee in his book, *Sit, Walk, Stand*, points out that while the sabbath was the seventh day for God, it was the first day for mankind. Adam and Eve were commanded, as their first task, to rest in the work that God had done. Nee pointed out that we are to remember that all that we do, first, depends on the work of God. Before we try to "walk" with God, or "stand" our theological ground, we must "sit" and appreciate God's work. The sabbath is to remind us, to put us in our place, firmly seated in what God has done for us. It should be a time to reflect, to give thanks, and to enjoy the blessings of God which are always a gift to us.

I think it is also important to notice that this means God is not a workaholic. He was not driven to create and neither should we be driven. He did not have to create in order to feel fulfilled, He was overflowing with creativity, and when He had finished, He took time to enjoy what He had accomplished.

Are you observing a sabbath in your life? Are you taking time to be grateful, to remember who has blessed you and enjoy what He has given? He takes this very seriously. Will you?

# Day 32
# Exodus 32-34

A stiff-necked people. This is a phrase that has always been a curious one to me. I could understand God calling the Israelites stubborn, or even stupid, but "stiff-necked" seemed like an odd choice of words. Yet, when you think about it, there is something very appropriate in that description that fit the Israelites, and all too often, us.

You can still do a great number of things with a stiff neck. You can walk, even run, drive a car, go to work, but the one thing you cannot do readily with a stiff neck, is to turn around. And turning around is a very important part of life. The Bible has a word for it: repentance.

To repent, is to turn around, to change directions from going the wrong way, to the right way. But repenting, turning around, is very difficult when you have a "stiff neck." You cannot easily swivel your head around to check first, where you have been. It is not even easy to look a little left and right to see things around you, to get some perspective. With a stiff neck, the only easy thing to do is to keep looking straight forward and keep going. But this is precisely the trait about people that really aggravates God, this refusal on our part to look around and check on where we are going.

Very few of the sins we commit are immediately fatal. It is our stiff-necked insistence on continuing to commit them that is our demise. If we will but turn and repent, we will find our loving and patient God, right behind us, willing to help us back on the right road. But if we will not turn, it becomes very difficult, sometimes even impossible, to get our attention.

I do not believe that God is put off by our sins, as if He were too pure to associate with filthy people like us. He sent His own son to prove this was not true. But I do think He is put off by our stiff-necked attitude, that refuses to see anything except that upon which we have fixed our gaze.

Will you look around your life today? Loosen up those pride-cramped neck muscles and check out where you are and where you are going. It's never too late to repent until you start thinking it is. Look around, there's a gracious God right behind you!

# Day 33
# Exodus 35-36

nce again the call goes out for those *willing* to do the Lord's work in building the tabernacle. As a pastor, I am constantly forgetting that God's work is really best done by those who want to do it. There is no excuse for using guilt, or clever marketing techniques to elicit gifts that do not proceed from the heart. The cheerful giver is the one to be sought. The other gifts come with so many strings that they almost never get unwrapped.

There is an important lesson in seeing the way in which God works with His people. The passage says that the call was issued to all who wanted to contribute, and then later, it says that God put the desire into the hearts of those who wanted to give. Which is it? Do we serve God because we want to or because He wants us to? Could it really be both?

The question of who is really in charge of our lives, is a perennial one. There are those who would argue that God could have nothing to do with our wills, if they are truly to be free. Others say, that we have no real will at all, but are determined by genetics and circumstances to make decisions as God has foreordained. I am not sure you can come up with an answer to which it is. And perhaps it misses the point anyway.

We seem to always be trying to build a house for God. We want to get Him in His right place. No matter how large or small that place might be, we want Him *in His place*. But God instructed the Jews to build a tabernacle, not a house. God cannot be contained by a house, or our conceptions of Him. He simply will not fit: He is too big. And He does not want to be *in His place*, if by that we mean somewhere a safe distance from our lives. There is no safe distance from God. He has chosen to love us. That means He will be as intimate a part of our lives as our own thoughts, and as basic as the work of our very own hands.

The tabernacle was to be a sign that God was with His people and so He is - closer than we think. He will not remain a safe distance from us and why should He? He made us that we might love Him and be loved by Him, for us to be in His Spirit, and His Spirit in us. Why settle for separate condos? God is offering a great deal on a tabernacle. Won't you build one with Him? He takes only volunteers - sort of.

# Day 34
# Exodus 37-38

lind obedience, blind faith. Some people say that these terms are synonymous, that all obedience and faith are blind. Kierkegaard called faith a blind leap and argued that if it were not blind, it could not be faith. But is this necessarily so, and what does that have to do with the directions for the building of the tabernacle?

God was going to give Israel a whole new way of thinking about Him. The religion of the Jews was going to be in stark contrast to the religions around it. The whole sacrificial system for the Jews was to be different from the pagans around them. This was a difference not only in form but in substance and it needed to be reflected in the architecture of the tabernacle: their holy place. God could not explain all the differences first. That was to be what the tabernacle communicated. He simply needed it built to certain specifications for reasons that He could only later reveal (in Leviticus). So, He had to be specific, and the builders had to build as they were told, even though they did not understand all the reasons why.

This is the essential character of faith. It is true that when we "obey" God because we understand and agree with Him, one could say we are not really obeying, we are merely following our own understanding. This was the test in the garden. Adam and Eve were to "obey" by *not* eating the fruit. It would have been "true" obedience, "blind" faith, doing as they were told even though they had no real reason to do so, no real reason except that they trusted God. But therein lies the difference.

How "blind" am I if I obey, not because I understand everything, but because I trust someone? My trust is not in my understanding of the circumstances, but rather in the character of the person I'm choosing to believe. Whether or not they are trustworthy is something I can "know." I can get a lot of information before deciding to take their word. That does not seem blind to me at all. It does mean that I must look more to my relationship with them than to my own understanding. That may not be easy, but it is certainly not "blind."

Sometimes, following God will mean knowing why we are doing what we are doing. Other times, it will only mean knowing for whom we are doing it. Do we really need to see more?

# Day 35
# Exodus 39-40

ow do you know the will of God? This is a question that I am asked frequently by people coming into my office. It is usually not in relation to the minor things in life, but the major ones: should they get married, or take a certain job, or move to another state. The need for divine guidance runs very deep in people. But I often wonder if we really know what we are asking for.

These passages about the making of the tabernacle are certainly an example of one kind of divine guidance that many people seem to be hoping for. They want explicit instructions on exactly how to live their lives. In their owns words, "I just want to know what God wants me to do!" Do we really want that? Do we really *need* that?

I confess to sharing those feelings sometimes. I would like to have that degree of certainty about my decisions. But would I really want God to treat me that way? Would I really like getting up every morning to pray with notebook in hand, to take down the details of what I was to wear, who I was to see, what I was to say, etc.? These last few chapters have been a bit tedious to read. I cannot but think that living that way would be more than just a bit tedious, it would be oppressive.

Fortunately, God had a much better idea in mind for us. He was not interested in creating robots who couldn't do anything other than exactly what they had been programmed to do. Nor did He want to have a lot of little simple minded dependents who had to be told what to eat, what to drink, what to wear, what to think every moment of the day. No, instead He wanted people, created in His image, beings with a free will and a strong character who could learn to make their own, good decisions. So, if that is what He wanted, He could not always lead us around by the nose. At some point we must learn that balance between independence and dependence.

What are *you* looking for? Is it divine guidance or guaranteed success? God has given us plenty of broad guidelines to live by: principles upon which to base our decisions. But He makes no guarantee that all our decisions will work out. The only guarantee is that He will be with us no matter what we decide or do. Isn't that enough?

# Day 36
# Leviticus 1-4

Animal sacrifices seem very brutal and primitive to our modern minds. The idea that God would order such sacrifices usually keeps people out of the book of Leviticus. Yet there are important lessons for us here in these pages of the laws that were to govern Israel. The worship in the tabernacle and later the temple, was of a very different character from the pagan ones of their contemporaries, and quite different from what most of us see at face value.

I am a city boy myself. I grew up in San Diego, California, and aside from a few insects and one gopher, I have never killed anything with my own hands. That kind of background tends to give one a rather sanitized view of life. I like to eat steak and chicken and lamb, but when I see them in the supermarket, they have already been killed, cleaned, butchered and wrapped in plastic. But meat doesn't come that way, and there is no pretty way to slaughter an animal. Still, the killing of animals is a fact of our everyday life.

I am detached from the reality of the process because *I* don't have to kill the animals. That is why, for the Jews, the sacrifice was done, not by the priest, but by the person bringing the sacrifice. In many pagan religions, the animal was killed by the priest, because only they knew how to kill it in just the right way to please the gods. The whole point of the sacrifice for the Jews, however, was not the effect it had on God, but the effect it had on them. They were to lay their hands on the animal's head, to reinforce the understanding that the animal was taking their place. Then, *they* were to kill it, not the priest. It was for *their* sin, so the sacrifice ought to be by their hand: no easy, clean, detached ritual to placate the gods. It was a very personal, warm-blooded act, to drive home the seriousness of sin and the price of broken relationships between ourselves, each other, and God.

I am glad that, through Jesus' sacrifice, I no longer have to kill animals to atone for my sins, but I sometimes wonder if I might take my sins a little more seriously if I did. The fact that I do wonder means I have not fully understood just how much more precious was the blood of my Savior that has already been shed for me. No greater price could have been paid and *no more is needed.* My prayer is that we all might realize that more fully.

# Day 37
# Leviticus 5-7

t is important to remember that the sacrificing of animals was not for the purpose of purchasing God's forgiveness through the blood of some animal. The point was always to drive home to the one who had committed it, the cost and seriousness of sin. The one that was to be changed by the sacrifice, was not God, but the person who had committed the sin.

The whole system was in fact designed not so much to have an eternal effect, but a temporal one. We need to remember that God is not playing some kind of sick, blood-thirsty game with us. Our sins have a real effect on us, and on our society. Just as certainly, forgiveness needs to be more than just a detached concept. We are in need, not only of being forgiven, but feeling that way too.

The sin and guilt offerings described in these chapters are very similar. The only real difference is that the guilt offering required restitution whenever possible. The sin offering was to repair one's relationship with God by changing the perspective of the sinner. But between people, when something wrong has happened, there is often more that can and should be done to try to make things right. God's justice requires not only that we "feel" sorry, we must *act* sorry too.

The action of repentance has a twofold benefit. It helps to restore the community broken between people when there has been some wrong done. The victim is truly of concern to God, but so is the victimizer. The act of restitution not only makes repentance more believable for the one wronged, but for the wrongdoer, too. We are often less able and willing to forgive ourselves for our sin than God is. If we are to believe our own repentence, we too need to see concrete evidence that we have changed.

How do we "know" today that God has forgiven us? Penance is a concept that was lost among the Protestant denominations because it carried the danger that we would feel we somehow earned God's forgiveness. Perhaps it is time we realize that repentance without action is so cold and thin that we don't believe it ourselves. Are you sorry for your sin? How will you show it? How will you know it?

# Day 38
# Leviticus 8-10

Whenever I read about Aaron or his sons, I never cease to be underwhelmed by their performance. It would be safe to say that they were never in danger of winning a contest for strength of character or depth of understanding. From Aaron's first priestly act of making a golden calf for the people to worship, to his sons offering the sacrifices improperly, to his later siding with Miriam against Moses, Aaron comes across as one of those people you can count on to desert their post when the invasion begins.

I think that I am entitled to say this as an ordained clergyman myself, that there is an important message to us all in the lineage of the priesthood going back to Aaron. I am afraid that the legacy of a questionable character has been handed down almost as faithfully as has the message of God's love and forgiveness. I am not saying that clergy are worse than most people, but neither are they necessarily any better. Unfortunately, being ordained to a holy office does not guarantee that one will end up being holy themselves. Aaron and his sons have been offering us that lesson from the beginning.

Rather than being so terribly disappointed in them we need to develop the ability to separate the medium from the message. This does not seem to be a very well developed skill in our society. The fact is that the worst among us can be right about something, and the best among us, in spite of all our good intentions, can be terribly wrong. Truth, like God Himself, is no respecter of persons. When we are in search of the truth, we must learn to seperate it from the means by which that truth has come to us - we must distinguish the medium from the message.

I don't think we necessarily need to be suspicious of our religious leaders, but neither should we blindly trust them. We are human, and ordination confers a special responsibility, not additional righteousness.

So, support your clergy, especially in prayer, but do not follow them uncritically. And when they fail, as we all do, remember that your faith was always supposed to finally be in the God whom we all serve, not in His servants. It is very possible to tell the truth without being able to live it - just look at Aaron, or yourself!

# Day 39
# Leviticus 11-12

Germs were not "discovered" until more than two millennia after these laws were given to Moses. Yet, it is easy to see that a good deal of what is written in Leviticus concerning clean and unclean things, is good basic hygiene. The prohibition regarding touching dead animals, eating blood or entrails, and avoiding the meat of animals which died on their own, shows a concern for contamination and disease that protected the Jews from many a plague.

This illustrates a rather general principle about our relationship with God. There are things that we must learn to take on faith. There are times and places where we need to obey, not because we understand fully what is going on, but because we trust the teller. It would have been ridiculous for God to have tried to explain about microbiology 3,500 years before the microscope - and unnecessary. The Jews did not have to understand about germs to be protected from them. That understanding could come later. But the protection was needed then and it was given.

This principle of obedience as a fundamental part of our relationship with God has been illustrated earlier, but not more graphically than in the food laws. It was never really defined for the Jews in just what way the food was unclean. They took it to mean some spiritual or moral character. We can see that in most cases, it was literally, physically, unclean. We do not have to understand everything, though, in order to understand enough. Most often, when God says "no" about something, it is to protect us, or because He has something better in mind. Both were true for the food laws. Take a look again at what kind of diet is described. It has only taken science several centuries to determine that the low fat and low cholesterol diet prescribed in Leviticus, is healthy for you!

This illustrates another basic Biblical principle - progressive revelation. God has continued to reveal more and more of His purpose and plan for creation. But we do not understand it all yet by a long stretch. So, when in doubt, it is far better to obey! It may be quite some time before we know why, but we need to be safe in the mean time!

# Day 40
# Leviticus 13-14

The thing that strikes me about these laws concerning leprosy is the calm and deliberate fashion with which they are handled. In a time when the treatment was limited to virtually nothing, the concern for both the victim and the community at large, are evident in these passages. There is caution for the community but at the same time concern for the sick. Our own society's hysteria over communicable diseases should tell us that this was quite an accomplishment for any community - now or then.

It is also worth noting that there is no suggestion here that leprosy was a punishment or judgement from God. The offerings prescribed for declaring someone clean were the same for anyone giving offerings at the temple. Those who had been unclean would not have been able to participate in community activities. The sacrifices were therefore not unusual, but those which would be expected from one who had not worshipped for a time.

The sacrifices were again in proportion to the ability of the person to afford them. All throughout the sacrificial system, this equity is evident. The offerings given were not to please God, as if large animals were more acceptable than small ones, but the sacrifice needed to be in proportion to the ability to give. Once again, the objective of the offerings was not to change God, but the person giving the offering. This is the whole basis of the tithe, that the giving is equitable because it is in proportion to the ability to give. The total "dollar" amount was not important, but the percentage was - it should be a sacrifice - one that would be felt, but one that would not cause undue burden. There need then be no cause for pride or envy. Each person could know that they had given an equal amount - in proportion to their ability.

These kinds of evenhanded and equitable relationships are critical for a healthy society. We do not need to return to the practices of Leviticus in relation to leprosy, but we do need to see the kind of balance between concern for the community and individual represented there. The idea that we are all obligated to share equally in the burden of civic responsibility rich and poor alike - is a healthy one that we need to return to. "Welfare" cannot make anyone "well" until it recognizes the responsibilities of the recipients as well as their need to receive help.

# Day 41
# Leviticus 15-17

Yom Kippur - the Day of Atonement. This is the holiest day of the year for the Jews. It was (and is) the annual event that marks the removal of the sins of the people. The whole sacrificial system finds its basis in this idea, that God has provided a way for the sins of the people to be removed. Every part of this ceremony had symbolic significance.

One of the things that is so obvious that it almost escapes our notice, is that this day came only once a year. It is crucial to realize that the ceremony itself did not constitute some kind of spiritual cause and effect chain. The offering of the sacrifice, done properly, did not compel God to forgive the people. If forgiveness was something that had to be purchased, or acquired after each offense, a person's salvation would certainly be the most fragile of things. We commit sins that we are hardly aware of. The sacrifices would have to be performed daily for each person and the whole community if that kind of legalism were represented in the sacrificial system. But that was not the case. The ceremony showed the graciousness of God, it did not cause it. And once a year was sufficient to be reminded and renewed.

The second obvious thing that gets missed, is that this was an annual sacrifice for all the people, not the individual. We are all guilty of the sins of our society, for we are all members of it. Even if we did not commit the sins ourselves, we bear a measure of the guilt - we *are* our brother's keepers.

There were two goats used in the ceremony. One was sacrificed as the gracious substitute for the people. The other was released into the wilderness. The term "scapegoat" comes from this second animal. God not only forgives, He also removes the sin, as David will later write in the one hundred and third Psalm, ". . . as far as the east is from the west, so far does he remove our transgressions from us."

The New Testament writers will talk later about God nailing our sins to the cross in Christ. We should remember, however, the whole of scripture belongs to us. God has not only forgiven, but removed our sins. We truly can feel that we have a new start - and we should do this at least once a year. Our sins are forgiven and gone! Praise be to God!

# Day 42
# Leviticus 18-20

The first sixteen chapters of Leviticus are usually seen as setting forth the ways in which sin, once committed, could be accounted for. These were the laws that reestablished a right relationship with God. The second part of Leviticus is usually seen as setting forth the laws by which you could maintain a right relationship with God. This is usually called the holiness code.

The formula is repeated over and over again. You are to do, or not do something, in order to remain holy; that is, set apart from the rest of the world. Over and over it is repeated that the people of God are to be holy even as God Himself is holy. They are not to be like the nations which were to be driven out. Repeatedly, this is stated and finished with the reminder that God is the one who delivered them out of Egypt - that He is the Lord. Holiness finds its source and purpose in the very character and nature of God. We are to be like Him, if we are in fact going to be His people.

The sacrificial system was not so much superseded by Jesus' sacrifice, as it was fulfilled. The food laws and sacrifices are no longer needed and we are told so in the New Testament. However, the laws of conduct for a holy life are neither changed nor "fulfilled." They continue to be descriptions of what living a holy life should look like. A holy life is exemplified by concern for justice at every level, especially the personal one. People are never to be objects, but always treated with the dignity due them as creatures made in God's image. Relationships are to be valued and respected. You do not violate the relationships of close family, between husbands and wives, or your neighbor. Sexuality is to be expressed properly or not at all. Contacts with spirits other than God Himself is dangerous and prohibited.

Some people believe that just like the sacrifices, the laws of a holy life as described in Leviticus, no longer apply. There seems to be very little support for that understanding in the New Testament. When asked to sum up the law and prophets, the part of Jesus' answer, to love your neighbor as yourself, comes from the holiness code in Leviticus. We should read these verses carefully - Jesus did. They are a description of what a holy life and a just society look like. The Lord is God - these are His rules.

# Day 43
# Leviticus 21-23

ithout blemish. This is a phrase that is repeated over and over again in these chapters. The priests, the sacrifices, the offerings, were all supposed to be the first fruits and the finest that there were to offer. Why this preoccupation with purity? Is God really such a snob that only the best will do?

This does not seem to be a difficult question to answer from the perspective of a minister. God wants to be God in our lives. He wants to occupy the first place in our hearts, minds, and souls. We consistently want to put something else in His place. We have our own agendas and values, and they usually mean that we would like God to take care of Himself and we will take care of ourselves.

God commanded the first fruits and the best offerings so we could show that He is valuable to us. As Jesus will say himself, where our treasure is, there our hearts will be also. I see it in the church all the time. We receive donations of items that people no longer want, everything from old televisions to used carpet. They have used them and are through with them, and rather than throw them away, they give them "for the work of God." This sounds noble, but is it?

God deserves our best. Without Him we would not only *have* nothing, we would *be* nothing. Yet, He has not asked of us that we turn over everything. He has asked that we give of our first and our best to show our gratitude. If we are not willing to do so, we might as well not bother at all. God Himself has no need of our money or the sacrifices and offerings described in Leviticus. He already owns everything and He could create at a word anything else He might want. But we have a great need to show what our priorities are - to show how strong is the hold that our possessions have on us. It is clear that while a great many people think they possess things, their things really have possession of them.

God invites us to be free and cheerful givers - to give with the gratitude and confidence that God has blessed us and will continue to do so. This requires we give of our first and our best - of our time, treasure and talent. Anything less isn't worth bothering with!

# Day 44
# Leviticus 24-25

The year of Jubilee! What a fascinating socio-political concept! Many have accused the Bible of not having a particular form of government and social order, but it is clearly stated here. It is neither communism in which everything is owned by the state and private property is non- existent, nor is it unbridled capitalism in which the rich get richer and the poor pay taxes. It is Jubilee - a cycle for society even as there is a cycle of the seasons.

It has long been recognized that as a social theory, communism lacks the ability to adequately account for the sinfulness of people. The fact is that people will not work very hard for the "good of the whole." Centralized control, not only of production, but of distribution, gives no incentive to individual effort or creativity. Collectivism, in any form, tends to bring everything to its lowest common denominator, not the highest.

On the other hand, it has also been recognized that pure capitalism can be enormously cruel. Pure self interest by each individual cannot be a binding social theory. We do need to consider others in society, both those who are less gifted, and less motivated. The rights of the individual cannot be separated from the rights of the group. "Let the buyer beware" may be good stoic advice, but it cannot be a sufficient basis for a social contract.

God offered the principle of Jubilee as the proper middle ground. The creativity and initiative of the individual could be rewarded. Those who worked harder, deserved to prosper for their efforts. But, in some matters, especially business, having a head start can translate into a perpetual unfair advantage. So, every fifty years, the scales were to be rebalanced. This reshuffling would bring new vitality, even to a stagnant economy.

Beyond even the genius of the plan, the witness of an entire society that took every seventh year off, redistributed the wealth every fiftieth year, and still prospered, should surely have attracted the attention of the world. Sadly, there is no evidence to indicate that the Jews ever celebrated the Jubilee as defined, even once.

Yet the principle is still good - cycles of activity and rest, of opportunity and redistribution. One wonders if it might still work. We can almost be certain it will never be tried.

# Day 45
# Leviticus 26-27

As the book of Leviticus draws to a close, the whole nature and understanding of the covenant is reaffirmed. The language here is clear and specific. What will happen if they are faithful is spelled out and what will happen if they are not faithful is spelled out - in vivid detail. Through it all, God repeats His faithfulness to His promises, to the people and to their fathers, Abraham, Isaac, and Jacob.

It cannot be overemphasized that this covenant was not based on the performance of the Jews. It is repeated several times just in this passage, that God is the God who delivered them out of the land of Egypt. This gracious action of God is the basis of the covenant relationship. The new relationship defined in the covenant on Mount Sinai, was still based on this graciousness. It would be new only in the sense that there would be a new purpose for their relationship. They were to become a priestly nation, an example to the world that Yahweh was God. This is not why God loved them or chose them. But, since God loved them, He gave them an opportunity to enter into a great new work with Him - one that would be an example to the nations.

The definitions of the covenant are therefore not definitions that create the covenant, but ones that operate within the relationship. Both the positive and negative definitions were not a case of the Jews getting what they deserved, but what they had been promised. When they obeyed the covenant, God would bless them beyond what they could normally expect. The rains would be favorable, the animals would be tame, and their enemies would flee. These would all be the action of God, and we will read about these events as we go further. When they disobeyed, however, they could expect to suffer, not what they deserved, but what God had promised. But even the punishment was always with an eye toward their repentance. In either case, they were to remember that what happened was both a response to their actions, and the hand of God at work.

God's grace and love are not products of the New Testament times - nor is His justice and discipline only Old Testament qualities. If the church is the new Israel perhaps we should consider our covenant more carefully!

# Day 46
# Numbers 1-2

These may be two of the most boring chapters in the whole Bible for most people. We can be glad that we are done with them. We should also be aware that they have caused more controversy for Biblical scholars than almost any others, because of the numbers of people in the Exodus recorded here. I think we should also be glad these chapters are included in scripture beyond just providing something to keep the scholars busy.

Most of the controversy centers around whether or not the numbers of people could have been accurate. The size of the group described in these chapters would certainly have been enormous. Only the men were counted here, so the accompanying women and children would have swelled it to a staggering number. For some, this stretches the limits of credibility and makes them question the accuracy and authenticity of the Bible. Others feel that if we do not believe the numbers exactly as given, we cannot believe anything the Bible has to say at all.

The sad thing is that we cannot prove it one way or the other, but we let the debate tear us apart. We cannot go back in time with our computers and do a recount. It is an argument that cannot be resolved but also one that need not be avoided. If we could learn to live with the idea that we are limited in our ability to know some things, we would do better, not only in Biblical scholarship, but in life. There are some things we cannot know, some things we were not meant to know, and some things that are not worth worrying about. I will leave it to you to decide wherein this one fits.

Yet, I think there is a reason to be glad these chapters were included. Whatever else we might conclude from them, we must certainly know that the writer was trying to be historically accurate. Our Bible is, from the outset, claiming to be an historical book. The sacred writings of some other religions are story, myth, or metaphysical in nature. The Bible claims to be history. These people were not merely characters in a story, they were our ancestors. The God they worshipped was not a mere idea, they believed He was really God.

That is at least the claim that is made. Only faith can confirm it. Let us at least not try to make it something it is not.

# Day 47
# Numbers 3-4

Logistics played a large part in the wandering in the wilderness recorded in the book of Numbers. It was quite a task just counting the tribes and assigning them places and duties. I have lead several mission trips with youth groups myself, but the idea of being responsible for that many people for that long a time would give me night sweats.

No matter how grand and glorious one's dreams may be, when they get down to becoming reality, the problem of logistics rears its ugly head. Every person must be accounted for, not just for food and lodging, but for jobs. People are unpredictable and everything they do, or don't do, will have an impact on the project. Every great undertaking must master the control of the details or fail as a result.

As the Jews were setting out from the foot of Mount Sinai, the first thing that had to be done was to take account of themselves - literally and figuratively. This kind of inventory is necessary in every endeavor if you are to anticipate problems and be ready for them. It is amazing how difficult this can be for us as humans on the level of the physical or the spiritual.

When was the last time you took an account of yourself? What assets do you have? What do you own materially? What do you owe? Do you have the things you really need? Do you really need the things you have? What do you really use, and what could you give to someone else who might use it?

Beyond the material things, what assets has God given you within yourself? How healthy are you? What skills, talents, abilities, knowledge, special training and experience do you have at your disposal? How valuable are your relationships with your family, your friends, and your co-workers? When you put this picture together, what has God equipped you for?

When we think seriously about all the blessings that have been given to us, it is humbling to realize what potential we have. In a world so full of need, we should not underestimate the resources that are at our disposal to help out. We are far better equipped than we think. But we need to manage our resources. And that starts by taking an account of your life. Will you try today - now?

# Day 48
# Numbers 5-7

**J**ealousy. We usually think of jealousy as more of a vice than a virtue, but it is spoken of in rather supportive terms in the Old Testament. In the Ten Commandments, God calls Himself a jealous God, and here we see provision made for dealing with jealousy within a marriage. Why is this emotion so strong and yet so divided?

Jealousy certainly has its negative side. Unreasonable jealousy can cause the kind of paranoia and suspicion that is the antithesis of trust. It can quickly destroy the intimacy that love requires. No matter how much of a compliment it might seem, jealousy soon focuses on the feelings of the jealous person rather than those of the beloved. This is the opposite of what love does, which is to focus not on itself, but on the good of the beloved.

On the other hand, jealousy seems to be, at times, a function of love itself. It is not wrong for love to want to occupy its proper place in the heart and life of the beloved. To be displaced from that position should cause jealousy in the heart of the lover. Love, even freely given, deserves its due. To deny love its proper place in our lives, is to do it an injustice it does not deserve, for real love is always worth receiving.

When I was in college I had a friend who was so close that she was like a sister. We talked many hours sharing our hopes and dreams about the future and listening to each others joys and sorrows. One day, she starting dating my roommate, and suddenly, all her time was taken up with him. Some time later, the night they broke up, she called to talk to me. I went and listened and we renewed our close friendship. I went home angry though. I was angry because I had been jealous. Not jealous in a romantic sense, for we would never be anything but friends, but jealous that my roommate had taken my place in her life. The truth be told, I loved her more that he did, and she had turned to him for the care and understanding that I had to offer, not him.

As I said my prayers that night, God mentioned that I make him feel jealous too. I often keep my hearts joys and concerns to myself, or take them to others who cannot understand or frankly, do not care as much. God does not want to be our mate, He wants to be our God. It is a very special relationship, very personal, very intimate. He is right to be jealous. We should be too.

# Day 49
# Numbers 8-10

obile Army Surgical Hospital. M\*A\*S\*H was a hit movie, a hit T.V. series and before that an important military branch. You can almost see the concept here in Numbers as the Israelites camped around the tabernacle and moved as the cloud of the presence of God instructed them. When the cloud stayed, they stayed. When the cloud moved, they broke camp and moved. The MObile People of God - MO\*P\*O\*G.

Actually, God was doing something very important in this exercise of moving the people. While it appeared to be very arbitrary to them, it *was* purposeful. Before they were to enter the land, they had to be prepared for what lay ahead. They had received the law, been given a new system of worship and government, had counted off and learned the relative positions of their tribes when they camped and when they moved. They had taken inventory of themselves and their goods. What remained now, was to practice: to drill. All armies must train for battle. They must know how to break camp and how to make camp. Setup and teardown must be routine procedures.

Armies also need to know how to take orders. Commands seldom have the luxury of arriving with explanations. There must be faith between the foot soldier and the commander, so that when a command is given, it is obeyed precisely and with dispatch. For an army, delay can mean defeat.

God is a masterful planner. Look at the order and symmetry in our universe. Details are important to God, and He has taken them all into account. He never gives His people a task that He does not prepare them for, and prepare them fully. He gives not only talent, but training. The problem is that we sometimes have a hard time remembering that we are always in God's school, and so we miss the lesson: the training intended for us.

Do you feel that you are wandering in the wilderness? Does it seem to you that you are stuck or running around in circles while others are getting what they want? Perhaps it is time to change your questions. What is God preparing you for right now? Have you checked with the General (God) lately to find out what your marching orders are? Don't you think you should? How about today?

# Day 50
# Numbers 11-13

One of the truest tests of character is how one handles challenges to one's authority and position. Moses met this challenge with the kind of grace and confidence that befits a great leader in any time. He had changed a good deal over the years, from the headstrong man who killed an Egyptian, to the hesitant man who tried to refuse his calling at the burning bush, to the leader we see in the desert.

Perhaps it missed your notice, but Moses' life can be divided into three, almost equal periods. His first forty years were spent in the household of Pharaoh. During his second forty years, he was in the country with his father-in-law, Jethro, where he had escaped after killing the Egyptian soldier. His final forty years were spent leading those whining, complaining people. While he was no longer a spring chicken, he had developed into one of the most able leaders in history.

Moses had grown a great deal from his encounters with God. He had come to understand the true nature and purpose of the One who had called him. When God poured out His Spirit on the seventy, to help share the burden of leadership, Moses showed no sign of insecurity. When Joshua wanted to stop the two who went into the camp to prophesy, Moses stopped him and said he would be glad if everyone could experience God's Spirit in such a special way. When Aaron and Miriam turned on him, it was Moses who pleaded with God for his sister. Moses was no longer threatened by what was happening because he had finally learned where his confidence belonged - in God and His call, not anywhere else.

These two traits of exceptional leadership, the desire to share power rather than protect privilege, and compassion for those who oppose you, are rare qualities indeed. Moses had been attending some very advanced classes in God's school and he had learned well. We should not underestimate the difficulty or importance of that.

Have you learned from your encounters with God? The Israelites are proof that it is possible to run headlong into the power of God and remain unaffected. What lesson has God been trying to teach you lately? Are you ready to learn it?

# Day 51
# Numbers 14-15

gain the people complained. They wished they were back in Egypt, they forgot the miracles God had done to bring them out of the land of bondage, and again Moses had to intercede for them. But this time, they had gone too far, and they would suffer the consequences. This story fairly reverberates with tension, pathos, and sadness.

There are certainly many things to consider in this story. We do not dare miss seeing the dangers of living in the past. The Israelites were prime examples of the crippling nature of nostalgia. They looked back at Egypt and forgot all the slavery, the murdering of their male children when Pharaoh tried to kill the baby who turned out to be Moses, the bitterness of being told what to do and when to do it. Instead, they remembered only the few comforts that had been theirs. The lenses with which we see the past with are so often rose colored.

What seems almost incomprehensible, is that when they looked back, they didn't remember the power of God shown in the ten plagues, a parted sea, a drowned army, and food delivered each day. What kind of strange disease afflicted their memory that they so quickly forgot the mighty works of God?

Perhaps it comes from the kind of loss of hope that slavery can bring. Dreamers and visionaries do not make good slaves. Those are either beaten into submission, or killed outright. The ones remaining have so little hope, they lose their ability to have faith, even in the present. No looking to tomorrow, just don't beat them today.

The Israelites of the Exodus appear to have had no ability to have hope or faith, with just a handful of exceptions. Caleb's plea falls not on deaf ears, but numb ones. The eyes can no longer look forward, only at today and yesterday - and they see neither of those clearly.

What might be even more sobering, is to realize that this is no game we are playing with God. It is possible to resist the good which God wants to give us. Another lesson to be learned from this is that while God's love is infinite, opportunities to do His will are not. Are we so different from the Israelites? Can we afford not to be?

# Day 52
# Numbers 16-18

Amazingly, some people think that faith is not really a very important or practical part of life. I find this amazing because nothing else is so foundational to our very beings as our faith. The rebellion of Korah, Dathan, and Abiram is a perfect example of just how critical faith is to everything we do and all the decisions we make in life.

At face value it may appear that this rebellion was founded in high principle. Korah made the point well, that the whole of Israel was to be a holy people, not just Moses and Aaron. The covenant had been with all the people, not just a select few. And the judgement of wandering in the wilderness instead of entering into the promised land had to have seemed a particularly bitter one to those two hundred and fifty leaders who rose against Moses and Aaron. But that was precisely the point at which their lack of faith had caused their undoing.

It had been lack of faith that had caused the bitter complaining among the people ever since Moses had first appeared. They complained during the plagues, even though they were spared from the effects of those plagues, they complained during the exodus, even though they left carrying the gold and jewels of Egypt, they complained in the desert, even though food and water were miraculously provided each day, and they complained when they were sentenced only to wander the desert instead of being killed outright. How quickly they had forgotten that their wandering was itself an act of grace. They should have all been dead. The fact that they were not was a gift from God, but one that only the eyes of faith could see - eyes which they quite obviously lacked.

We all have our complaints with God. Maybe He didn't make us rich enough, or smart enough, or tall enough, or talented enough for our liking. But, perhaps we had better take a closer look at our lives. Perhaps what we have seen as curse, has really been kindness. Certainly, the most important thing is that God has given us Himself - He is with us. If we could just see that, our faith could transform the rest of the view of our lives, and we might be quite surprised at the picture we see. Look again - was that a desert or a dessert?

# Day 53
# Numbers 19-21

T he decline and fall of the Jews is almost complete in this passage. The great people that God had sought to bring out of the land of Egypt and into the promised land have fallen into disbelief and disobedience - even the great Moses himself. Aaron and Miriam had died and the leaders who had brought them out of Egypt were almost gone. There is a weariness about the time that lingers in these pages even centuries later.

It seems unfair that Moses should not be allowed this one "slip up" at Meribah. After all, the people with whom he had to contend, were far more unfaithful, far more disobedient, and far more unruly, than Moses. Isn't it only fair to be graded "on the curve?" We should be compared to other people: "Well, at least I wasn't *that* bad!" We never want to be held up against an inflexible standard. We are like the two men who were being attacked by a bear. The one started to put on track shoes and his companion said, "What are you doing, you can't outrun a bear!" The first man replied, "I don't have to outrun the bear, I just have to outrun you!"

God does not grade on the curve, and we should be glad. It is really a miserable lifestyle to have to compare yourself to others all the time. God has a standard by which we will be measured, regardless of how our neighbor has done. I hope by now, that you have seen that the standard is faith, not works. Moses had disqualified himself as the one who would lead the people into the land because he had finally given into the temptation of which Korah had accused him - he began to see himself as better, on a higher level of being, on God's level. Working with the likes of the Israelites, could God afford that kind of pride in their leader? They had already shown how easily they were misled. Anything short of unwavering faith would have led to disaster.

Yet, Moses did not fall out of God's love. In fact, when you consider what was to come, not leading those people anymore could almost be seen as a gift, not a curse. But leadership must be judged with greater severity for the sins of the leaders will be multiplied many times. What we must remember is that we do not serve in order to be loved, we are loved and therefore can serve. Moses forgot that, and it cost him - but maybe not that much.

# Day 54
# Numbers 22-24

I am sure that this story of Balaam and Balak must have made for good telling around the Israelite campfires. Balak, the bad guy, tries to get Balaam, the prophet, to curse Israel, but God thwarts Balak at every turn. The reluctant Balaam even has a close encounter of the Dr. Dolittle kind, with his beast of burden. No doubt, the humor was not lost on the Israelites - score: God 1; Moabites 0.

But what was the flap all about? Would it really have made any difference what Balaam said about Israel? For that matter, is there really such a thing as a curse, or a blessing?

One thing seems clear from this account. The reputation of Israel, and her God, had already proceeded them. It does seem hard to believe that a group of people that size could have gone unnoticed by the countries around them. There seems to have been an understanding too, that this strange group wandering in the desert, had escaped the clutches of Pharaoh. The Jews had also scored several military victories and exhibited some sense of purpose driving them. The surrounding nations had heard the rumors of how they managed to stay alive in the desert, and there was growing anxiety about what they could and would do next.

Moses had pleaded several times for just this reputation. This was to be the people of God. They were to be an example of His power and greatness. There is no suggestion that they needed Balaam's blessing, nor that they should fear his curse, for God was with them. But God had chosen to show that they could not even be cursed without His permission. Not only would this people of God not be stopped, they would not even be slowed down a little.

There was no power in Balaam's words, only in God's purpose. Balaam knew that and tried to tell this to Balak several times. Balaam had no particular love for Israel, but he had no real say in the matter anyway. No external force would have been able to stand up against the purpose of the covenant God and His people. Only an internal one could do that.

There is a lesson here for the Church to learn. What kind of reputation do we have as a people of God? What does it take to stop us from accomplishing His purpose? Just how unstoppable are we? The world is watching.

# Day 55
# Numbers 25-26

srael had really done it this time. They had gone beyond mere whining and complaining. They had turned their backs on the power of God which had thwarted the attempts of Balak to defeat them. No external enemy would have been able to defeat the purpose of the God of Israel, but an internal one could. As it has been repeated so many times in history, danger comes not from without, but from within.

It seems unbelievable to us as we read this passage, that the Israelites could have been so blind. But temptation can be a more formidable enemy than many armies. The worship of Baal Peor was gay and exciting. Baal was a common Canaanite name for the god of the harvest, or more broadly understood, fertility. Baal Peor was the Moabite version which was worshipped in the "high places" with ritual and festive prostitution, both male and female. This was a "feel good" religion in its truest sense: if it feels good, do it!

The trouble with that kind of "feel good" religion is that it doesn't really "feel good" for very long. Those who have been involved in prostitution for any time at all, find it is anything but an uplifting experience. Prostitution inevitably treats both parties as things, a means to an end, and not as noble creatures made in the image of God. We should never treat each other as only a means to an end. People are an end in themselves. To treat them as less is always a degrading experience.

Make no mistake, it is enticing at the beginning. There is an excitement and frivolity that is very attractive about the "if it feels good, do it" philosophy. Unfortunately, the payment for our actions eventually comes due, and we are often unpleasantly surprised at the cost.

We cannot have it both ways. If we want to be treated with the dignity of beings made in the image of God, we must act and treat others as such. If we want to use them only as means to our own ends, we will degrade ourselves in the process and enter into a battle which we will have lost from the beginning.

Israel played the harlot, figuratively and literally. But with harlotry, there is very little "play" involved. This is no game. God takes us very seriously: can we do less?

# Day 56
# Numbers 27-29

Just when you thought it was safe to go back to reading, along comes another listing of the feasts and festivals that the Jews were supposed to keep! How many times does this have to be repeated? If we are measuring by how well these rites were observed, the answer would be even more times than this. The Jews fell away from practicing the covenant like most of us do our diets.

It does me good, though, to see the list of things that the people of God were supposed to celebrate. Sometimes when I look at our modern calendar, with some "special" occasion every month except August (and after all, that's "back-to-school") I wonder when we ever get any work done. It is comforting to know the tradition of celebrations goes back so far.

There is something in all of this that tends to get lost: the people of God were supposed to be a celebrating people. Not all of the ceremonies were high solemn affairs. The Jews had a reputation among the nations as being very austere and perhaps compared to the debauchery that went on at many pagan ceremonies, they were. But celebrating and giving thanks was not only supposed to be part of their life, but central to their religious life.

Some might accuse me of trying to build a theology for parties, and there is some truth in that. The idea that life is cruel and austere is a stoic doctrine, not a Christian one. God made the world a beautiful place, full of lovely and fun things to see and do. Mountains were meant to be skied, forests to be hiked in and beaches to be walked. Smiling requires far fewer muscles than frowning. The rejection of enjoyment in this life is a rejection of the very intent of God. There is a time for work, and there is a time for giving thanks and expressing joy.

It is a responsibility of the faith to stop and remember the saving acts of God, and also His original good plan for what life was meant to be. The festivals and celebrations described here in Numbers, may look to us as massive slaughters, but they were instead, holidays in the truest sense. They were "holy" days when you gave substitutionary sacrifice, remembered the gracious acts of God, and rested. Do our modern holidays measure up to this standard? Shouldn't they?

# Day 57
# Numbers 30-31

holy war. There have certainly been many claims to this throughout the centuries. Conversely, many people claim that there is no such thing. I fancy that I am a typical modern man in that I would much rather speak of a "just" war than a "holy" one. The claim itself begs for proof, and it sounds hollow and not a little foolish to hear both sides claiming it in a conflict. But if ever there was a holy war, the one Israel was beginning certainly deserved the title. This account of the defeat of the Midianites without the loss of one Israelite is just the first of many miraculous victories that give credence to their claim.

Perhaps it is time to face some unpleasant truths about the Scriptures. There seems to be a sense among many people today, that a God of love could not be involved in anything so bloody and senseless as war. Most certainly, He would not order a war much less the extermination of every man, woman, and child. It just wouldn't be nice.

But, I am afraid that the Scriptures paint a different picture of God's view of things. God does not value human life less than we do, but He does value it differently. He sees us, not just as creatures whose life ends at death, but creatures who will live an eternity after death. That does not degrade the value of this life, but it does change it. The fact is that we will all die. It is not a question of *if*, but only of *when*. If there are things worth dying for, there must be things worth killing for. This may not sound nice, but that does not make it bad.

I do not believe that God is nice, but I do believe He is good. A nice God would not allow people to die of starvation, or to be born with birth defects, or allow rapists, child molesters, and murderers to assault their victims. Apparently, a good God does. But a nice God would also have had nothing to do with wretched and filthy humanity. Niceness either ignores mess, or leaves it for someone else to clean up. Goodness has the strength to roll up its sleeves and get dirty in the process of cleaning things up.

I cannot give a final answer as to how God can allow so much evil to exist in the world. But I can give thanks to know that He is intimately involved in the pain and mess. It isn't nice, but it is very good.

# Day 58
# Numbers 32-33

Poised and almost ready to go into the promised land, this new generation of Israelites was already showing signs of lacking the fortitude to carry out God's agenda. The tribe of Reuben had already become comfortable where they were and wanted to settle for the land they already possessed. And there was an eerie warning of what would come to pass in the promised land, as the Israelites would fail to eliminate all the Canaanites who dwelt there.

I am struck on one hand, by the flexibility of God's plan, and on the other, by its undeviating nature. The tribe of Reuben asked to be allowed to stay. This *asking* was not sinful in itself. Moses warned them about what happened to their forefathers when they would not obey God. Yet, a compromise allowed the tribe of Reuben to return to the land east of the Jordan once the promised land was secured for the other tribes. The plan was modified to meet the new and changing demands. I think this is a mirror of much of God's plan for us. There is an overall purpose which must be served, but within that, there is flexibility for personal preferences.

On the other hand, taking the land completely, and being both the judgement of God against the Canaanites as well as the fulfillment of the promise to Abraham, were the main purposes of God's plan that could not be compromised without drastic consequences. There are some things that cannot be done by half measure. You cannot "mostly" give birth, or "mostly" stop the car in the garage, or, apparently, "mostly" conquer a people. Any part left unaccounted for will eventually lead to your own undoing.

It is hard for us to carry through with things. We either get tired, or distracted, or discover we really didn't want to go through with it, in the first place. We must remember, however, that the race is not won by being the first one out of the gate. It is won by being the first one to cross the finish line. And life is much more like a marathon than a sprint. If we wish to find the will of God and do it, we had best pack a large portion of perseverance in our backpacks. Without that essential supply, we will not achieve the goal for which we set out. And some things, left unaccomplished, can turn out to be very dangerous failures.

# Day 59
# Numbers 34-36

ustice and mercy do not necessarily have to be strangers. We see the balance of the two here at the end of the book of Numbers. Still, it seems like a curious way to end this rather choppy book. Like waves on a stormy ocean, the Israelites years of wandering were far from quiet. Yet, between the swells, there were times of tranquility. Perhaps it is fitting for this book to end with a look toward the future of the people, the way things ought to be in the promised land.

Once again, reading the description of Old Testament justice gives me a strong sense of the impact it has had on the western culture's understanding of law. There was a concern for equity before the law for the rich and the poor. Provision was always made in the sacrifices so as not to favor the rich or overburden the poor, and the land was to be divided equally among the tribes. There was even great care to make sure that marriages did not cause an inequality in land holdings. These may seem like obvious things to us, but that is because we live with the benefits which have come from centuries of these understandings. However, throughout history, money and power have been able to buy privilege. In many parts of the world (and some say here too) it still can. But the belief that it should not be that way, and laws to back up that belief, are a direct legacy of the justice declared here.

There was mercy available too. The sacrificial system was the prime example, but it shows up too in the concept of the refuge cities. They were not to thwart justice, but instead, to guarantee that it was done evenhandedly, and in public. But they could not harbor the guilty. Murderers would receive justice. Those guilty of manslaughter could be safe but confined until the priest died. Then they were free to go home. In no case could they buy their way out early. God's law, not money, would wield the power in their society.

These may seem like unimportant matters, but not if you have ever been a victim. The benefit of a just society is too often appreciated only by those who do not live in one. We are the beneficiaries of a tremendous tradition of clear and just laws. How well are we taking care of our legacy?

# Day 60
# Deuteronomy 1-2

**S**ummaries and repetition are important tools for teaching. Moses was using both these tools in this book to reinforce the lessons that Israel should have been learning all along. The name itself - Deuteronomy - means "second law." It is the name given by the scribes who translated the Old Testament into Greek from its original Hebrew - called the Septuagint. This was not a new law, but the second "giving" of the law to the people.

We should remember, that some of what Moses related, was new to this generation of Israelites. Their elders had all perished in the wilderness because of their disobedience. Those who would enter the promised land were just children when many of these great events had taken place. Moses wanted to send them off with the proper understanding and perspective.

A lot can be learned from a person's summary of events. Moses wanted to make sure that two things were perfectly clear. First, that God was the one who had called them out of Egypt and had been with them all through their wanderings. It was God who had delivered them, God who sustained them, God who had given them their victories, and God who would be with them in the future.

He also wanted to make it clear that the difficulties they had encountered had been a result of the lack of faith and obedience by Israel, not by God. God had called them to be a priestly people, and they had accepted that call. The call came with promises, both of help and discipline. Not following that call would not derail the purpose of God, but it could be very costly to them indeed.

Have we learned these lessons in our own lives? When you look back on your life, can you see clearly that God has been at work? Are you remembering those answered prayers and drawing strength to believe today from God's faithful actions of yesterday? If not, you are missing out on the power of the past to help in the present.

Have you heard His call? Do you believe that He has given you a purpose for your life? Why else should you have been chosen to know of the love of God if not to spread that message to others? You know, won't you tell?

# Day 61
## Deuteronomy 3-4

 as anybody really watching? Moses argued that the people should obey the commandments so that the other nations might know that Yahweh was God. God had led them out of the land of Egypt with signs and miracles, had sustained them in the desert and given them victory over their enemies. He had also killed those who had rebelled and those who had worshipped the gods of the Moabites. But was anybody really watching?

It seems that in fact, they were. One of the things that seems to be continuous, throughout the centuries, is that people are busy bodies. We like to keep track of what our neighbors are doing. Long before the Evening News or Entertainment Tonight, people were keeping an eye on each other and what the "other guys" were up to. Call it gossip, or call it news, or even call it history, we have a positive addiction to finding out how the people next door go about their business.

Reputations can be powerful things. Moses argued for God's reputation several times when Israel had transgressed to the point that God was ready to wipe them out. It was not just the reputation of Israel on the line, but the reputation of God. This was the people God had chosen just for this purpose, that they might be known as His people. They were to be of the highest moral character, obedient to laws far superior to those of other nations. They were to have a system of politics and economics that would be the envy of the world. They were to have military success unparalleled in any time. Their actions were to speak as clearly as their words.

The other nations were watching - and they still are. We will find out in the New Testament that the Church is the new Israel: the people of God. We are to be all these things too. We should be unparalleled in our justice, unrivaled in our ethics, above reproach in our politics, and without peer in our economics. Are we? Do we even try?

It's not easy to be priestly people. The standards are as high as the stakes. We do not cease to be God's people when we fail, but we drag God's reputation down with our own. People are watching. What will they see? They will not see perfect people. Let us hope they see humble ones.

# Day 62
# Deuteronomy 5-7

t is almost unfortunate that this book is called Deuteronomy. Aside from the fact that most people don't really know what the name means (deutero - second, and nomos - law), those that do, can be mislead by the title. There is a great misunderstanding about the Old Testament and the law to begin with, and it is not particularly helped here.

The problem is that most people think of the "law" as being a kind of contract. A covenant, however, is something very different from a contract. In a contract, the performance of the people in the contract, is dependent on each other. One person promises to do something *if* the other does something else. If either party does not fulfill their end, the contract is void.

A covenant, by contrast, is the establishment of a relationship that is not based on the performance of the people in the covenant, but upon the character of the people in the covenant. You make a promise of performance based on your character. In that respect, a covenant is never any better than the word of those who enter into it. For some, this does not amount to much, but for others, there is no greater assurance.

The Ten Commandments, reiterated here in these chapters are not the terms of a contract between God and Israel. They are the descriptions of the covenant relationship. They spell out how God would treat them depending upon how they obeyed the law. Their obedience did not earn them the covenant relationship - that had been granted graciously. Their disobedience did not release God from His commitment. He promised what He would do, one way or the other - and He has proven throughout the centuries to be good to His word.

That is why the "Shema" ("Hear, O Israel: the Lord your God is one Lord; and you shall love the Lord your God with all your heart, and with all your soul, and with all your might.") is not a duty, but a privilege. We do not have to love God to be loved by Him. We are free to love Him, because He has loved us first. This was as true for Abraham and Moses as it is for us.

Can we finally believe this is true? Can we really get off the treadmill of legalism into the freedom of God's covenant love? We can. Will we? Will you?

# Day 63
# Deuteronomy 8-10

Prosperity can be a very difficult thing to handle. Moses seemed to be very concerned that the Israelites would be quick to lose their perspective once they had become prosperous. He had reason to be worried. There is an old saying that nothing succeeds like success, but it appears that in the world of the human heart, nothing fails so quickly as success.

Moses wanted the people to remember that the blessings they enjoyed were the gracious gift of God, not their due. He repeats several times that it was not because of their righteousness that God had chosen them or sustained them or delivered them or set them up in the land. God was removing the other nations because of their disobedience, not because He loved Israel more or because they were somehow inherently better. If fact, they were disobedient, even after greater grace had been shown to them.

I think there is a sober warning to us in these chapters. We are certainly quick to think that when things are going well, they are doing so solely as a result of our good effort. Throughout the centuries, peoples who prosper are quick to become proud. Not only do we conclude that our success is due to our genius, but we assume that God is rewarding us in a special way, that in fact, He has chosen us because we are just plain superior - a master race, set apart to rule the lesser peoples of the world. How proud and wrong we become.

Especially in America in this century, we have inherited extraordinary blessings. Why should we have been so fortunate as to have been born here rather than into the abject poverty of so many other nations of our time? However we want to answer that question, it had better not be because we think we are better. We, like Israel, have not been chosen because we are more righteous. If God has blessed us more it is certainly not for the purpose of rewarding us for our superior righteousness. He has had a very different purpose in mind.

How quickly the Israelites forgot that the reason they were set apart - a priestly nation - was for the purpose of making God known to the other nations, not thumbing their noses at them. They were called to service, not privilege. So too, are we. How easy that is to forget and how dangerous.

# Day 64
# Deuteronomy 11-13

The spiritual well being of their children is a primary concern of every parent, or should be. We have all struggled to understand our faith, and we want to help our children to understand theirs too. How can we pass on our hard-fought understandings to our children that they too might know the love of God?

Moses again encouraged the people to remember the mighty acts of God. He told them to recite them and repeat them often, to make them like things written on the insides of their eyelids. They were to speak of them when they got up, when they walked, when they ate, and before they went to sleep. Remembering the acts of God was to be continual.

I certainly think that there is good advice here to parents, but we need to understand it fully. As a pastor, I see many families that try to follow this advice to the letter. In these families, no church meeting is ever missed. Bible verses are read, reread, written, colored, done in macaroni art work and memorized. Yet these are not always the children who later come to love the Lord and who are found regularly in His house of worship. Why should this be so?

There is most certainly nothing wrong in telling our children of the mighty acts of God recorded in Scripture. But that is not the only thing Moses told the people to remember. He also told them to remember their own mighty failures - the ways in which they turned from God, and His gracious acts of discipline and forgiveness. They were to tell of their sins, the consequences, their repentance and God's forgiveness and restoration.

It is too easy for us to tell of the sins of other people long dead from Biblical history. The message Moses has for us today is not just to remember what God did so long ago, but what has He done in *our* lives. How well have we told our children of the mighty acts of God in our lives? Have we told them of our failures, the consequences, our repentance and God's forgiveness of us? These are the mighty acts of God, no less than the Exodus, and, for our children, perhaps more important to know. It is fairly easy to share *the faith* with our children. It is much harder to share *our faith* with them. The latter encompasses both and is what I think Moses really meant.

# Day 65
# Deuteronomy 14-17

T he Jews got a reputation for being an austere people, but this was no fault of the definitions of God's covenant with them. When we read the descriptions of the covenant set forth in these chapters, we cannot conclude that these were to be an unhappy and sour people at all. Quite the contrary, consider the command of what to do with the tithe of the first fruits. They were to gather together, eat them and celebrate! I have heard many a sermon on tithing in my day, but never one from this passage! I wonder why?

As I read these passages I was impressed by the message that we are to remember constantly who is the source of our blessings. Not only are we to remember it is God who is the source of our blessings, but we should be living lives that depend on Him as the source. The Israelites were told time and time again they were to keep the commandments and God would keep blessing them. If they obeyed, they could count on the early rains and the late rains. They were to free their slaves every seven years and this should not be seen as a burden to them. 15:18 They were to give to the poor because God would provide abundance for all. They were to rest every seventh day, have a week-long feast seven weeks after the harvest, to rest every seventh year and redistribute the wealth every fiftieth year!

Of course, all this depended on God's constant blessing. That seems to have been the hard part for them. It is a frightening thing to trust in God. What if He doesn't come through? We had better make sure we have done some things to take care of ourselves - or so we reason.

Trusting is, of course, the hard work of faith. We should not underestimate the difficulty of living the risky life of faith. We want so much to be done with this religious stuff and God so much wants us never to be done with Him. But then, God doesn't want us to be religious, He wants us to be relational. He calls us to trust in Him and believe that we will be blessed beyond what we deserve.

This can rightly be called hard - for it is certainly hard to do- but not austere. Life with God is to be full of rejoicing and getting more than we deserve. It is life *without* Him that is truly hard.

# Day 66
# Deuteronomy 18-21

I can hardly say how thrilling it is for me as a minister to read that the portion due to the priest from any ox or sheep is the shoulder, two cheeks and the stomach!

The system of rules governing the people of Israel certainly seems very foreign to us on many fronts. But what are the underlying assumptions about the "State" of Israel, and do they still apply for our modern "State?"

I continue to be impressed with the impact that these laws in Deuteronomy have had on the western world's idea of justice. No one could be convicted of anything on the word of only one witness -two would be required. Justice should be "blind" with regard to whether or not the persons involved were foreigners or women or rich or poor. Justice was always to be administered in light of the fact that God would ultimately judge, not only the people involved, but the judge too.

One way in which we seem to have differed has been in our concept of responsibility. We have come to think of all behavior as the result of some cause other than choice. Therefore, we should pity the guilty for they could not help themselves. This was not so for God's people. Justice was to be without pity. If pity *were* going to enter into the equation of justice, it had to have some source other than the State. Even the individual who was wronged, was under no obligation to dispense mercy. This did make the society "pure" in one sense, but brutal in another.

I think we will find in the New Testament, God revealing reasons why, as individuals, we should be showing mercy, and even pity, on those who have wronged us. But I am not at all convinced that this is a quality that is supposed to be exhibited by the State. We have become so concerned about the "rights" of the criminal that we have forgotten about the needs of the victims. A society cannot continue to operate when justice is undercut in the name of pity.

Can a society be both just and merciful? I am not sure I am qualified to answer that question. I do know that we will not achieve such a society by letting people blame their bad behavior on someone or something else. Justice and mercy both require responsibility on everyone's part. Without it, there will be no justice, and finally, no mercy either.

# Day 67
# Deuteronomy 22-25

ith so many "laws" that could be given, why were these the few chosen to be singled out? It looks almost like a random collection rather that a purposeful arrangement. It seems to welcome our critique on an individual basis. I have my favorites, how about you?

I am particularly fond of the one in 24:5 that says a man, newly married, should be free from military service or business for a year, to stay at home with his new wife! Even though I'm already married, I think it would be a wonderful idea for our society to institute. I would have *loved* to have that first year of marriage at home to spend time appreciating my wife and for us to just get to know each other better. (I would appreciate that now!) I wonder what impact that practice would have on our divorce rate?

This opens a larger issue, however. There is some sense in which we feel we can "pick and choose" among these laws of God. I think there is some truth to that. These are, after all, the descriptions of the covenant God made with Israel. Some of them are specific to their call as a priestly people, inheriting a particular land, during a particular time. Some of them refer to cultural practices that are no longer around or viable. But what about the rest of them, and how do we tell the difference between the ones we should pay attention to, and the ones that no longer apply?

I think the clue is in remembering that these "laws" were never seen as exhaustive. These were not all the rules that one needed to live by, but only some examples of the great principles of the "law" worked out in detail. Even the Ten Commandments were summed up into two by Jesus. The *principles behind the laws* have not changed from the very beginning, and those still apply to us today.

What are those principles? This too, is open to debate, but it is precisely the kind of debate worth having. These laws show an abiding concern for both the individual and society. There was to be equity and respect for each and every member. Before we "pick and choose" among these various expressions of God's law, let us make sure we have understood and adhered to the principles behind them. Those truths never change.

# Day 68
# Deuteronomy 26-28

The clarity in these chapters is almost overwhelming. If ever the Israelites wanted to complain about the covenant, it could not have been that they did not know what it entailed. The blessings are listed specifically, but with such open-endedness as to suggest heaven on earth. If they had obeyed, the blessing would most certainly have been the talk of every nation.

Likewise, the promise of the curses, if they did not obey, is frighteningly graphic. The curses would be relentless and merciless. It was to be abundantly clear to all, that these were to be punishments. They were not merely consequences of their disobedience, but curses imposed upon them which were to have been as much of an example of God's faithfulness to His promises as the blessings would have been.

It is very important to see the historical and covenantal nature of these blessings and curses. Many people throughout the centuries have thought they could assume this same kind of arrangement with God. They have tried to live according to the definitions of this covenant with Israel, assuming that the blessings would thus be guaranteed. This is a dangerous and faulty assumption.

God has never been in the business of playing "let's make a deal" with His people. The covenant with Israel was not a covenant of works but a covenant of grace. It was established by grace - they had not earned the right to be in a special covenant relationship - and sustained by grace - since they constantly broke their end of the covenant. The covenant's purpose was to show the world that the God of Israel was the only true God (remember the *Shema*) and it was peculiar to Israel.

While it is undeniable that obeying God's laws as set forth in the Bible will benefit any individual or nation, we cannot assume that the promises or curses necessarily apply. God is doing a new thing since the time of Jesus. His gracious covenant is now available to everyone in a new and better way.

But let us be very clear that He has never been involved in the game of trading our righteousness for His blessing. The covenants of God have never been based on works. We can and should thank God for that!

# Day 69
# Deuteronomy 29-31

How do you sum up a life's work in a few paragraphs - especially a life like Moses'? I find these chapters to be among the most moving so far because of the eloquent way in which Moses appeals to the people for the last time, and how he is foretold by God that they will not obey. This would be tragic if it were a Greek play. It is all the more so because it is history.

Moses had certainly seen the heights and depths of life. He had come as close as any person to seeing the face of God. He heard God's voice in a way we can only dream of, and he was the conduit of miracles that almost defy reason. Yet he had also seen the ignorance and hard heartedness of the people God had tried to deliver. He had known their lack of faith, their rebellion, and even been the object of their mutinies. There was certainly more living packed into his years than any of us will ever see.

All these things make him a person worth listening to. At the end, he sums up his message by telling the people that if they obey the covenant they will be blessed, and if they do not they will be cursed. Simple. Straight forward. "... I have set before you life and death, blessing and curse; therefore choose life..." (30:19) How simple and yet profound - choose life!

The choice is set before us too. People often go to a minister to talk because they feel they have lost their way in life. They do not know what to do anymore. They go looking for some kind of divine guidance. Many times it turns out they *do* know what to do, they just don't want to do it. I never cease to be amazed at how unhappy they are if you try to point this out. What they really want is some other kind of alternative that will allow them to go on doing what they want without having to live with the consequences. I don't know how you do that - I suspect it can't be done. We must choose and live with the consequences of our decisions.

Choose life. It is not really a complicated decision - Moses pointed out, it has been laid out before us. But do not underestimate the difficulty of that decision. It is a hard decision because you don't make it with your words, you make it with your life. Whose laws will you live by, God's or your own? Choose life - He'll help. Ask Him.

# Day 70
# Deuteronomy 32-34

The song of Moses. This one is going to need a *really* catchy tune! I give it a ten for truth, but how do you dance to this one! It seems to be a kind of strange send-off to the people just before they lose their leader and commence to go into the promised land. Is this prophecy, prediction, or just warning? If it had been up to me, I would have closed with that great "choose life" phrase - it's catchy and upbeat. Yet God Himself orders Moses to give the people this song. Why?

Whenever you are going to begin a great venture, you need to enter into it with the greatest enthusiasm you can muster. There is probably no time during the adventure that you are going to be more hopeful or more positive than when you begin. This song of Moses looks to be a big wet blanket thrown onto the people at precisely the time when they needed to be pumped up. Can you image this song as a locker room talk just before the big game? "Well team, you will be going out there to face the number one team in the nation and you won't run the plays I send in, you'll screw up the defensive strategy we practiced and more than half of you will get career ending injuries in the first half! But, I'll send in our best player in the fourth quarter and we'll mop 'em up! Now, go out there and get slaughtered!"

I think it does have a positive message in it though. Rather than being a self-fulfilling prophecy of failure, I think it is a warning to be heeded and a promise to be clung to. God never says when the disobedience will happen. Perhaps the disobedience and resulting disaster need not happen in this generation. If they obeyed the covenant, it would not. That a generation would come that did not obey the covenant was predictable. But no generation had to be the ones to disobey. One would choose, not be forced.

I hear many young people today saying, "I don't want to get married, all marriages end in divorce." "I don't want to have children, the world is too terrible a place in which to raise children." Nonsense! It does not *have* to be that way. If it is, it will be our doing, not God's. And remember, His team will win in the end - guaranteed. In the end, the song is one of hope! Press on!

# Day 71
# Joshua 1-4

hirty-eight years of wandering in the wilderness was finally over. Israel was entering the land. The spies brought encouraging news. The reputation of the God of Israel and the way He fought for His people had preceeded them to Jericho and there was great fear there. To top it all off, God had miraculously brought them across the Jordan as He had brought their ancestors across the Red Sea forty years earlier. It was a great time to be an Israelite!

They had finally arrived in the promised land. It must have been exhilarating to be a part of such an achievement. After so many years of waiting and preparing and striving, their goal was now realized - they had entered the promised land. Fateful challenges awaited them, but for the moment they could celebrate and rejoice - they had arrived!

I frequently hear people saying that life is like a journey. They say that what is really important is not the destination, but the traveling itself. I don't agree, and I don't think Joshua would have either. The traveling is important, but the point of any journey is its destination, and the nature of the destination is of paramount importance.

I do not believe that life ever has a *final* destination. It is the nature of our creative God that He always has new ideas and new directions to go. Life, to be life at all, must always be going on to newer and better things. To suggest that the goals and achievements that constitute life as it develops are of no particular importance is to devalue the experience of living itself. Life is not simply activity, but purposeful activity. It is not just striving, but achieving things worth doing and worth having.

That is why it was important for the Israelites to stop and mark the place of passage with the twelve stones. Not only had God brought them into the land miraculously, He had brought them into the land finally! This was a day long awaited and to be remembered and celebrated. It had been worth the doing and was done. Now, on to what was to come.

Do we have a similar sense of arriving in our lives? We should. What have you strived for and achieved? Did you mark the event? Before you go on, get out that diploma or whatever it is, look and remember, and give thanks!

# Day 72
# Joshua 5-8

oshua fit de battle ob Jericho, Jericho, Jericho; Joshua fit de battle ob Jericho, an' de walls come-a-tumblin' down. That's how the old spiritual goes. I can still remember the words from learning them in the second grade in Sunday School. It is an amazing story which has captured the imagination ever since it happened. As we become adults though, do we still believe such things?

The story of this miraculous victory has engendered some of the most creative explanations I have ever read. Some suggest that there was an earthquake that knocked down the walls of that great city. Others have conjectured that the people marching around the city for six days, in rhythm (where did they get that?), weakened the structure, and the sound vibrations from the horns and the shouts shook the walls apart. Even the old classic song seems to have missed the point. It was not Joshua, but God, who knocked down the walls and how He did it is not only unimportant, but distracting. The whole point of the marching in silence and then the shouting was that it couldn't have had anything to do with anything except obedience to God. He wanted to show His power, not His mastery of structural engineering!

It seems astounding to me that people would grant that God is the all powerful creator of the universe and have a hard time believing that He does miracles. The real question about God should always be, not what *can* He do, but what has He *chosen* to do, and why. He chose to defeat the people of Jericho, not to teach us a lesson about believing the absurd (as some have suggested), but to show that He is alive. God is not a concept or a force, but a spiritual being - *The* Spiritual Being - who does not sit back and watch His creation like some theatre critic. He is the author and lead actor in this drama. We are the supporting cast, not vice versa.

Before we dismiss these passages as irrelevant, we should note that Joshua's curse came true. Jericho was rebuilt by order of King Ahab 500 years later by a man named Hiel. His son Abiram died when he began. When the gates were set, his youngest son, Segub, died. (I Kings 16:33-34) God is alive, and He is acting in His world today. What is He doing in your life?

# Day 73
# Joshua 9-11

Are you bound by a commitment made under false pretenses? The people of Gibeon had deceived Joshua and the elders regarding who they were. Why did Joshua and the elders feel they were still bound to keep their end of the bargain? Considering that God had ordered Israel to destroy all the inhabitants of the land, shouldn't Joshua have ordered the destruction of Gibeon and the three other cities who had deceived them?

The answer to this question is perhaps the best illustration of the difference between a contract and a covenant. If Joshua had made a contract with Gibeon under false pretenses, he would not have been bound to honor the contract. Remember, contracts are based on the performance of the other party in the contract. Covenants are more binding precisely because they are not based on the performance but on character. A covenant is never any better than the character of the person making it, but in the case of Joshua, that was more valuable than anything else for which the people of Gibeon could have hoped.

A covenant is therefore not a thing to be entered into lightly. Joshua's mistake was in not consulting with God before entering into the covenant with these deceitful people. But it did not leave Joshua in a helpless position. The people of Gibeon had gained their lives, but they would be servants to the people of Israel all their lives. A covenant binds, but it does not imprison. We cannot be forced into a covenant, therefore, whatever the requirements are, they come as a result of our free choice to enter into the relationship. The consequences can be far reaching, but we do not lose our ability or responsibility to continue choosing them.

Some people might say that because of this, you should never make a covenant with anyone. But if you do not you will miss out on the benefits of a covenant relationship. In an uncertain and unstable world, covenant relationships are one of the few things strong enough and stable enough to endure the unexpected. They should not be underestimated or undervalued. There is at least one covenant relationship that should never be missed - the one with God through His son. Have you made it? Will you trust it? It has been thoroughly tested and it is thoroughly reliable. Ask Joshua.

# Day 74
# Joshua 12-14

istory or theology? Which is the Bible? Passages like these bring this dichotomy to mind. But the Bible claims to be both, in fact it is theology through history, and that is part of its unique claim. God has chosen to reveal Himself, not by writing His own best seller (which He certainly could have done) but through action. Action speaks louder than words, you know. Unfortunately, for some, even action doesn't speak loudly enough.

It has certainly been one of my own long-standing questions as to why God does not act more directly and explicitly in history. Why doesn't He appear personally in all (at least some) of His glory? Why not speak in a voice loud enough to be heard by all nations and peoples simultaneously? Imagine the effect of what would be the worlds largest PA system, a voice booming from out of the clouds saying, "Hey! All you people on earth, stop! Just what do you think you're doing anyway? Now sit down! I want to tell you a few things! And pay attention, I don't like repeating myself!" Then, He could follow it up with a smaller voice that went around with each of us every day saying, "Hey! Knock that off! Don't say that! Don't do that! What are you thinking about doing now? Well, don't. What's the matter with you anyway?"

Well, maybe that isn't such a good idea after all. I wonder what the effect of all that direct intervention would be. I certainly don't think it would help us know Him better, trust Him more, or love Him much at all. In fact, I think that the kind of God described above is exactly the one that many people fear - a heavenly nag.

God has revealed Himself in history in a way clear enough. He gave the Israelites an inheritance in the land, miraculously delivered them out of Egypt and gave them success over the Canaanites. It took faith for them to see their history that way, but without faith, no actions on God's part would have been sufficient to prove the case.

He has blessed us too. Do we have the eyes to see it? You have at least been given the blessing of having enough education to read and enough time to do so. You have a rich inheritance. There is theology in your own history. Have you read your life lately?

# Day 75
# Joshua 15-17

These are difficult chapters to read and find interesting. They make up an important legal history for Israel (for many centuries back), but are not particularly important for salvation history. Deeds and titles to property have never been fascinating reading, unless, of course, it is *your* land and *your* title!

The dividing of the land was vital to the Israelites because it was the basis of their social and economic system. If we remember, there was to be a system of cycles for the resting of the land - every seven years - and a redistribution of the wealth - the Jubilee - every fifty years. This cycle was also to influence the cost of land and property between Jubilees. If land was "sold" it was really only "leased." It had to be returned in the Jubilee. Therefore, if there were many years before the next Jubilee year, the price would be high, if only a few, the price would be less. In all these things, there was to be a basic equity. Individual enterprise was to be rewarded, but there was to be no permanent advantage. Therefore, the records of land transactions were crucial. Hence the space given the matter here in Joshua.

There is a balance in this system between the rights of the individual and the needs of the society that is not easily achieved. Our society has tried to guarantee this kind of balance through laws intended to protect the individual and society. I am not at all sure it has been very successful. I do know that it has resulted in the making of so many laws that no one can keep track of them all. The idea of wiping the slate clean (at least back to some fundamentals) has a lot to recommend it, but I have no idea how we could accomplish it.

The use of families to guarantee social equity could work on the numerical levels of ancient Israel. It is doubtful if it could work for the millions on earth today. Interestingly enough, there is no record that it was ever really tried by the Israelites.

How could our society be more effective in rewarding individual enterprise and still be responsible to the needs of all in our society? The rich should not always get richer and the poor, poorer. Communism has failed on paper and in fact. But has democracy really succeeded? Tough questions. Do you have any answers?

# Day 76
# Joshua 18-19

"So they finished dividing the land." 19:51 Thank goodness! What a process that must have been! I'm sick of reading about it and what's more, trying to find something to be "devout" about it in these pages! There was an interesting process used here at the end that is worth reflecting on (I hope!).

Joshua had become frustrated at seven of the tribes for not going out and conquering any of the territory so they might finish dividing up the land. God's plan had called for a slow and systematic conquering so the land would not be uninhabited in the process. They had not conquered as ordered and Joshua was getting old. However, they needed to get the process done, at least on paper so to speak.

Their answer to this problem was the casting of lots. The land was spied out and divided into seven parts, and each remaining tribe would draw out the name of one of the territories. This was *not* understood to be random chance. They believed that God would be at work in the process and each tribe would pick according to what God wanted them to have. It was simple and quick, but how sound is this theory?

I know many people, myself included, who have wished that God's will could be so easily determined. Whether it is selecting a college to attend, what shoes to wear, or what person to marry, the big and small decisions of life cry out for some divine guidance. Can we trust God will work that way? Would He?

I think the idea of casting lots does have some place in our lives. First, it does not negate doing our homework. Joshua sent out spies to collect information. In our decisions, we need to gather as much information as possible. Second, they were already sure that this was part of God's plan for them. We too can determine if any of our choices contradict God's laws. Those that do can be eliminated. Third, it finally makes a choice. There will be times in our lives that we will get no more direction. The information is in, the possible choices could each fit God's plan - so choose! It may be impossible to determine which side of the fence will grow the greener grass, but we do know you can not plant on a fence. Choose and trust that God will be with you no matter what. You know He will!

# Day 77
# Joshua 20-22

"Not one of all the good promises which the Lord had made to the house of Israel had failed; all came to pass." 21:45  This is a key verse in Joshua.  Israel had entered the land, but it was not exactly what they had expected.  So it was important for Israel to know (and us too) that all the promises God had made *had* come to pass.  He had been faithful to His word.  He was and is reliable.  The covenant was and is kept.  That God is always faithful in keeping His promises may seem so obvious as to not need saying, but is it?

There is a strange thing about the promises of God.  They do all come true, but not always as we expected.  It is like the experience of ordering something at a restaurant and when we receive our request, it is not precisely what we thought it would be - in fact, sometimes it is hard to recognize it as food - especially at the more expensive "gourmet" places!  So, too, when we ask for things in prayer, even the affirmative answer is not always what we expected.  This does not mean it is not something good, but it is certainly not what we thought it would be.  God's gifts are always good, but good as He knows it, not necessarily as we envision it.

Someone once said that there are only two tragedies in life - not getting what you want, and getting it.  There is a good deal of truth in this rather cynical aphorism, but what makes the difference again is not so much the gift as the perspective of the recipient.  When we go in search of God's blessings in life, it would serve us well to look carefully at what we actually receive.  Often we think God has answered *no* when in fact He has seen past our shortsighted desires to our needs, and sent us the things we would have asked for if we had more wisdom.  One of the most important skills in life is learning to recognize a gift when we get it - to open up our perspective and see our world anew, with eyes of faith that know God always answers, and gives even when we have not had enough faith to ask.

God is faithful to His word.  It does need to be said again.  What have you been wanting and asking from Him?  Has He really said no, or has He already answered *yes* and you missed seeing it?  Look again - that blessing may just be in disguise!

# Day 78
# Joshua 23-24

Joshua's appeal here at the end of his life is one of the classic passages in the Scriptures. "And if you be unwilling to serve the LORD, choose this day whom you will serve, ...but as for me and my house, we will serve the LORD." 24:15 At the end of Joshua's life, this summation and challenge still rings clearly centuries later - choose whom you will serve.

I read a quote many years ago in a church bulletin from a man named A. Leonard Griffith. I don't know anything about him, but the thought was so profound and well-said, I saved it and now share it with you.

In religion we are not asked to make up our minds; we are asked to make up our lives... We may refuse to make up our minds, but our lives get made up one way or the other...Whatever we believe with our minds, our lives are committed either to God's way or to the God-denying way, and what matters in religion is the act of commitment.

I do not sense a judgmental attitude in what Joshua or Griffith are saying. I hear the clear sound of reality ringing in both statements. We *must* choose - we *will* choose - looking back we must admit that we have already chosen. We will serve something with our lives. Human beings are inherently religious - we will worship something. If not God, then money or power or sensations or philosophies or myths of our own making, but something. Our lives and actions are a result of our choice each day. That is the point Griffith makes clear. Joshua is calling us to make the decision purposefully. If we must choose, then let us do so deliberately.

Making the wrong choice is not necessarily the worst thing if we do so deliberately. Those who choose to worship something that isn't God, and truly worship it, are more likely to be disappointed and turn to the real God than those who want to avoid the decision for whatever multitude of reasons. Jesus will say in Revelation that it would have been better to be hot or cold toward him than luke warm. There really is no fence to sit on. Choose. Make up your mind. Your life gets made up anyway. Oh, and yes - choose God!

# Day 79
# Judges 1-3

here is an abrupt change of tone to the book of Judges that is apparent from the outset. The time spans covered in each chapter are much greater than any since Genesis and the great figures the likes of the Patriarchs, Moses, and Joshua, are gone. This is a new era of less high drama and more plodding along by the people.

Yet there is a consistent thread running through this book and the time it covers, that should not escape our notice. The author takes great pains to make it clear that God was always true to His covenant promises and would remain true to them (see 2:1,2). But the plan had changed from what it was supposed to be when it was announced at Sinai.

In one sense, however, the plan was not different at all. God had made a covenant with Israel and had been very specific about what that would be like when they worshipped Him, and what it would be like when they went chasing after other gods. The book of Judges records the faithfulness of God to those covenant promises. Unfortunately, most of that faithfulness was keeping the negative promises, but promises were kept nonetheless. The plan was still in effect - God was still good to His word.

But in another sense the real intent got lost somewhere along the way. Where were those covenant people, those priestly people who were to be an example to the world? The blessings of the covenant never went unnoticed by the other nations throughout the Exodus and the conquering of the land. God had intended Israel to be an example of His existence by the blessings He showered on them. They became an example of how He can love us in spite of ourselves. That just doesn't seem like what God started out trying to do with them.

There is a lesson here for us too. God is not playing a game with us that when we are good, He blesses us, and when we are bad, He punishes us. He was not doing that with Israel, and He is not doing that with us. He has a plan and a purpose for us, one that calls us to be a priestly people in our world. But we have an affect on that plan. We do not lose our responsibility to choose and to act in accordance with that plan. No matter what we do, He will not stop loving us. But we can have a tremendous effect on our ministry. What kind of example do we want to be?

# Day 80
# Judges 4-6

"That the leaders took the lead in Israel, that the people offered themselves willingly, bless the LORD!" 5:2 What a simple description of success. And yet this rather simple formula is not at all easy to achieve in real life. Leaders who lead, and people who follow willingly. It is a winning combination almost every time.

It of course presumes that the leaders know where to lead. As a leader you must not only have a vision, you must be able to communicate that vision. It is also very helpful if you happen to be right about what you want to do and where you want to lead. Those are some of the things that make it very difficult, and not a little risky, to be in leadership. Very few things about life are guaranteed, so taking the lead in any venture comes with great risk. If you turn out to be wrong, there is a high price to pay, and those who follow will share in the penalty.

Perhaps that is why Gideon was so reluctant, and why he asked for such a clear sign before he was ready to commit. He needed to be absolutely convinced himself that this was what God was calling him to do, and not an aberration or his own imagination. Gideon believed and moved forward as he was led, which was what made him a great leader.

Many people envy Gideon his answer from God. They would like to be able to get the same clear sign about what they are to do. However, I wonder how many would feel that way if they knew it meant attempting an enterprise as perilous as Gideon's. And remember, even before confronting the Midianites, he had to face the wrath of his own family and friends when he pulled down their idols. What should really amaze us in this story is not God's answer to Gideon about the fleece, but Gideon's response to God's answer - he believed and obeyed. When we ask for direction, are we really willing to accept an answer and follow through with it? From that viewpoint, it is risky even to ask!

Leaders who lead have always been in rather short supply. It is a difficult position to occupy. Especially in our time, leaders draw a lot of criticism. Perhaps as much as our criticism, they need our prayers for vision, wisdom and courage. They need all they can get.

# Day 81
## Judges 7-9

he second part of the formula from the *Song of Deborah*, is people who follow willingly. This idea of willingness has shown itself many times already in the Old Testament, but it is perhaps never better illustrated than by Gideon and the troops he was to command. Send home all those with other commitments, other priorities, the anxious, the indifferent. Take only those who want to be there.

Some people call this "total" commitment but the Scriptures refer to it as "willing" commitment. Is there a difference?

A number of leaders throughout time have tried to command "total" commitment. Some have been military, some political, and not a few religious. Their call for total commitment almost always includes the idea that you give up your will and surrender it to the leader. You are to obey and not ask questions. Having any other value or commitment in your life makes you unworthy of the call - commitment must be total. Yet there seems to be a lack of this kind of rhetoric in the Scriptures.

I think the idea of "willing" commitment is somewhat different. I do not think that you are any less committed as a willing follower, but you do not give up your will when you obey. The difference is that as a willing follower, you know and agree with the principles for which you are fighting. To be sure, there must still be trust in the leader and obeying of commands (especially in battle) but it is not a blind obedience - it sees very clearly and never stops looking toward the common goal.

Gideon was to take only those who were willing. One great advantage to leading those kind of people is that they do not just take orders, they can think for themselves. They understand the goal of the operation and will obey, work, and be innovative in getting the job done. The Israelites understood that God had guaranteed the victory to them. Their numbers did not matter. Willing followers bring all they have to the task. The commitment is not only total, it is theirs. That makes them more determined, not less.

Both leaders who lead and people who willingly follow are necessary for God's work to be accomplished. We have prayed for our leaders. We should not neglect to pray for ourselves. Without our willingness, no genius on their part can make up that deficit.

# Day 82
# Judges 10-12

A story of triumph and tragedy was the life of Jephthah. Born an illegitimate son of Gilead and cast out by his own brothers, he became the hero of Israel by defeating the Ammonites. But the sweetness of his victory turned bitter because he made a foolish vow to sacrifice the first person he saw when he returned, if God gave him the victory. That first person turned out to be his only child, his daughter. In a show of unbelievable character, she agreed to be sacrificed and he carried through with his vow.

I cannot imagine the grief of a father who makes that kind of a sacrifice. Of course, the fact that it seems worse because it was Jephthah's own daughter betrays our shortsightedness. No matter who had come out first, they would have been someone's son or daughter. The vow was a brutal and senseless one. God did not ask for this and in fact, had Jephthah known the Covenant, he would have known that human sacrifice was forbidden. That he thought God would require such a sacrifice or in any way be pleased by it, shows the degree to which the Israelites had been corrupted by the Canaanite's bloodthirsty religion. We are never bound by honor to do wrong. If Jephthah had only known.

There is a sad lesson here about the price of ignorance. How do we know what God does and does not want of us? This is the great value of God's revealing Himself to us in mighty acts in history, through His Son Jesus, and through His Holy Word that we are reading together. This is why we have the Scriptures - the Canon. The word canon means "reed" which was used as a measuring stick. When weighing the alternatives of actions, the Scriptures are here to help us measure our ideas of what is right and wrong - what is pleasing to God and what is not.

Our best intentions, our strongest gut feelings, our dreams, our visions, our vows, all must be measured in light of God's Word. We will still have to struggle to understand what the Bible is saying to us, but what an advantage it is. We have the benefit of being able to see God's nature and purpose as it has been revealed across the centuries. It is a light to guide us through the dark muddle of messages we get from all different directions. We need so much to learn to let it shine for us. If Jephthah had only known.

# Day 83
# Judges 13-16

amson and Delilah. Truly one of the classic stories from the Old Testament. Almost everyone has heard at least parts of this story at one time or another. Yet, as I read it again my attention was drawn more to the world around them than to their story. It was such a different Israel from the one that had been drawn out of Egypt. Samson and Delilah are representative of the people of their time - tragically lost characters belonging to a lost generation.

Many people have used Samson as an example of outer strength and inner weakness. This is certainly true, but there have been better examples of this truth. Samson was not the most vain or foolish person ever to have come along. Delilah was not the most cunning seductress either. Her attempts to get the truth out of Samson were far from subtle and had he not been such a fool, she never would have succeeded. They were not the epitome of arrogance and betrayal, the essence of epic tragedy, but two pathetic persons whose characters could be cheaply bought or tempted.

Samson was a fitting judge for his time. The people of Israel had never cleared out the land as they had been instructed. Far worse, they had abandoned the covenant and gone after other gods to worship. Samson's own father tried several times to worship the angel who was sent to tell him of Samson's birth. Israel had lost its identity as the people of God. The people no longer knew who they were, why they were there, or what they were to be doing. Without that sense of identity and purpose, living was reduced to doing whatever it took to get you through another day.

Samson, as with the other judges before him, showed no sign of understanding the purpose of Israel as a nation. Each threw off the immediate oppressor, but none tried to lead the people together to fulfill the covenant, take the land, and worship God as He had instructed. They failed for lack of vision. God was great enough; their desires were not.

Do we know why God has called the church into being? Do we remember the purpose for our nation coming together? As a church and a nation, have we yet learned the crucial lessons Samson and the Judges have to teach us? I wonder.

# Day 84
# Judges 17-19

"In those days there was no king in Israel, and every man did what was right in his own eyes." 17:6 No truer statement could be made to sum up this period of the Judges. What is sad is they were not without guidance. God Himself had told them He would be king. He had given them the law to keep them in right relationship with Him and with each other. But they had failed to keep up the sacrifices, had lost their relationship with God, and finally, forgotten the law all together. Everyone had become a law unto themselves. Can any society so constituted survive?

It is important to note, that in spite of the moral degradation, morals of some kind still persisted. Situational ethics (by any name) have always been a castle built on air. Even when everyone does what is "right" in their own eyes, they want to universalize that moral judgement somewhere along the line. It seems to be inherent that we know there must be limits somewhere - usually a little further than we have gone ourselves but certainly limits crossed by some people.

Such was the indignation raised by the action of the Levite cutting up his dead wife and shipping her parts to the tribes. In spite of the general laxity of morals, this got everyone's attention. If everyone can do what is right in his or her own eyes (we call it "doing your own thing"), there can be no limits - right and wrong are just what *you* want and *you* don't want. But while right and wrong may not always be clear, there are those things so clearly right or wrong, they are unmistakable and undeniable. That should be the kind of evidence that convinces us that there is a right and a wrong - and it does not just apply to the large things but the smaller things too. If there are limits - and there are - then right and wrong are not just what we want them to be, they *are* what they *are* - what God set them to be.

This should be obvious, but reading the news, it appears that it is not so clearly understood in our time. It is no longer wrong to lie, or embezzle, or cheat, just wrong to get caught. But God did not make the world that way. There *is* right and wrong, and they are not a matter of anyone's opinion except God. Unless we want a society like that of the Judges, we had better start remembering this lesson.

# Day 85
# Judges 20-21

As we finish the book of Judges, we find Israel in disarray. The tribes, who never were particularly close, now went to war against each other. It would not be fair to say that theocracy had failed, because it had never really been tried. The nation that was to have been the model of righteousness for the rest of the world had become as corrupt as the other nations. The once mighty people of God, who had marched out of Egypt, crushed Jericho, and routed the mighty Canaanites, were warring even among themselves. This was a sad time in their national history.

There was, of course, no reason to despair, because God had remained faithful to the covenant. In spite of all of their disarray, their continued disobedience, their lack of vision, and finally their moral disintegration, they were still the chosen people. God had promised, back in Genesis, that He would send a savior. Through the centuries He had revealed that this blessing would come through the descendents of Abraham and then through the family of Jacob (Israel) and that purpose endured even through the dreadful times of the Judges. The good news is that God remains faithful even when we do not.

This is very good news indeed and in spite of the dark picture of God's people, the light of that hope should still shine brightly for us. We have often heard from the naysayers and prophets of doom in our country (maybe even in these pages occasionally?) how bad things are and how hopeless they have become. It is easy to become discouraged in the face of so many bad things happening. But if we are to learn any lesson out of the book of Judges, it should be that it is never too late to return to God. As long as we still have breath, our prayers will be heard and answered. Not because we deserve to be heard - we do not and never have. And that is precisely the point. When we are at our worst we clearly see that we need God's grace. Perhaps that can also help us see that, at our best, we still need God's grace. The good news in life is God and His love. It is wonderful when we occasionally get it right and love Him back, but no matter, we can count on is His enduring love and grace.

If you are discouraged with your own discipleship, remember this lesson from Judges, and take hope - God lives!

# Day 86
# Ruth

Ruth comes like a breath of fresh air in a coal mine. The time of the Judges embraced so little that was good and wholesome, whereas the character of all those involved in Ruth's story reflects the nature God would have us all exhibit. The story begins with great personal tragedy; it ends with great joy and honor. And the link is this virtuous woman with a great heart - who was not even an Israelite.

That is a key element of the story of Ruth. Just because God had chosen Israel to be a priestly nation did not mean He was not at work in the others. Something of the greatness of God's character had become imbued in Ruth, and she would not depart from it. She is truly one of the laudable people in the Scriptures.

There must surely have been something warm about Naomi too. Both her daughters-in-law remained with her and the one does return to her own people only after much entreaty by Naomi. The weeping at their parting sounds every bit genuine. Yet Ruth's devotion speaks more of the depth of her character. She risked everything because she loved Naomi. Love like that should not be underestimated - it is truly the most precious thing on earth.

Ruth's faithfulness brings out the best in everyone else too. In spite of Naomi's bitterness when she returns to her home, the faithfulness of Ruth prevents her from falling into a depression. Naomi could not curl up in self pity, for Ruth's kindness needed to be returned. Naomi had to think of someone other than herself. She had to try at least to help Ruth find another husband.

Boaz was so impressed with their story that when he met Ruth, he too, treated her with kindness and when she went to lay at his feet, in obedience to Naomi, he wanted her, but would not act until it could be done properly. Her honor deserved it, and demanded it.

This is the effect that good character can and should have on others. We do not need to go around telling everyone how wonderful we are. When we are truly the honest and noble people God made us to be, people notice. What fitting great-grandparents to David. The story of Ruth should help us to believe that greatness is not something that comes from without, but from within. Therefore it is within the grasp of us all. It knows no nationality or station in life. Won't you grab for it today?

# Day 87
# I Samuel 1-3

I f they gave out Caspar Milquetoast awards for Bible characters, Eli would have been a sure winner. The weakness of his backbone is so astounding as to be almost legendary. Not only would he not stand up to his sons and insist they stop corrupting the priesthood, but when God announced His judgement against them, he does not lift even a small prayer in protest or lament.

It is a testimony to the character of Samuel that he could be raised in that kind of an atmosphere and still become a man of vision and courage. It is also a testimony to his kindness that he could love Eli in spite of his obvious weakness. That is a skill we would all do well to develop.

It is difficult, especially for youth, to accept the flaws of their elders. It is particularly hard to accept those shortcomings when the elders acknowledge their existence and still seem unable or unwilling to change. Such was the case with Eli. He knew very well he was not controlling his sons, either as a father or as chief priest. None of this could have escaped Samuel's notice and its effect could have been devastating. Idealism can be very fragile. When it is disappointed it can become bitter, cynical and vindictive. Not so with Samuel. He loved Eli and learned from him what he had to teach.

Just what do we expect from our leaders - spiritual and otherwise? Certainly, being in a leadership role carries with it added responsibility and burden of living the best we can. When leaders fail, their followers cannot help but suffer too. But how dependent should followers be on their leaders? Whatever answer we come up with, it must not be 100 per cent dependent. Leaders are human and they will fail. If we have leaned too heavily on them, we will be tempted to dismiss the good they had to offer when we discover their bad side.

Samuel loved Eli and saw him for who he was. It is possible to do both - to see people as they are and still love them. When they are our elders or leaders we would do best to remember as Samuel did, we are not following them as individuals, but the things they represent. Samuel could love Eli because Samuel was following God all along, not Eli. Can we do the same for our leaders?

# Day 88
# I Samuel 4-7

The Ark of the Covenant. It has enjoined mystery and curiosity for centuries. The story of its capture and subsequent return is among my favorites in the Old Testament. There is such a marvelous sense of mischievousness about the whole affair. It speaks to that sense deep within us that feels that God should act more directly on His own and not so often through people. If Israel was so inept as to let the Ark be captured, then God Himself would defend it.

Of course, the idea that the Ark itself was anything special to God - like a favorite piece of jewelry or furniture might be to us - has very little to recommend it. God was not yet finished using the Ark in the history of Israel. Still, it was not the piece of wood and gold itself that was important, but what it represented. Its loss or destruction (since we have no idea what its fate was) did not in any way harm the purpose of God in bringing the salvation of the world through His Son. Jesus initiated no movement to find the Ark. To treat it as if it had some special power is to turn it into what it was to testify against: idols. We are to worship the Creator, not the creation. It was the foolishness of the Philistines to think it was an idol. But even the Philistines recognized the power of the God associated with the Ark. They had felt it first hand and wanted no part in displeasing the God it went with.

Many people wish God would act like this more often. Why does He leave so much up to the actions of His people? I have a great deal of sympathy for people who ask this question, for I often think that if I were God, I would not waste days, weeks, years, centuries, millennia, waiting for people to get things done! I'd do it myself! This is just one of many reasons we can all be glad that I'm not God!

I do not think I can fully answer why God doesn't act more directly. But as I have grown older, and hopefully wiser, I am more grateful for His patient purpose that insists upon working through people. Sure, He could do it Himself, and much faster no doubt. But He has chosen to work through us. The Arks in this world are few and far between. What we find instead is an incredibly patient God who has given us an important part in His plan. What a God!

# Day 89
# I Samuel 8-10

t is obviously difficult to break with our past history; we keep repeating the same mistakes. Samuel was able to rise above his teacher Eli in his own discipleship, but he was no better at fathering than Eli. His two sons were as bad if not worse than Eli's. Moreover, they rejected God's sovereignty and contributed to the call for an earthly king. Given the quality of leadership the Judges provided, the request for a king did seem reasonable. But as is often the case, the cure can be worse than the disease.

As a child, I knew the pressure of the uncomfortable present. I just knew that what my parents or teachers wanted me to do or learn was going to take too long or not work out anyway. I had a better idea. My idea could be implemented right away and would pay off immediately and in the long run, if only I would be permitted to act on it - to do it my way. I requested, I reasoned, I argued, I pleaded, I worn them down, until at last they agreed - and I turned out, more often than not - to be dead wrong. The voice of experience had spoken and the ears of inexperience had been deaf.

As a parent, I now get to experience this process from the other end. Now I am the "establishment" who is too cautious, sees only the negative side, is too pessimistic or cynical, who just doesn't want to admit he is wrong. Now I get to bear the incessant requests, reasons, arguments, pleading, until I am worn down and give in too. And in like fashion, more often than not, the voice of experience turns out to be right. It is a strange process this growing up, but it does not seem to have changed much over the centuries.

The people wanted a king, and little did they know the price, even though they were clearly warned. But far too often we insist on learning lessons the hard way. When we do, our loving parents, and God, have no alternative left but to let us try it our way. With a lot of love and effort, maybe something else can be worked out in the end. It may not be the good that was intended, there may be scars and pains to suffer that could have been avoided, but love endures, and it is creative. No human king was ever going to be the answer - so God changed the plan.

What have *we* been asking God for consistently that hasn't come about? Perhaps we should reconsider our requests.

# Day 90
# I Samuel 11-13

amuel was one of those figures in the Old Testament who walked more closely with God than most people in history. He was given a special call which he observed faithfully. He obeyed the Lord from his youth and in spite of difficult times, seems to have been very much at peace with his life. He was the kind of person I would very much like to have been able to interview. His insights into the heart and mind of God were sought in his own day and would be welcome in our own.

I am impressed with the advice and perspective that have been preserved for us. After the people realized what they brought upon themselves for having asked for and getting a king, they cry out to Samuel to speak to God on their behalf. 12:19 His response is practical and hopeful. It could be paraphrased, "Even though you have sinned against God, do not cease to turn to him and follow him. Avoid vain things and instead look to those things of God which are never vain. And do not think I would sin by not praying for you. In short, never give up!"

This is such wise and prudent advice. We either want to minimize our sins by saying, "Well, everybody does it," or "It doesn't really hurt anybody but me," or "Nobody else will ever know" or we become so obsessed by our sins we cannot accept forgiveness - "God could *never* forgive me for this," or "Nothing could ever make up for what I have done." Neither of these responses properly understand God. He does take sin seriously, but His forgiveness is always available to us - we never trust Him in vain. How I wish I could learn that more deeply myself. How I wish we all could. So much of our time is spent running away from God either out of denial of our sins or fear of His retribution. I can almost hear the gravelly old voice of that seasoned servant of God, named Samuel, saying - "Face the reality of yourself and God and never give up, because God *is* who He *is*!"

What a wonderful thought too, that those closest to God know it is a sin for them to stop praying for us. We are not to give up on ourselves, and we are not to give up on each other. Praying and hoping and trusting in God are *never* in vain. If Saul had been able to believe that, his life might have been very different. If we can, our's most certainly will be.

# Day 91
# I Samuel 14-15

aul is deserving of some sympathy. He lacked a
component it takes to be a good leader. The Bible
provides little direct information about him, but,
reading between the lines, he has always appeared to
me a rather tragic kind of figure. His fall seemed
inevitable and therefore almost not his fault.

It's that "almost" word that catches us though. Saul is
almost tragic. To be truly tragic one must be of the highest moral
character and yet suffer anyway. It is this injustice that makes the
tragedy. For Saul though, his failings were his own. He had not
been caught up in circumstances over which he had no control.
The kingdom had been given to him. It was not his to take, but it
was his to lose.

Saul had many opportunities to learn his lesson about
following God. But for Saul, religion was just a part of one's life
that had to be done properly. If you presented the sacrifice the
correct way, that was all that counted. If Samuel wasn't there to
present the sacrifice, then Saul would. If God ordered all the
Amalekites slaughtered and their goods destroyed he could keep
the best and give God his "cut," as it were. He never understood
what God was all about.

Samuel tried to tell him and we should not miss the lesson.
To obey is better than sacrifice. 15:22 What Saul never
understood was that the sacrifices were not for the purpose of
appeasing God. God's love is always gracious - it cannot be
bought by sacrifices or good works. The purpose of sacrifice was
to change the attitude of the sinner. Obedience is not the currency
that buys God's love and forgiveness, it is the fruit of a changed
heart. To obey is better than sacrifice because sacrifice should
lead to obedience. Obedience should come as our response to
God's grace, not as some kind of payment to achieve His favor.
Saul understood neither sacrifice nor obedience.

We do not practice "sacrifices" in the literal sense any more.
But I find many people trying to offer up their good works to God
in order that He might bless them. Good works are a reward in
themselves, and God has loved us while we were yet sinners.
There is great freedom in this understanding of God's grace. If
we miss it, like Saul, it will be rather tragic.

# Day 92
# I Samuel 16-17

avid stands out in sharp contrast to Saul immediately. Saul was the big, strong, attractive leader that people expected would be king material. But he proved to have little understanding of the heart of the God who had made him king over Israel. Samuel was sent to the house of Jesse to anoint a new king over Israel. Samuel looked at Jesse's sons as they were presented, and starting with the eldest, looked for someone much like Saul. Even Samuel did not understand fully the heart and mind of God.

Finally, God told Samuel to anoint David. At this point God says something that is perhaps the most important observation about Himself since revealing His covenant nature. He told Samuel that He did not see as men do, with eyes that look only at the outward being, but He looks at the heart. 16:7 God measures the heart, for therein lies the true worth of the person. Greatness does not consist of power or position or wealth or intelligence, but in the heart. Why should this be so? Because the heart is the seat of love, and love is, in the final analysis, the greatest power of all.

This is true of the nature of God Himself. His majesty is evident in the power to create out of nothingness, and His greatness is seen in His justice, creativity, wisdom, and purpose, but without love, where would all those attributes be? We must give thanks to God that He is loving, for if He were not, all that power would be more than dangerous - it could be fiendish.

John (the apostle) will tell us in his first letter in the New Testament, that God is love. This is not the same as saying love is God. God is not some force or sum total of feelings. He is the wholly other Being, the Creator of all that is, and the best news is that His most important character trait, indeed His very being, is love. All the things He is and does come from that motivating factor. This is the good news, without which, no other news could ever be good.

So God measures us by our hearts too. David was a man of great heart. David did many things outwardly that were worse than Saul. However, what matters is not what is on the outside, but on the inside. We will see this played out in many arenas with Saul and David. It is a lesson we cannot afford to miss.

# Day 93
# I Samuel 18-20

**F**ear and jealousy make formidable bed partners. Saul started out being jealous of the acclaim David was receiving and with the addition of fear, his condition turned into pure paranoia. Such is the nature of sin in our lives. It grows and multiplies, finds other sins to which it is cousin, and finally blooms into the kind of evil deeds that make up our nightmares.

What a sharp contrast Jonathan's character is to Saul's. The story of the friendship between David and Jonathan is one that exemplifies the best human relationships have to offer. Love for one another knows no fear. Jonathan knew David's heart and knew that his father's fears were unfounded. Saul's attitude toward David put Jonathan in the kind of conflict to which none of us should be subjected. Jonathan loved his father, but he could not support him in his attempt to destroy David, who had done no wrong. It is a sad choice to have to make, but there can be only one right decision in those situations. Jonathan chose the Lord, honesty, nobility, and his beloved friend David. It was the right choice to make.

The friendship between two young warriors for the Lord is the kind of stuff of which legends are made. We all long to have that kind of a friend, who is closer than our family - one with whom we share interests, perspective, and a joy and excitement for life. Most of the time these are friendships from our youth, when we are still idealistic and full of promise. We draw energy and courage from these relationships and when they die, their loss is immeasurable.

These kinds of friendships seem to be hard to come by in later life. Perhaps we get more cynical and less idealistic. Or perhaps we have so many other conflicting loyalties and demands on our lives that it becomes hard to have the kind of commitment and vulnerability these friendships require. Whatever the case, our lives are much poorer for their absence.

How are your friendships doing? Have you ever had a friendship like David and Jonathan's? Where is that friend now? Did years or miles cause it to wane? Did you just loose contact? Whether you spoke to them yesterday or ten years ago, why not call them today and check in? I think I'll go call my friend now.

# Day 94
# I Samuel 21-24

Almost everything about David's life became an important lesson or precedent for the Israelites, even so small a thing as his asking for and receiving the showbread from Ahimelech the priest to help him escape from Saul. No less than Jesus himself (in Matthew 12) quotes this example of how God is not concerned with ceremony and ritual, but the realities of the heart. David continues to be an example, even to our day, of the kind of relationship with God and our own destinies, that we should all enjoy.

I suppose that is what I find so attractive about David. He is the small town shepherd who made good because he had the credentials that really count - a heart for God. While he is one of the greatest figures in the Old Testament and the history of Israel, there is something very real and down-to-earth about him that speaks to us all.

No theologian, David successfully argues (and lies) his way into getting the provisions he needed from Ahimelech. He was busy obeying the laws of God and did not have time for the petty interpretations men had put upon them. Jesus points this out himself and expands the lesson, reminding his listeners that if you obey the letter of the law, but not the intent, then you have not obeyed the law at all. Even such a small thing from David's life was useful for instruction.

David's understanding of the heart of matters has made him an appropriate role model throughout the centuries. In spite of his weaknesses (and he had some critical ones) this virtue of being wholehearted, served him well. There are many lessons to be learned from the life of this shepherd boy but among the most important is how we too can live our lives in wholehearted trust in God and His purpose for our lives.

David was a man of destiny - but we, too, are people of destiny. It is a hard thing with which to come to grips, but God has a plan for us no less than He had a plan for David. If we are to discover it and live it as David did, we will need to start in the same place David did, giving up playing religious games with God, and approaching Him with trust and abandon. It is that simple - but it is certainly not easy!

# Day 95
# I Samuel 25-27

David was stuck between the proverbial rock and a hard place. He was pursued continually by Saul, and yet he could not kill him. Twice he had the occasion to kill Saul personally, or at least let one of his men kill him, and yet he would not. This must have mystified his followers, and perhaps it mystified him at times, too.

Following God can often be that kind of an experience. While others may lie or cheat or steal to get ahead, following God's plan cannot include breaking God's laws along the way. This seems like a disadvantage too great to overcome, yet it is not, for those who will obey God will be able to count on God's intervention.

Abigail wanted to remind David of this. He did not need to respond to Nabal's foolishness by being equally foolish. God would take care of Nabal in His own way and in His own time. In the mean time, God would take care of David, too.

How short are those short cuts really? It often looks like the little lies or oversights are the fastest way to get things done. But God takes obedience very seriously. After all, if we want Him to be active in the process of our lives and decisions, we will have to leave Him something to do. He operates under the strictest of standards, nothing short of love and justice will do for His contribution. So, it may seem like a small thing, or something no one will notice, but God sees it all, and it matters very much to Him. Most of these decisions turn out to be more important for our character than for the events themselves. Will we prove to be trustworthy and patient as we wait for God to act?

This does not mean that we are to be sitting ducks. Prudence is one of the cardinal virtues. David's escape to the land of Israel's enemy, the Philistines, was both prudent and shrewd. We need to act on our own initiative within the confines of God's laws. The philosophy that says "let go and let God" often falls into the error of trying to force God's hand. We can not decide what His contribution will be and march out into traffic, against the light, sure that He will intervene in events to guard us. Faith is neither taking things into your own hands, nor acquiescing to fate. Somewhere in between we will meet God's deliverance. Count on it!

# Day 96
# I Samuel 28-31

The transition from Saul's rule to David's was a sad one. It exemplifies the difference between these two kings. Saul faced his adversities with a lack of confidence in God and the people around him. David faced his trials with faith in God and those around him. If only Saul could have trusted God and David.

Iffy history can be a fun, if uncertain, game to play. What would have happened if Saul *had* trusted David? Could the prophecy that David would replace him have come true without the loss of Saul's and Jonathan's lives? Theoretically, yes. Saul could have lived to a ripe old age, at which point, the love between David and Jonathan could have allowed Jonathan to cede the throne to David without bloodshed. This may seem an unlikely scenario, but it was possible.

Those in search of the will of God should heed the warning of Saul's life. His tragic end illustrates the result of taking too narrow a view of God's will. Saul could conceive of only one scenario for the fulfillment of the prophecy: the death of himself and his sons. Consequently, he helped fulfill the prophecy in precisely the worst way. He even risked calling up Samuel from the dead rather than trust God (no, I'm not going to discuss the theological implications of that!). He was still the Lord's anointed and that still meant a lot. Failing to trust, he contributed to his own downfall. Unfortunately, he took his sons with him.

David faced his mistakes differently. He had left Ziklag unprotected and paid the price for that oversight. When his followers began to murmur against him, he did what Saul did not - he strengthened himself in the Lord his God. 30:6 Some people feel when times are bad, they are embarrassed to turn to God because they didn't turn to Him when times were good. While there may be some validity to those feelings, the point is that if we will not turn to God when we need Him, when will we? If we fail to ask His help when we need it, will we even recognize it when it comes?

Prophecies from God always come true, but the way in which they are fulfilled may be quite different from the way we first expected. God's will does not preempt our will. We do have a say. Won't you at least ask?

# Day 97
# II Samuel 1-3

olitics by murder - an interesting but brutal form of statesmanship. One wonders how quickly Congress would change using the same techniques. Before we become too historically arrogant, we should remember that this political methodology is still with us - Lincoln, Kennedy, Sadat, Gandhi - all assassinated. We have not come nearly as far as we might like to think.

David mourned the death of Saul and Jonathan. Not only had the Lord's anointed died, and his beloved friend Jonathan, but David knew that whenever leadership changes violently, there will be more violence before order can be restored. It is not just the person who is killed, but a portion of the position dies with them. That is one of the sad truths about the politics of assassination - killing someone seldom accomplishes the desired outcome, for ideas and movements in history are larger than the people who are involved in them.

David's reign did not begin immediately after Saul's death. There were still many battles to fight and allegiances to be settled. Politics are always more complicated than they first appear, and yet there are some simple truths that endure throughout. David had been anointed by God to be King and that would happen regardless of the intrigue involved. In the final analysis it is the great ideas and purposes of life that move the world. The politics of any culture cannot be separated from its spiritual life. It would be interesting to see history as it appears to God and not just as historians see it. We might find the things that made the most difference were not always the ones that made the headlines.

What can we learn from David's time with its bloody politics? Perhaps the most important thing is the need to have good people involved in the political process. Many people feel that politics is such a dirty, compromising business that no one in their right mind would want to get involved in it. But it is not inherently bad. Not all kings or presidents or senators are corrupt. We should hope that some of our best people would aspire to serve God and their country in politics. If they do not, then it will be left to those whose motivation is nothing more than selfishness. It would be no small thing to start by praying for those already in public office.

# Day 98
# II Samuel 4-7

The relationship between David and the Lord is one of those which is rich in lessons for us. The shepherd boy who became king had a unique relationship with God, and yet it also had elements that all our relationships with God should share. There was an intimacy and friendship between David and His Lord that should be the hallmark of everyone's personal relationship with God.

Surely, this is one of the most surprising things about our Creator, Redeemer, Deliverer - He wants a personal relationship with us. Most of the world's religions see their deity as an awesome power to be feared and served - a demanding god who wants and expects obeisance from its subjects. The God of Israel is such a different God. His attitudes and actions toward His people speak of something entirely different.

God has no need of a fancy house. In fact, He has no need of anything we could offer. All *things* are at His disposal. Let us remember, this God whom we worship, can bring entire galaxies into being out of nothingness at a word. He could no more fit in a house than our solar system could fit in our living rooms. He is not in search of our time, or talent, or money, as if without them He would be poor. He is in search of our love - open hearts, open minds, open souls. He is so fabulously wealthy that it is His great joy to share His riches with these strange, frightened, hairless bi-peds (as C.S. Lewis calls us) with which He has populated the earth.

So, when one of His beloved, if misguided hairless bi-peds, wanted to build Him a house, He looked past the silliness of the gift, and accepted the thought. In fact, God promised David that He would build a house for him - a kingdom that would never end. What an unexpected God we have - who wants to give, not get. He wants nothing we have, but everything we are. Sending a representative will not do - building a building, painting a picture, writing a song or a book, sending a priest, will not suffice. He wants our hearts.

Can we, too, give something to God? There is a temple which we can build for Him too - but not one that is made with hands. The grateful heart is the only temple He wants. Will you open up yours to Him?

# Day 99
# II Samuel 8-10

There is such great freedom in faith. David was a king who knew the freedom of his faith in God and it made him an extraordinary monarch in his time or any other. He was free to do the right thing and to show kindness, because his confidence was in God's promise, not his own cleverness. What a marvelous attitude toward the future.

David had never feared Saul or his family. Twice he killed those who had come to him with news of their participation in the death of Saul and his family. Most kings would rejoice to hear of the demise of those who would contest their thrones, yet David did not. When he had the opportunity, he went searching for any heir left from Saul's family - not to do them harm, but to treat them with honor and care for them. This had to be a difficult attitude for others to understand and apparently, many of them never did.

This kind of generosity which proceeded from his faith, extended beyond Saul's family. When the king of the Ammonites died, with whom David had been at peace, he sent representatives to express his sincere condolences. Loyalty was one of the results of David's confidence in God. He could afford to be loyal to his friends and good to his word, for God was watching over him. He only needed to do his part in the present, and God would take care of the future.

None of these lessons are new, however they are still outstanding traits whether they are found in a king or a commoner, ancient or contemporary. The testimony that these virtues are not common place is that so few people are willing to believe they exist in others. David was loyal, while so many others were not - and they were suspicious of any who looked to be loyal. It is a common human frailty to assume that others are, at heart, really no better than we are ourselves. It keeps us from accepting gifts from those who are better and wiser than we because our fear makes us suspicious. It is sad but true, evil begets more evil, and suspicion begets more suspicion.

On the other hand, good begets more good. Loyalty will engender more loyalty. Doing the right thing will not necessarily make you well understood. Suspicious people will still suspect your motives. But do the right thing anyway!

# Day 100
# II Samuel 11-14

ere begin the sad stories that would haunt David the rest of his life. As much as he loved the Lord and as much as the Lord loved him, David had set into motion events which would bring suffering on countless others. For as many blessings as David brought to the position of king, he also brought disaster.

As so often happens with people, it was not the time of trouble and crisis that proved to be his undoing, but the time of prosperity. David's kingdom had never been larger or more secure, but when the time came for him to be out doing his job as king, leading the battle, he stayed at home and was idle and restless. So in that time, temptation was not resisted, and he gave in, not only to adultery, but to deception and treachery. To commit adultery with another man's wife was bad enough, but to send Uriah back carrying the orders that would cause his death was premeditated murder.

However, we have benefited from David's sin. Western jurisprudence has been based on this legacy that no one is above the law. For oriental monarchs of David's time, this was not true. The king was the giver of the law and was, therefore, not bound by it. Not so with the Israelites. God was the giver of the law, and not even the king could transgress with impunity.

David's response shows the depth of his understanding of God. He offered no excuse or argument, but admitted his guilt and sought forgiveness. Even in the face of the judgement against his unborn son, he turns to God. What a different response to that of Saul. But even his repentance could not change the consequences of his actions. The sword had entered into his house, and it would haunt him and his family from then on.

There is a sobering lesson for us in this account. God's love for us is not based on our performance. His forgiveness is not conditioned on our being worthy of it. On the contrary, to receive it, we must recognize that we do not deserve it. But being forgiven does not turn the hands of time backward - it cannot undo all things. Before we lightly disobey what we know is right, we would do well to remember the consequences of David's life. We will not lose God's love, but we may lose a blessing we very much wanted to keep.

# Day 101
# II Samuel 15-17

People who live in glass houses, shouldn't throw stones! This is an old adage to which David would have subscribed had glass houses existed in his time. David was an adulterer and a murderer, so when his son Amnon raped his daughter Tamar, and his son Absalom subsequently killed Amnon, David was rather quiet during the whole affair. It is hypocritical to condemn others for things of which you are also guilty.

Hypocrisy aside, the truth is still the truth. David failed to condemn Amnon and left Absalom to seethe over the injustice. After Absalom killed Amnon, David neither truly forgave nor punished Absalom. David was paralyzed by his own guilt. As a role model, his sons were following along in his footsteps. Unfortunately, they were the wrong footsteps.

Absalom's revolt against David must have come as a crushing blow to him, but it should not have come as a surprise. No longer was David revered by his son Absalom for David had proven to be indecisive in family matters. Leadership that will not lead will eventually create its own opposition out of the frustration of those whose legitimate needs go unanswered. David had proven to be an able conqueror, but as a ruler, he had left much to be desired.

The process of repentance is a long and costly one and there is no shortcut around that process. The need to admit to guilt is seldom over with just one admission. It usually has to be admitted many times, before many different audiences, if the consequences of our sins are to be changed. David needed to admit to his own sin when he and Amnon shared the shame of a sex drive gone wrong. He needed to admit again his own guilt as killer when Absalom and he shared the role of premeditated murderers. No doubt this would have been very hard, but how much different the results might have been if he had.

It may not be easy to tell our children that they should not do what we have done, but is it not hypocritical if we admit to our own mistakes. The alternative to our discomfort may be our children following our example and walking down a road we know goes nowhere. People who live in glass houses should not only stop throwing rocks - they need to rebuild and warn others.

# Day 102
# II Samuel 18-21

bsalom is a study in what happens when you will not forgive. As the firstborn son he was in line to receive the throne from David and yet his bitterness and vengeance cost him not only the kingdom, but, finally, his own life.

Absalom was right in being outraged that there was no justice in Amnon's immunity from punishment for what he had done to Tamar. But there is a very big difference between justice and vengeance. Absalom wanted revenge, not justice, and as so often is the case with vengeance, it has more than one victim.

Revenge is a cold emotion. It seeks its own satisfaction no matter what the cost. It can become a consuming passion which locks its host into an event in the past and makes them unable to go on with life. Absalom's whole life got locked to the event of Tamar's rape, even though he had no direct part in it at all. His inability to forgive Amnon made him as much a captive of that event as Tamar and Amnon. The only thing that could have released him was to forgive Amnon.

But forgiveness does not preclude justice. It is very possible to forgive someone and still seek to see justice done - especially when the injustice was perpetrated against someone else. Justice demands its due, but does not make a victim of those who seek it. Amnon should have paid the price for his deed. If Absalom had been seeking justice for Tamar, there were other recourses for him. David needed help in doing justice for Tamar, but instead of encouraging his father, Absalom kept his own counsel of revenge and took matters into his own hands.

As is so often the case, Absalom's revenge was not sweet, but bitter. His heart, unwilling to forgive, was unable to let go of the past. Justice served, can walk away from the past knowing that all that could be done was done. Absalom passed the ultimate judgement of the law on Amnon, but that was still not enough.

It is a difficult balancing act to walk the line between justice and vengeance. What distinguishes them may seem like a very fine line, but it is a very important one - forgiveness.

Is there someone in your past you need to forgive? Doing so will not release them from justice, but it may release you from a vengeful prison of your own making. Think about it.

# Day 103
# II Samuel 22-24

obody likes a census. This seems to have been a universal dislike going back to ancient times. The census taken just before Jesus was born probably gives us a clue as to the reason. Then the census was for the purpose of taxation. The census David ordered was probably for the purpose of finding out how many men were available for battle. In any case, governments have a common purpose in taking censuses - to find out information on the population so they can know how much can be gotten from them and how much will be needed by them.

Why the census was such a terrible thing in the eyes of the population is fairly easy to see. Why God was so offended is a bit more obscure. Considering the other things David had done, why did this one act engender such a harsh response?

As David grew older, his confidence in the Lord had begun to fade. It had long been the pattern in Israel that military service was voluntary. Back as far as Moses and the Levitical laws only those who really wanted to fight (not the newly married, nor the faint hearted) were *allowed* to go into battle. That had changed somewhat with the introduction of kings in Israel (which had been one of the things God had warned them about - conscription), but there was still the fact that part of doing battle was first estimating how many men would show up to be part of your army. David wanted to rely on the census and troop availability rather than God, to decide what battles to face next.

This was a fundamental shift from David's usual trust in God to trusting in his own judgement. God did not take this lightly. So much of the success in David's life could be attributed to his trusting God with his future. Now was not the time to become "conservative." It is always too soon to stop trusting God.

Taking stock and counting the costs are important elements of discipleship. But there seems to be a difference between these steps of stewardship and taking a census. Perhaps it lies in the fact that we tend to limit ourselves when we take a census, because we forget to figure God into our equation. We assume we can travel no further than our stocks will take us - but have we included God in our inventory? How different our estimates will be if we do!

# Day 104
# I Kings 1-4

I have to admit at the start that Solomon is not one of my favorite characters in the Old Testament. There are several reasons, but primarily it is because of the sense of disappointment I feel about him. When in high school and reading about Solomon for the first time, I was impressed with his choice of asking for wisdom. Being a cognitively-oriented person myself, I thought wisdom to be the greatest thing you could ask for. Yet Solomon turns out to have had, on balance, a rather sad life. For all his wisdom, it did not help him to do the right thing.

Fallen idols seldom engender sympathy and I am afraid I have little for Solomon. He had inherited a kingdom almost at its zenith. He made smart political moves at the beginning of his reign that assured a stability during his life time unusual for any king. He had followed God from his youth and finally requested a special blessing from God that guaranteed him fame and fortune, although these were, admittedly, not his goals in asking for wisdom. So how did he go so wrong?

It is a difficult lesson to learn in life that knowing the right thing to do does not guarantee that you will do it. The problem people have had since Adam and Eve is not that we are ignorant or stupid, but that we are fallen at heart. We will know the good and not do it. Education is not the answer to the world's problems. There must be something done to our hearts so we will make the right choices - the choices that benefit ourselves and everyone else.

In the final analysis, obedience is more fundamental than wisdom. To know the good is certainly "higher" than simply doing the good and not understanding the reasons. But, finally, it is doing the good that counts - for whatever reason, because if you will not do what is good, you will do what is bad. Solomon knew that it was wrong to allow his wives to set up idols and allow the worship of other "gods." His intellect led him to a cynical attitude (that we will read about later) and finally disobedience.

Solomon is an excellent example of the fact that we do not need to know more about the will of God in order to do it. We need to do the will of God that we already know. It is our hearts more than our minds that need changing.

# Day 105
## I Kings 5-7

The temple would become a national treasure and a source of great pride. It would do so at the cost of tens of thousands of forced laborers over more than seven years, and a significant shift in misunderstanding of the God it was intended to honor. The temple became the embodiment of what the people did for God - the opposite of the tabernacle, which embodied what God had done for people. There was great rejoicing at the building of the temple, but from our New Testament perspective, it should have been a day of mourning.

It seems strange that God would have given David and Solomon permission for a project that He had to know would corrupt the nation's religious understanding. The God of Israel was not a local god. He needed no house to live in. He needed no central shrine for people to serve Him. He needed no mystical place wherein His people could beg His favor or placate His wrath. Other "gods" required such things, but not the God of Israel. Yet the temple represented all these things in the minds of the people. How could God agree to such an obvious mistake?

Perhaps it was because of Israel's track record with the tabernacle. Despite all of the correct symbols, Israel had managed to misunderstand God quite thoroughly, for centuries. Visual aids are not always effective in the long haul. David had wanted to do something for God. He felt it was wrong for him to live in a house of cedar while it appeared that the ark was devalued by being housed in a tent. It was a foolish gift, but it was heartfelt. Apparently, that was enough for God.

Notice though, how much the original purpose of Israel had been lost even by Solomon's time. With the building of the great temple, and Solomon's reputation of being a wise man, the emphasis had turned from Israel being a priestly people to the other nations, carrying the message of the one true God, to the idea that they were the "apple of God's eye" - favored because of some national greatness. By Solomon's time Israel felt that if the world wanted to know God, it had to come to them. What a far cry from what Moses announced back in the wilderness. God had remained true to His covenant with them, but if His message was to be carried to the world, it would have to find another vehicle.

# Day 106
# I Kings 8-11

e will meet the legendary wisdom of Solomon in the Proverbs and Ecclesiastes, but I find it informative to note what happened to the man before reading his wisdom. We should distinguish the medium from the message. Truth is truth, no matter what its source, but there is value too in knowing the character of the bearer.

I have always suspected that for all Solomon's wisdom, he must have missed something somewhere along the line, to have gone so terribly wrong. I think that you see some of it in his prayer that is recorded in these chapters. Although he admits the house he built cannot contain God in any real sense, he asks that God treat it in a special way - that when anyone prayed in it, or toward it, that the petition receive a special hearing, that any oath which included mention of the temple, should be, somehow, more binding. Why? The only possible answer is pride.

Solomon was proud, not of what God had done, but what he had accomplished. The author of Kings says that so many animals were sacrificed on that day of dedication that they could not be numbered. How sad. God loved those animals. The sacrificial system had not been established for the sake of a blood-thirsty God, but for the sake of the sinners. Solomon seemed to understand that intellectually. In his prayer he says that no sacrifice can be sufficient, and yet he ordered the slaughter of all those animals, offered up for his pride, not the glory of God. Solomon wanted God's house to be the best, but not only for God's sake. This mixed motive would come back to haunt him.

Perhaps Solomon was trying to help those with simpler minds, meaning all the rest of us, by providing a central "shrine" to focus our worship rather than depend upon our understanding of the more complex reality of a God who is everywhere. God even grants his petition and says that the City of David would forever be a special place to Him. But was Solomon right? Is it better to have an artificially simplistic faith rather than a complex real one? Do we ask God to do the same thing? If only He would speak to us directly - tell us what to do. Would it really be better? Perhaps before we ask God to change the way He works, we should consider that He might know what He is doing after all!

# Day 107
# I Kings 12-14

To select which of the first kings of the divided kingdom was the worst, Rehoboam or Jeroboam, would be difficult. Both worked unceasingly at undoing whatever good David and Solomon had done for the nation. Each brought his own fatal character flaws to the office that set a course for disaster which would vary little over the following centuries.

Both Rehoboam and Jeroboam stood at the crossroads of the history of their respective kingdoms. They each had the privilege and responsibility of being the first kings of their new, albeit smaller, nations. Rehoboam had already proven that he was unfit for the task by taking the wrong advice thereby providing the means by which the kingdom could be split. Each of them had that unique opportunity to be in at the beginning of something and each laid the foundation for disaster. Did it have to be so?

Rehoboam was counseled wisely, to serve the people who would in turn serve him. But he chose to ignore this formula for leadership. He would not give the people what they needed, instead he would do what he wanted. He tried to command a respect that can only be earned. He would prove that leadership which ignores the needs of the followers will find an insufficient foundation to keep going.

Jeroboam on the other hand, made the mistake of trying to meet the needs of the people without regard for whether or not the means were right. The people of Israel needed a new place to be the center of their worship. Instead of reinstituting the old places of sacrifice from the days of the judges, and reminding the people that the temple could not contain God anyway, he set up an alternative religion and pagan sacrifices. What he did was popular, but it was not the right thing to do. Good leadership must be concerned with both.

God has called each of us to be initiators of things in this life. The foundations we give these endeavors (or people, since we give our children their start) will be critical to their success. As leaders, have we been concerned both with serving the legitimate needs and with doing the right thing? If we do not do both then the foundations we lay, however popular, will not stand the test of time.

# Day 108
# I Kings 15-18

lijah burst onto the scene in Israel like a comet. Ahab was in no way prepared to deal with the likes of this prophet. Elijah stands as one of those strangely intriguing and yet repellent figures in the Old Testament. A great man of God, and not a little bit scary.

This story of his confrontation with the prophets of Baal on Mount Carmel is one of my favorites. After seven long years of drought, he appeared to challenge the pagan system that Ahab had built and to stand firm for the Lord. What a scene to have witnessed! It is the classic drama we all long for - the decisive confrontation between good and evil - with good prevailing in total victory and humiliation of evil. Why doesn't God do this more often?

Why indeed? Elijah's question comes to us across the centuries. How long will we go limping with two opinions? If the Lord is God, then follow Him; if Baal, then follow him. 18:21 Moses had called the people to the same decision in his time; I set before you the choice of life and death - choose life! Joshua had issued the call to decision; choose this day whom you will serve, but for me and my house, we will serve the Lord. Elijah asked the same question - how long will you go limping with two opinions? How long indeed?

Perhaps we should be glad that God does not smash evil outwardly and openly every day. What if He did the day before you or I were ready to make that decision to follow Him? Then we would surely be crushed with the evil we had not yet chosen to give up. Not every day is the day of decision and for this we should be grateful. It is that grace period that has allowed so many centuries to pass and for us to be born and have the opportunity to decide.

But let us be very clear, the day of decision comes for everyone, and one day, for the whole world. We cannot go on forever limping along with two opinions. Eventually we must choose. Whom will we serve? When all else is accounted for, this will be the single most important choice we ever make. Let us choose whom we will serve and serve Him with a full heart! May God grant us the grace to make the right choice today!

# Day 109
# I Kings 19-22

Elijah's life has many lessons to teach us, but perhaps the most important one comes not from his victory over the prophets of Baal, but from what happened afterward - how he faced his despair. After winning such an obvious victory over the 400 prophets of Baal, it was certainly reasonable for him to think that everything would be different and better. Ahab and the people had seen for themselves that Yahweh was the true God and Baal was nothing. So how could Jezebel threaten his life after such a great victory?

I think this story should tell us something about the impact of the miraculous on most people. I often hear people wondering why God doesn't do more "flashy," more obvious, shows of His strength. However, those miracles do not affect the human heart as much as we might like to think. The Israelites who witnessed the ten plagues in Egypt and the parting of the Red Sea, quickly lost their faith when pursued by Pharaoh. The crowds that witnessed the victory over Baal's prophets, even though they cast the prophets off of the cliff, quickly returned to the status quo as the rains came and the drought ended. But Elijah had sold out his expectations of God's deliverance to the "big event" theory. If God would just show them, how different it would be. God did, and it was not so different.

Elijah was exhausted from the confrontation with the prophets, and ran deep into the desert. He was tired and his expectations had been shattered. These are the times that despair can really get its grip on us. God sent an angel to give the best advice for facing discouragement - eat, rest and withdraw. We are physical creatures as well as intellectual, emotional and spiritual. What happens to us affects all the parts. The first thing to do is rest - take care of the physical needs. Then, the intellectual, emotional and spiritual ingredients can be dealt with.

God sent Elijah a living parable. Up in the cave, withdrawn, God sent the fire, and the earthquake - the show of force. But God was not in those, instead He was in the still small voice. And the message was that God had more going on than Elijah knew.

When we are discouraged we need to remember Elijah's lesson - eat, rest, and remember that God is at work in ways that we may not yet know, but if we ask, He may reveal them to us!

# Day 110
# II Kings 1-3

lijah and Elisha were the kind of prophets that give prophets a bad name. They were strange looking, poor dressers, intense, antisocial, and downright dangerous! They were also seldom bearers of good news to the kings who reigned during their ministries. It is understandable why people would think that if this was what it meant to follow Yahweh, they would be happy to follow some other god if they could. Who wanted to wear rough clothing and hang out in the wilderness all the time?

What lessons are we to learn from these "great men of God?" In what ways are we to be like them? I think many people still have the same fear today - that to be really close to God will cost them their lives, and they will have to wear strange clothes and preach to people on street corners. Perhaps the clue is to see the people the prophets stood in contrast to - the kings.

If Elijah and Elisha were intense and fanatical, then the kings were certainly the picture of the moderate and the carefully religious. Like so many other people, the kings wanted to give the gods their due, whatever that might be, and be done with the religious part of life. We should make the appropriate sacrifices, and just to be safe, sacrifice to whatever god the religious nuts warn us is out there. Those religious fanatics are probably all right in their own way. Let's not rock the boat. We'll give a little devotion wherever necessary, and hope for the best. After all, we aren't really any worse than anybody else, so god, or the gods, will probably treat us fairly - don't you think? There certainly is too much risk in going with just one religion. Better to cover the bases, hope for the best, and try not to think about it. I think the kings would have been pretty average in our day.

But faith in Yahweh is a risk. He is a jealous God, and He simply will not tolerate us chasing after other gods. He wants our full devotion. Were Elijah and Elisha really so strange, or did they just appear so because they lived in a world full of hypocrisy and compromise. One thing is certain. They remind us that you cannot mix worshipping Yahweh with other religions - either He is God or He is not, it cannot be both ways. Believing that is not fanaticism, it is facing the facts. It only looks fanatical to a world that cannot make up its mind. What about our world today?

# Day 111
# II Kings 4-6

The encounters of Elisha with the Shunammite woman and Naaman are very important changes in the flow of salvation history. The New Testament authors picked up on the shift and the significance had not been totally lost on the Israelites themselves. We need to make sure that we see the change here too.

In one sense, of course, this was no change in the modus operandi of God at all. He sent his prophet Elisha to respond to those individuals whose faith had made them open. As with Abraham, their faith was counted to them as righteousness. But neither of them were Jews, and what was worse, God was sending no miracles to the Jews at the time. To the Israelites, this looked like He had abandoned His people and was, inexplicably, working for their enemies. Why would He do this?

We have spent many hours by now, reading about this people of God called Israel. From our vantage point it seems reasonable that God should have become disgusted with them by now and it is surprising He continued with them at all! But we need to remember some of the plot in this story of salvation so we can understand clearly what God had been doing.

Remember, God had called Israel to be a priestly nation. He did not hate the other people of the world, He loved them, and they were not being ignored by Him all these centuries. We know for a fact that they came under His judgement from time to time - remember Israel's receiving the promised land was as much a judgement *against* the Canaanites as a judgement *for* the Israelites so we must assume that they had also received His grace in some fashion. Naaman and the Shunammite woman are just examples of individuals whose heart had been measured by God as all hearts are, and found to have faith.

God had not abandoned His covenant with Israel when He sent mercy to Naaman and the Shunammite woman. He was acting consistently with His character as He always has. It was Israel who had ceased to understand the covenant. God has always measured the heart and dealt graciously, not legalistically, with people. With Naaman and the Shunammite woman it starts becoming clearer what we will see in the New Testament - being an Israelite is more a matter of the heart than the body!

# Day 112
# II Kings 7-10

How does one go about changing a society? The nation of Israel had become incredibly corrupt. Droughts did not seem to have any effect. Miracles of deliverance (like God's intervention with the Syrians) brought no appreciation for the God who had delivered them. What would it take?

The answer seems to be amputation. If you are going to remove the corrupting influence, one sure way is to eliminate those who are doing the corrupting. Jehu becomes the vehicle by which God does this for Israel and Judah. His was a bloody, but effective means of changing the nation.

Many people find these accounts of the brutality of political change by mass killing to be foreign and primitive. But there is a rather naive historical myopia behind those feelings. If you read of the slaughter in Russia under Stalin, or in Romania under Ceausescu, you must realize that brutality as a vehicle of political change is very much with us. The fact that violence as a means of political change is abhorred in our country, is quite the exception rather than the rule.

It should not really surprise us that the kings in the Old Testament used the only means of social change they had available - force. It is still quite common today, but there is another way. Societies can also be changed from within, by changing the individuals who make up the society.

In history, there would come a man who would present the perfect alternative. His life and work would bring about a change in the lives of the people he touched, and the lives of the people they touched, until, like a little leaven, the whole world would be a different place. His power would be such that it would forever change the hearts of those who love him, and would topple nations and empires, only to rebuild them with a new sense of justice and a growing ability to allow freedom and political change without violence. His influence has been felt for many centuries and it is still fighting against the forces of hatred and violence, but it has made more difference than we will probably ever know.

Of course, He hadn't been born in Jehu's time and we must remember that difference. What a difference it has made!

# Day 113
# II Kings 11-13

hese chapters remind me of the old saying, "You can't tell the players without a program." This is the program, and I still can't tell the players apart! I'm not sure, but Benhadad in Syrian must be like Smith in English! As for the kings of Israel and Judah, it becomes impossible to keep track of them unless you have been making a scorecard!

What value are all these people and events to us anyway? Do we really need to know this history? I suppose in one sense, the answer would be no. It is not necessary to know all the details of this history of Israel. Many Christians have a deep and meaningful relationship with God without ever reading any of II Kings.

Yet Christianity claims to be an historical faith, therefore, the history is important. Many of these kings did very little that was noteworthy from the viewpoint of salvation history, yet they are links, and it is good to know that all the links in a chain are present and accounted for. It also provides us with some interesting object lessons along the long road of salvation history.

One of the side bars of this narrative is the impact of women throughout this history. Both for good and ill, women also effected the flow of salvation history. The effects of Jezebel, directly and through her daughters, were felt well past her death. Her daughter, Athaliah, even ruled briefly over Judah as Queen (after her son died and she had the rest of the royal family killed). Power, greed, cruelty, and violence are no respector of gender. The women as well as the men took part in the evils of their time.

I confess that I find little uplifting in reading about these people and their time. Perhaps the most we can get out of them is to look and be glad for the time into which we have been born. And maybe we should realize that we are not just a product of the time we are in, but also architects. We have been influenced and we will influence. Each generation must not only deal with the past, but decide again what kind of character their lives and their society will have.

When our children's children's children are writing about us and our time, what will they say? Will it be glorious, hideous, or nondescript. It's up to us.

# Day 114
# II Kings 14-17

he ten tribes of the North were carried off by the Assyrians and have never been heard from again. The Assyrian king decided the Jews had caused him too much trouble and he would repopulate the area with other people. It was an extremely effective strategy. But it was really a sentence that Israel had brought upon itself. If God had not been fed up with them, this would never have happened.

This brings us to some rather disturbing questions that have confronted us many times now in the history of Israel. Is it really possible to wear out the patience of God? Having once received God's grace, can we really fall from it? If we can, just where is the dividing line?

These are difficult questions that we must answer ourselves, but there is some perspective offered in these chapters that can help us. First, we should recognize that this judgement against Israel is for them as a nation, not necessarily as individuals. There is a difference between a society and the people that make it up. The whole is something different from the sum of its parts. To be certain, the two are intimately involved with each other, but they are not synonymous. It seems clear that societies can and do fall from grace, but that does not necessarily mean it is true for individuals. The argument for what is called "eternal assurance" or "once saved, always saved" will be made later in the New Testament, but what happened at this point was a judgement of the nation of Israel, not necessarily each individual.

We should also take note that to fall out of grace, even for societies, is not a matter of inches but miles. Israel had not forgotten to cross a few t's or dot a few i's, they had sacrificed their own children on alters made to honor other gods. God's patience may not be forever, but it is certainly *very* long indeed! Invoking the wrath of God is not because we stray a few inches off the straight and narrow, it is because we travel miles and miles into the territory of the evil, vile, and disgusting acts of life.

Finally, let us not forget that God's grace was operating even in this judgement. He was still being consistent with what He promised He would do if they rejected Him. At least for those victims of Israel's sins, this was good grace indeed.

# Day 115
# II Kings 18-20

ezekiah came as a breath of fresh air after a long confinement in a musty cave. For the first time in the record of the kings since David, this king is said to have followed David in all his ways, and finally tore down the "high places," those places where idols were set up and worshipped. Hezekiah had them all destroyed. So why was this not enough to change the fate of Judah?

It seems that what has taken centuries to do is not easy to undo. There is an accumulative effect, both for good and evil, that makes either difficult to overcome the longer they are allowed to go on. Hezekiah's reforms were good, but they were fighting a trend that would not die easily and he did not have the foresight or ability to make lasting changes. His ambivalence was obvious when he was told by Isaiah that the kingdom would be carried off to Babylon. He made no attempt to change that judgement, being satisfied it would not come during his own lifetime.

What is it about human beings that we so readily allow future generations to suffer? It seems we are not only selfish but lack faith in the grace of God. Hezekiah had just experienced God's grace by being given fifteen more years to live when he should have died. God grants him this extension, we are told, because of Hezekiah's earnest prayer to live longer. Why didn't Hezekiah pray for the nation? Why did he not beseech Isaiah to ask God to change this judgement? How often have we read that God did so when earnestly asked?

We seem to be so terribly fatalistic about history. In one sense, God has ordained that the outcome of salvation history will be the remaking of the heavens and the earth, but the nature of how it will be until then seems to be much in our own hands. God will win this game, but the final score has yet to be determined.

Each person and each life is of importance to God. Hezekiah's life should teach us the value of turning to Him and serving Him. But it should also teach us not to give up seeking His grace for ourselves, our children and our children's children. Our doing so may be just the trend they will need to make the difference in their own generation. It is always too soon to give up seeking God's grace for everyone!

# Day 116
# II Kings 21-25

One of the most amazing things about the reign of King Josiah was that the book of the law was rediscovered. It is astounding that the Scriptures could have been lost to begin with, and that they should have been lost for so long a time. Josiah's zealous devotion to the covenant brought the last time of peace and prosperity that Judah would see for centuries to come.

In the United States, we revere the Declaration of Independence, the Constitution and the Bill of Rights as those documents and ideas which have formed the basis of our society. How much more should the book of the Law have been revered by Israel? It contained their charter as a people of God, their laws by which they were to function and rules by which they were to keep their relationship right with God. How could it have come to be ignored?

Before we criticize the Israelites, perhaps we should consider our own record with the same book! The Bible has been the number one best seller ever since it was first published. There have been more Bibles printed and distributed than any other book in history, and by no small margin! But how well read is it?

Having persisted in this course for one hundred and sixteen days, reading three or four chapters a day, you have seen for yourself one reason the Bible is not all that well read - it's so long! Yet we still believe it is the book that gives us the understanding of our faith - don't we? It is a resource, not just for history, but for reflection and the comfort of God Himself. Why is it so under utilized by God's people?

I believe that one of those reasons that the Bible is not more used is because so many people have never read the whole thing. That is what this course of study is all about. People have spent hundreds of hours studying the Bible in its parts without ever having read it as a whole. I believe that once you have read it through, you will never be able again to relegate it to the shelf with the old college text books or the knick knaks that Aunt Clara sent you. This is God's word alive today! After you have finished this year, you will find a new sense of ownership about your Bible, and studying its parts will be much more meaningful. Keep on going, the best is yet to come!

# Day 117
# I Chronicles 1-3

ow you know why I wrote the pep talk for yesterday's devotion! Yikes! These are the chapters that can just kill you! The bad news is that these genealogies will continue until chapter 9! The good news is that it can help us remember the good old days when we were reading the explicit instructions on building the tabernacle! These chapters make those look positively fascinating!

Before you despair and decide simply to skip these chapters, I would encourage you to take a quick run through them and notice how many names you are familiar with! I have no idea where the author of Chronicles got all these names, but I was pleasantly surprised at how many were familiar and I think you will be too.

Since it shouldn't have required much time today to read over these chapters, take a little extra time to think about the larger picture you have been seeing through the life stories of these people. God has been slowly and methodically bringing about the promise of the Messiah that He gave back in Genesis 3, right after the fall. Although we have come some distance in salvation history, this understanding of a Messiah is still being developed at this point. Why did God take so long? I honestly have no answer. But I can say that I am truly glad He has continued His plan through the ups and downs of His people throughout the centuries.

Who have been your favorites: Adam, Noah, Abraham, Isaac, Jacob or Joseph? Did you feel closer to some of the lesser known figures like Caleb, Jesse or Naaman? I hope some of these people will have become friends to you by now, for they are the faithful who have preceded us. It may seem odd, but it is the promise of Scripture that we will one day actually meet them! I wonder if they will be as curious about our lives as we have been about theirs.

We do share something in common with them that binds us together - not just that we are all descendents of Adam and Eve, but that we will all inherit the kingdom together. We are family after all - family of faith. Before we become too bored, perhaps we should remember that this is, in part, our genealogy too!

# Day 118
# I Chronicles 4-7

amily names and nicknames can be difficult things to live with. There was a song quite a while back that was popular for a time, called "A Boy Named Sue." The ballad told of a boy who had been named Sue by his father because the father knew he wouldn't be around to help the boy grow up tough, so he gave him that name to guarantee he would learn to defend himself. Jabez must have felt much like the boy in the song. His mother named him "pain."

We have looked many times at the legacy we leave to our children - good and bad. Jabez certainly would have had room to complain about his mother's legacy. But as is so often the case, it is not the cards that we are dealt in life that determines how well we do, but the way in which we play them.

I am probably stretching (what else is there to do with these chapters?!) but it must count for something that in this long, boring genealogy, that Jabez gets a few lines about his character. Obviously Jabez did a remarkable job of playing the hand he was dealt. We might not catch the impact by calling him Jabez, so let's use the name he was given as the allegory it was intended to be - "pain."

"Pain" was good - in fact exceptionally good. While he had been trouble to his mother at birth, "Pain" became a real blessing. "Pain" cried out to God for a blessing and received it. While we might not normally think of "Pain" as good, in this broken and fallen world, "Pain" can often be a real asset.

There is of course a place for pain in our lives. If we did not know pain, we would not know to move our hand when we touch a hot stove. Without pain, we might not know when we were terribly sick inside, but could not see it. Without pain, we might go on living lives of quiet desperation, unable and unwilling to face the hard realities of life.

Pain is not an unqualified good, nor is it an unqualified bad. It can be a message. It should neither be sought nor ignored, but given its due. Whatever else it does for us, it should, like it did for its namesake, Jabez, get us to turn to God. He alone can take away our pain. And He might just have an important lesson and blessing to share with us at the same time!

# Day 119
# I Chronicles 8-10

The author of Chronicles gives a slightly different perspective of the history of the kings of Israel. While much of the content of Chronicles duplicates the books of Samuel and Kings, there will be a different emphasis, another perspective that can be helpful in understanding the events. It will also give us the opportunity to look at some things again that might have escaped our notice the first time through.

It seems likely that I & II Chronicles were written after the exile in Babylon. There was a need to make sure that it was clear the people who returned from the Babylonian exile, were a continuation of the line which traced back to David. The author does not concern himself much with Saul, but jumps past the first king of Israel to the great king of Israel. You might also notice as we go along, that the failings of David and Solomon will be down played in this retelling. It seems that the author felt no good was to come out of tarnishing the memory of the nations heroes. In addition, the northern kingdom of Israel is virtually ignored by the Chronicles.

How should we feel about pre-digested history? In our society, we value the truth and almost take a sort of perverted pleasure in finding the faults of our national heroes. What best serves the interest of people?

We must remember that these are part of the Scriptures, and as such, are part of what we believe to be the inspired Word of God. That doctrine of inspiration does not mean we have to be blind about them. We have been given not only the Chronicles, but the Samuels and the Kings too. God has seen to it that we have these altogether to provide some balance. Perhaps that is why we have more than one gospel account - no one perspective would have done justice to the richness of the reality.

History simply cannot be told without some interpretation. The teller must decide what facts are important and what the events mean. While we may find a somewhat different perspective on the events, let us look carefully before we declare them contradictory. They may just be a different perspective that notices or draws out different things. Given a fair reading, I think you will see the work of the one real author - God!

# Day 120
# I Chronicles 11-14

One of the problems with reading other people's mail is that they will sometimes make an inside joke or reference that only makes sense to the person they were writing too. The author of Chronicles makes several of these kind of "inside" references. It can make it very difficult to understand just what was really going on.

One of these is recorded in chapter eleven when the three mighty men were credited with risking life and limb to go and get David a drink of water from the well in enemy territory. When they returned safely, David, apparently to honor them and God, refuses to drink the water and pours it out on the ground. Perhaps I'm missing something here, but if I had just risked my neck to get my commander a drink of water and he didn't even drink it, I would be experiencing many emotions, but honor would not be among them! Even if he was trying to say that my life was more important than his thirst, I would rather that he share the water - not just pour it out!

The account of Uzzah and the Ark is another example of an "inside" meaning. When the ox cart began to tip over and Uzzah put out his hand to steady it, the author of Chronicles says that God struck Uzzah dead for touching the Ark. I have read some commentators who have suggested God struck Uzzah dead because he lacked the faith to believe that God could take care of His own Ark. God had delivered the Ark out of the hands of the Philistines, He could certainly deliver it out of the mud! This seems like quite an interpretive stretch to me! I have a feeling that there must be more to this story than is recorded. God isn't generally that touchy!

But these are two good things to remember when we read passages like this. First, in one sense, we are reading other people's mail when we read the Bible. There will be references which are not clear to us because we no longer live in that society and time. The second thing is that we are not always told the whole story, in part, because we do not *need* to know the whole story. Remember, the Bible is not all there is to know, just all we need to know for our salvation. We will undoubtably have many questions to ask when we get into the Kingdom of God - maybe we'll remember to ask about Uzzah - or maybe not!

# Day 121
# I Chronicles 15-17

hese chapters remind me of what I like most about David - his wholehearted abandon - his love of God and the life God gave him. You can hear it in the song he had Asaph sing for the occasion of bringing the Ark into Jerusalem. "For great is the Lord and greatly to be praised, ... Ascribe to the Lord, the glory due his name; bring an offering, and come before him! ... O give thanks to the Lord, for he is good; for his steadfast love endures for ever!" No wonder he danced in front of the Ark as it entered, but his exhuberance offended some people, even his wife, Michal.

It doesn't say why Michal despised David because of his dancing. She was Saul's daughter and perhaps she had been upset that David should rejoice so much now that he was king and Saul was dead. But she knew that Saul had betrayed David, not the other way around, and she knew that David had not rejoiced at the death of Saul and Jonathan. I think it is more likely that she thought it was beneath him as a king to make such a spectacle of himself in public over something like the Ark. How common and bourgeois to be so carried away with emotion over religion! What would the people say?

There is most certainly something very risky about giving our whole hearts to God with such abandon. Why, we might even shout out loud, or cheer, or (heaven forbid!) act like we do at football or basketball games! People might think we were excited about God and what He is doing! They might even take us for religious fanatics or something! Best we should be very careful about that sort of thing - emotions can't really be trusted, you know.

To be sure, emotional highs can be generated by many different things other than devotion to God, and having to be on a constant emotional high can lead to hypocrisy. But make no mistake, there are times and places for most everything, and those who will never get excited have missed out on one of the best things about being human - passionate emotions.

God is very pleased when from the true depths of our hearts, we give thanks to Him for His graciousness. Go ahead and take a chance. If God is happy, the rest of the world's opinion doesn't matter!

# Day 122
# I Chronicles 18-21

**W**hat impresses one person can be quite different from what impresses another. In contrast to the author of II Samuel the Chronicler makes no mention at all of David's adultery with Bathsheba but gives great attention to his numbering of the people, the subsequent plague, and the purchase of the future site of the temple. The fact that we would probably agree with the author of II Samuel as to the importance of David's adultery says something about our frame of reference as well as that of these authors.

The author of Chronicles might have mirrored more accurately the prevailing attitudes of the people during David's time. A king's infidelities were a common practice and not likely to cause a stir. Now a census was a different matter. David's adultery may even have been unknown generally. He did marry Bathsheba, and their sons who lived were all "legitimate." But for the author of II Samuel, we might also be ignorant of the episode. But taking a census would have been known throughout the kingdom and opinions on it would have run very high.

From our vantage point centuries later, we know that in fact, the author of II Samuel was correct, David's sin with Bathsheba was much more important than the census. The lesson it had to teach about the king not being above the law is more important, but also, within David's own family, his sin brought a curse with it that would affect the whole history of the nation. The whole kingdom might not have known of his sin, but his family most certainly did, and it seriously undercut his ability to be a role model.

I wonder how often the same is true of our lives. Is it the things we do that bring us some measure of notoriety that make the real difference in our lives? Or is it those things of which only we, our family and closest friends and God know, that make the real difference? I think it is the latter. We are really the people God knows us to be. But before we get too guilt-ridden, let us remember that we can even be mistaken about ourselves. David was still one of God's favorites, in part because David accepted God's judgement of his actions - he did not seek to punish himself more or less than God required. Can we say the same?

# Day 123
## I Chronicles 22-25

The temple was always a mixed blessing for the people of Israel. David wanted to do something for God and God honored that desire even though it was a silly request. God could not fit into any house, but David had been sincere in his desire to do something for God, and that was good enough for Him.

On the positive side, David wanted it to be the best shrine to any god anywhere. Why? Because David believed that God deserved nothing less than the very best - the best of our time, treasure and talent. David was a wholehearted lover. When he gave, it could not be what was left over, or what he didn't really want anyway, or his spare time and energy, it had to be the first and the best - giving from love and gratitude is always that way.

How much different would the Church be if all its members gave with the same kind of attitude? No more second hand couches, or TVs that have lost one of the three primary colors (the kind where the faces look blue!) or filing cabinets with one drawer that won't open. The first and the best for the work of God. That is an ingredient sorely missing in many congregations. I wonder how impressed the world would be if our churches reflected that kind of giving.

When the temple was completed it was without parallel, and yet it wasn't all wonderful. On the negative side, there seems to be an aspect inherent in monuments that reflects more on the builder than the one memorialized. David and Solomon's temple reflected more on them than it did on God. So it is with us, since God never comes and takes the present home, we often fall victim to feeling awe about the gift rather than the one to whom it is given.

What might David have given to God instead? God is, after all, the worst nightmare for the conscientious gift giver. What do you give to the person who *literally* has everything? J.S. Whale wrote, "God does not need our sacrifices but he has, nevertheless, appointed a representative to receive them, namely our neighbor. The neighbor always represents the invisible Christ." Helping build other grateful hearts by giving is the greatest monument that we can erect to God. And it will outlast all the temples and cathedrals ever built.

# Day 124
# I Chronicles 26-29

 avid's final speech here in I Chronicles reviews the highlights of what he had learned in his own life with God. He had loved God with a whole heart, if not always with wholehearted obedience. He had been greatly blessed, but still remembered that this life was one of the sojourner - a brief time compared to the eternity to be spent with God in His Kingdom. Both of these are valuable lessons for us all to learn.

Some people have a problem understanding how God's love for us can be gracious if the promise of blessing is tied to obeying God. David tells Solomon that God will establish his kingdom forever, if he will follow God faithfully. That seems like a conditional arrangement, doesn't it? Our problem is that we too often confuse love with approval.

I love my two children. They are a great joy to me - most of the time! I will always love them. Nothing they could ever do would stop that. But I do not, and will not, always approve of what they do, or even what they may become. Approval will be dependent on whether or not they grow up to be the persons that God has made them to be. If they do, then I will not only be able to love them, but rejoice in them too. If they do not, I will still love them, but I cannot approve or condone that which is wrong for the sake of my love. God always loves us, but that does not mean that He always approves of what we do or who we are. That will depend on what we choose to do and become. But He, for His part, will always love us.

That is why it is so critical that we come to know God and trust Him in this life. If we do not come to understand that His love is not conditioned on our actions, we will most certainly make the error of mistaking His approval for His love. When Judgement Day comes, we will discover just how little claim we can lay on His approval. If we do not know by then that it is His love which counts, we will most certainly be lost in our own self-imposed guilt from which no power will be able to reclaim us.

This world is, at last, not our home. We are just pilgrims passing through. May God grant, that like David, we will be able to say that we loved God with a whole heart and appreciated the blessings that come from an obedient life.

# Day 125
# II Chronicles 1-3

The wisdom of Solomon was legendary. He was known throughout the world for being the wisest man of his time. God even congratulated him for his choice of wisdom and knowledge and blessed him, not only with both, but with fame and riches and honor. What was this wisdom that made him so great?

We get a clue from the things God mentions that Solomon could have asked for instead of wisdom. The wisdom and knowledge of God are greater than possessions, wealth, honor, victory over one's enemies or long life. (1:11) We ourselves know this is true.

Certainly, the wisdom and knowledge of God are greater than possessions or wealth. The fact is no matter how rich we become, we will die, and we cannot take it with us. But the wisdom and knowledge of God remain ours for eternity - etched into our very beings. He who gains the whole world and loses his soul will have gained precisely nothing.

Honor and victory over one's enemies are valuable assets. However, both are fleeting glories in this life. We see many examples on television, of people who have achieved great fame and victory, yet after the battle is done, and the awards given, the spotlight moves on, and many cannot bear the loss of it. The public's adoration is a fickle thing. It is not only more important to know God sees all we do and rewards us, it is the only notoriety that lasts.

Solomon chose well in asking for wisdom and understanding. The two together are a powerful combination. We must have some knowledge in order to be wise, but wisdom is more than just the accumulation of facts, it is knowing how to apply them.

We possess the same knowledge as Solomon. We know that the knowledge and wisdom of God are more valuable than riches or fame or victory or long life. But if we are going to be as wise as Solomon, we must learn to apply this truth in our lives - to live, not only like we know this, but also like we believe it. Are we willing to live as if knowing God is better than fame, fortune and long life? It is the wise thing to do, but as Solomon discovered, it is easier to know than it is to obey!

# Day 126
# II Chronicles 4-6

O ne of the most wonderful things about prayer is that you can be completely honest, dead wrong, and things can still turn out all right because it is God who is doing the listening. Solomon's prayer at the dedication of the temple is an example of just how that principle works. Here we find him praying that God will give special attention to prayers and requests made in or toward the temple. How like Solomon, how unlike God.

I have had my share of theological discussions with people which have ended in their rather disdainful closing remark, "Well, I'll pray for you!" I never really mind that kind of "threat." I may not agree with what they will be praying about for me, but I know that the One to whom they pray can be trusted. Who knows, they may be right, in which case it will probably take an act of God to change my mind! In any case, I cannot lose.

That is one of the strange and wonderful things about being a follower of this God of the Israelites, Yahweh. He works with and through imperfect people to bring about His perfect will. It is a feat that no one less than God could or should attempt. Yet He has done it throughout the centuries, even into ours.

Solomon was so right in his prayer that there is no other god like Yahweh, who keeps His covenants, and practices steadfast love. 6:14 Yet he was so wrong in thinking that God would listen any the less to the heartfelt cries of His people because they were not in, or directed toward the temple. Even though God agreed to make the temple and Jerusalem a special place, He did not change His nature of omnipresence to suit the limited ideas of His servants. God hears our prayers always, not because He has such good hearing, but because we are never out of His awareness. He is always so close that He knows all our thoughts and feelings, not just those directed to Him in prayer.

Prayer is not like a long distance phone call. Prayer is turning our limited attention to the ever present mind of God. That is why we need not be pretentious in prayer - he knows what we are really thinking anyway. It is also why we can afford to be wrong - He makes allowances. When we pray little, He does not know us less, but we understand Him less. That is the one mistake we cannot afford to make. Have you prayed today?

# Day 127
# II Chronicles 7-10

The fourteenth verse of chapter seven is one of the most poetic in the Scriptures. "... if my people, who are called by my name humble themselves, and pray and seek my face, and turn from their wicked ways, then I will hear from heaven, and will forgive their sin and heal their land." It was set to music in a beautiful hymn. "If My People Will Pray," which is one of my favorites.

God makes many promises in the Scriptures but few are more poignant than this one. Herein is the understanding that we are united as a people. Our sins and our righteousness have a combined impact that make us a people. Furthermore, what we do as a people has an affect on our land, either for good or ill. We cannot separate the destiny of the earth from the destiny of its people.

There were many accounts of the downfall of communism in former East Germany and Romania, and the full story of the horror may never be known. Much occurred that is yet to be documented. But we do know the toll on the people and the land of these former communist countries was devastating. The pollution from outdated and inefficient factories poisoned lakes, rivers and towns. The lack of such basic health care as clean needles made AIDS among Romanian orphans an epidemic the effects of which have yet to be estimated. When it is written, the legacy of atheistic communism will scorch the pages of the history of infamy.

What turned the tide? There will be many opinions, but in any fair account the Church will have to be recognized as among the most important forces in changing the course of history. Often banned, more often persecuted, the Christians behind the Iron Curtain kept believing and kept praying and God heard and answered. Even from what little I have read, we are in store for many amazing accounts of the power of God at work changing the face of Europe and bringing new freedom and healing to sin-sick and oppressed people.

God is still faithful to His promises. We should not forget, that for all of our technology, ours is not the power in the world that makes the difference. History is still in the hands of God, and the most powerful thing we do, is pray!

# Day 128
# II Chronicles 11-14

ivil wars are always bitter, especially religious civil wars. I can understand why God would forbid Judah and Israel from entering into such a conflict. But, as so many times before, they ignored His commandments and set brother against brother and family against family.

Jeroboam made civil war inevitable by establishing a new religion for his people. The more difference he could create between Judah and Israel, the less it would feel like a civil war, or so he must have reasoned. Unfortunately, this strategy cut him off from his own real source of power - God.

The author of Chronicles spends very little time talking about Israel - the ten tribes of the North who had ceased worshipping Yahweh. We may feel this is not a good historical approach, somewhat like the United States refusal to recognize mainland China in the early 1960's - one billion people who were just "ignored" - but unlike the United States, the author of Chronicles had a point regarding Israel. The fact is, that with Jeroboam's rejection of God he had set the course of his nation toward oblivion. The national identity of Israel was based on its relationship with God, not that it held some particular piece of earth. When Jeroboam rejected that, he took the ten tribes out of the stream of salvation history and into an historical tributary that would dry up, never to be seen again.

As so often happens, he won the battle and lost the war. Not all of our mistakes are recoverable. In some matters the decisions we make are more important than the reasons for the decisions. Jeroboam had good reason for not wanting to depend on Judah for his religious center. Rehoboam was more faithful, but not by much, and more out of default than design. The difference was that Judah's God, Yahweh, was real, and Israel's gods, the Baals, were not. That is more than a little bit of difference - it is all the difference.

Some people think it is not important what you believe, only how well you believe it. I do not agree. Especially in matters pertaining to God, what counts is not how much faith you have, but who you have your faith in.

Jerobaom was wrong. Thus saith the Lord!

# Day 129
# II Chronicles 15-17

The accounts of the kings of Judah are relatively brief but telling summaries of their reigns. It is a bit sobering to think that even kings can have their lives reduced to a few paragraphs. How much more our own lives? Yet, perhaps this is something we need to understand about life. Greatness is not to be measured by fame or public acclaim, but by how much we contribute to the movement of God's kingdom in this world. This is, finally, His story, not ours. We are just a part of it.

Of those parts we can play, it would seem that prophet is one of the tougher roles. Asa, who had otherwise been a pretty good king, became angry with the prophet who announced God's displeasure with his alliance with Benhadad and so he had the prophet thrown in prison. All too often this is the fate of the bearer of bad news - when we don't like the message, we blame the messenger. This of course makes no sense, but we do it anyway, and it somehow makes us feel better - at least for a while.

We will read in more detail later on about the life of prophets, but here we get a glimpse of how difficult their task was for them and the people to whom they prophesied. They so seldom had any good news for the people, and their own level of frustration generally made them less than diplomatic in presenting it. This brings up an interesting question: do the messengers bear any responsibility about how they present their message? I suppose that the answer is yes and no.

Yes, if they truly care about the message being delivered, they must be concerned not just about the telling, but the hearing of their message. They must try to present it in a way that it is most likely to be understood. To deliver the message in the wrong "language," literally or figuratively, is not being responsible.

On the other hand, they can be so concerned about what people are hearing, that they change the message to be more "acceptable" and fail to recognize it is primarily the responsibility of the hearers to accept the truth when they hear it.

It is not always an easy thing to follow God and participate in the movement of His Kingdom. It will not always make us popular, and we will not always do it well. But in the end, it will be the only thing that was worth mentioning about us.

# Day 130
# II Chronicles 18-21

Jehoshaphat was one of the few good kings of Judah. His reforms made his reign a blessing to his people and an example to those who followed him - even to our day. He had a sense of the presence of God we would do well to recapture for our time and society. For Jehoshaphat, what counted was what God thought and what God did. Everything else was of relatively less importance.

It is interesting to see Jehoshaphat charging the judges he set over the people to remember that all their judgements were done, not for the sake of people, or the king, but for God. And he reminded them that God was watching what they were doing. Their judgements must therefore be truly just - no bribes, no favoritism - just honest justice.

How many people need to remember this today! When I was attending seminary I worked briefly as a morning security guard (if you can believe that!) for a department store where I got to know some of the people in management. One of their regular topics of conversation concerned the high cost of what they called "shrinkage." I was not familiar with the term so I asked what they meant. They informed me that it is the corporate euphemism for theft. What I found saddest was, according to them, the largest factor in "shrinkage" is not shoplifting, but theft by employees. It is amazing how much money has to be wasted to protect businesses from their own employees - security, surveillance, investigation, and prosecution, all of which has to be passed on to the consumer in the form of higher prices. Not to mention the loss of revenue from those employees who are just plain lazy and take twice as long as they need to do their job. How much could be saved if we all worked as if we were working for God! The fact is that as Christians, that is precisely the truth for us.

Jehoshaphat also showed unusual insight as a king when he was beset by enemies all around. Instead of panicking, he turned first to his greatest asset - God. He turned to God in prayer *first* because he knew if God would act, the rest would fall into place. How often we turn to Him only as a last resort!

Some people feel the idea that God is watching them all the time is oppressive. Jehoshaphat found it to be a motivator and a source of strength. How do we find it?

# Day 131
# II Chronicles 22-24

 hat a difference one person can make! For good or for evil, we can have an impact quite a bit beyond what we might expect. Athaliah, the wicked queen and granddaughter of the equally evil king Omri, murdered the royal household. Yet, Jehoshabeath, Athaliah's granddaughter, saved Joash by hiding him with Jehoiada, the good priest. Jehoiada took care of Joash until he was seven. Then Jehoiada arranged to have Joash safely declared king, Athaliah deposed and killed, and the temple restored during Joash's reign. Jehoiada lived to be 130 years old, but almost immediately after his death, Joash was swayed to evil, and died under the judgement of God. This stuff has more action than most modern motion pictures or soap operas!

There are some important lessons for us to learn from these people and events (other than never to trust a person named Athaliah). The flow of history is not always determined by the great armies or businesses, but by singular individuals - in this case, one baby and one priest. But what a difference that one baby made to the nation and what a difference that one priest made to that baby! That is the nature of individuals - we each have more potential than we realize. Changing a person, for good or evil, will have implications we cannot imagine.

There was a young man who started attending a church in Boston in 1855. After several weeks, he informed the deacons that he would like to join and be a member. However, he was so illiterate and ignorant of what Christianity was all about, that the deacons told him that he would have to go to some classes at the church for a year, and then he could come back to be examined for membership.

The boy agreed and began attending the classes. At the end of the year, he was examined again, and was found to still be woefully ignorant of many basic Christian truths. Yet, his obvious sincerity and willingness made the deacons decide to take a chance on him. And so, telling him that if he applied himself and attended more classes, God *might* be able to do something with him, Dwight L. Moody was finally admitted to membership and went on to be one of the most influential Christian leaders in American history. You just never know about people!

# Day 132
# II Chronicles 25-28

hat goes through the mind of someone like Amaziah, who was given a great victory by God, and then immediately turns around and worships other gods? I know people are fickle, but I would think that even the worst "what have you done for me lately" attitude could manage enough gratitude to last through the day!

Perhaps the answer is in seeing that it is not what goes through our minds but our hearts that makes the difference. It was written of Amaziah that he did what was right in the eyes of the Lord, but not with a blameless heart. What does that mean?

In our modern times we have come to think of the heart as either merely a biological organ, or the seat of our emotions. "Matters of the heart" now refers to our strong and passionate feelings, but little else. However, for the Jews, the heart was much more than just feelings - the heart was the seat of the will. Your heart was not just what you felt, but what you chose. To "set your heart" on something meant a devotion that encompassed your whole being. The act of choosing, whether that went with your feelings or not, was a matter of the heart.

Perhaps that is why it was easy for Amaziah to turn to idols rather than God. God's deliverance may have moved Amaziah's emotions, but not his heart. Idols are actually more attractive in that way. They can command our feelings, but they do not require our wills. We can serve them, and still keep our hearts to ourselves. God requires that we give our hearts to Him.

Why should God be so demanding? The fact is that while we might think we can worship idols and still keep our hearts, we cannot. Our hearts will belong to someone or something else. We cannot keep them for ourselves. We will be devoted to something. If not God, then pleasure, or money, or power, or something. We will become like that thing we worship, what we have given our hearts to. God wants that to be Him, because only He will give us back ourselves. Everything else we could worship, would take all we have to offer and in the end, return us nothing. Amaziah learned this too late. Idols cannot save us, and we cannot save ourselves. Only God deserves our heart. Will we give it to Him today?

# Day 133
# II Chronicles 29-32

know it sounds rather silly, but as I read about these kings I find myself cheering for the good ones. Even though I know how the story turns out, I cannot help but wish they could have been faithful, could have shown that the Lord is God by the great victories He gave them. I long to see the fulfillment of the blessings of the covenant for God's people rather than the curses.

Hezekiah provides a wonderful chance to cheer in the midst of this otherwise bleak period. He not only repaired the temple again, but he set Judah back on the course from which the people strayed. He offered the required sacrifices for the people (not thousands upon thousands) and then invited the individuals to come and bring their sacrifices as they were supposed to do. He even invited Israel to come and celebrate the passover as they should have, as one people of God.

When the arrogant Sennacherib came to attack him, Hezekiah and his people turned to God and allowed Him to give them a great victory without having to do anything themselves. The speech of the taunting Sennacherib recorded for us adds to the excitement of the victory. Like David facing Goliath, the arrogance of the unbelievers provides the sharp contrast to the deliverance of the Living God. It makes me want to cheer!

Some people might object to the use of sports terminology as if we were cheering for our favorite team. But there is certainly an element of drama to life. The stakes are high (the hearts and souls of men and women) and even though we know who is going to win in the end, the score has yet to be determined. In each family, in each generation, God will finally prevail, but the number of casualties and victories is still very much in our hands, too.

I know I have mixed my metaphors but I beg your indulgence. None of the analogies, not sports, nor games, nor war, can truly do justice to the conflict we are all born into and live in every day. I think that someday, in the Kingdom that is to come, we will finally be able to appreciate fully the seriousness of the struggle of which we have been a part. Then we will know that the battles and struggles have been worth cheering for, and agonizing over. Until then, I'll risk sounding silly. Go Hezekiah!

# Day 134
# II Chronicles 33-36

hy is it that people are so easily corrupted? It is said of Manasseh that he seduced Judah into worse evils than those of which the inhabitants of Canaan had been guilty. And God had cast them out before Israel. It is recorded that he even sacrificed his own sons to the Baals. How can that kind of "religion" possibly compare to the worship of Yahweh, the God who loves and forgives and gives graciously to people?

It would seem the desire to do whatever we want to do without regard for the consequences or impact on others runs very deep in the human heart. We will try to get away with *as much* as we possibly can. God's patience with Manasseh is astounding when you consider how long and how low he was allowed to sink before judgement caught up with him. Perhaps that was what was so seductive about him. For a long time it looked as if he could do whatever he wanted, loot the temple, set up altars and sacrifices to other gods, participate in the licentious and bloodthirsty rituals of Baal worship, even sacrifice his own sons, and the God of Israel would do nothing. Either God wasn't really there, or He wasn't really powerful, or He didn't really care, but whatever the case, the strict rules and ethics that went with worshipping Him, could be ignored with impunity. Or could they?

Why do the wicked prosper? David will be asking that question repeatedly when we come to the Psalms, but we encounter that question ourselves long before then. I think there are several parts to the answer, but the one Manasseh reminds me of here is that the wicked do not prosper in the end. You may be able to take advantage of God's patience for a long time, but not forever. Eventually, judgement day arrives. Sometimes we get a foretaste of it in this life, as Manasseh did, courtesy of the Assyrians. With some grace, we can profit from that reminder of judgement, but whether we do or not, judgement will come.

It really cannot be any other way. Many people do not like to talk or even think, about judgement, but the day will come when God finally puts an end to the horror and violence. God must stop it, because we have proven time and time again that we will go on "getting away" with as much as we can for as long as we can. It really is good news that this won't go on forever.

# Day 135
# Ezra 1-3

"It was the best of times, it was the worst of times." Thus begins the *Tale of Two Cities*, and what might be an apt description of life all the time. For some people things will be going very well, while "just around the corner," things could hardly be worse. But in history, for any given people, the times do have an over all character. For Ezra, these were not the best of times by a long shot, and he wanted to be part of altering that.

The ten tribes of the north had been carried off, never to be heard from again. The two tribes of the south, Judah and Benjamin, had endured the captivity of Babylon, and through the gracious work of God through Cyrus, were allowed to return to Jerusalem to rebuild the temple. It was clearly not the best of times for Israel, but things were looking better - or at least there was that hope. As the foundation rose to rebuild the temple, the old men cried bittersweet tears, remembering the glory of the temple of old, yet glad there would again be a temple in which to worship. The young men shouted for joy that there would be a temple for them at all. There is a great deal of pathos in these chapters.

Not many civilizations can rise out of their ashes. Israel again proved to be a testimony to the presence of God in that it did not just disappear. There are no more Edomites, or Moabites, or Hittites, but there are Israelites. The tenacity of this people who have survived so many centuries without a land or political system to tie them together is a testimony to the Covenant God to whom they belong.

The world has witnessed the dissolution of the former Soviet Union without a war or even a "revolution" to speak of. How many of us foresaw or guessed this would happen in our lifetime? What will happen to the countries of the "old" USSR is yet to be seen. But one of the most astounding developments in it all has been their open desire to recapture their lost faith. Atheism has failed. Religion has proven to be, not the opiate Marx claimed, but the source of strength and hope.

Like Ezra, we can hear the crying. These are not the best of times, yet they hold such promise. We can rebuild the foundations of a society that turns to God. Will we try?

# Day 136
# Ezra 4-6

**D**oing something for the right reasons, and in the right way, is a "sea of troubles." Many people will not understand what you are doing or why, and even those interested in helping can become opponents of the project once their help, or ideas, have been turned down. Such was the case with the temple at Jerusalem.

Zerubbabel and Jeshua showed unusually good sense in turning down the help of the "other peoples" who wanted to help in the rebuilding. Even though this caused them to oppose and finally succeed in stopping the work, it was better to have it delayed than done the wrong way. How can I be so certain that their help would have been bad? I can't be certain, but it should be noted that this time, after the temple was built, it remained free from offerings to other idols for centuries. Had the surrounding peoples helped, would they not have demanded something there to represent them, or perhaps their gods? On some things, compromise can be a very dangerous thing, and intolerance a positive virtue.

As Christians, our lives (and even our bodies) are to be temples to the glory of God. Many people will offer to help us build them, and offer suggestions in the process. In our time, it has been suggested that monogamy is simply too restrictive a rule, especially for men. What is really wrong with a little, well managed, extra-marital activity? Or, certainly, for young people, we can no longer seriously expect that they will not be sexually active before they get married, now can we? Isn't it just more reasonable to want them to be "responsible" with their premarital sex? And while you're at it, how about putting that small graven image over in that corner?

There are some things for which compromise is no virtue: particularly the world of virtues. Courage only when there is no danger, faith only when there is no question, truth only when it serves our purpose, justice only when it favors our cause, are not virtues at all. If our lives are to be of any real use to God, ourselves, or others, then there are things which we will have to try to do as well and as correctly as they can be done, even when that is not popular. Let us build our lives according to His design, even if we get a little less help from others!

# Day 137
# Ezra 7-10

here are many opportunities to take things out of context in the Scriptures and these chapters offer yet another one. Ezra decried the actions of the men of Israel for marrying foreign wives until they agreed to divorce them and denounce their children. How can this have been the will of God?

We need to go back and remember why this prohibition about intermarriage with the Canaanites was given. God was not clearing out the Canaanites just to make room for Israel, but because of the horrible practices of the peoples of Canaan. Theirs was a brutal and bloodthirsty society that offered up even their own children as sacrifices to their gods. The fact that the hedonistic religion had the ability to corrupt people had been proven in their own culture and in Israel throughout the period of the Judges and Kings. Giving up the beliefs of the culture that you grew up with has never been an easy thing to do. How much less possible was it for people who could not read and had never been exposed to other ways of thinking and believing. Back then (and perhaps more now than we care to admit) when you married someone, you married their religion too.

In Ezra's time, the stakes were even higher. Israel was no longer a nation. There would be no more kings. They were subjects of foreign rulers. The land that was supposed to be an inheritance to them, was once again heavily populated by peoples of different religions. If Israel was to survive as a people, their common bond would have to be something other than politics, it had to be their faith. The temple and the sacrificial system, so long abused or ignored by the Kings of Israel, would prove to be the force that kept them alive as a people of God.

Yet they had still lost the original purpose for their being the people of God. God did not want to keep them "pure" because He loved them and hated the other nations. Remember, Israel was to be a priestly people, set apart for the purpose of reaching the other nations with the message of the great and gracious God.

Perhaps the "reforms" for Ezra were necessary for the purpose of keeping Israel alive. But the purpose of Israel was to reach out to the nations. God is not a racist. Any other interpretation of Ezra is not to see the story in its proper context.

# Day 138
# Nehemiah 1-3

Nehemiah must certainly not have been the first person in his time to pray for the restoration of Jerusalem. Why did God choose him? Was it the depth of his caring? Did he pray more fervently than anyone else? Was he so uniquely gifted for the task that no one else could have accomplished it? Why then, and not earlier? Or, why then, and not later?

There is no escaping the mystery of God's will. We simply do not understand Him well enough to be able to predict accurately what He is going to do and when He is going to do it. I never cease to be amazed at the number of people who are very uncomfortable with the idea that God has free will too, and that He exercises it according to designs to which we may not be privy. He acts so much like a God who is out of our control, and that indeed can be a scary thought.

This is, of course, exactly what God is - a God who is out of our control. That does not mean He is out of control, He is fully in charge of Himself, but He is most certainly out of *our* control. Yet I see scores of people who attempt to control Him all the time. I do not think we can look at Nehemiah and conclude that because God chose him, he was more righteous, or more intelligent, or more gifted, or more deeply committed to the task, than anyone else in his time. God simply chose him and we do not know all the reasons why.

The idea that if we pray harder, give more generously, treat people more ethically, then God must bless us in some way, is really a pagan one. It is an attempt to control God, and it doesn't work. More than that, it can be a tyranical belief that steals the joy out of our life, as we try to earn God's favor with the proper combination of penance and prayer. We will not really love a God whose love must be earned, we will resent Him. Love must be freely given and freely returned, or it is not really love at all.

That is not to say we know nothing of God's will in life. He has made it abundantly clear that He does love us, has a purpose for our lives, for the history of the world, and is actively accomplishing that will Himself. God graciously chose to use Nehemiah and He graciously chooses to use us. We can trust His will, but that does not mean we will be able to predict it!

# Day 139
# Nehemiah 4-7

ehemiah's life is a study in itself of how good leadership can overcome opposition and coordinate a badly divided community. In spite of what I wrote yesterday, I admire Nehemiah and think that he was a special individual whose faithfulness and wisdom are well worth emulating.

There are many principles of good leadership which can be learned from the way he handled his ministry for God. One of those is that he saw his work as a ministry. He was not just rebuilding a wall, but participating in God's plan for His people. Do we understand our work in the same way? We should.

God does not need more people getting into the clerical ministry. The church has long recognized that service as an ordained cleric, requires a sense of calling from God. I do not dispute that understanding. However, we seem to have missed the point that God calls His people to minister for Him in *all* other areas of life too. Nehemiah was not called by God to serve as a Levite to lead the worship in the temple. This did not mean his contribution to the faith of Israel was less important. Indeed, we can clearly see that without his contribution, there might have been no worshipping in the temple or anywhere else. All of our jobs can be done so as to serve God and, in fact, that is the key to ministry. We must finally rid ourselves of the mistaken idea that if you really love God, you should become "a minister." If you love God and seek to serve Him, you *are* a minister. The tasks may vary, but the calling is no less valid.

Nehemiah also understood the source of his power to serve God was God Himself! He was opposed by Sanballat the Horonite and Tobiah the Ammonite who tried to taunt and intimidate him into submission. Their taunting reminds me of an apocryphal story about Nietzsche, the German philosopher and atheist who proclaimed that God was dead. As the story goes, Nietzsche was supposed to have written on one of the walls of St. Peter's Basilica at Rome, "God is dead" and signed, " Nietzsche." After Nietzsche's death, someone else is said to have written on the same wall, "Nietzsche is dead" and signed "God."

Where are the Horonites or the Ammonites now? Nehemiah, his people, and his God, have had the last laugh!

# Day 140
# Nehemiah 8-10

I wonder if Ezra skipped reading aloud those long lists of the names of people? Can you image being there for the reading of the law on that day? Remember, the "law" was not just the Ten Commandments, it was the term used for the first five books of the Bible. It was also variously called the books of Moses and the Pentateuch. The whole history from Genesis to Deuteronomy made up "the law." God's relationship with Israel had always been more than just the book of Leviticus.

I think it is important to notice at this place in the history of salvation, that the understanding of God's gracious covenant love was not a theology made up by the New Testament authors, but the clear and plain understanding from the Old Testament itself. We can not be sure at all when those first five books were first written down, but we know they date back a long way in written form. Still, having the Scriptures was no guarantee that they had read them. With the lack of resources to publish them in quantity and the level of illiteracy among the common people, they had considerably more excuse for not reading "the law" than we do today! The ability to avoid dealing with one's relationship with God has been present in every generation and is with us still today.

That is one of the problems with faith. It must be embraced by each individual and each subsequent generation for themselves. It cannot be inherited like blue eyes or red hair. We must each ask the great questions of life. Who are we? Why are we here? Is there a God? What is God like? What happens to me after I die? God's revelation (the Scriptures) are invaluable in developing answers to these questions and can be handed down to us (as they indeed have been), but we must each finally make those answers our own, or not. We may try to avoid them, but they will not go away. From the first day they present themselves to us, they will require answers and will follow us all our days, even after we think we have answered them.

So how do you answer them? Who are we? Is there a God? Is He really like the one described in the Bible? Was Ezra right about Him being a God of covenant love and grace and forgiveness? What do you believe?

# Day 141
# Nehemiah 11-13

ehemiah records for us just how fickle and forgetful people can be. After all the effort to get the wall rebuilt, and to restore the temple and the sacrifices, when their leader departed, they quickly reverted to form. Even the simple task of not working on the sabbath was too much for them.

Nehemiah returns and restores order to the temple, the sabbath and the city. He is compelled to use some force in doing so, and no doubt, made more enemies in the process. But order needed to be restored. If they had continued to ignore the laws and the sabbath, how long would it have been before they had slipped into as much sin and ruin as their forefathers? That is precisely what Nehemiah argued, and he was right.

Our society seems to be fond of saying that you cannot legislate morality. In one sense, that is true. Nehemiah could enforce the rules about not working on the sabbath, but he could not force people to observe the good of the sabbath. The sabbath was supposed to be (*is* supposed to be) for the purpose of resting and remembering to give thanks to God. It is to be the time when we remember that all we have is a gift, and reflect on the goodness of God the Giver. Yet as the Puritans discovered, you can force people into the church, but you cannot force the church into the people.

On the other hand, all legislation enforces morality. The idea that we cannot disregard the rights of others with impunity is a moral decision. The idea that all people are equal and valuable is an ethical one - it cannot be proven empirically. Laws exists to enforce a morality, at least on the outside.

That is all Nehemiah, as a civil leader, could hope to do. He could work hard to provide a just and safe society where, for the most part, honest commerce and community could go on unhindered. He could prevent and punish some of the bad, but something else had to provide the basic motivation for the good.

The people in the former Soviet Union are finding this to be true in our century. Force can control people, but it cannot motivate them very well. I am afraid in our country we need to learn the other side of the equation. Without basic justice and safety, a society cannot prosper either. Nehemiah, we need you!

# Day 142
# Esther 1-3

The story of Esther starts out like a kind of bad soap opera. King Ahasuerus was having a stag party with his "guy friends," and after a couple of days of drinking, sent for his wife to show off how beautiful she was. She refused to come and parade in front of a bunch of the King's drunken buddies. But refusing a royal command, even a stupid one, can be hazardous to one's health, and Queen Vashti was deposed and a young virgin sought to take her place. It sounds more like a plot from a soap opera like *The Young and the Restless* than an incident in the Bible!

I could not help but notice in this account the amount of concern and energy necessary to "keep women in their place." What really got Queen Vashti in trouble was that she might have set a "bad example" throughout the kingdom. Women might have thought they were more than merely the property of their husbands! Imagine what that might have led to!

Fortunately, King Ahasuerus had his trusty "guy friend" advisors there, and they knew just what to advise him to do. Trade in that uppity wife for a new young virgin! After all, there were many beautiful women besides Vashti, and they would certainly know their place after what happened to the ex-Queen.

God certainly works in mysterious ways. Ahasuerus will not win any awards for strength of character. He appears, at least in these accounts, to have been a shallow fellow and easily fooled. Yet God worked through his vanity and foolishness to bring about the safety of His people.

Some scholars have rejected the book of Esther because it seems to be an account that is too simplistic in its interpretation of events. They want to argue that people and political situations are more complex than those portrayed here. Perhaps they are right. Perhaps the writer of Esther did not know of some master plan by King Ahasuerus or perhaps Vashti. On the other hand, the reasons people act the way they do can be surprisingly simple. We often act from the most meager and petty of motives, if for no other reason than we have no strong motives.

It is comforting to think that God can and does work through us even when we are not aware of it. Let's just hope we are more often like Mordecai than Haman or Vashti!

# Day 143
# Esther 4-6

Esther is revered for her courage. But is it really courageous to take the only reasonable course of action? Mordecai had to argue with Esther to help her decide the right risk to take. He pointed out that even if she did not act, she could not expect to be spared. She would have to risk, but not to act would surely have been to die in the slaughter with the other Jews.

This raises the difficult question of whether or not we are exhibiting faith when we obey because we see the sense in obedience. If we obey God because we can see that His will is right and just and benefits everyone, have we obeyed God, or only our own reasoning?

In one sense, when we obey because we agree, we have obeyed our own reasoning, and not necessarily God. I think this is why obedience to God's laws does not always guarantee that you will be close to God. You may benefit from living according to His word, but that does not automatically deepen your relationship with Him as a person. We can relate to Him as the maker of the laws, as our creator, but miss finding our relationship with Him as our Father, our Redeemer, and our friend. At some point, in order for faith to truly deepen our relationship with God, we must trust Him, not because we have understood everything, but because we know in our hearts that He is trustworthy. Like a flier on the trapeze, we must let go of the bar and trust that when we have started down, the hands that catch us will be there, and be strong enough to hold us. Esther's actions were the most logical choice given the circumstances, and in that sense, were not a matter of faith, but of reason.

However, this analysis splits some very fine hairs, and on the whole, is rather bloodless. No decision that involves one's death is ever merely logical. Esther's decision was a courageous one, in spite of the fact that her alternatives were limited. The temptation to wait and do nothing is always powerful. It may have made sense for her to act, but many people would have done nothing in her place.

That's the hard thing about faith - to be real faith it must commit itself and act and that is *always* a risk. How much risk have you taken lately?

# Day 144
# Esther 7-10

The book of Esther has long been a questionable addition to the Scriptures. Even before New Testament times, Hebrew scholars were bothered by the lack of use of the name of God, Yahweh, anywhere in the book. Indeed, it has a quite different tone from the other books we have just read, especially the Chronicles. In Esther, deliverance does not come from God's actions, but from the cleverness of Mordecai.

Why then has it been included in the Scriptures throughout the centuries? One reason may have been the times in which it was written. We should remember that this was the period after the Jews had ceased to be a nation, politically speaking. They needed a new sense of identity. Under Ezra and Nehemiah, that identity had been forged around the temple and the law. This story of the Jews being able to defend themselves against their enemies in the many lands into which they had been scattered, had to be one of the best morale boosters available. Even though the book was questioned for centuries, the celebration of Purim has been a constant since it was first started.

The question is really whether we need to have it spelled out explicitly that God made the events in Esther occur in order to accept that they were His will? This is a question that is larger than just the book of Esther. How do we know that what happens has been the action of God or just our own clever manipulations?

Remember this is a devotional and, therefore, I can ask questions I do not pretend I can answer! How do we know when God has acted? Only through faith can we answer that question, and we might very well come up with different answers. That is not to say it can be both ways. God knows what He has done and what He has not done. We can only choose to believe one way or the other. Proof will have to wait for the next life. In this one, we will have to content ourselves with choosing to believe one opinion or the other.

For my part, I choose to believe that God works through us all the time, and frequently without our being aware of it. I have no problem believing that God worked through Esther and Mordecai even if that is not explicitly stated. It helps me believe that He can work through servants like us!

# Day 145
# Job 1-4

he book of Job is one of the most read, debated, and perhaps misunderstood, in the Old Testament. It is considered an epic poem by literary standards and the question of whether or not there really was a person named Job is still hotly debated in scholarly circles. The time setting is agreed to belong back in the days of the book of Genesis, probably some time between Abraham and Jacob.

Historical criticism aside, Job deals with an issue that is more problematic than the book's origins. If God is good, why is there evil and suffering? This is a universal question we must all face and answer. It has been such an enduring problem that theologians have given it a name - theodicy. The problem can be stated in this way. God is all powerful. God is all good. Evil exists in the world. All three appear to be true, yet they appear to be contradictory. If God is all powerful and all good, how could He let evil exist? If He cannot stop evil then He must not be all powerful, or all good. How then do we understand our world and God?

These are no small questions. The writer of Job made a good choice in dealing with these questions by using the life of Job as a vehicle to deal with issues this complex. Many things can be said in literature (or poetry) that are very hard to say in prose. This understanding of the use of genre is also key if we are to avoid making the mistake of asking questions of this book that it does not intend to address. Many people are thrown off by focusing on the issue of Satan talking in the court of God. Whether or not Satan makes accusatory visits before God is not the point of Job. The primary question is why is there suffering. This question is difficult enough without clouding the issue with other questions about the genre and not the story itself.

The question Job asked, and we must too, is why do the good suffer? His friends came to offer answers and Job struggles himself with his answer. As we read along, we should not miss the pathos of the characters. In no small measure, how we feel about Job, his friends, and his struggle, will contain more of an answer for us than the arguments presented. As you read, try to ask yourself what you thought and felt when you have suffered unjustly.

# Day 146
# Job 5-8

E liphaz was the first to bring his argument to Job. His argument is a common one, especially among religious circles. As with most things, there is some truth in it. But there is also some dreadful error and Job rightly rejected his friend's counsel as not accurately accounting for the facts of his case.

Eliphaz wanted to remind Job that none of us are without sin. We all stand guilty of one thing or another and have no claim to being favorably treated by a Holy and Righteous God. He wanted to speak this bit of advice as delicately as possible, because when people are suffering, they are generally not in the mood to be reminded of their sinfulness. For whatever truth there may have been in his point of view, even Eliphaz knew that it would not really comfort Job to be told that he deserved whatever bad might have befallen him.

The problem with this argument is not that we are not sinful. Job does not claim to be sinless. There is no question that we are not righteous, and we are certainly deserving of punishment for the things which we have done wrong. The difficulty is not that Eliphaz insulted us as sinful humans, but he impugned the justice of God. Job knew that he was sinful and deserving of punishment, but God is just and does not apply punishment that does not fit the crime.

Justice, if it is to be deserving of the name, must seek to balance that which has been unbalanced. Simply to return hurt or pain in kind is not justice but vengeance. Eliphaz thought that since Job had sinned, the consequences of his sin had found him out. But Job knew that the evil that had befallen him was not a consequence, however remote, of any of his sins. You do not stab your children for not taking out the trash. Consequences are the results of the actions which cause them. The idea that God visits punishments upon us with no relationship to our actions is not justice and is no part of the Scriptures. Evils that befall us must either be connected consequences or else must find their source elsewhere than a just God.

Job would not accept the idea that God swats flies with a bazooka, and neither should we. The explanation of pain and suffering must find its roots elsewhere. Sorry, Eliphaz!

# Day 147
# Job 9-11

Zophar, Bildad, and Eliphaz all essentially presented the same argument to Job. They felt that surely the calamities which had befallen him were a result of Job's own sin. They felt he needed to accept the reprimand, look closely to find out his sin, repent, and throw himself on the mercy of God. The idea that Job would complain against God was, from their point of view, sacrilegious, hypocritical nonsense.

What should we tell people who are suffering? As a minister, it has been my sad duty at times to join a family at the hospital as they waited outside an operating room to see if their child would survive a car accident. At those times I could not imagine interrogating them for the purpose of finding out what sins they committed to warrant the punishment of the death of their children. Yet that is precisely what Zophar, Bildad, and Eliphaz were saying to Job. Apparently they hadn't read their Scriptures. Remember in Leviticus where it says that the children cannot be punished for the sins of their parents? God does not make others suffer for our sins. Our sins may indeed make others suffer, but that is quite a different thing.

Sad to say, there are still many religious groups that offer the counsel of Zophar, Bildad, and Eliphaz. They argue that whatever ills befall us come as judgements from God. By implication, they suggest that all blessings are a sign of God's approval. To be sure, our blessings (like intelligence, musical talent, or good health) come to us as gifts, not things we have necessarily deserved. But there is no connection between gifts and special status with God. He makes His rain to fall on the just and the unjust. He is no respecter of persons. Even great faith is no guarantee of an easy life. In fact, those who seem to be closest to God often suffer some of the worst tragedies.

Why should this be so? That is what Job was asking. In Job's case, we know there was at least some sort of purpose behind his sufferings. Even in his case, it seems hard to believe that they were sufficient reasons. That is the struggle of the book and of the questions it raises. But as hard as they are, the answers cannot be found in the neat and simple answers of Zophar, Bildad, and Eliphaz. God's grace must be taken into account.

# Day 148
# Job 12-15

 " an that is born of a woman is of few days, and full of trouble. He comes forth like a flower, and withers; he flees like a shadow, and continues not." 14:1,2 This is one of the famous passages in the Scriptures. Why should this be so? Perhaps because suffering and lament are indeed a part of each and every life. No one escapes pain in this life, no matter how hard they might try. The key to handling pain is not in denying it, but in facing it.

Job had so much trouble and grief that he had cursed his birth and longed for death. Perhaps more of us than we would care to admit, have felt the same way. We need not have faced the death of our children, the loss of all our wealth and our own sickness to feel the cold grip of despair. There is a small and desperate person inside each of us, a lonely and frightened creature, unsure of itself and terribly vulnerable. No matter how large or strong the exterior may be, this inner person needs a protection and assurance that must come from outside itself or it will collapse and die in despair. We cannot save ourselves.

One of the very common charges against Christianity is that it is a crutch for those who cannot face life. Indeed it is a crutch. But a crutch is not bad when you are lame, and we are all lame inside. We need a saviour and a redeemer for we surely cannot save ourselves. We did not bring ourselves into being, we cannot forever maintain our health and we cannot control what happens to us after death. On all the issues that really count, we find ourselves not strong and independent, but weak and ineffectual. Without help, we find no meaning in the struggle and no victory that death cannot steal. Without God, we are without hope.

Job's pain may have made him more aware of his condition, but it did not create it. Had his life been easy at every turn, he would still have needed God in that deep inner self, to give him meaning and hope for life after death. The need for God is always with us. Sometimes it is easier to forget that than at other times, but our lack of awareness does not change our real state of being. Job knew there was no where else to turn but to God, even though he could not understand why God was silent. If our pain can teach us the same it will not have been in vain.

# Day 149
# Job 16-18

Eliphaz and Bildad again argued that the wicked will not prosper but instead be cast down. Perhaps that will be true in the next life, but there are more than a few examples of the wicked doing quite well in this life. I dare say there are many very successful businesses whose owners are more than wicked and they live quite comfortably. From a strictly pragmatic viewpoint, their argument seems to be quite weak.

Why should this argument still be so pervasive? Perhaps it is because those who try so hard to be good, want to believe their opposite numbers are not having as good a time as it appears. We have heard (or perhaps said ourselves), "Well, sure, they look like they are enjoying themselves, but I'll bet they aren't *really* enjoying themselves!" Perhaps this is a matter of semantics, but I think there are many people who truly enjoy being bad! Even Jesus will say that the evil people in the world are better at being bad than the righteous are at being good! So, maybe we only want to believe the wicked do not prosper.

Then again, from the testimony of those who have walked deeply into the way of the wicked, we are told that while being bad can be fun up to a certain point, it cannot fulfill a person the way being good can. Malcolm Muggeridge, a British journalist who was an atheist until becoming a Christian late in his life, entitled his autobiography, *The Chronicles of Wasted Years*. There is a depth of living which cannot be experienced from the restrictive borders of selfishness, conceit and self absorption that goes with the way of the wicked. So, perhaps in that sense, the wicked never do prosper.

But Job was right in rejecting the counsel of these friends because they had turned the equation around. They had equated evil with punishment and success with blessing. That can be refuted by the evidence we have at hand. The wicked do often prosper, at least outwardly, and perhaps more, and the good suffer through no fault of their own.

There is a wideness in the freedom which God let enter into our world that makes it possible for it to be very unfair. That is not to say there is no justice or that there will be no judgement day, but prosperity is no sure measure of the quality of character.

# Day 150
# Job 19-22

In chapter nineteen, Job makes an astounding discovery about his afflictions. First, as he continued in his arguing with his friends, he made note of the fact that it was more important to them to make their point with him than it was to accompany him in his grief - even if they believed he was wrong.

I wonder how often I have been guilty of the same sin. In well-meaning zeal we can often add to the burden and grief being experienced by others. We want to teach, they need to be comforted. We want to reform, they need to be reassured of God's love for them, in spite of everything else. And I wonder how often I have turned out to be wrong anyway, and they, like Job, have been suffering through no fault of their own. Perhaps Job was right, and we should be more concerned with showing love and compassion in spite of sinfulness, real or suspected, rather than trying to assign guilt and dragging people to "willing repentance." After all, Jesus walked with sinners long before he expected them to respond.

The other amazing thing that comes out in this chapter is Job's faith that, in spite of his suffering, God would still receive him into the kingdom of heaven. "For I know that my Redeemer lives, and at last he will stand upon the earth; and after my skin has been thus destroyed, then from my flesh I shall see God, whom I shall see on my side, and my eyes shall behold, and not another." 19:25-27 Job did not understand why things had gone so terribly wrong, but he knew that, in the final analysis, God would make things right; the only right that really counts, and it is not ever in this life, but the next.

The doctrine of the resurrection is latent in the Old Testament but comes clearly to light in the New Testament. However, it has always been part of the understanding of God's people. Even though the Sadducees abandoned the hope, the Pharisees, who were better versed in the Scriptures, knew well the resurrection of the body was a fundamental part of their faith. If this life is to be any more than a vain and tedious exercise, there must be something after this for us. Therein is the hope that sustained Job and can and should sustain us. It will not eliminate suffering, but it is the only true comfort that makes it bearable.

# Day 151
# Job 23-25

*J*ob himself picked up the theme about the wicked, but from the perspective of the injustice that the wicked prosper while the good suffer. Why should it be that those who do wrong not only benefit, but live long and easy lives, while the innocent and the righteous suffer from the ruthlessness of the wicked? Where is the justice in that?

These are not easy questions to answer. Job complained eloquently for the poor and downtrodden and asked why God pays no attention to their prayers. Do we as yet have a sufficient answer to Job's questions? I don't know. It is easy to say yes from the comfort of my home and loved ones about me. But what answer would I give if it were one of my loved ones who had been robbed, raped, kidnapped, or killed? I may be guilty of being morose at this point, but I do not want to be guilty of being smug. I thank God I have not had to answer these questions from the perspective of the victim, and I sincerely hope I never have to do so. But for those who have, they know this is no academic exercise, but a huge burden of faith.

Bildad's answer was wholly unacceptable. For him, whatever might befall us, we have not been righteous and, therefore, we are all deserving of destruction. That still begs the question of why those who do wrong should be allowed to prosper. We are all guilty of sin, but if God is already judging us, then how can *any* escape, especially those we know to be wicked? Job's question was not why we are worthy of punishment, but why we aren't all receiving it. If this is justice, then there is something terribly amiss, for many of the wicked are favored not punished. No, whatever the answer, it can not be Bildad's.

But let us remember, even though Job remained faithful, he did not remain flawless. His understanding had kept him from believing the wrong thing, but not necessarily commending the right one. He knew what wasn't the right answer, but not what was.

We may not know where all the evil comes from in our world, but we can know one place it does not - God. We may not understand why He does not answer all prayer in the affirmative, but we dare not conclude He answers none. Faith may be difficult, but unbelief offers even fewer answers.

# Day 152
# Job 26-29

I n spite of the fact that Job felt it was unfair that the wicked should prosper, there was no longing to change places with them. He was not really very far from Zophar, Bildad, and Eliphaz in his assurance that the wicked would not prosper in the end. It is from Job's perspective that we first hear the truth that in spite of their prosperity, what do the wicked have to turn to if they fall on bad times? To whom will they turn? To God? Job felt certainly not. Then if not to God, they would find no help in their suffering. Job did not envy them that fate, nor should we.

Perhaps there is more to this understanding than first meets the eye. Just how valuable is our faith, as hard as it is to understand and maintain? Where would we be without it? We may not know why God does not follow our agenda, but where do we go if we conclude that there is no God? Nietzsche wrote that when there is no God, there are no absolute values. When there are no absolute values, then we are left feeling only anguish, because there is pain, despair, because we cannot stop it all, and forlorn, because we have been abandoned by a God who should be there but isn't. I think that is a fair description - if there is no God. Given that choice, I choose to believe.

Then Job reminisced. He remembered the good old days that were really good. He did not envy the wicked, but he did miss his blessings. And let us remember what this test had been all about. God had said of him, "Consider my servant Job," and Satan had claimed that Job was righteous only because God had been good to him. Was Job's love for God only a function of a need for God? Was his faith solely a condition of prosperity? That was the question. Put another way, was Job's faith really no more than the wicked's indifference in their prosperity?

Job is a lesson in the value of our faith. Faith is valuable in prosperous times; it is *in*valuable in difficult times. It may not provide us a place where all our problems are solved magically, but it does give us a place to turn to; a place outside ourselves when we know we are insufficient.

In the truly difficult times, faith may feel real anguish, and even a sense of being forlorn, that God seems so distant. But it does not despair. And that is no small difference.

# Day 153
# Job 30-32

f ever anyone had the right to complain about fair-weather friends, it was Job. He had been kind to all, fair to everyone, good to his family and friends, hospitable to strangers, and dealt honestly and fairly with his business partners. But when calamity struck, they all left him, afraid that too close an association could be dangerous to them. With friends like that, who needs enemies?

Just how conditional are our friendships? When we are growing up, we seem to think they will last forever. During adolescence we often feel our friends are more reliable and trustworthy than our families. Sometimes it is even true, but often we come to discover those friendships are not as deep and abiding as we hope or intend them to be.

Those friendships that do endure share a common element. They are based not so much on our common experiences, but on a shared knowledge of each other's true character. The friends who truly know us, and are known by us, are the ones whose characters are an open book for us. We know their real strengths and weaknesses, and they know ours. That is why when we hear stories about them from other people, we "know" whether or not they are true. "I just *know* he wouldn't do that!" And we do know, if we are good friends.

This makes me suspect that Job did not have any really good friends. For all his wealth and kindness, no one came to Job's defense. No one was there to agree with him that none of these calamities were a result of Job's failings. No one came to his aid, insisting he had not done anything deserving of what he was suffering. "He just couldn't have; he just wouldn't have! Not my friend!"

Perhaps it was part of the test that all of Job's friends desert him. Or perhaps he had that all-too-common experience of people being friends with what you are rather than who you are.

Real friendship is costly and rare. Perhaps the reason it is rare is because it is so costly. It takes time to get to know someone's character, and vulnerability to reveal one's own. We can not have very many of those kinds of relationships, and we don't need too many. But how valuable are those few. Give your friend a call today!

# Day 154
# Job 33-36

Elihu moved the argument back to the central issue. Job's friends could find no other reason than God was punishing him according to his sin, and Job would not accept that argument. But for his own part, Job went too far when he argued that it made no difference whether or not one believed in God; both saint and sinner suffers, so what advantage does the saint have?

Elihu did not argue with Job that the evils which had befallen him were punishments for Job's sins. Clearly that view leaves God being inconsistent and capricious; justice can be neither of these things. But Elihu wanted Job to remember that God had already been gracious and forgiving to him in the past. Job did not claim to be sinless, and Elihu reminded him that God had blessed him in the past when he had not deserved it. How often and how quickly we forget those things which we have been forgiven, and focus on those times we feel have been unjust.

Elihu had no answer to all of the whys of Job's situation. He only knew that we cannot call God unjust and we cannot think God punishes for every transgression. Both of these ideas lead to grievous errors. This does not mean we can understand our suffering all the time, but we can know some things which our sufferings are not, and that is something.

Put quite simply, Elihu left room for not knowing. In this case, that is precisely what had to be done. None of them knew all of what God was doing. For his part, Job had been right, it was not a punishment and Job had been wrong, it had not been capricious.

There is a general principle here that is very important, especially on issues of this magnitude. What we don't know and cannot explain, does not necessarily negate what we do know and what we can explain. As Elihu pointed out, this is a problem inherent in being creatures. If we are to admit that we cannot know everything, we must be ready to identify those points at which our wisdom stops without concluding we don't know anything at all.

I do not know all of why God allows suffering in the world. But I do know He has not sat at a comfortable distance and just watched it all. He knows about suffering. He lost a son.

# Day 155
# Job 37-39

od had been silent up to this point. Job had cried out to Him and He had not answered. When He did answer, it was not what Job had expected. The voice Job had wanted to hear did not bring the message he had wanted to hear or in the way he wanted to hear it. Far from joining into the argument as a speculative or defensive member, God entered authoritatively and took the role of the questioner Himself.

"Gird up your loins like a man; I will question you, and you declare to me." 40:7 What a shocking challenge. God did not come with hat in hand, hoping to justify Himself to Job or to us, but rather as the Sovereign Lord He is. God put Job in his place by reminding him that the question of why these things had befallen him are but a few of the questions Job could not answer.

The language here is among the most beautiful and powerful in all of the Scriptures. Where were we when God stretched out the heavens and the earth? While some might find the idea of a storehouse for rain rather unscientific, we should remember that for all our scientific advances, we still cannot explain why protons with the same electrical charge stay in the nucleus of atoms, or whether light is a wave or a particle, or how to stop the common cold. Measured by any terms, the amount we still don't know dwarfs all of the advances of mankind.

Some feel that God begged the question with His response to Job. He gave no explanation to Job about the circumstances of his predicament, and appears to feel that He does not need to explain Himself. Instead, He puts Job essentially on the defensive by asking him, "Who are you to question me?" But I don't think the implication is that Job was impertinent in asking only overly optimistic in thinking he would be able to understand the answer. If Job could not understand even the simple physical origin of things, how much less capable of understanding the origins of metaphysical things. In other words, the questions of *what* the universe is, are easier than *why* it is. If Job could not understand the former, how much less the latter.

We long for understanding, but how much will be enough? At some point we must be willing to stop seeking to know *about* God and settle for knowing Him instead. It is enough.

# Day 156
# Job 40-42

or many people, the ending of Job leaves much to be desired. Job was never told of the "test" he was put through, and we are never given any more information as to how this kind of "testing" can be consistent with a loving and just God. God simply answered by appealing to His authority as the Omnipotent God, to do what He wants to do, when He wants to do it, and the way He wants to do it. He does not answer to us, we answer to Him.

This idea that God has free will too, and exercises it according to his own designs, is a frightening one for theologians in particular. Many theologians seem to want to understand everything about God so that they might be able to predict His every move and decision; like the weather, if we could figure out all the intricacies, we might at least be able to prepare ourselves for it.

But just because we can not and will not understand all of what God is doing, much less why He is doing it, does not mean we have a reason to fear Him or His purpose. We may not understand all His methods, but He has revealed enough about His character to know that His decisions will all be for our good - in the long run. That again is what is so hard for us, because we see only the short run. God knows us, not only as we are now, but as we will be 100 million years from now. From that perspective, we may well agree that whatever suffering we had to go through to arrive there was more than worth it. But now, we can only anticipate that perspective.

There is one other thing to consider before we leave Job. Job "repents" after God speaks. Of what did Job repent? It could not have been the sins which caused the evil to befall him, because he was right about his having done nothing to deserve those. Of what was he guilty? He had not cursed God as his wife had said he should. But he had begun to believe that God did not care and that was just not true. In the end, faith will not be an idea we have, but a decision we make. Will we trust what and who we do know, or throw it all away because we cannot have all our questions answered? Job's lesson must still be learned by each of us. Will we keep believing? I hope so.

# Day 157
# Psalms 1-4

The Psalms hardly need the company of a devotional. They are devotional by their very nature. Perhaps one of the most unusual things about them is their ability to communicate so profoundly and personally after so many centuries have past and so much change in culture. They speak fervently of the things that are both eternal and perennial in human life.

In these first four psalms alone we find David during times of great rejoicing and deep despair. His ability to be honest with God and himself were a gift to his people, and through the Psalms, to people throughout history. We can, and should be encouraged, to see the "man after God's own heart," singing praises, and crying out in anguish. There is no real reason to hide from God, He knows all our thoughts and feelings anyway, yet most of us try to do precisely that. But David was an open book to God and we are blessed for him to have been so open in his psalms.

The first psalm sets the tone for the whole collection. They were written to consider the eternal questions of the universe. What is good and what is bad? What will last, and what will be washed away? Blessed is the one who does not walk or stand or sit with the unrighteous, but delights in the Lord. What wonderful imagery. Evil is transcient; good is enduring. Life belongs to the godly; the wicked will perish. Why? Because God is just and loving. He will win in the end. So all life must face this reality or suffer the consequences.

Why should this even have to be said? Many other psalms will deal with the fact that the wicked do prosper, even if only for a while. We need to be reminded of the eternal truths about God, ourselves, and others. That is the "law" which David wrote so much about. The "law" is not the Levitical ordinances, but the order which God placed into the whole of creation, the spiritual as well as the physical universe. And the character and nature of that law is what binds us together and makes life the deeply profound experience it should be. We are to meditate on this plan of God which encompasses not only all the good we know, but leads us into all the good we have yet even to imagine. It does not matter how many centuries ago David learned this, it is still true today and will be even into the age to come.

# Day 158
# Psalms 5-8

There is a significant difference between the kind of faith expressed in the psalms and what our society seems to value so much. In our day and time, we hold out the ideal of the balanced and moderate life as being the greatest accomplishment. We want to be able to face all of life's successes and failures with the cool composure of one who is in control.

This may explain why so many people (especially Presbyterians) have a hard time relating to the psalms. It seems that David was always overreacting. He was either at the heights his mind could conceive or the depths his soul could suffer. And whether he was at one extreme or the other, the implication is that this kind of seesaw, up and down lifestyle, was not only the norm but somehow the ideal. How can that be?

There are innumerable things in our cultural history that find their roots in the Scriptures. The value of the individual, the concept that no one is above the law, are but a few of those ideals that have shaped our society and find their basis in the Judeao-Christian faith. But the concept that the ideal human life is one in which we are always in control is borrowed from the Greeks, not the Scriptures. The whole message of the Bible is that God is in control of life and history, not us. The idea that we are in control does not stand up to much examination. And the idea that we should therefore deny our deep feelings of disappointment or gratitude is positively tyranical. David was more "human" in his crying out, both in anguish and ecstasy, because we are not in control, but we are loved by God, who is in control.

In Psalm 5 David cries out in pain, calling on God to bring forth his vindication against his enemies. He consoles himself with the knowledge that God does not reward the evil-doers, but in the end will bring judgement. He vents his frustration that this judgement seems to be delayed but he does not try to tell himself not to feel frustrated.

In Psalm 8 he marvels at the greatness of God's creation and the wonder that God has given humans such a large place in it. He did not try to control life but to live it. This was the great abandon toward life and God that made him so great. May God grant us that same freedom to be fully human.

# Day 159
# Psalms 9-11

he Lord is holy and righteous. He is just and will recompense the wicked for the evil they do. This is the clear message of the psalms. But if this is so, why do the wicked ever prosper and the righteous suffer? This was not only the basic question in Job, it was also a preoccupation in many of the psalms.

We have just read how the book of Job offered no final answer to this dilemma. In our culture we say that justice delayed is justice denied. There seems to be an injustice in God's patience that allows the wicked to prosper at any time. Why doesn't He stop the wicked *now*?

There is no answer in the psalms that was somehow neglected in Job. We do find the tension that Elihu articulated, that the wicked are still wrong, even if they prosper, and God is still just, even if His judgement is delayed. We cannot understand all the reasons for the delay, but we can know the end result.

There is an extra element we find in the psalms with regard to the question of the righteous suffering. Even though David affirmed the tension, he felt the freedom to express his unhappiness with it. He complained - loudly. And he seemed to feel that it made a difference for him to do so. That difference was more than just a psychological one. He felt that it was part of God's decision-making process; that he could influence God. He believed that God responded to the cries of His people - so he cried. His crying was not out of despair, but an honest expression of hurt to his Heavenly Father to speed up the process of sending deliverance. David prayed, and he prayed hard.

This is a difficult concept for Calvinistic types today. If God is sovereign and He moves according to His own agenda, why should we pray? What do we need to ask? He knows our thoughts, He knows our needs, why should we bother?

I do not know all the reasons, nor can I tell you why it makes a difference to God that we should have to pray to Him about things He knows better than we do. I do know that to do so draws us closer to God - even those painful prayers. He does not want us to live our lives like actors in a play for His own amusement. He wants to be part of our lives, even the hard parts. So pray - even if it is only to complain!

# Day 160
# Psalms 12-15

"The fool says in his heart, 'There is no God.'" 14:1 This is one of the most often quoted passages in the psalms. Many a sermon (both in the pulpit and out of the pulpit!) have started with these words. Yet its true meaning often slips by those who quote it the most. They read it as if it said, "The fool says in his mind..." but instead it says "the fool says in his heart..." What is the difference? A great deal!

We live in a society and time that values knowledge above almost all else. We want to know the answers to problems and understand the workings of all things so that we might properly control them. To this end, many seek to know the truth about God. Many even know a great deal about God, but do not know Him personally. And probably even more know God personally, and yet they still act like fools; acting as if God did not exist or did not care what they did, thought, or felt. That is truly foolish behavior.

What we think with our heads, and what we actually do, are often two very different things. That is because our wills, that part of us which makes our choices, is more intimately connected to what we call our hearts than what we call our heads. It is not merely a matter of knowing the right thing to do, but having that mysterious inner strength which allows us to actually choose to do the right thing.

Remember, David was called a man after God's own heart. He knew what counted in life was not what we thought as much as what we choose, because actions show what is in our hearts. The fool who thinks in his heart that there is no God will go around doing evil whenever it pleases him, because he fears no judgement. When we act as if we thought there is to be no accounting for our deeds, we too play the fool. We may know with our heads that God is there, but in our hearts we have shown little knowledge of Him.

What do we believe about God, and where do we believe it? How deeply are we convinced that God is just? How certain are we that He is gracious? At what level are we willing to trust that He forgives us? If we stop at answering these questions with just what we think, we will risk being fools.

# Day 161
# Psalms 16-18

here is a sort of pattern that emerges in the psalms, whether they are psalms of complaint, or psalms of praise. David cried out to God and spoke from his heart. He was not afraid to tell God what he thought and felt, whether despair or joy. He stated his case and closed with an assurance of God's love and deliverance.

Some may feel that he was overly optimistic. After all, what else could he have said? If you are going to write something religious about a God who loves and sacrifices, then no matter how bad things may get, you will have to end on an optimistic note. Right?

I am surprised at how often I have heard people dismiss a sermon or a lesson or some "advice" from me as a pastor, because, after all, I have to think things will work out! Well, guilty as charged! If God is the God described in the Scriptures, an all powerful, all knowing, all loving God, then things will have to work out all right in the end! Why dismiss this truth just because it is obvious?

Billy Graham told a story once about attending a luncheon with Senator Magnusen. The Senator was seated at another table and called across to Billy to ask him if he were an optimist or a pessimist. Billy responded that he was an optimist, of course. Senator Magnusen asked why Billy would say "of course" when there were obviously so many bad things that happen in the world. Billy responded, "Well Senator, you see, I've read the end of the Bible, and God wins!" As followers of a gracious and loving God, we cannot lose hope. Complain or not, rejoice or not, the one constant of faith is holding on to that one last hope - we are not alone in this - God is with us.

Perhaps the thing that made David able to have this perspective, even in the face of unfair persecution from Saul such as most of us will never know, was his ability to express honestly his feelings toward God. Believing that God will make things right in the end does not make the sting of injustice go away. We can cry out, and we must cry out. God does not ask us to deny the reality of the pain, but instead to recognize the greater reality of His love and purpose, mysterious as that may be.

Where do you hurt? Tell Him. He can take it!

# Day 162
# Psalms 19-22

"Let the words of my mouth and the meditation of my heart, be acceptable in thy sight, O LORD, my rock and my redeemer." 19:14 This is one of my favorite prayers from the psalms. It exemplifies a sense of just how intimately we are known by God, and the pure desire that such knowledge of us by God, would be a joy to Him and not a discouragement.

I heard that some scientists theorize that the sound energy of every word we speak, goes out from us into space, travelling for an eternity, and if there were instruments sensitive enough, they could still be heard millions of years and miles away. The person giving this illustration was suggesting this was some reason to be careful what we say. I don't know if I really care that some creatures may be out there eavesdropping on my conversations, but I do think we should care that God hears all our words whether He wants to or not. It is easy to forget that He is constantly subjected to the stream of insensitive dribble that so frequently comes pouring out of our mouths.

Perhaps even more sobering is the realization that He is also subjected to knowing every thought that comes pouring into our consciences. David called them the meditations of our hearts. What are they like? What would it be like if you could hear, not just the words, but the thoughts of those around you? Mind reading sounds like a real gift until you think of what a constant barrage of rubbish that goes pouring through most of the time. Hearts at peace that are filled with gratitude and wonder at the world, must surely be a real gift to God. Perhaps it is the only gift we can truly give to the God who has everything!

I should be remiss if I did not call attention to the 22nd psalm. This is the one that Jesus begins to quote as he is dying on the cross. Many who have read that account in the Gospels, wondered if Jesus had despaired and believed that God had abandoned him. Read the whole psalm. From his pain and agony, he turned to the most appropriate psalm of all. David must surely have been inspired to have written so perfect a cry for the occasion of the sacrifice of the saviour. But it was not, and is not a psalm of despair. Read the end. Jesus knew he had not been abandoned. But what a sacrifice to give. Let us meditate on that!

# Day 163
# Psalms 23-25

The 23rd psalm. What is there to add to this? It has been one of the most beloved and most quoted passages of Scripture for centuries. Why does it speak so clearly and deeply to people? What chord has it struck in people that has made it, aside from the Lord's Prayer, the most widely memorized passage in the Bible?

Perhaps it is because it comes from a young David, surrounded by God's creation, reflecting on things eternal and immutable. David is looking out at life from the perspective of one who is just beginning to realize the profound nature of having been brought to life out of nothingness, made in the very image of God, with all of life and eternity set out before him, still to be experienced. Oh to feel young again, as when the earth was new, and all things were still possible. It is a longing that runs as deeply as any in our being.

There is a peace here, with David's shepherd, that we all long for and need. There is the confidence of having all our needs met - I shall not want. To be at rest in our souls is a profound experience. No clamor of screaming, conflicting, obsessive desires that drive us continually to seek a fulfillment which alludes us, but the comfort of a cool stream and a gentle pasture that feeds and nourishes us until we want no more. This truly must be a description of being in the presence of God Himself. It will be an end to all agonies and struggles and the acceptance of gifts that fulfill us and build us up into creatures of such greatness and nobility that we have yet even to imagine them.

The Shepherd is with us even now. Peace is available to us, at least in part, even in this life. No valley or shadow can drive Him away. No enemy or evil can defeat Him. He steadies us and strengthens us and guides us all our days. No far-away God who watches from a distance. He is as close as a staff in our hand; nearer to us than our very thoughts.

Not even death can separate us from Him. We are His, and no power can wrench us from His loving hands. And when we are done here, He will make for us a new place where we will know Him better than we have even known ourselves. This is our journey, and it is safely determined, not by our will, but His. The 23rd Psalm is truly a vision glorious. Know wonder we love it!

# Day 164
# Psalms 26-29

"ait for the LORD; be strong and let your heart take courage; yea, wait for the LORD!" 27:14 This is not welcome advice to a world rushing everywhere it goes. Waiting must be one of those virtues lost in the fall. For us today, the faster we can go, the faster we want to go. It used to take forty-five minutes to bake a potato. Now, with a microwave, you can do it in just over four minutes. Yet you see people standing in front of their microwave ovens, tapping their toes and trying to figure out how to make it go a little faster.

We desire the thirty minute workout that can be done in only twenty minutes, or the "quality time" relationship that doesn't interrupt our work, or the daily devotional time we can do over the tape player in the car on the way to work (you know you *can* pray with your eyes open!). Just what are we in such a hurry for? We aren't quite sure where we are going, but we want to make sure we get there first.

Why is it so hard to wait for the LORD? There is an old joke about a fellow who is speaking to God and asks, "God, is it really true that a billion dollars is to you as a penny, and a million years as a minute?" God answers, "This is true." So the man asks, "Well God, how about giving me a billion dollars?" And God replies, "Ok, in a minute." This is part of our fear of waiting on God. What if He takes longer than we want to wait?

It must certainly be a great advantage to have God's perspective, to be able to see things, not just in the here and now, but in the there and then. Much of our anxiety would melt away if we could see that what concerns us so much today will in fact be resolved and life will go on to bigger and better things. But what keeps us from having that perspective now? Nothing but ourselves.

Perhaps that is why God told us to set aside one day a week to rest and remember. The Sabbath is supposed to be that day when we regain our perspective, when we learn to wait. What have most of us done to our Sabbaths? If we are so poor at patience perhaps it is because we lack practice. Remember, he who has God and everything else, has no more than he who has God alone. So, hurry up - and wait!

# Day 165
# Psalms 30-32

Sin is not a particularly popular twentieth century topic. Many people have argued that one reason for the decline of the mainline denominational churches in the later part of our century, has been a result of hanging on to the commitment of preaching and teaching about sin, in an age that no longer needs that kind of a guilt ridden concept. They argue that we should not speak of needing forgiveness for our sins, but instead the need for personal fulfillment that can only come through relationship with God.

I suppose there is some truth to that argument. Much of the kind of puritanical preaching of two hundred years ago, depended on the picture of a wrathful God who watched our every move and thought, and smiled very little. And I believe that picture of God to be a false one. I think we must realize that God does not drive us to Himself by incessant nagging, or guilt, or punishments. If this were the case, we should all be far more guilt-ridden, haggard, and crippled. The fact is that if God wanted to make our lives absolutely miserable in order to drive us to Him, I know He could do a better job, because I could do a better job at that task, and He is much smarter than I am.

The problem of going to God out of fear or guilt is that if it is God (or our perception of Him) that is causing the guilt or fear, we will want to get away from Him as soon as the guilt or fear is gone. Fear and guilt may be good short term motivators, but in the long run, their effect fades as soon as they do. In that sense, I suppose that the need of fulfillment is of more value than the need for forgiveness.

On the other hand, David was quite right when he observed that when he didn't admit his sin, his body suffered. Feeling guilty is not always the result of somebody's overactive conscience. We are most certainly guilty of many things. The guilt we feel is not only real, but right; it tells us that we are not so far gone that we do not recognize the right from the wrong. At those times, there is no fulfillment outside of confession, repentance, and forgiveness. We cannot go on to the future until we have made some accounting for the past. If yesterday does not count, then neither does tomorrow. We will be able to stop talking about sin as soon as we all stop doing it.

# Day 166
# Psalms 33-36

"Let all the earth fear the LORD, let all the inhabitants of the world stand in awe of him! For he spoke, and it came to be; he commanded, and it stood forth." 33:8,9 There are many psalms that praise God for His creation, that lift up for our consideration, the majesty of God displayed in the wonder of creation. But this psalm goes beyond that, to consider the power that brought existence into being out of nothingness.

God is not merely great because He has been clever in His creation. We are discovering and building new things all the time ourselves. As I write this, computer scientists are just now making machines that will be able to process information in teraflops - that's a million, million floating point operations per second. With that kind of power, they will begin to tackle such projects as predicting the weather or running simulations of air turbulence. When it comes to making new things, we are beginning to build things that astound even us. And all these technical advances have come in this last century. Remember back at the tower of Babel when it was said that nothing would be impossible for mankind if we kept cooperating? The fulfillment of that prophecy looks closer than ever.

Yet, for all that we can do and might do, there is one thing which remains beyond our capabilities - to truly create. We are makers and builders, but only God can create out of nothing. We are clever with those things we have at hand. God brings them into being through His own will. That is truly awesome power. No matter what we discover or make, we are simply not in the same league as the Creator. He is as far above us as we are above the amoeba (or further!). What sheer arrogance on our part to think that we could ever impress Him with any of our accomplishments.

Yet what is more awesome to me than all of this, is that God should care so much about us. His real greatness is still not in His incredible ability to create, but in His astounding desire to love. C. S. Lewis wrote that the true measure of greatness is not how tall one can stand, but how low one can stoop. God has proven His greatness by all measures. He has stooped all the way down to us. Let all that lives and breathes praise the LORD!

# Day 167
# Psalms 37-39

"Take delight in the LORD, and he will give you the desires of your heart." 37:4 This is another of my favorite verses in the Scriptures because it has spoken so personally to me of how God works and how I am supposed to be.

When I was an adolescent and read this psalm for the first time I thought that I had come upon a wonderful promise of God. "Take delight in the LORD, and he will give you the desires of your heart." As a teenager, my desires ran along the lines of popularity and girlfriends. I was not going to be so crass as to desire cars or money, but peer approval and romance seemed almost worthy enough to invoke God's help. I am sure that we have all, at one time or another, prayed those prayers to God, asking for the job, house, car, yacht and discovered that He is not about to put Sears out of the mail order business. Yet the passage stands, and I do not know why it does not plainly apply to some things. What about those times (why are they so hard to remember?) that we did ask, and God said, "Yes"? He delights in seeing us happy, as any parent would. He will also not give us what is not good for us, as any good parent would. But does that mean we shouldn't ask?

There is another, perhaps deeper way, of understanding this passage. "Take delight in the LORD, and he will give you the desires of your heart." This can also mean that when we delight in the Lord, He will put in our hearts the desires He wants there! That means that I can live my life, not out of sync with my desires, but in harmony with them! If God gives me those desires that are pure and noble and worthy, then instead of living a life of duty and drudgery, always at war within myself, I can do what I want, because I will want to do the right thing!

I am convinced that having the right and proper desires and following them with a whole and happy heart, is precisely the life God intended us to have. David mentions the wicked. We are often jealous because the wicked seem able to pursue their desires (evil though they may be) with more abandon and commitment than the saints. If that be true, it is because we have not yet desired the right things. But take heart! "Take delight in the LORD, and he will give you the desires of your heart!"

# Day 168
# Psalms 40-43

avid frequently "wrote" to his "soul." He spoke to himself as if there were an inner self able to talk to another inner self. Psychologists do not consider this strange, but rather indicative of maturity. To be "self aware" is that unique sensation in which we can not only experience things, but reflect upon our experiences of those things.

Most of us are aware of this capacity. We watch ourselves carefully most of the time. When we are meeting new people at a social function, we are careful to monitor what we are saying and doing as compared to what we are really thinking and feeling. At home and with good friends, we like to get away from some of that vigilance and just "be ourselves." But there are other, more intimate times we use this dialogue.

Modern psychologists would probably call what David was doing in these psalms "self talk." They are the things we tell ourselves that we believe (or want to believe) as opposed to what we feel. David was trying to find comfort for himself by reminding his "soul" that, in spite of current circumstances, there had been reason in the past to praise God and there would be reason to do so again. This can indeed be very powerful medicine for the aching heart.

What we tell ourselves to believe about circumstances can have a profound affect on how we feel. Events are never merely static facts, but facts as they are interpreted by those experiencing them. This is why some people are able to flourish in the worst kinds of circumstances, and others fall apart in the most favorable of circumstances. Some modern "self help" books would have us believe that as long as we say positive things to ourselves, things will work out all right. That is not what David was doing, and I do not believe it works that way. We must have *reason* for believing positively or we will only be deceiving ourselves foolishly.

Accordingly, David was reminding himself of the good reason he had to believe things would get better. God was still there. God is still here. This is not false comfort. And we need to tell it to ourselves again and again and again, until we believe it. It is the most important truth we can learn.

# Day 169
# Psalms 44-46

n Psalm 44 the sons of Korah reflected on the source of their strength and confidence. "For not in my bow do I trust, nor can my sword save me." 44:6 This is the testimony of faith: it is not our strength, but God's strength that delivers us. Therefore, we should trust in His purpose and not our own devices or defenses - right?

The problem with that affirmation is that God does choose to work out His will through what we do. Calvin referred to this idea as "human agency." God does not always (in fact some would argue seldom) intervene directly but instead works through people. What if God intends to save you through your own sword? Is the old maxim, "Speak softly but carry a big stick" inconsistent with the affirmation of faith that it is God who delivers?

During the 1960's, a comedian (and Harvard math professor) named Tom Lehrer wrote a song entitled, "Who's Next?" It poked fun at nuclear proliferation. In the song Lehrer mentioned some nations that had "the bomb" and those who wanted to be next in line. One of the verses went, "Egypt's gonna get one too, Just to use on you-know-who. So, Israel's getting tense, wants one in self defense. 'The Lord's our shepherd,' says the psalm, But just in case, we'd better get a bomb. Who's next?" This is a dilemma for the faithful. How do we know the difference between relying on our own strength and being the "human agency" through which God is going to act?

This debate raged all through the cold war, and the arms race went on, and some would argue now that "deterrence," "mutually assured destruction," has proven to have been the right option. I don't know if you can ever resolve that debate unless God wants to answer it for us. Faith can and should know, that whether through proliferation or disarmament, God controls the outcome.

Perhaps we must consider that the purpose of faith is not to be an infallible guide to decision making, but instead the foundation upon which we build our hopes. We do not and can not know all of what God is doing, but we can trust in His ultimate motives. God is our refuge and strength in victory and in defeat. Psalm 46 gives us perhaps the best direction. Whatever decisions we make, let us first be still, and know that He is God. *His* will be the deciding vote. That *should* cause us to worry less!

# Day 170
# Psalms 47-50

**I** was raised to be careful about the things I believed and claimed to be facts. What we believe ourselves is crucial to our own well-being, nevertheless, what we proclaim as the truth to others must be guarded even more carefully, because they may also believe it as a result of our testimony. It is one thing to stumble and fall, but it is quite another to become a stumbling block to others. This is what Jesus meant when he said that it would be better to have a millstone tied around one's neck and be cast into the sea than to cause another person to stumble.

So I try to be very careful about saying that something is "true" or "undeniable." It seems that as soon as you do that, some clever person out there thinks of some exception and shows you to be a fool. But Psalm 49 does speak to us about one of those truths I have found to be undeniable, and, therefore, a foundation for all the rest of my understanding of things. It is an old adage and the source of many jokes, but it is as true as anything else I have known: you can't take it with you.

Death is the unequivocal. It is the one universal fact of life. One hundred percent of people do it. Even Jesus died. But that is what is so important and unique about his death; that he rose again. That is, of course, what Christianity is all about. If the resurrection is not true, then all of this is rather a vain exercise. We cannot take it with us, no matter how good or bad, how wealthy or poor, intelligent or talented we may be. If nothing can be done about death, then it will have the final say and it will not only close the book, it will eliminate the book altogether.

I have never understood the Sadducees of the world. The Sadducees were the religious officials of Jesus' time who performed the temple sacrifices and did not believe in the resurrection. For them, immortality was experienced only through one's descendents. But their death will steal that away too. You cannot take it with you, and until you have settled where you are going, the journey is of little value, and in the end, no value.

On the other hand, I choose to believe that there is life after death. And for that life, I don't believe I'll need any worldly goods anyway. That truth changes our perspective on everything - or should.

# Day 171
# Psalms 51-53

I t is from David's life we first read the passage which makes it explicit that God measures the heart. Back when Samuel was directed to go to the house of Jesse and anoint a new king for Israel, we find that even Samuel was surprised at God's choice, for even Samuel did not fully realize the criterion that matters most to God. That criterion, a heart for God, was the story in miniature, of David's whole life, and ours too.

The fifty-first psalm is among the most famous because David wrote it after the sorry episode with Bathsheba and Uriah. He had committed adultery and murder and was found out. His repentance is astounding for an oriental monarch of his time. To admit wrongdoing was a shock to everyone. But David knew he was not above the law, and that there was no path back to God and godliness other than full confession and turning to God for gracious forgiveness.

"For thou hast no delight in sacrifice; were I to give a burnt offering, thou would not be pleased. The sacrifice acceptable to God is a broken spirit; a broken and contrite heart, O God, thou wilt not despise." 51:16,17  God measures the heart, and His forgiveness is a matter of grace. Our confessions do not earn us forgiveness. No payment can be made to balance out the scales of justice in our favor. We do not deserve forgiveness, we cannot command it or demand it; we can only ask and trust in His love and forgiveness. All other arguments and offerings must be muted. We must stand before God, not to justify ourselves, but to be justified by Him.

This seems like standard fare for Christians. We have heard this truth hundreds of times from the pulpit. Yet we still have trouble believing it. We fear going to God confessing, hoping we can instead say, "Well, I've done better lately." We would gladly sacrifice anything to avoid confessing, "Again and again I have chosen the wrong - forgive me."

But if we can learn a lesson from David's life and heart, let it be this: if God could (and did) forgive David for adultery and murder, can we not believe He can forgive us too? Do not be afraid, open your heart to Him, and let Him heal and cleanse it too.

# Day 172
# Psalms 54-57

etrayal is always a bitter pill to swallow. Of all acts of treachery, none can cut as deeply as friends turned enemies. They know us better, our strengths and our weaknesses, and not only are they more dangerous because of it, they cut at our own self-confidence. Betrayal by our friends will make us worry that we are either not worthy of loyalty, or, at least, a poor judge of character.

All that considered, it still seems a bit much for David to be praying for their death and eternal damnation. There is a harshness about the calls for judgement in the Old Testament that is too strident for our New Testament ears. We may be able to pray for our defense, but to pray for their demise seems to be "sub-Christian" in some sense. "Let death come upon them; let them do down to Sheol alive;" (55:15) has crossed the line from justice to hatred.

C. S. Lewis, in his book *Reflections On The Psalms*, suggests that we consider a couple of things before rendering judgement on these psalms. He points out that to accuse them of being "sub-Christian" is to be accurate, but not fair. We believe in progressive revelation. David did not have the advantage of knowing Jesus, or his teachings. It becomes much more clear through Jesus' ministry that God calls us to love not only our friends, but also our enemies. That teaching is not explicit in the Old Testament and it is not surprising that David would not have understood enough to know it. The fact is that David spared Saul, which is more than most of us would probably do, no matter what we might say now. David may not have understood as much, but he most certainly lived closer to the limits of his understanding than most of us ever will.

Lewis also points out that David was expressing his feelings, not necessarily justifying them. The psalms come from the heart as an expression of self to the Lord. That does not mean they will always be right. David expressed his anger, despair, hatred, and even loathing because that was what was in David. There is much to be said for that kind of honesty with God. It is perhaps much better to be honest with our feelings and wrong, than to be "proper" and duplicitous. God knows anyway. We need to be honest with Him for our sakes, not His.

# Day 173
# Psalms 58-60

There are many times when I am reminded of how blessed my life has been. As I read through these psalms which speak so fervently of the pain of injustice, I realize how historically unusual our lives are who have suffered no such injustices.

The Jews have been a persecuted people for almost as many centuries as they have been a people. From one culture to the next, one nation to the next, they have been a minority, usually not well liked. The pain of prejudice is part of their heritage, and these psalms will always hold an appeal for those who have suffered that particular brand of hatred.

Prejudice has never been the exclusive property of the Jews, however. The "minorities" in our culture and every other culture throughout history have had to consume a steady diet of the unfairness that goes with prejudice. To be hated, not for anything you have done, but because of someone's perception of what or who you are, must be a bitter experience. And injustice goes beyond that.

Even in our own time, the people who have suffered under the cruel dictatorships across our planet have known the sting of rights being denied or trampled. "It is unfair!" is a cry that comes to the lips of nearly all people at one time or another.

I am pointing this out because I fear some of us, who have never known that kind of violation of our God-given rights, fail to feel the passion that is rightly ignited in those who have so suffered. I have not been betrayed by a friend, had my life threatened by those whom I have done no harm, been denied a job, or housing, or food, or services, because of my race, creed, or color. Mine has been the "American dream" and I can only look on and guess at the anger and indignity of prejudice.

I do not feel guilty that I have been the gracious recipient of such blessings, but I do think I need to be reminded of the cost that has been paid, and may need to be paid again, to secure those liberties I so often take for granted.

Those who have known these injustices first hand can certainly identify with the Psalmist's cry of anger. Those of us who have not, might do well to listen carefully to the anguish expressed and be moved to do more than just listen.

# Day 174
# Psalms 61-64

 soul that thirsts for God. What interesting imagery David used in the sixty-third Psalm. He was in the wilderness of Judah when he wrote this verse. Perhaps he had finished several days of travelling and experienced the need that can become a compulsion we call thirst. In any case, he used that metaphor for his longing for God - a desire that effects our very beings - a need which must find fulfillment or there will be no joy.

How often have we felt that kind of desire for God? A desire for God would hardly be called a thirst or even a longing for most people who have learned to get along well enough without giving God so much as a second thought. But is that a mark of callousness or confusion?

I have to believe that at some time every person, has thirsted after the knowledge of God. As we grow we must all come to that point where we ask the questions; why are we here, where did we come from, and where are we going? The need to ask those questions and the desire to have answers is universal to our race. St. Augustine said that each of us are born with a God-sized hole in our hearts, and nothing but God can fill that void. The thirst is built in.

Sadly, many people find no answers to those questions, and like all unfulfilled needs, they must either be satisfied or denied. Many take the route of denial, not always because they did not have an experience with God, but that the experience was not what they expected or wanted. Our problem is not that God neglects to satisfy our thirst for Him, but that any such satisfaction must, in this life, always be temporary. And most people do not like that aspect of life. They want to find something that will satisfy once and for all; they dislike the thirsting and want a one-time fix.

Thirsting after God is not always a pleasant thing, but it is almost always a good sign. It means at least we still want the right thing. The quenching of that thirst, the experience of the power, majesty, and love of God, is far better than the thirst, but it cannot last in this life. No matter how glorious, we will lose the sensation and we will thirst again. That may not be pleasant, but it is not bad. How thirsty do you feel?

# Day 175
# Psalms 65-67

*et's Make a Deal* was a popular television game show when I was young. Monty Hall would roam the audience, which was dressed in ridiculous costumes, to offer one "prize deal" after another. There was, however, always the risk with each deal that the contestant would hit the "stopper" and have traded a week in the Bahamas for a four foot ball of string.

People like playing *Let's Make a Deal*. It is a particularly popular game to play with God. "Lord, if you'll just ... then I promise to ..." The trouble is that God seems to be less adept at the game than was Monty Hall.

"May God be gracious to us and bless us and make his face to shine upon us, that thy way may be known upon earth, thy saving power among all nations." 67:1,2 This can look like *Let's Make a Deal*. Some people feel it would be more honest to say, "May God be gracious to us and bless us because we like being blessed!" Does it really add any weight to suggest that if God did bless us then we would be much better witnesses for Him? "Ok, God, if you'll just heap those blessings on us, just think of all the good press it will mean! Even people in Poughkeepsie will hear about it! Really, we're not asking for ourselves! Think of the benefits for You and for others!"

But perhaps there is a better motive behind the Psalmist's reasoning. As I have gotten older I see more and more how brief this life really is. Even at thirty-six, it seems like yesterday that my five-year-old daughter was in her cradle. I can look forward and appreciate what some of you know now, that even eighty years is a short time and all the good and bad times are not as important as those things which contributed to God's kingdom. There is an old saying, "Just one life, 'twill soon be past, only what's done for Christ, will last." Perhaps there is more wisdom than selfishness in praying for God's blessing that His name might be known throughout the earth. That is, after all, what it said He had been trying to do with the covenant with Israel; to bless a nation and a people so much that others would be drawn to find out why. The Sabbath day, the Sabbath year, the Jubilee, were not just for Israel but for a testimony to the nations. May God bless us, that we might be a blessing and a witness to others!

# Day 176
# Psalms 68-71

"**Z**eal for thy house has consumed me." 69:9 Thus begins the verse Jesus quoted after he had turned over the tables of the money collectors in the temple at Jerusalem. The psalms are in fact full of zeal. David's highs were a bit higher and his lows a bit lower. That is not always a welcome temperment for those of us more staid (stiff?) Presbyterian types. We are not exactly sure what we should do with our emotions, but we are quite certain we don't trust them.

Yet there is a whole-heartedness to David's life and psalms that speaks of a depth of experience that cannot be without feelings. I worry sometimes that we have made Christianity into a bloodless and cold system of beliefs instead of a warm and living relationship with God.

Martin Kaplan of Emory University wrote this twenty years ago as he reflected on the graduates of that day: "In the seventies the new conformists, perhaps soon to be our new professional class, have chosen relativism as the best game in town. Instead of doubt, irony, inquiry and foolish dreams - the dreams that made our older brothers and sisters cry - they have chosen the rewards of privatism, self-fulfillment, personal gratification, individualistic autonomy, and burgherly hearthside virtues of coping, acquiescence and accommodation. ... The real flower children of the seventies; their ontology is clear and crisp: 'Yoko and me, that's reality.' They haven't acceded dumbly to this world vision; its the key moral tactic for the decade. They've chosen cynical relativism as the shrewdest strategy for operation within our premised economy; in so many ways, their choice is a wise one. With some persistence and some luck they'll be financially rewarded.... What they will lack is the dimension of outrage, the capacity to thunder 'No' when some injustice has been wrought on something other than their own self interests."

I wonder how often the Church has been guilty of the same thing under the guise of wanting to be "in control." Being "cool" is not a Biblical virtue. Righteous indignation may be dangerous for most indignation feels righteous whether it is or not, but self-interested disassociation is no substitute. Outrage at injustice is a virtue and it is never a quiet one.

# Day 177
# Psalms 72-74

 salm seventy-three is a psalm of Asaph. In it he considered the theme repeated so many times before in the psalms and is still on the hearts and minds of God's followers. Why do the evil prosper? Why is justice delayed? Where is God while the wicked oppress the poor and have health, wealth, and ease?

Asaph knew what a meddlesome question this could be. He even described his anguish over the question as having made him "well nigh slip." The slip he referred to was envy. Oh, how we, who are trying to be good, can envy those who take the unfair advantage that accompanies the breaking of rules.

This is one of the problems in dealing with the wicked. They not only commit acts of injustice, they also conjure up in us the green-eyed monster of jealousy. But why should that be?

Asaph wrote that trying to understand this was a "wearisome" task, until he went into the sanctuary of God and "perceived their end." In the sanctuary of God, he was reminded that you do not win the race at the beginning or the middle; only at the end. If you cannot cross the finish line, then no matter how far ahead you have been, you will not win the race. The wicked will one day have to stand before the throne of judgement. If, in that day, they have no one to speak for them, no saviour, then it will be a terrible day indeed, and all the fine days up until then will not matter one little bit.

There is another reason, however, that we tend to be envious of the wicked, which is that they are generally better at being bad then we are about being good. Jesus made the same observation himself in the parable of the unrighteous servant. There is more wholehearted seeking after wickedness than there is after goodness. But before we hang our heads in shame, or feign to defend ourselves against this charge, let us consider that this too can be a blessing in disguise.

Instead of wishing we were more like the wicked, we should wish we were more like ourselves. Let us control what has been given to us - not envy or jealousy - but joy of friendship, strength of loyalty, and peace for our souls. These can be as real and tangible as forbidden pleasures. Let us free ourselves from the bane of envy and start having more fun!

# Day 178
# Psalms 75-78

saph, in the seventy-seventh Psalm, wrote of the need to find comfort in the day of despair. We are not told what his particular problem was, and it is probably not important for us to know. We all face times in our lives when our souls refuse to be comforted and God seems to be so far off and trouble so close at hand. What are we to do in these times of distress?

Asaph said, "I will call to mind the deeds of the LORD; yea, I will remember thy wonders of old. I will meditate on all thy work, and muse on thy mighty deeds." 77:11,12 This is one of the keys to getting through difficult times: to have the perspective of faith. And how do we get that perspective of faith? We remember.

The Passover was one of the most important celebrations of the year for the Jews because it was to remind them of how God had made them into a nation. It was His mighty acts in the ten plagues that took them out of the captivity in Egypt, His fire and cloud which guided them into the wilderness, and His great power that parted the Red Sea and subsequently drowned the Egyptian army that pursued them. We build faith to get through the difficulties of today by looking back and remembering faithful times in the past. Those faithful memories build trust in the relationship by reminding us that there is good reason to believe God will come through in the future since He has done so in the past.

This not only applies to our relationship with God but with each other. Faith and trust are essential components of any relationship, which is why it is so difficult to repair relationships when there has been a violation of that trust. When we violate a trust, instead of having faithful memories, we have painful ones. But part of the solution, even in those situations, is to look back and remember the faithful times.

The past can be either a liability or an asset. With God, we can always look back and see those faithful promises kept. Why is it that we so often fail to do so? We should consider that it is not only the faithful promises of God which He kept through the sacrifice of His son, but those which He has kept in our individual lives. What mighty deeds has He done in your life? When was the last time you considered them?

# Day 179
# Psalms 79-81

Psalm eighty-one is the story of Israel in miniature. Many people believe the Old Testament portrays God as a legalist while in the New Testament, His grace rather than the law, takes over. We have seen for ourselves that this is not true. God's grace was made clear to the people of Israel and understood as such, albeit not by everyone, throughout the centuries. Covenant is not law, but grace.

Asaph repeated the familiar formula in this psalm. "I am the LORD your God, who brought you up out of the land of Egypt. Open your mouth wide, and I will fill it." 81:10 God chose Israel not because they were better or more faithful, but because He chose to. They were to worship Him, not so that He would love them, He had already done so, but because He did love them and had already delivered them out of slavery. Our "work" is never the prerequisite for God's grace, but the response to His grace. He gives first, and the force of that goodness alone should command our grateful response, but the gift is already given. We return, not payment, but praise and worship.

It may seem as though I focus on this point too often, but I do not believe we can focus too often on the message of God's grace. There have been scholars who have wanted to discount the message of the Old Testament because they did not see the graciousness in its pages. Conversely, there have been scholars who dismiss the New Testament, arguing that there is really nothing "new" in the New Testament, but only what is contained in the Old Testament made more explicit! The answer, as Jesus said, is that he did not come to do away with the law and the prophets, but to fulfill them. The message of God's grace is in the Old Testament as well as the New Testament, because it is the same God proclaimed in both. But, oh, how much more clearly do we see it in the New Testament than in the Old. The sacrificial system in Leviticus was gracious, but how much easier to misunderstand that than Jesus' sacrifice on the cross.

God has loved us before He has asked anything of us. That was true for Israel and it is still true today. You cannot earn God's love, and you do not need to because it is already yours. That message cannot be told too often or too well. Believe it!

# Day 180
# Psalms 82-85

The eighty-fourth psalm is one of the great praise psalms. It looks forward to the vision glorious of the Kingdom of God that is still to come. It is a reflection of the hope of glory about which we still have only hints. That hope was once the great hallmark of Christian faith, but in our modern times it has been characterized as a false and vain hope; in Marx's words, an opiate of the people.

I am quite certain many believers have abused the idea of eternal life in the Kingdom of God. It has been used alternately as a threat and a promise. If you do not obey or do certain things, you were told, you would never see this great reward. And if you gave up certain things or did others, your reward would be great in the Kingdom which is to come. So endure poverty or injustice, because you will get your reward later. While there is some truth in each position, neither encompasses the truth of the Kingdom. But remember, the most dangerous thing in the world is not a lie so obvious that everyone can see it, but a partial truth that takes great wisdom to discern the truth from the error.

While it is clear from the Scriptures that not all will enter into the Kingdom of God (or want to be there for that matter) it is also clear that you cannot earn entrance. No amount of good works will qualify you. You must enter at the gracious invitation of God or not at all. Likewise, while it is true that eternal life in the Kingdom of God will be immeasurably more valuable than anything on earth, that does not mean that what happens in this life is unimportant and injustice a matter of no concern. If the values of the Kingdom to Come are real, then they must apply here too. God intends the good for us, and now is not too soon to start. Why has that been so hard for people to understand?

There is a promise to us in the psalm that we would do well to claim. "For the LORD God is a sun and shield; he bestows favor and honor. No good thing does the LORD withhold from those who walk uprightly. O LORD of hosts, blessed is the man who trusts in thee!" 84:11,12 This is not a promise of the future, but of the present and all "presents" that are to come. We may not receive all the things we want, but the promise here is that we shall have all those things which are good for us. That is the nature of God both now and into eternity! Praise God!

# Day 181
# Psalms 86-88

s I read through the psalms again, I am reminded of just how difficult David's life was much of the time. His days as a shepherd must have been just the kind of preparation he needed for an adulthood which was lived at the front lines of so many battles with friends and foes alike. Perhaps before we envy great people like David, we should consider the prices they have had to pay for that greatness.

In Psalm eighty-six, David again calls out to God for relief from those who persecute him. He asks that God hear his petition and praises God that He should be willing to hear such petitions. He then makes an interesting request. "Teach me thy way, O LORD, that I may walk in thy truth; unite my heart to fear thy name." 86:11 Why would it be a benefit to have a heart united in fear of God's name?

To have a heart that is united is an obvious benefit in any endeavor. We are all familiar with the term "half-hearted" and just what it means when we have one. No athlete can afford to have their loyalties divided. To win, one must be dedicated to the task, given over to the pursuit in any and every area of life, for any victory worth having will require the intensity of a whole heart. But a heart united in fear?

The fear of God is not the same fear we have of the mugger. The fear of God is the respect and awe due to a being of God's power, authority, and majesty. But what other fears do we have in our lives? I think they are many, perhaps legion.

We fear death, our own and those whom we love and depend upon. We fear injury, loss of a job, failure, ridicule, sickness, aging, war, pollution, disease, and the list could go on! Fear is not merely a universal experience, it is a daily companion to us all. How we handle our fears not only has a lot to do with our mental health, but how well we function at every level of life.

David asks God to teach him his ways, to unite his heart to fear God's name. In a world full of dangers it can sometimes be very helpful to know what you have to worry about first. If we could learn to fear nothing but that which displeases God, we would find a clarity to our thinking and decision making for which most people long. If God is pleased, what more need worry us?

# Day 182
# Psalms 89-92

I am quite familiar with the Ninetieth Psalm as it is one of those which is frequently read at funerals. Of course, in the Presbyterian Church we do not call them funerals, we call them "witnesses to the resurrection" and I think this is more then just "politically correct speech." There is an important difference between focusing on death and focusing on life after death. One is despairing; the other is hopeful.

Funerals are among those times in life when we are forced to face those realities we spend most of the rest of our lives trying to avoid. They are times when we must ask and seek answers to the questions of the meaning of life and death. They are hard times when we must face just how fragile life is and how much we need God for all the important things in life. This psalm serves those times well.

Before anything else we need to remember that God is from everlasting to everlasting. While our lives come and go, the constant in all creation is the Creator Himself. Our lives seem long to us at times, but those who have lived longest know what a false sense that is. All our accomplishments and records, no matter how great, will one day be forgotten or undone; only the Lord's work will endure. So the psalmist asks that we would learn to number our days "...that we may get a heart of wisdom."

Part of that "heart of wisdom" will be to see the shortness of our days on earth, but another part must also be to see the almost incomprehensible length of our days in the Kingdom of God which is to come. On one hand we fret too much about what happens to us in these years on earth and are filled with a false sense of importance. We struggle, build, compromise our ethics to make enduring contributions, and they all pass so quickly. On the other hand, we underestimate the impact we will have as creatures who will outlive not only the buildings we build, but the continents they stand on, and even the very planet and solar system itself. We are so very young!

How does this change our thinking about this life, death, and the meaning of what we do? I think the implications are great. We must not think too highly of ourselves; neither must we not think too lowly. We are creatures whose true nobility has only begun to be revealed. That is no small comfort - and challenge!

# Day 183
# Psalms 93-95

"The LORD, knows the thoughts of man, that they are but a breath." 94:11 This is not particularly the most important point that the psalmist is trying to make, yet it strikes me as one of those times when the obvious and yet profound has been laid out for our attention.

The idea that God can "read" our thoughts is not an especially surprising one. After all, God is supposed to be omniscient, that is, all knowing. If He knows everything, then He would obviously know our thoughts. This is in fact, one of the three great attributes of deity: omniscience (all knowing), omnipotence (all powerful) and omnipresence (being everywhere at once).

What is not so obvious is that these are attributes belonging *only* to the deity; only God can be those three things. There is no indication anywhere in the Scriptures that anyone other than God can read our thoughts. Now, if Miss America walked into a bar wearing only a string bikini, you could probably know what was on the minds of the men there, but that is not the same thing as reading their minds. True mind reading, to know the very thoughts of another as they are thinking them, is a power which is restricted to God (and we can thank Him for that!).

Likewise, only God can be in more than one place at a time because He created time and space and is not limited to its restrictions. We cannot really conceive how He accomplishes this, but it is not beyond our comprehension to understand that He would be capable of it.

Finally, only God is all powerful The one who called all creation into being at a word has no rivals. God alone is sovereign.

Who would disagree with such obvious theology? Oddly enough, there are some people who do not realize they are doing it. There are those who would have us believe the Devil knows all our thoughts, tempts each and every one of us and is so powerful that we cannot stop his influence in our lives.

Whether you believe in a personal Devil or not, we must be convinced that he cannot be God's equal. He cannot read our thoughts, be everywhere at once, and do anything he likes. But if we think so then it will have the same effect as if he could. Don't be fooled. Deceit can be a powerful weapon.

# Day 184
# Psalms 96-99

"**M**ake a joyful noise unto the LORD!" This is a phrase that we read over and over again in the psalms. Whenever I read it I cannot help but think of all the old jokes about the singing that goes on in church and its comparisons to the clay creations of special treasures elementary school children make for their parents. But there is no denying that those creations, and our songs, are beloved by the givers and the receivers. And what is so wrong with that?

One of my primary beliefs is that our experience of life is more profound than our understanding of it. Put in other words, we can and do experience things that we cannot fully explain or comprehend, but we experience them none the less. In some way I feel music is one of those things. Music is not merely an aspect of life or an analogy or allegory of existence, it is a part of life itself. The idea of melody and harmony, of beauty itself as some relationship of similarities and differences balanced in a pleasing fashion, is not just a description of life but an essential element of living itself. There is rhythm in all that is around us and in us, and life is full of things that simply resonate with the song which is God's living creation, or are at discord with the flow of it all. C. S. Lewis in *The Screwtape Letters* described heaven as, "... the regions where there is only life and therefore all that is not music is silence."

So much of modern life and religion is not a song or even a joyful noise, but a discordant cacophony. Our communications, our sleeping, our eating, our building, our work, our play, are all out of sync and off key. Life lived as it was intended, is more like a dance than a march, more like a song than a sermon, more like a hug than a handshake. We know this not because we have to be told, but because it is written inside us all, where we feel the flow of this experiment of God's we call life.

If that does not come out of your heart and your mouth sometimes you are blocking up what God intended to flow forth from you with joy and ease. It does not matter if it is a pure note or shout for joy, God has made us a deep well of being, and that should at least occasionally rise up to overflowing and let go! Let all that lives sing praises to God!

# Day 185
# Psalms 100-102

Psalm 100 is probably more familiar than most of the others. It can be heard as a responsive reading in hundreds of churches on any given Sunday. It is a psalm of praise, thanks, and rejoicing that suggests the note of security and happiness which should attend our Sunday services of worship. How sad it is that it is so often spoken like a dirge followed quickly by a service most noted for its general lack of any hint of joy.

What is the worship of God? The word itself comes from the old English word "worthship." It means to show forth the worth or value of something to you. In our modern times it would probably be more akin to cheering for your favorite sports team than what we do on Sunday in church. How can we do a better job of truly worshipping God?

There was once a time when Christians were instructed to prepare themselves on Saturday evening to attend worship on Sunday mornings. I think there is great value to that kind of discipline, but now more people in church Sunday morning probably stayed up and watched reruns on one of the cable channels than made time for meditative prayer. Is the answer to get out our old guilt-generating machine and try to recreate the Puritan society in which ushers roamed up and down the isles with polls to poke those napping after only the first two hours of the sermon?

David wrote, "Serve the LORD with gladness." You cannot worship a God of joy by forced obedience to a routine. Gladness is a matter of the heart and it proceeds from the inner being which has known rest for its weariness, healing for its pain, and forgiveness for its transgressions. Worship is not always a shout for joy, but it is always an openness to the God who loves us and reads the attitudes of our hearts as easily as we do the billboards on the side of the road.

If our modern worship has fallen into disrepair I have to believe it is because we have mistaken worship for what we do instead of what we are. God is a spirit and He must be worshipped in spirit and in truth, or not at all. Our best worship comes from the abandonment of hearts open to God whether that brings cheers or tears.

# Day 186
# Psalms 103-106

There are days when I find living around me very tiring. I am sure that my wife would tell you she finds the same thing to be true! But she has the advantage of being able to get away from me some of those times, and I have to follow along wherever I go. That can be a real handicap.

Those days I find myself most tiresome to me are usually the times when I have once again fallen victim to my own sinfulness, whether sins of omission or commission. My sense of frustration with myself is not helped by the realization that I have had more blessings and advantages in my life than most people in this world. I have been the beneficiary of a happy childhood home with parents and a sister who loved me, plenty of food and clothing, good schools including college and seminary, a lovely wife (you're welcome dear!) and happy and healthy children, and still I find the feet I would stand tall upon, to be made of clay. Quite frankly, if it were up to me, I would have written myself off long ago as one of those human projects that just keeps absorbing resources without giving back a reasonable return on the investment; like one of the old gas guzzling "luxury" cars whose fuel efficiency was measured in gallons per mile. Or so I feel on my dreary days.

At those times I like to reread the One hundred and third Psalm. "He does not deal with us according to our sins, nor requite us according to our iniquities. For as the heavens are high above the earth, so great is his steadfast love toward those who fear him; as far as the east is from the west, so far does he remove our transgressions from us. As a father pities his children, so the LORD pities those who fear him. For he knows our frame; he remembers that we are dust." 103:10-14 Forgiving is not an easy thing to do, even when you are trying to forgive yourself. That is why it is so important that we recognize the greatness of God, that He can and does forgive us, more often than we forgive ourselves. He has known us and loved us and removed our sins from us as far as the east is from the west. We cannot wear out His love or His patience as long as we will trust that fact. We may feel unfortunately stuck with ourselves, but God does not share our perspective. May we learn to share His!

# Day 187
# Psalms 107-109

The One hundred and seventh Psalm can be called a psalm of praise to a God who delivers. Again and again the formula is repeated. People should praise God for His gifts, but instead they sin against Him and He chastens them. They then cry out for deliverance, and God delivers them from their trouble and they praise Him. Why should life be so patterned?

"Whoever is wise, let him give heed to these things; let men consider the steadfast love of the LORD." 107:43 What is there to consider in all this?

For one thing, the steadfast love of the Lord does not preclude justice. Just because God is willing to forgive us does not mean that our actions have no consequences. I may be forgiven my sins, but it does not follow that I will not suffer the consequences of my actions. God will not change the hearts of those whom I have disappointed nor restore to me the lost time and energy that was wasted. To assume that God's forgiveness will change the past is to believe you can jump off the Empire State Building, decide half way down it was a mistake, and expect to find your self miraculously back at the top of the building. If our lives are to be meaningful, God cannot be constantly following us around and magically undoing all our wrong choices and actions.

But the steadfast love of the Lord does mean that when we have learned our lesson and cried out to Him for His help, He is always there to hear us and answer. This is not to be mistaken for the idea that God is tapping His foot waiting to hear us cry "uncle." Swallowing our pride and genuinely seeking God's help is not some kind of game God plays, but a description of repentance itself. We do not earn God's consideration when we have humbled ourselves. The truth is that we will not be ready to accept His help until we have humbled ourselves. The latter is quite a different thing than the former.

It takes wisdom to see the steadfast love of the Lord in our lives. It takes the eyes of faith to see God at work in the bad times and the good times. But look and consider the steadfast love of the Lord. He is just, but He is also forgiving and redeeming. He delivers! Praise His name!

# Day 188
# Psalms 110-113

The One hundred and tenth Psalm is considered a "messianic" psalm. It is considered so by no less an authority than Jesus himself who quotes it as referring to himself (Matt. 22:44). The author of the book of Hebrews also makes use of this psalm and its reference to Melchizedek. What are we to make of this rather cryptic psalm?

I have long wondered why God has chosen to go about revealing His salvation in the way He has. It is said that the Messiah came in the fullness of time, but what made the time so full? Why not earlier or later? And why does it look here like the Messiah was to come "conquering," not like a lowly child in a manger? If God was not going to be any clearer than this about what His purpose is, why mention it at all?

Perhaps it is to be a comfort for us when events do happen as foretold. It is hard to know in this psalm, for it has certainly not come true in a very real sense; at least not yet. But if it does start happening, it would be no small comfort to know that this too, is part of God's plan.

Perhaps too, it is enough to know that God's plan for us is not in our hands, but in His. He has plans for human history, and while we may participate in them, even significantly, we are in no danger of thwarting God's plan for things. In the final analysis, when history is complete as God knows it now, we can be sure the most important moves in the game will not have been made by us, but by God. What may be surprising will be finding out how much of what we considered important will have had no lasting impact at all.

One thing we can know for certain is that while God is supremely interested in us as individuals (this is what His first coming was all about) He has also not forgotten the nations. There will be an accounting and all the enemies of God will be laid at the feet of the Messiah. It may not come as such welcome news (although it should) but history is not about us as individuals or even as nations; it is about God creating, and redeeming for purposes not all of which have been told to us. But we can know that He is not finished with us yet, and while some may have missed His first coming, they will not miss His second!

# Day 189
# Psalms 114-116

**M**any people find it difficult to talk about their faith because they do not know how to answer those who want proof of God's existence. It is usually a dreadful time for parents when their children first say, "If God is there, why can't I see him?" We all fear that we will not be able to give a sufficient answer to this question. And the problem grows worse when adults ask it, for adults feel they are somehow more enlightened simply for asking the question; children at least ask from a genuine curiosity. But in either case, how do we answer?

In Psalm 115, David surprises us by turning the question around on those who would ask it of the followers of Yahweh. He taunts the worshippers of idols to show their god. If the idol is real, why can it not speak or hear or smell or feel? If it is not alive, then why in the world should we put our trust in it?

That is perhaps the most important thing to understand when we face the questions about "proving" God's existence. We cannot "prove" it in a material sense. We cannot say some magic words and make Him appear. He chooses, for His own reasons, not to do so. But does that mean that He is not there? The fact is that if God is the God who is described in the Scriptures, then we should not be surprised if He fails to "perform" as we like. His will is His own. As creator of all things He is not bound by all the rules of His creation (what is impossible for us is unequivocally possible for Him). It is not stupid or illogical to believe that what governs the infinite and all-powerful would be different from what governs the finite and the limited.

And what of the other choices? If God is not the one described in the Scriptures, who or what is He? Believing there is no god leaves you with nothing. You came from nowhere, you are going no place and in between what happens to you is of no particular importance. Few people worship stone idols anymore, but many worship the god of money or power or fame. Yet all these, like idols, are dumb. Fame will never sacrifice itself for you or keep you from death. Money and power care nothing for their possessors for all are only temporary owners.

It is clear that we need a God and a saviour. Whose choice is the more foolish?

# Day 190
# Psalms 117-120

"Oh, how I love thy law! It is my meditation all the day." 119:97 How many of us echo David's feeling about the law of God? How many of us are really happy when conversations turn to the topic? How many of us can say we look forward to opportunities to take time to reflect on God's laws, each and every day? How do most of us really feel about God's laws?

I would guess if you asked most people on the streets about their general impressions of the laws of God, most would respond that they are probably too strict ("Nobody does THAT anymore!") and living according to them would be boring and you would have no fun at all in life. God's laws are all those things we should do and don't, and what we shouldn't do but do. No wonder we don't love God's laws or want to think about them much, if at all. But what is the "law" of God that David loved so?

We have read for ourselves what the law of God is, and what it is not. It is not merely the Ten Commandments. It is not a list of do's and don'ts that govern our every thought and action. The law of God, given to Moses, was not a means by which we earned God's forgiveness, love, or salvation. All those things are products of God's grace, not our obedience to "the law." The law David loved, and which God has given to His people, is the description of a proper response to His grace. It is the guide to a personal and communal life that draws the best out of us all. It is the demand for a system that carries the highest regard for personal dignity and purpose. Both rich and poor, slave and king, are equal before "the law." The law provides repentence, penance, and restoration for trangressions. The law of God demands our best efforts to worship Him, to live at peace and in cooperation with our neighbor, and to make the most of the gifts God has given to each of us. We may not cheat, or lie, or be unfaithful or untrustworthy, not because God is a prude, but because anything less than everyone getting the most from life, falls short of the greatness of His plan.

To the Pharisees "the law" became a living death; an attempt to live up to a standard that was impossible to achieve. But for those, like David, who know that God's laws grow out of His grace, they are the wisest of guides to life that we possess.

# Day 191
# Psalms 121-123

Not all of the readings each day are of equal length. (Did I really need to say that?) The chapters in the Bible were not created for the purpose of making it easy to study. So, after the long readings for yesterday (especially Psalm 119), today is a welcome rest of just a few verses over which to ponder. Still, as my mother always told me, good things come in small packages.

The One hundred and twenty-first Psalm is called the song of ascents. Our spirits are lifted up to consider the source of our strength and salvation. The law may provide us with wise counsel to guide our lives, but our help is always from the Lord Himself. Christianity is not merely a set of beliefs or right- thinking (dogma), it is a personal relationship with God, our savior and redeemer.

This is one of the hardest parts of understanding our faith. Belief *about* God and belief *in* God are two very different things. The former may make us wise, but the latter gives us life. The reason is not always so obvious, but we must be reminded that no amount of knowledge about God can substitute for knowing Him. You can read volumes and volumes of information about a man, but it will not tell you some things that meeting him face to face will. And even if you could know everything about him, it would not substitute for spending time with him; talking about everything or nothing in particular. We need not just the knowledge of God, but a real experience with Him wherein we become the human creatures we were meant to be; beings made in His image to be in fellowship with the divine creator. That we can experience His fellowship in small amounts now is amazing; that we will know Him for an eternity in the Kingdom to Come is glorious.

We lift our eyes to the hills, from whence does our help come? It comes from the Lord who made heaven and earth. What more can we ask? What more do we need? Perhaps only the reminder that what really counts in the end is not our knowledge of God but His knowledge of us; not that we cry out for help, but that He is willing to answer. To know that about God comes not from years of studying His character, but from the experience of being touched by His Love. Have you let God touch you today?

# Day 192
# Pslams 124-127

Anxiety is one of the main causes of stress in our society. In Psalm 127, Solomon says it so poetically, "It is in vain that you rise up early and go late to rest, eating the bread of anxious toil; for he gives to his beloved sleep." 127:2 What an important lesson for our fast food, fast lane, modern times - the comparison of the over-booked day of the anxious achiever and the restful sleep of the beloved.

I heard a radio psychologist once define anxiety as the fear of future loss. That struck me as perhaps the best definition I had ever heard. At the root of our anxieties is the fear that we will do, or have already done, something that will cost us in the future. If we choose "this" job, we cannot take "that" job; if we choose "this" car, then we cannot take "that" car; if we don't make the "right" decision, we will lose out later. The trouble with this kind of game is that it keeps us constantly afraid of multiple "possible" realities. Of course, only one of the possibilities we fear can come true, but we can worry about all of them and more, if we have time to dream them up. It also seems increasingly difficult to see that something good is also a possibility and perhaps as likely or more likely than the bad. But fear can be an awesome force. Emotionally it can come very close to the impact of reality itself. If you believe something enough, it is as good as real for you because you will act as if it were true whether it is or not. And so, with anxiety, we can suffer many more losses than are really possible, and find ourselves drained, driven, and unfulfilled.

How does one get off of this treadmill of despair? Solomon suggested that we remember the source of our confidence - especially about the future. If God is on our side, then we do not have to be anxious about the future because it is secure in His hands. Jim Elliot, a missionary martyred by the Auca Indians, once wrote, "He is no fool who gives up what he cannot keep, to gain what he cannot lose." We cannot keep anything from this life. Death will steal it all. We need not be anxious about our lives, for the only guarantee in this life is that you will lose it all - unless you have been able to give it all up to God, who desires to give it all back to us, and eternal life too. Believing that, we can sleep at night with the rest of the beloved.

# Day 193
# Psalms 128-130

he One hundred and thirtieth Psalm has been popular from the early centuries. It was one of Luther's favorites because it speaks so well of the forgiveness of God. For those who feel the Old Testament is a book of harsh judgement and a wrathful God, this psalm argues that the understanding of God's forgiveness and mercy came long before New Testament times. God's covenant of grace and forgiveness are founded in the nature of God Himself, not the imagination of the New Testament authors.

What is rather striking about this psalm is not so much that it identifies the lack of righteousness in people (if God did mark iniquities, who could stand?) but in crediting His forgiveness as a reason for God to be feared. What did the psalmist mean by saying that God's forgiveness was a source of the fear of God?

We should remember that the term "fear of God" does not necessarily mean being afraid of God. Fear, in this Old Testament sense, is akin to respect, to the awe and circumspection due great power. The power of God to have created the universe out of nothingness, to order its nature and movements by His will alone, to know not only all that is, but all that might be, is not to be taken lightly.

Yet there is perhaps a greater sign of the majesty of God - that He forgives. It is one thing to have the power to prevent anyone or anything from harming you, for certainly, there is nothing that we can do that could seriously damage God's being or existence. But it is quite another thing, and the true measure of greatness, to have the ability to crush one's enemies, and instead, to convert them into one's friends. God shows the awesomeness of His power not so much in the flood, but at the cross. To be "big" enough to forgive, to be even "bigger" enough to pay the price for the sins of those who have hated you, that is unpararlleled greatness.

God's goodness knows no equal. He is just, and will not let guilt go unpunished. Whether in this life or the next, justice will be served. But He is "fearsome" all the more because He is also forgiving and gracious. He has taken the burden of sin upon Himself, and remakes even His enemies into His loving children, if we can but finally trust in His real greatness.

# Day 194
# Psalms 131-134

A s a child of the late twentieth century, I have been raised to believe that the search for knowledge is the highest possible good.  It is the value that has driven the western civilization mind set ever since the Middle Ages and was present throughout history before that.  Such long standing and cherished assumptions often go unquestioned by individuals. Yet Psalm 131 presents an alternative to that search for knowledge which our type A society should consider.

The search for knowledge is certainly an admirable goal. But how do we understand "knowledge." Most of the time we define "knowledge" in our culture as "facts."  We want to know what makes things work so that we may modify and control them. Yet "knowing" a person is more than just having a lot of facts about them, it is being in a living experience with them. Knowledge of God is something to be sought, but it must also be something which we already possess.

David uses the analogy of the child and the parent.  There are certainly many things my children do not know about me and my wife.  But there are other things which they already know about us; things which they might well understand better now than they will when they are teenagers.  They know they can trust our love for them.  They know they can come to us in their times of need and confusion and find safety for themselves.  When something frightens them or they are in a new situation, confronted by things they cannot understand, they run to their parents, for they know we are there for them.  They find peace and security, not in their own understanding of the situation, but in the certainty of their knowledge of our relationship.  What they do not know about the situation which frightens them, does not change what they *do* know about us.  Likewise, what they don't know about my wife and me does not change what they do know about us from the years of hugs and kisses and love.

We want them to grow up and understand the world they live in.  We do not want them to remain children all their lives.  I believe God wants the same for us.  But if we are to "grow up," we will have to relearn that childlike trust in our loving God and find peace in the knowledge of Him we already possess.

# Day 195
## Psalms 135-137

hese psalms reflect on the great acts of God in the history of Israel. They are reminders to the people that God has intervened in history on behalf of His people and therefore nothing can ultimately defeat them. They seem rather nationalistic in that sense and do not have nearly the attraction for us that they must surely have had for Israel in David's time.

Still, they remind me of something we seem to have lost sight of in our modern church era. These psalms speak of God in very concrete terms. There is no "spiritualizing" of these historical events. What made them great in the minds of the people in the Old Testament was not what they said about the existential conflict of the forces of evil and the forces of good but the fact that they were concrete, measurable, historical acts of deliverance for the nation. For them, God was not a concept, but a person and a person who was both powerful and on *their* side. For them, faith was not just some positive mental attitude, but a real experience with the powerful God who is really there providing measurable proof and results.

Some people think that this kind of "what-have-you-done-for-me-lately" attitude is the antithesis of faith. There was, however, something very pragmatic about Israel's religion that seems quite intentional; not only the intent of Israel, but of Israel's God. The God of Israel likes to act in history. It does take the eyes of faith to see it, but let us make no mistake, God's choice is not merely to watch us or coach from the sidelines. The testimony of the history of Israel is that far from being a spectator, God is *the* active participant. His are the decisive moves, and He makes them according to His own counsel.

Perhaps that is why we so often have trouble with our prayers. We try to spiritualize our relationships with God when He is quite willing and able to be very practical with us. In Jesus' great prayer we are told to pray for our daily bread. How willing are we to do that? What is at risk for us if we try? Perhaps we do not pray for specifics because we are afraid of what it might do to our faith if we did not get an answer. Or perhaps we are simply more afraid the answer would be "no" which might require a real change in our desires! Prayer and faith are risky business!

Check Here
When Read
❏

# Day 196
# Psalms 138-141

ohn Calvin is generally given credit for developing the doctrine of predestination. Whether or not that is an accurate assessment, it is clear the doctrine did not originate with him. It is not even a New Testament understanding, but it goes back throughout the Old Testament, and Psalm 139 is one of the clearest statements of the belief.

Predestination is not what you would call a "popular" doctrine in most circles. The idea that God has already foreknown and foreordained life gives many people fits when it comes to understanding how there can be evil in the world. If God has ordained everything then He must be responsible for everything too. If He is responsible, because we can only do what we must do, then He becomes the author of evil and we become helpless victims of the fate assigned to us. It is easy to see why this doctrine is no longer widely preached!

But just because we do not understand something fully, or like the implications it has, does not mean we can ignore the clear testimony of Scripture. After all, we claim the Bible is revelation - that which has been revealed, not deduced. So then how are we to understand this doctrine?

As with all things which we cannot fully understand, we must be careful not to exceed the limits of the things of which we can be sure. David says, in positive fashion, that God is sovereign. He has known us before we were yet made, even before our birth. He knows the process by which we have been called out of nonexistence into existence. He knows everything about us, even our very thoughts; even the desires of our hearts which lay hidden from our own consciousness. Nothing takes Him by surprise.

How this can be and we can still have free will is not explained. That we do have free will and are responsible for our own sins is also clear. That the wicked deserve punishment and will receive it is also clear. How all these fit together is not so clear. But what should not escape our notice is the idea that God being in control, however that actually works, was a comforting idea to David. It can be for us too. It is far more frightening to think that nobody is in control. Someone needs to be in control, and if it makes any difference, I vote for God!

# Day 197
# Psalms 142-144

The One hundred and forty-third Psalm is yet another psalm of David's from a time of distress. It is from one of those periods in his life when things were not going well. For David, those times were not infrequent. But he was a man who knew how to handle the times of trouble and we can learn a great deal from his approach to faith and life.

In this troubling circumstance, whatever that was, David says that he turned to mediation to find strength. Meditation is not widely practiced in our western culture, but that does not mean it is bad. In fact, throughout the centuries, mediation has not been an exercise practiced by the mystics only, but by devout people from all walks of life. We have come to associate meditation with "eastern" religions, but that is more out of our own historical ignorance than truth.

The word meditation carries the connotation of considering an idea or thing over and over again, like a cow chewing its cud. That is one of the significant differences between "eastern" meditation and meditation as presented in the Scriptures. Much of "eastern" meditation is an attempt to empty one's mind of everything except perhaps of a word or phrase repeated over and over. The Scriptures tell us that instead of emptying our minds, we are to fill them by considering something carefully and fully. This is, in one sense, the essence of observation. Scientists know the need to examine all the details of something, to make sure that all angles and perspectives have been considered. This is the Biblical ideal of meditation. Not to be empty, but to be as fully aware as we can be.

Meditation is, therefore, not a mystical experience as much as a skill for appreciating fully what we are already experiencing. It is meant not to take us out of this life, but to help us understand our lives more deeply. Like Sir Arthur Conan Doyle's detective Sherlock Holmes, whose skills of observation let him see clearly things hidden from others, meditation should sharpen our senses, increase our awareness, sensitize us to the importance of detail, and make our lives richer. God would not have us miss any good thing from life, and He has given us the great gift of our minds to consider things carefully. Meditate on it!

# Day 198
# Psalms 145-147

raise the LORD! Those of us who come from one of the more "restrained" denominations, often have a difficult time with the practice of this concept. To praise the Lord by speaking of His mighty deeds, to tell of the greatness of His love and forgiveness, to proclaim His righteousness to all the earth, is just fine, but don't ask us to raise our voices, or our hands, too high!

I have grown up in a church where, if you stood up and shouted "Amen" during the sermon, you would not be asked to leave, but no one would want to sit next to you the following week. I have also attended sporting events with some of these more stoic fellow members and listened as they shouted themselves hoarse for their favorite team. I am not at all sure I would feel comfortable in a church in which the congregation decided to do a "wave" during the sermon, but there seems to be a longing for some kind of middle ground not many churches have been able to achieve; that balance of order and ardor.

But however we choose to praise God as a community, I think there is an important sense we often miss in which we can praise the Lord as individuals. Praise is not merely saying "praise" or "glory." We praise one another regularly without resorting to such religious sounding terms. Saying "thank you" or "I appreciated that" to members of our family or co-workers, is thought to enrich our relationships. Saying "nicely done" or "good job" are part of our everyday vocabulary. Am I suggesting that God would like our telling Him we thought He had done a good job, or that we appreciated something He had made? Precisely. When I have looked at the mountains from the vantage point of a ski lift and watched as the snow collected in large flakes on my lap, I have been moved to say, out loud, "Nice work, God!" I will admit that people don't just fall all over each other to ride with me again, but none the less, I think God knew I honestly meant the compliment and He graciously accepted it.

Perhaps an even more important kind of praise is that which we share with others. To praise God to someone else, to tell, as any lover would, of the greatness of His virtues and the richness of knowing Him, is important praise indeed. And you don't even have to raise your hands if you don't want to!

# Day 199
## Psalms 148-150

"When all is said and done, more is said than done."
I don't remember where I first heard that little bit
of wisdom, but it certainly describes life here -
with one notable exception - God. With God,
there is much more done than said. God is
supremely a God of action, not talk. Let His creatures speak
volumes with regard to His will and purpose, God doesn't talk a
lot about what He is going to do, He just does it.

That alone should make Him worthy of our praise. Here is
someone who does not talk a good line of promises of what He
could or might do. God has acted according to His purpose, and
set into motion all we know of in existence (and perhaps more we
have not been told of). When all is said and done, it will be what
God has done, what God has chosen, what God has accomplished,
that will make all the difference. Perhaps the best news of all, is
that with God, all can never be said, because God will never be
done. He is creative, and there is no reason to believe He will not
go on for an eternity continuing to be creative.

Without God there would not only be nothing, there would
never have been anything. With God, the possibilities are as vast
and endless as His knowledge and power. What is yet to come
has not even begun to be revealed.

What possible good is all this lofty anticipation?
Perspective. We are in need of perspective in our daily lives. The
pressure of the ordinary and mundane chores threaten to steal
from us the joy of being creatures created in the image of the
Living God. We act so often as creatures whose lives are
desperately in search of some kind of meaning. The fact is we are
children of the King! We are the beloved of the Creator of the
Universe who has not abandoned us, but has purposed us to
greater things than we have yet imagined. There is nothing
ordinary about us! Someone once said it is not *who* you are that
counts, but *whose* you are. We are His. Whatever else may be
true about us, we must come to grips with the fact that we are *not*
meaningless little insignificant creatures - we are children of God.

So let us be the ones to lead the praise of our Creator,
Redeemer, Comforter, Guide, Friend and God! Let all the earth
praise the LORD! Praise the LORD!

# Day 200
# Proverbs 1-4

"The fear of the LORD is the beginning of knowledge; fools despise wisdom and instruction." 1:7 This is one of the verses about which I am frequently questioned. From the New Testament perspective, we often have a problem understanding fear as something positive. If God is all loving and gracious, if He has forgiven us and even sacrificed His own Son for us, then how can it be good to be afraid of Him?

First, we should realize there can be such a thing as a "healthy" fear. While I was working my way through seminary, I spent a year and a half working as a carpenter. I learned a lot about construction in that time. As a result, I usually tackle repair projects with a fair measure of confidence.

Unfortunately, as a carpenter, I did not learn much at all about electrical wiring. I proved that recently by being propelled from the top of a ladder I was standing on while trying to replace a light fixture. As I sat on the floor recovering from a jolt that made my ears buzz, I informed my wife that I guessed I hadn't switched off the correct breaker after all. Now, when I cannot call an electrician, I shut off the power to everything I can, up to and including my next door neighbor's house. I have learned a healthy fear of electricity. If you ignore the power of something truly powerful, you are foolish, and may very well end up embarrassed, hurt, or worse.

This is what Solomon was trying to tell us, with "the fear of the LORD is the beginning of knowledge." But we must also remember that this is just the beginning of knowledge, not the end of it. The electrician has no less "fear" of electricity than I do - perhaps in a sense, even more. Yet an electrician is less afraid of electricity because he knows more about it; he knows what to "fear" and what to do to make it useful. For him, electricity is a friend. But without that initial "fear" he would not live long enough to know anything else.

The fear of the Lord is the beginning of knowledge, but the end of knowledge is the love of God. Those who know God can be trusted and that we need not be afraid of Him, must remember that for those who do not know Him, a healthy fear of His power may be the first step to the greater knowledge of His love.

# Day 201
# Proverbs 5-8

Solomon is dealing here with the topic of sexual sins. It might seem odd to heed the advice of a person who obviously ignored it himself, but a part of wisdom is knowing how to separate the medium from the message. Solomon's counsel is valid, and the wise will not ignore it because of its source.

In chapter 5, verse 15, he advises his son to "Drink water from your own cistern..." and in verse 18, "Let your fountain be blessed, and rejoice in the wife of your youth..." I think here Solomon is trying to help us see the importance of being able to live in continuity with our past. In verses 16 and 17 he says "Should your springs be scattered abroad, streams of water in the streets? Let them be for yourself alone, and not for strangers with you." This might seem a little odd because usually we are told to give and share of ourselves. But this is an area where we should keep our lives to ourselves. Here Solomon is telling us that we must live our lives not for the approval of other people, but on our own principles. We cannot listen to what everyone else tells us is good for us - especially the adventuress, the wicked and evil. We must, as he says elsewhere, take our own counsel, and chose in favor of actions which maintain continuity with our past (assuming, of course, that our past was full of good ways).

In verse 23 he explains why. The person who does not follow this counsel, "... dies of lack of discipline, and because of his great folly he is lost." This is an insightful thought. When we choose to take the counsel of everyone else, we try going in all different directions at once, we lose our discipline, our water runs out in the street. There is great strength in wholeness, in singleness of purpose, in moral purity, in discipline, in continuity with our past. I am using these all as synonyms. We must make decisions to go one way or the other; we cannot go in two directions at once. The "pure" life might seem boring compared to the life of the "adventuress" but it is not so. The "adventuress" has lost her direction, her past, and having lost her discipline, the ability to see something through to the end, to commit oneself, she dies. When we try to live for the opinions of others, we find ourselves in the same boat, pulled in different directions, and we lose our direction, our discipline, and we die.

# Day 202
# Proverbs 9-11

There are scores of proverbs that tell us the righteous prosper and the wicked suffer. I sometimes wonder how much we really believe that. When we look around, it appears many of the wicked are doing quite well and many of the righteous are suffering quite badly. But what does wisdom tell us? What is the real end of the righteous and the wicked?

Of course, the first thing to consider is that in the end, when judgement day comes, the wicked will not have prospered at all. If you spend one hundred years here on earth in the lap of luxury, but an eternity outside the Kingdom of God, you will not have prospered in the least. The time we spend here is so short compared to the time we will spend in the next life, this life pales by comparison. We must remember that we win the race at the end, not before. In this life, the most important thing is to come to know the love and forgiveness of God. If we fail in that, we will have lost the only race that finally counted. This is wisdom, to know that we must first account for what happens after our death. If we do not, then death will have its final victory, and the last and best laugh will not be ours.

But Solomon also wanted us to consider that even in this life, the wicked do not prosper so much as we might think. "The righteousness of the upright delivers them, but the treacherous are taken captive by their lust." 11:6 There is a kind of sad irony about wickedness. When you sell your soul for thirty pieces of silver, you do get the silver, but you lose the ability to enjoy it. When we make something else God in our lives, it will become "god" for us, but it will never love us as God does, only possess us. Our lusts will bring us some pleasure, but they will in turn, demand more and more of our time, energy, and devotion, seldom giving us back the same pleasure we got at first, and eventually, no pleasure at all. This is true, not just of drugs or alcohol, but of the love of money, power, or fame. The untrustworthy finally have no one to trust, the greedy never have enough, and the treacherous have no safe place to turn.

The righteous are saved more than once. The inability to desire things in life without becoming captive to those desires is a trap for which no amount of pleasure can compensate.

# Day 203
# Proverbs 12-15

art of the usefulness of the proverbs is that they are simple, yet profound. It does not take a theological genius to get their point, and they are perhaps least understood by theologians for they have less to do with eternal things as with living each day. The most difficult thing about them is that although they are easy to understand, they are very difficult to do.

"He who spares the rod hates his son, but he who loves him is diligent to discipline him." 13:24 Children need discipline. We all do for that matter. Without clear limits and guidelines, the world is a scary, arbitrary place in which to grow up. I knew that as a parent, disciplining my children would be one of the responsibilities; for their sake as well as the world's. What I did not understand well enough is how easy that is to say, but how difficult that is to do. I can remember my parents saying to me, on those occasions when I was being disciplined, that this was much harder on them than it was on me. I knew they weren't enjoying having to discipline me, but I did not understand that they were being very accurate in that description. As a parent, I now know the agony of having to choose some form of discipline and then second guessing myself as to whether or not I was too strict or too lenient, was this the right time to do something or not, ad infinitum. It really is much harder (now that I've seen it from both sides of the fence) but I also love my kids and will do what is necessary for their good.

What it finally comes down to in this life is this: It is not what we believe that makes the difference, but what we choose. Belief can be very calm and comfortable, but faith has to put on its working clothes and exercise the will in order to do anything. I may believe in disciplining my children, but they will not know that unless I am willing to back it up with my words, actions, and tears. I think it is quite alright for me to let my children see that it is agonizing for me as a parent to make those kinds of decisions (my parents let me see that) but I must not shy away from the responsibility and the possibility that I will be too harsh or too lenient. I don't think that as a parent I have to make the *right* decisions all the time, but I must make them. I think my kids will understand and appreciate that. I did.

# Day 204
# Proverbs 16-18

o many of the proverbs give cause for reflection that it is hard to focus on just one or two. But these little pearls of wisdom come with each successive verse, so I can only pick a few that stand out to me. It is easy to see why some of the great saints have spent so much time pondering the proverbs.

Perhaps I am just tuned in to looking for these references, but I cannot help but notice the number of times that Solomon reminds us that God measures the heart. "The crucible is for silver, and the furnace is for gold, and the LORD tries hearts." 17:3 It is not what we do in our outer actions that is so important, but what proceeds from our hearts, which is to say it is very possible to do well but not to mean well. With that in mind, Solomon wants us to remember that God is not so simple as to be fooled by just what we do. As the crucible refines silver and as the furnace refines gold, so God tests and refines our hearts, for it is in our hearts that our true selves are revealed. God looked at David's heart and found it to be one truly in search of Him. God looks into our hearts too, hoping to find the same desire. What does He find?

"A cheerful heart is good medicine, but a downcast spirit dries up the bones." 17:22 Again it is the heart which is of concern to the wise. I wonder just how well Solomon understood the truth of what he wrote. It has taken centuries, but medical science now has the hard evidence to prove that happy people live longer and healthier lives. We have discovered that our bodies do in fact respond considerably to our attitudes. Those who are bothered and worried constantly, produce chemicals that increase their blood pressure, harden their arteries, and age their major organs faster. Those people who are "happier" have lower blood pressure, healthier organs, and stay "younger" longer. The evidence continues to come in, but it is clear already that our bodies respond chemically to the stresses we perceive in our world. The more stress we perceive, the more stressed we are, and depression goes even further to degrade our health.

How is your heart? Not just the one that beats blood throughout your body, but the one God knows. Their health is tied together.

# Day 205
# Proverbs 19-23

"The horse is made ready for the day of battle, but the victory belongs to the LORD." 21:31 This proverb reminds us that no matter what we do, the deciding factor will always be what God does. But does this mean that what we do is of no particular importance? What is it in most of us that wants everything to be of one extreme or the other? Why do we feel that the explanation for what happens either needs to be only what we do, or only what God does? Can't it be both?

The proverb does not suggest in any way that preparing the horse is unimportant. Calvin called this idea "human agency." God chooses to work through people and what we do. Most of the time He does not work in miracles (although working through us could be considered a miracle), but through the ministry of people just like you and me. When someone needs to be comforted, to have a sympathetic ear, God does not send the "counseling" angel (although perhaps we wish He would), He sends one of His followers, one of us, to be His ear for that person. Perhaps you can see the enormous chance He takes in doing so. What if we won't go? What if we turn out to be insensitive and boorish? What if we say the wrong thing?

It is odd that we should at once both overestimate and underestimate ourselves in these matters. On the one hand, God has not taken so great a chance since He is not sending us alone, He goes with us. No matter how poorly or how well the horse has been made ready, it is still God who gives the victory. In other words, God sends us, but He does not abandon us to the task. We overestimate our own importance when we think that we have been the deciding factor, whether we have been at our best or our worst.

At the same time, we underestimate the value of our going out into "the battle." Someone once said that fifty percent of any victory is just showing up! We must learn to trust that while doing our part may not be the deciding factor, it is none the less a critical one. Especially in the area of serving people in God's name, we fail to see how often people will be tolerant of well meaning incompetence. Our trying makes things possible, and with God, that is more than enough.

# Day 206
# Proverbs 24-27

hen we read a chapter like the twenty-sixth, it is good to remember that in the proverbs, *fool* is almost a technical term. It does not refer to someone who is stupid. The fool may be very intelligent indeed. But the fool in proverbs is someone who shows a deliberate disregard for morality and ethics. The fool says in his heart, there is no God, and therefore concludes that he can make up any rules he chooses providing he can muster the strength to enforce them. "Might makes right" is the proverb of the fool but in the final analysis, God is there and He is the mightiest and that makes the fool foolish.

I am not quite sure what to make of Solomon's consistent advice to avoid dealing with the fool. From the New Testament perspective it would seem this individual is precisely the kind of person who should be reached with the gospel. The question is what would be the most effective way to go about doing this. The answer, even in the New Testament, might be much closer to the advice of Solomon than we think at first glance.

How do you reach someone who has deliberately chosen to disregard ethics? "Answer not a fool according to his folly, lest you be like him yourself." 26:4 What does Solomon mean here? I think he is trying to warn us not to try to argue with someone who has deliberately chosen to disregard morality. Arguing has seldom convinced anyone of anything: it generally gets the issue confused with a lot of extraneous issues and solidifies a person's resistance. Besides, trying to argue with a fool is to act as if God were not there, or not concerned with the life of the fool, to act as if it were our job, and not God's, to reach them. That is foolish itself.

"Answer a fool according to his folly, lest he be wise in his own eyes." 26:5 What does this mean? I think it means that we are to answer the fool not by arguing, but by pointing out to him that he is acting as if there were no rules or morality; not arguing, but disagreeing with him by challenging his decision to act as if he were the source of morality and ethics.

This may seem like splitting hairs, but I think too often as a society, we have tried to argue about ethics instead of standing up for what we do believe, which in itself is quite foolish.

# Day 207
# Proverbs 28-31

The virtuous wife is praised in chapter thirty-one and in many other proverbs. It may sound a bit condescending to our modern ears, but it is an important lesson for our time. It is a tremendous benefit to be married to someone of good character, regardless of their gender, and we need to be reminded of that in our day perhaps even more than they did when this was written.

It is not just individual marriages in our day that have suffered, but the whole concept of marriage itself. Cohabitation outside marriage is not only generally accepted, but many college people feel it is a wise decision to try living together before getting married; like leasing with an option to buy. If you decide not to purchase, it is much simpler than selling and you will have only had to "pay" for what you used!

But you cannot "test drive" a total commitment. No level of conditional commitment can simulate an unconditional commitment. Marriage requires courage; courage to make the commitment knowing that you cannot guarantee the future, but promising to do your best anyway. What most people who live together lack is not knowledge, but guts. And guts is what you most need to make any relationship last.

It is not just marriages that have suffered but the family as a unit and a concept, too. So many people now are concerned with the way in which marriage and children interfere with their own personal self fulfillment. They are, of course, right in one sense. Marriages and children require lots of your time, energy and commitment. They are not hobbies or special interests, they are the most demanding relationships and responsibilities we have. They are also, by far, the most rewarding and fulfilling. To avoid them because of the need to find something else in your life to fulfill you is a fools errand. No job or career will ever come running to you shouting your name when you come home wanting no more then to sit on your lap, or hold you close when you have failed or lost someone close to you. Single or married, it is the people in our lives that make the difference, not our occupations.

Is it hard to find a good wife or husband, to have a good family? You bet. Is it worth the effort? Unquestionably. If you have them are they a blessing from God? Undeniably.

# Day 208
# Ecclesiastes 1-3

"Vanity of vanities, says the Preacher, vanity of vanities! All is vanity." 1:2  This is not exactly the typical "upbeat" message you expect to hear in church!  It sounds not like the voice of wisdom but of despair.  However, the term here is almost a technical term and the message, while sounded with a low note, is not one of despair but of facing reality.

It is not certain who the author of Ecclesiastes was, but it is fairly certain he was writing in response to the misconception that wisdom always brought prosperity.  The book is well placed.  After reading Proverbs, one gets the impression that wisdom will always bring blessing.  We know from our experience, however, that this is not true.  Part of reading the proverbs requires the wisdom to know the limitations of knowledge.  The proverbs are observations, not formulas.  Not all of the wise prosper and not all fools come to ruin (at least in this life).  The writer of Ecclesiastes wants us to remember that in the end, this life, whether it was filled with pleasures or pains, will cease.  The ultimate meaning of this life will come in the next or not at all.  For good or for ill, this life will pass and in that sense, it is all vanity to be overly concerned about it one way or the other.

This is a message our modern world desperately needs to hear again.  In the 1980's in America there was a prevalent attitude that could be summed up by the bumper sticker "He who dies with the most toys, wins."  This is foolishness and vanity.  He who dies with the most toys, dies.  The show "Lifestyles of the Rich and Famous" held out a fantasy picture of life that somehow found meaning in the accumulation of wealth and leisure.  But the Preacher tells us that he has searched the depths of pleasures and desires and found no ultimate meaning there.  Happiness is neither with the yacht nor without it, but in being able to enjoy what one has when one has it, for it will all be taken away one day.  To everything there is a season.  If we are not given new life after this one, then life will pass without being of any particular importance.

What then are the wise to do?  The good news is that we may enjoy what we have and quit chasing the end of the rainbow.  He who has God and everything else has no more than he who has God alone.

# Day 209
# Ecclesiastes 4-6

here is an underlying theme in Ecclesiastes that is often lost in all of the negative statements. It is itself a negative statement, but it finds its foundation in a positive value. "This is a grievous evil. . ." is a negative statement used in these few chapters, but it points to a positive idea about life.

One might consider that if all life is vanity and all effort meaningless and futile, it is also vain to be upset about evil. Indeed, if there is no meaning to life, then life is neither good nor evil, it just is. But there is something deep down in our souls that will not let us escape the belief, at least the feeling, that life is meaningful and that good and evil do exist. The Preacher cries out in frustration at the injustices in life. All the fruits of our labor are not ours to keep, but must be handed over to the next generation with no more guarantee that they will be well cared for than that they will be neglected. There is an unfairness to death that positively screams at us for restitution. And so it should.

Let us remember that this life is not as God intended. It was many months ago that we read Genesis, but we must not forget that God did not intend the world to be full of sin and death. The evil and injustice in creation was not God's doing, but ours, and the promise of the Kingdom that is to come is that it will again be the world as it should have been - no evil or death or injustice or sin.

I never cease to be amazed at how many people begin to think of death and destruction as part of the natural order. I do not believe that this is what the Scriptures teach at all. Death is an unwelcome and unnecessary guest at the party we call life, and it has changed the nature of the party into a mixed affair at best. But we need to remember that God is the host of this party, and trust that He has not intended it to go this way, and will not allow it to continue thus forever.

There is grievous evil in this life to be sure, but there are also marvelous joys. And as far as we know, this is the only path for us into the next life which will be the fulfillment of what for us now is only the promise. For all of the vanity that surrounds us now, there is at least one thing which is not vain and that is life itself. It is a gift we have only begun to unwrap.

# Day 210
# Ecclesiastes 7-9

believe that it was Woody Allen, paraphrasing Ecclesiasties 9:11, who said, "The race is not always to the swift, nor the battle to the strong, but that's the way to bet!" The wisdom of the Preacher has a rather cynical twist. It is so cynical that even a modern cynic like Woody Allen has to take a lighter view of the analysis! We must remember that part of wisdom is knowing the limits of knowledge, and I think that occasionally the Preacher himself exceeded his own limits.

Yet I think that Ecclesiastes has a great contribution to give to us. The end of things must be taken into consideration and cannot be avoided. The Preacher sought to see things from their end and give them due weight. "Because sentence against an evil deed is not executed speedily, the heart of the sons of men is fully set to do evil." 8:11 What a wise description of most people's lives. The Preacher did what most people refuse to do; to look at the end results of their actions and choose accordingly. But because the sentence against evil deeds is delayed, people go about doing evil as if the sentence will never come; in this life or the next. As the Preacher says, that is folly, for the sentence against evil does come, both in this life and the next, no matter how long it may be delayed. Like jumping off of a ten story building without a parachute, no matter how much you enjoy the experience during the first nine floors, the tenth one will be your undoing.

This is because our actions *do* have consequences. What we do does matter. Life itself is not vain, but rather the pursuit of ultimate meaning in this life is vain. We must take into account where our actions and decisions will lead us. Once we do this, our actions and decisions do not lack meaning, they have the *proper* meaning. As the Preacher says, there is nothing better than to enjoy life with the wife whom you love. 9:9 That enjoyment is not necessarily a function of the kind of house in which you live. There are many mansions within whose walls there is little enjoyment and many tiny apartments which contain the warmth of a love that makes the world a much better place. To enjoy the gifts that God has granted to this life is not vain, but to place all our hopes there is folly itself.

# Day 211
## Ecclesiastes 10-12

 oody Allen once said, "I do not want to achieve immortality by being famous, I want to achieve immortality by not dying!" That is, of course, the only immortality that will really count, and it cannot be achieved by us alone; it can only come as a gift from God, not in this life, but the next.

Having said that, then what good is this life? That is the question with which the Preacher struggled. He came to the conclusion that the only meaningful thing in this life was to enjoy what you have while you have it. There are no guarantees to be had in this life. Wisdom is to be sought, but it cannot promise success or happiness. Those things seem to come and go according to some design other than our own. If we will accept that the meaning of life does not come from ourselves or our activities, we have the hope that we can receive this too, as a gift from the hand of God.

One of the favorite verses for seminary students is Ecclesiastes 12:12b. "Of making many books there is no end, and much study is a weariness of the flesh." There is a wonderful practicality to the Scriptures. Life is more profound than our understanding of it. What has been given to us in our existence is a gift that we will never fully understand or appreciate, for it grows as time goes on. What we will be has yet to be revealed, and when we have arrived there, God will have new horizons waiting for us. If we can accept this, it gives us a wonderful freedom to enjoy life which cannot be experienced by those who must make their own meaning out of existence.

There is a certain craziness to this outlook on life. Ken Kessey's novel, *One Flew Over the Cuckoo's Nest,* is about a red-headed Irishman who gets himself committed to an insane asylum rather than serve time in jail for a brawl. Once inside he discovers a world without humor, gone wrong by taking all things seriously. The main character, McMurphy, walks up and down the halls laughing and shouting that he is the "bull goose loony." To be a little crazy in an insane world is not necessarily a bad thing. We must laugh and we must cry and we must maintain our hope that this is not the only life. If we cannot, then this life will have been nothing but a crazy end rather than just a kind of crazy beginning.

# Day 212
# Song of Solomon 1-4

**I** am not alone in wondering why the Song of Solomon is one of the books of the Holy Canon. Throughout the centuries it has been questioned by scholars, both Jewish and Christian. Many theories as to why it has remained have been presented, but the fact is that it has continued to be included as part of the Scriptures as far back as any other book. What has caused its enduring appeal?

I must confess that it is rather lost on me. Some scholars have argued that it is symbolic of God's love for Israel or Christ's love for the Church. (?) I find that a little difficult to swallow. It looks to me like poetry about two people who are in love. Perhaps it is because of the translation, but it looks to me like some not very good poetry about two people in love. Comparing the hair of the beloved to a "... flock of goats, moving down the slopes of Gilead. . ." (4:1) loses a lot in the translation for me. But I suppose if some of the love letters I wrote to my girlfriends were put into print, the snickers would be at least as loud, and no one would accuse them of being poetry of any kind.

Perhaps therein is part of the lesson to this book. There are intimate exchanges between two lovers that sound not a little foolish outside their context. The things we say and mean and feel for each other as lovers are not intended for the rest of the world. In those personal and private relationships, we can all be beautiful and handsome, elegant and commanding, the epitome of femininity and masculinity - at least to one other person. It is a rare and precious gift in this world to be able to be lifted up above what others might measure us to be, into the seat of the hero or the heroine, at least for a time and an individual. It is not an experience that transfers well from the bedroom out into the streets, but given the nature of our potential as creatures made in the very image of God, perhaps it is closer to our true selves than we dare to admit publicly.

There is something very high and heady about love that makes it worth the sacrifice even of our pride. Our blushing or snickering should not be mistaken for shame but as a protection for that which should remain private. But if we have never loved or been loved to the point of this outrageous and embarrassing ecstasy, our life is the poorer, not the richer, for it.

# Day 213
# Song of Solomon 5-8

here is perhaps another positive message to be taken from this book of poetry that speaks so highly of love and that is, God is not a prude. Throughout the centuries, the Church has taken a very dim view of sex, as if it were some kind of necessary evil God permitted, rather than His chosen way to bring intimacy into marriage and children into the world.

We know that debauchery and promiscuity are not the plan of God for people, but are we as clear that neither is asceticism? The Church throughout the centuries has been as guilty of extremism as the pagans with regards to sex. Too little sex is a rejection of God's intention as well as too much sex. We have sought to define sex as only for the purpose of reproduction (if that is true, why did God make it pleasurable?) or as some kind of a spiritual or romantic experience best left to rare and exotic circumstances (candles anyone?). But sex is a whole being experience and that includes the body. There is absolutely nothing inherently wrong with physical pleasure. It is a gift from God which can, and should be, enjoyed in its proper time and place.

This creeping kind of asceticism pops up in many areas other than just sex. We don't like being physical beings. We find it limiting because we want to be more than people, we want to be gods. That was the sin of Adam and Eve and it is still with us. We twist it into a hope that in heaven we will be some kind of angelic creatures. Yet this is not the promise of the resurrection. Adam and Eve were part of the creation that God said was perfect - good. There is nothing wrong with being physical. The Greeks were wrong. We are not trapped in earthen vessels. We are both spiritual and physical creatures able to experience and enjoy the best (and worst) of both worlds. Being physical is not base and low, it is deep and warm and earthy. It is an experience intended to be as solid as the boulders in the Rocky Mountains and as full of surging energy as Niagara Falls.

Too much religion has been what goes on in the head and not enough of what goes on with the rest of the body. If we could recapture that understanding we might regain the attention of the world as being people who really know how to live life to the fullest.

# Day 214
# Isaiah 1-3

saiah stands out among the books in the Old Testament not only for its length, but for the contribution to the understanding of the great God of Israel and His plan for all people. The nature of God Himself is more clearly defined and the role of the servant, the redeemer, and savior is described with remarkable clarity considering its place in salvation history.

Isaiah's message was not an easy one to deliver. It was given to him to pronounce judgement against Israel for their abandoning the covenant. But there was also a new revelation that he had to deliver, that God was going to continue His plan to bring a blessing and deliverance to this broken world through the "stump" of Jesse, a remnant that would be faithful. Redemption is still ultimately God's work and He will not let His purpose be utterly thwarted.

After reading through Ecclesiastes which dealt with the world in "round" figures, it is a shock to move back to the specifics of Isaiah. Sin and righteousness are not merely concepts, but concrete actions which will receive concrete judgements. It is good to remember after all of the philosophical considerations of Ecclesiastes, that God takes the pains and the joys of this life quite seriously and so should we. Justice delayed will finally arrive and perhaps sooner than we think. Repentance and right living are never in vain, and Isaiah serves to remind us that after all our musings, we will have to choose and live with the consequences.

"Come let us reason together, says the LORD: though your sins are like scarlet, they shall be as white as snow; though they are red like crimson, they shall become like wool." 1:18   Isaiah holds up a mirror to the people and warns them that the picture they see will not be a pretty one. They have become as bad as the Canaanites who God had judged before them. Their sacrifices at the temple have been misunderstood and are not acceptable to God. They have clothed themselves in hypocrisy with their evil deeds and veiled sacrifices. God has not been fooled. But there is still hope, for God will have the final word and it will be one of redemption. May God grant that we can look into the same mirror and know we too can survive the view.

# Day 215
# Isaiah 4-6

There are two things which impress me in these particular chapters. In chapter five God is speaking and asking that we judge between the vineyard owner and the vineyard. Remembering that in the first chapter we are encouraged to reason with God that we might find salvation, it is significant that already we are asked to make a judgement as part of that process.

Seeing things from God's point of view is an important perspective. As a minister I regularly hear about people who have a complaint against God because He has not performed as they would like. People ask why God doesn't solve this or stop that or cure them. But we so often fail to see what God *has* done and in this parable of the vineyard, God is reminding us that from His perspective He has done more than enough. What more blessings did Israel want? The earth was fertile, God's commandments were just, and He had promised to bless them with favorable weather and crops. What more do *we* want in this world?

It is people with their greed, self-indulgence, materialism, pride, injustice, and immorality that have made the world into a mess. The earth, by all measures, is the garden spot of all the planets we know of, and if that were not enough, we have been given the intelligence to work to make it even more friendly. What is it that people want? Let us judge between God and Our World. Who has been unfaithful? Most certainly not God. Our complaint that God has not solved world hunger or over population or political tyranny has missed the point. God has provided so that none of those things had to happen. God has also already provided for their undoing - through us.

That brings me to the other thing which impresses me in these chapters and that is the call and response of Isaiah. When Isaiah saw the glorious vision of God, his first response was the recognition of his own unworthiness. But God solved that ("come let us reason - I, the Lord will make you clean") and then He asks, whom shall He send? Isaiah's response is the great response of the healed heart - "Here am I! Send me!" No matter the task, no matter how great or small, God's solution is to work through us. He has already provided all the tools, now He needs only the workers. Are you forgiven? Will you go?

# Day 216
## Isaiah 7-9

I t sometimes comes as a shock to people to discover that the prophecy about the birth of the messiah which has been made so famous by Handel's music, *Messiah*, in fact refers originally to someone other than Jesus. This kind of "prophecy" is referred to in theological circles, as antetype and type. The first occurrence of the fulfillment of such prophecy is called the antetype (ante meaning before) and the fulfillment of the prophecy in its fullest sense is called the type.

This should not cause us great concern to find out that God prepares people to understand what He is going to do. People need a great deal of preparing. Like throwing a ball to a child when they are first learning to catch, God has had to say to the world many times, "Now here it comes, I'm going to throw it, put your hands out, keep your eye on the ball, I'm not going to roll it this time, it's coming at full speed, get ready..." and we still let it hit us right between the eyes!

God loved and delivered His people many times before He did so through His own Son. What is so outstanding is that of all the ways He could have chosen to deliver us, He would have chosen this unusual way - through a child. Ahaz was given the opportunity to ask for any way he wanted deliverance. He could have asked for a legion of angels or that his enemies all dropped dead simultaneously - as deep as Sheol or has high as the heavens. He chose not to ask at all. So God chose for him and He chose a baby.

By Jesus' time, many people were still looking for a deliverance from God. They wanted a deliverance that came from overwhelming military victory. But God had already shown His best pitch once before, and while it amazed them, it should not have taken them by surprise. "For to us a child is born, to us a son is given; and the government will be upon his shoulder, and his name will be called, 'Wonderful Counselor, Mighty God, Everlasting Father, Prince of Peace.' Of the increase of his government and of peace there will be no end, upon the throne of David, and over his kingdom, to establish it, and to uphold it with justice and with righteousness from this time forth and forevermore. The zeal of the LORD of hosts will do this." 9:6,7 Steeerike three, you're out! End of game! Nice pitch God!

# Day 217
# Isaiah 10-13

"oe to those who decree iniquitous decrees, and the writers who keep writing oppression, to turn aside the needy from justice and to rob the poor of my people of their right, that widows may be their spoil, and that they may make the fatherless their prey!" 10:1-2

It is sad to think there are people who sit in the quiet and calm of well-heated and air-conditioned offices and devise injustice and oppression. We often think about the criminals who take the direct and warm-blooded approach and attack their victims face-to-face. These crimes are frightening, but there is a singular coldness to those criminals who sit at a distance and never see the faces of their victims. Woe indeed will be theirs in the Day of Judgement when they discover that God has seen all of those things and in His court no evidence can be disallowed - the truth will come to light for all to see.

C.S. Lewis wrote a book called *The Screwtape Letters* which is a series of fictional letters from Screwtape, an undersecretary in a department of Hell, to his nephew, Wormwood, a junior tempter assigned to the demise of a particular individual on earth. Lewis was often asked why he chose the metaphor of a bureaucracy for his picture of Hell. He answered that he did not feel that the worst evils were done in the "sordid dens of crime" that Dickens wrote about or even in concentration camps. There we see the final result. The orders to do such things were given in clean, well-lighted offices where nobody had to raise their voice, by people with white collars and cut fingernails and smooth-shaven faces. The cold-blooded nature of the scene matched well as a backdrop for Hell.

Just because there is not random violence in the streets does not mean a society is just. Legal oppression is still oppression and the judge is coming who "... shall not judge by what his eyes see, or decide by what his ears hear; but with righteousness he shall judge the poor, and decide with equity for the meek of the earth; ..." 11:3  Isaiah brought a message of redemption and salvation, but he did not confuse that with a suspension of justice. The Messiah was coming both to redeem *and* judge. If we are to be true to our Lord, the Church's message must be the same today.

# Day 218
# Isaiah 14-16

saiah had judgements to pronounce on more than just the nation of Israel. The common wisdom of his time was that when two nations fought, the nation which won had the stronger god. But the testimony of Isaiah's prophecies was that there was but one God, and that even in defeat, Israel's God was the one at work. The other nations were as much at His disposal as any, and after He used them to bring judgement upon Israel, He would in turn judge them.

This was a radical thought for Isaiah's time. Nonetheless, Isaiah pronounces judgement against the very nations that served as God's tool to discipline Israel. One of the most striking is the judgement against Babylon.

Babylon was one of the most impressive cities ever built. Its city walls were ninety feet thick and three hundred feet tall with towers rising much higher than that. The length of the walls was about fourteen miles on each side and a river flowed through the city providing a constant water supply. There was enough land within the city walls to raise enough food to live on. The city was siege-proof, but it was defeated in one day.

Jeremiah would also prophecy against Babylon and together, Isaiah and Jeremiah, pronounced seven judgements against Babylon. First, that it would be destroyed, second, that it would never be reinhabited, third, that the Arabs would not pitch their tents there, fourth, that there would be no sheepfolds there, fifth, that wild beasts would occupy the ruins, sixth, that the stones would not be taken away for other buildings, and seventh, that men would not pass by the ruins.

Babylon was defeated and destroyed in 538 B.C. and it has never been rebuilt. Although you can hire a guide to take you there, the Arabs will not stay the night and refuse to pitch their tents on the site. In spite of the fact that most other ancient cities had their stones reused, the rocks imported for Babylon at great cost have never been moved. There are no sheepfolds around Babylon and only wild beasts inhabit the ruins. Although most ancient cities are on prominent tourist routes, Babylon is not and it has very few visitors.

There is but one Lord, and He is God.

# Day 219
# Isaiah 17-20

he office of prophet was never an easy one to fill. Aside from the fact that you frequently had to be the bearer of unwelcome news there were those occasional "living parables" like going three years "naked and barefoot" to show what God was going to do to somebody else. If I were Isaiah I think I might have been tempted to ask God to consider saying it with a nice I'm-going-to-smash-you-flat bouquet from FTD instead.

There is another, almost cryptic reference in these chapters that should not go unnoticed. In chapter nineteen Isaiah prophesies that there will be a final deliverance for Egypt and Assyria. "In that day Israel will be the third with Egypt and Assyria, a blessing in the midst of the earth, whom the LORD of hosts has blessed, saying, 'Blessed be Egypt my people, and Assyria the work of my hands, and Israel my heritage.'" 19:24 We saw it ourselves earlier, but it has not often been emphasized that the other nations of the world also belong to God, and Israel was chosen to communicate with them, to be a priestly people, not a nation of favored sons.

It is perhaps one of the greatest temptations for prophets and priests, to begin to think more highly of themselves than they ought. The struggles it takes to try to know God, and to make oneself available and to be obedient, can easily begin to build up in one's mind the subtle idea that you are in fact better than those godless pagans who care nothing for God or His laws. How easy it is to forget the multitude of blessings which have come to you when you have been called to some kind of ministry - the numbers of wonderful loving people who contribute and the small amount of gratitude we show to them or the Lord. The fact is that many of those "godless pagans" might very well do a much better job than we do had they been given the same advantages. There but by the grace of God, go I.

Perhaps that is why, occasionally, God calls His prophets to such unusual extremes. Israel was not loved more than the other nations, but they were privileged to be given so important a role. As Christians, we are not loved more by God, Jesus died for us all, but we are privileged to be given such an important message for the world. Let's be glad we can deliver it with our clothes on!

# Day 220
# Isaiah 21-23

t is difficult for us to appreciate fully what a change in perspective Isaiah's prophecies represented in his own time. The idea that there were many gods was almost universally accepted, and each god held sway only within certain bounds. As nations and peoples fought, the struggle between the gods of one or the other, went along with the battle. When a nation conquered, they had proven not only that they were mightier, but that their god was too.

This was true even within the religious life of Israel. While God had been revealing Himself consistently as being the only God, this chosen nation had consistently missed the claim and understood themselves in much the same kind of "household" relationship with Yahweh as the other nations had with their gods. This is also one of the reasons that the kings of Israel and Judah so often turned and sacrificed to other "gods." They had not received the responses from Yahweh they wanted and therefore, they were pragmatically turning to the gods they thought would produce the desired results.

Against this, Isaiah's prophecies claim to be authoritative over all the nations because there are no other gods - only Yahweh alone. He exercised judgement and mercy to all as He saw fit. There are no "household" gods that vie for power for their followers. There is but one God who holds claim and title to all our lives.

This may seem like a far-off message for a long forgotten time, but I think it is closer to home than we might like to admit. The other nations claimed the right to worship their own gods in their own ways and Israel was willing to allow them that freedom - whatever worked for them. We are very willing to let people today worship their own way and say it's okay, whatever works for them. The trouble is that there is only one God, and it is not okay with God not to worship Him.

It is certainly a God-given right to worship as we see fit, but worshipping a god who isn't there is not okay - it's disastrous. As Christians our message has never been "believe in Jesus *if* it works for you," but believe in Jesus because nothing else *can* work for you. Anything less makes Jesus just another household god.

# Day 221
# Isaiah 24-27

ne of the difficulties about interpreting prophecy is that you can never be sure of your interpretation until the event is over with. Prophecy has 20/20 hindsight, but the view it gives of the future is difficult to ascertain. There may be different ways to interpret prophecy, but only one way in which it comes true.

In chapter twenty-four, Isaiah appears to be giving a vision of the final destruction of the whole earth - an apocalyptic vision. That is at least how it has often been interpreted. It is hard to say definitively since the world hasn't ended yet, but the belief the earth will end some day is an ancient one. If we cannot be certain, and we cannot do anything about it, what good are such visions of the end?

I suppose for those living at the time, it may be a comfort to know that it was expected. There is a value to knowing the inevitable. Ignorance may be bliss, but only for as long as ignorance lasts. In the day when the knowledge cannot be avoided, it may be quite a bit of help to know that God is still in control. Quite frankly, I hope I'm not around to find out.

Closer to home, I think there *is* a value in knowing that things will not go on like this forever. For all the beauty of this world, there is also great ugliness. The pains and sufferings of this life were not part of the original plan of God, and while they are worth enduring in order that we might be born and know Him, there is still a longing for the suffering to come to an end. The tears of the parents whose children have been killed water the flower of hope that there will be an end. The weariness of those whose whole lives are spent in toil to earn just enough to survive, groans for the day of relief when the work will be through. The aches of those who have never known a day of life without illness and pain, throb for the time when suffering will cease. It is good to know that that day will arrive.

It is even better to know that when that day comes, it will not only be an end, but a new beginning. The destruction is not the final word, but merely the means to put an end to that which could not and should not go on. A clean slate, a new canvas, fresh lumber, all new material for a new creation is the promise. When you think of it that way, it is not a bad idea at all!

# Day 222
# Isaiah 28-30

saiah's message to the ten tribes of Israel, who were about to be carried off by the Assyrians never to be heard from again, was that they had played God for the fool too long. They had done as they pleased, gone after other gods, and thought Yahweh was too weak or too foolish to do anything about it. They had been weighed in the balance and found wanting - judgement day had arrived.

It is certainly a sad fall from grace which Israel experienced. God had intended to make them a model nation, a nation for whom God was the King and government was by His law. They were to rest once every seven days, one year every seven years, two years every fifty years, to have "free enterprise" and yet every fifty years redistribute the wealth so that poverty would not become endemic, and in all these things God would prosper them above the nations that they might be an example of His love. God also, at the covenant at Sinai, had warned them of the kind of example He would make of them if they did not obey the covenant, an example of the wrath of a righteous God.

Moses had saved them from that fate as had Joshua, but the nation would not respond. The God who had prevented Abraham from sacrificing Isaac on the mountain to put an end forever to the sacrifice of Molech (sacrificing children) had to watch as even the Kings of Israel and Judah sacrificed their own children to a bloodthirsty god who did not even exist.

"Because this people draw near with their mouth and honor me with their lips, while their hearts are far from me, and their fear of me is a commandment of men learned by rote; therefore, behold, I will again do marvelous things with this people, wonderful and marvelous; and the wisdom of their wise men shall perish, and the discernment of their discerning men shall be hid." 29:13,14  The marvelous thing He would do was not to restore their nation, but to bring out of the rubble of a shattered covenant promise, a remnant people who worshipped Him not in a temple but in their hearts.

That lessons stands for us today. God does not care how many times you have gone *in* to church, but how much you have taken church *out* with you. Let us not make Israel's mistake. God is not fooled - He measures our hearts.

# Day 223
# Isaiah 31-34

The people of Israel were faced with a rapidly deteriorating political situation. Assyria in the north was threatening at their borders. They looked around for help. Judah, their brothers, were neither in a position nor of a disposition to help them. They decided to turn to Egypt for help and were condemned for doing so. If God does work through human agency, through other nations, why not through Egypt to deliver Israel?

That answer is, as it so often is, that it was not so much what they did as the way they did it. They did not turn to God to ask for protection, but instead relied on their own reasoning and political manipulations. It is very possible that God would have chosen to use Egypt to deliver Israel from the Assyrians. Or perhaps, as in the times of Gideon, He would have done so in much more dramatic fashion. We will never know, however, for they did not turn to God, thereby receiving God's judgement rather than His deliverance.

This seems like a foolish thing to do, and quite separated from our daily lives here in the twentieth century, but you can almost treat the historical Israel as an allegory for the servants of God in our world - us. How often have we failed to turn to God to ask for guidance or deliverance and instead relied on our own clever ideas and the Egypts of our lives? God does not want us to be independent of Him, or utterly dependent upon Him ("Lord, should I have cream of wheat or toast this morning?") but in trusting relationship. The key to maturing in relationship with God is to do the things which we know we can do, and turn the other things over to God, trusting that He will guide and provide for us. Too often we know what to do and don't want to do it, and we want to try to control in the future what is beyond our control.

What fears assail you today? What Assyria is on your borders making you afraid of tomorrow? What Egypts are there looking like a chance to handle things yourself? Have you honestly asked for God's help? Are you feeling guilty because you have not turned to God? Repent and trust. What you fear is as much in God's control as anything else. Instead of something that paralyzes, it can become something that deepens your relationship with the God who loves you.

# Day 224
# Isaiah 35-37

There is an old song by Jim Croce whose chorus goes like this: "You don't tug on Superman's cape, You don't spit into the wind, You don't pull the mask off the old Lone Ranger, and You don't mess around with Jim." Sennacherib could not have heard that song and heeded its advice, but I am sure there must have been some kind of Assyrian equivalent. The point is that you had better not mess with powers greater than yourself.

Sennacherib made the mistake of thinking that because he had defeated Israel in the north, the God of the Jews was weak and ineffectual. He did not make that mistake again. Isaiah had good news to report to King Hezekiah for a change. This man who had defeated Israel had also mocked God and God would defend His own honor this time.

Some people read this account and almost cheer. Certainly Hezekiah and the people of Judah must have shouted for joy. There is a sense in which we want the hero to defend himself and win the battle against evil. There are also those who find this kind of history to be questionable. Patriots always feel that God is on their side, while others think the idea that God would chose any side is ridiculous. The Prophets were always seeing everything from a religious angle and interpreting whatever happened to them as either a blessing from God or a punishment from God. Does everything always have to be about God?

Yes! We so often loose sight of this rather obvious fact because we are such proud creatures. The clear testimony of these Scriptures we have been reading is that this is God's story - He initiated it, He participates in it, He maintains it, and He will draw it to a final conclusion before He goes on to the next thing. God is God. He is the God of the Jews, the God of the Assyrians, the God of the Russians, the God of the United States, and everyone else throughout time. We do not always acknowledge the fact, but that does not alter it in the least.

We are not God. Our value and meaning are relative to Him. We may be part of His divine happiness (where we will find our true selves) or try to pretend He is not there, but in the final analysis, He is the main character and we are supporting cast. How is your part doing?

# Day 225
# Isaiah 38-41

ezekiah was a study in contrasts. He brought about the reforms which were so badly needed, but he lacked the ability to see them through all the way. When envoys came from Babylon, he revealed all he had to them; he not only tipped his hand, he turned over every card. When Isaiah pronounced God's judgement upon Hezekiah (which was more than a prophecy, it was obvious that nothing could be hidden anymore), Hezekiah's response was: "At least it won't be during my administration!"

When the prophecy came that Hezekiah would die, he besought God to change His mind, and God granted him fifteen more years. Yet, when doom for the kingdom was pronounced, he made no effort to make a similar plea for his people. He made two profound mistakes from which we should learn.

His first mistake was his blatant self-interest. When his life was to be affected he brought every energy to bear on the problem. When it came to things that future generations would have to face, he made no move but took comfort in the fact that he would not have to be there. This may seem unusual, but in America during the 1980's there was a lot of this same philosophy around. Sometimes it was motivated by fear ("The world is going to blow up anyway") and sometimes by sheer greed ("All I care about is getting *my* BMW"), but in either case there was a disregard for the duties of today that pertain to our tomorrows. Tomorrow has arrived, and those of us in it have few kind thoughts about those who did so little to prepare for it.

Hezekiah's second mistake was in seeing such a small God. We often look at the magnitude of the difficulties we face and find despair to be the only reasonable response. For Hezekiah, the power of the rising Babylonian empire was impossible to ignore. The prophecy that they would conquer Judah was not surprising but rather to be expected. But he was looking in the wrong direction. What is significant is not the immensity of the problem, but the vastness of the One who holds the solution. Who knows what might have happened if Hezekiah had sought God's favor for the nation with the same fervor he did for his own life. He did not, and we will never know. The challenge is the same for us. Will we make the same mistakes? I pray we do not.

# Day 226
# Isaiah 42-44

The servant of the Lord. This was a new development in salvation history. Israel was to have been a priestly nation, but the role of priest and the role of servant, while similar, have some significant differences. God had turned a new page in salvation history and the way in which He would communicate with people. Israel had proven to be ineffective in taking the message of the covenant to the world (or even keeping it themselves) and God was giving the job to someone new - His servant.

We will be reading more in the days ahead about the nature and mission of the servant of the Lord, but we should not miss the crucial changes announced in these chapters.

The servant of the Lord was to have a mission very similar to that of Israel. God's love and justice were to be proclaimed to all people, but the message was to be delivered in a distinctly different manner. Israel was to have been the showcase people, a nation whose very existence declared the graciousness of God. The servant of the Lord would be going forth to *all* the nations: "I have put my Spirit upon him, he will bring forth justice to the nations." 42:1 No more confusion about one nation being favored; God's justice is for all people, regardless of nationality.

Not only would the servant of the Lord be taking his message to all peoples, he would be doing so with tenderness and mercy. Many have wondered, throughout the centuries, why God does not establish His justice in the world through force. That is clearly not the mission of the servant of the Lord. "... a bruised reed he will not break, and a dimly burning wick he will not quench ..." 42:3 We must remember the nature of the message of the covenant - God graciously loves and forgives us. That is not a message which is carried well in the fist of an iron glove. God never intended to have Israel rule the rest of the world. The servant of the Lord was not being sent to dictate obedience through force, but to bring the message that Israel had failed to deliver - salvation by grace.

God's justice would still have to be fulfilled, and the role of the servant of the Lord would be different here, too. But justice and love together for all people would be the message of the servant of the Lord. It still is today.

# Day 227
# Isaiah 45-48

hapter forty-five reminds me a great deal of the parts of the book of Job where God is speaking. God is normally a person of action and not dialogue, but when He speaks, we should all be listening. These prophecies of Isaiah speak of great movements of salvation that span the centuries and the great purposes of God which reach across all creation.

There are many things about God that are difficult to comprehend. Aside from those issues of His being and nature, it is difficult to understand His patience with people. Why did He choose to send the message of salvation through Israel? Why did He endure their unfaithfulness for so many centuries? Why does He allow so many evil things to happen before He acts? The answers to these questions allude us still.

But, "Woe to him who strives with his Maker, an earthen vessel with the potter! Does the clay say to him who fashions it, 'What are you making?' or 'Your work has no handles'?" 45:9 I do not think this means that we should not ask such questions, but that we must not demand answers - at least as we might expect them. In a college art class I had the opportunity to make some pottery. As I worked, a friend came by and said, "Your pitcher hasn't got a handle." I replied, "That's because its not a pitcher!" I understood their confusion (I'm no artist!), but when you don't know what is being made, you should be careful about criticizing the work. I am not sure we fully grasp what God has begun with this creation of which we find ourselves a part, but I would not at all be surprised to discover finally that creation is much more than we expect - and well worth all the effort that has gone into it.

One thing is certain about this message of salvation - it is meant for all people. Israel was told so, but quickly forgot. Isaiah repeated the charge with greater clarity: "'Turn to me and be saved, all the ends of the earth! For I am God, and there is no other.'" 45:22 I don't know why God has chosen to communicate this message through people like you and me, but I know that He has done so. As the hymn goes, "We've a story to tell to the Nations..." and while we might think we're the wrong pots for the job, God does not. (Sorry about mixing my metaphors!) Perhaps we should have more confidence in His choice - He does!

# Day 228
# Isaiah 49-51

n the day of trouble it is good to be reminded of the help of the Lord. As Judah faced the Babylonian captivity, it must have been comforting for them to be told that God had not given up on them entirely. They would not be carried off because God was unable to help them, but rather as a result of their own sins. They would also be delivered, not because of their righteousness, but because God had promised to do so.

It is sad that so often we do not find out that God can be trusted until we have come to that day of trouble; sadder still that even then, some never learn this. "'I, I am he that comforts you; who are you that you are afraid of man who dies, and the son of man who is made like grass and have forgotten the LORD, your Maker, who stretched out the heavens and laid the foundations of the earth ...'" 51:12,13 This is, of course, a rhetorical question. God knows very well who we are, that we fear people, their opinions and actions. Faith is difficult for us because we cannot control what happens to us after death, and not all that much before then either. We must wait (patiently or impatiently) for the help of another. What makes the difference between those who wait with patience and those who do not?

Have we forgotten the past? The answer is yes! We are people who are usually so wrapped up in what is happening today that we find it difficult to remember what happened in the past. "What have you done for me lately?" is the question we most often ask of God. Israel had forgotten what God had done with Abraham and the other patriarchs, with Moses and the people delivered by the ten plagues out of Egypt, with Gideon and the other judges, with David and the kings; all yesterday's news. "What have you done for me lately?"

This is why God established one day a week to be a day of rest and remembrance. The Sabbath is the day that we are to remember the great acts of God and not all of those are ancient history. What has God done in your life? How many times has He saved you on the freeway, the fall in the yard, the slip in the tub, the incident with the power lines? How many times must He deliver us before we will "never forget"? Let us take the time to look back, remember, and be comforted.

# Day 229
# Isaiah 52-55

The role of Israel and the role of the servant of the Lord were similar, but also different. Israel, the showcase people, were to have proclaimed the gracious covenant nature of God, but they had nothing to do with atoning for the sins of people. The servant of the Lord was to proclaim the love and forgiveness of God, but more than that, he would proclaim *and* fulfill the justice of God.

These prophecies of Isaiah about the suffering servant had to be among the most difficult for the Jews to understand. How beautiful they are to us because we know of their fulfillment. How mysterious to them because they are such a change in the message of salvation history.

The sacrificial system described back in Leviticus was to have proclaimed God's graciousness - substitutionary atonement. But the sacrifices had to be repeated, and they did nothing to balance the scale, only to proclaim forgiveness. A sacrifice had to be made, and it had to be one that would fulfill the law.

This is one of the reasons the Church has always taught the idea of "progressive revelation." God has continued to bring a greater clarity of His nature and purpose throughout the centuries. Even for Isaiah, the proclamation of a savior was a repeat of the promise given in Genesis chapter three, but a much clearer picture. When we see Jesus in the New Testament, we will see that picture come into even sharper focus, and then these prophecies of Isaiah will reflect an astounding accuracy.

Why did there have to be such a sacrifice? There are several theories about the nature of the atonement, but we must not forget the cost of sin and the need for justice. Many have felt that God should just forgive us of our sins, as if they were not really that bad. Most of the people who feel that way have never had their child kidnapped or held the hand of a person who has been tortured. There are sins in this world for which even we can see justice must demand retribution. Nothing will undo the pain, but doing nothing will not suffice. God knows that, and He sent His servant to pay the price for our sins.

God's graciousness and love go hand in hand with His justice. The servant of the Lord came to proclaim them both. As his representatives, we should not shy away from the same task.

# Day 230
# Isaiah 56-58

Chapters fifty-six through fifty-eight repeat the proclamations of salvation to all people and judgement against the wicked. We should remember that these prophecies were not necessarily given one right after the other as we read them here. There may well have been considerable time between them. They also bear a message that would not have been welcomed readily by the people who received them.

Still, it is important for us to see how clearly the message of the New Testament is contained in the Old Testament. Jesus quoted from Isaiah many times. He came to fulfill the law and the prophets and we can see ourselves how well his ministry did just that. "Thus says the Lord God, who gathers the outcasts of Israel, I will gather yet others to him besides those already gathered." 56:8 There is but one God and the testimony of His purpose is consistent throughout all of His revelation - His salvation is intended for all.

Perhaps I have emphasized this point too often, but the impression that the God of the Old Testament is different from the God of the New Testament is wide spread - and false. That was one of my announced biases from the beginning of this study, that you might see for yourself the testimony of God's gracious covenant love from Genesis to Revelation. We are more than half way through and it is here for us again, in clearer form than before and we must not miss it.

Isaiah also makes it more explicit that the wicked will not prosper. Not only will the day of judgement come, but even in this life there will be no peace for them. "'But the wicked are like the tossing sea; for it cannot rest, and its waters toss up mire and dirt. This is no peace, says my God, for the wicked.'" 57:20,21 When we cut ourselves off from God we establish ourselves as the highest authority in our life. The problem with this is that we know just how unreliable we really are. If we are the best the world has to offer, then we know we must always be on our guard, for we know that we ourselves are not to be trusted.

God offers salvation and peace to all who would accept it. Those who reject the former will find out that they cannot get the latter.

Check Here
When Read
❏

# Day 231
# Isaiah 59-62

The sixty-first chapter of Isaiah is a special one. The first two verses are quoted by Jesus to describe his ministry. "The Spirit of the Lord God is upon me, because the LORD has anointed me to bring good tidings to the afflicted; he has set me to bind up the brokenhearted, to proclaim liberty to the captives, and the opening of the prison to those who are bound; to proclaim the year of the LORD'S favor..." 61:1,2

"The Spirit of the Lord God is upon me..." One of Isaiah's major contributions to Old Testament theology was the increased understanding of the role of God's Spirit in His plan of salvation. While the idea of the Trinity does not become clear until the New Testament, we begin to see more glimpses of it here. This work of salvation is always God's, no matter what other means He chooses to use.

The word "afflicted" that is used can also be translated (as it is in Luke when Jesus quoted it) "poor." "Good tidings" may seem an unlikely thing to give to the poor, but it is not. Many people who have been poor will testify that having few material possessions is not what is oppressive about poverty; it is the lack of hope for the future. To know that you will not always be poor, to know that there is more to life than just what we experience now, that is the hope that we all need. We betray our own short sightedness when we think of the "poor" or "afflicted" as only those physically poor. The poor in spirit are destitute no matter how expensive their houses may be.

Jesus said "to proclaim the year of the LORD'S favor" was fulfilled in the hearing of the people to which he read it. Jesus' life, death, and resurrection have ushered in the favor of the Lord in a greater way than ever before. It is interesting to note, though, that Jesus did not quote the entire second verse: "...and the day of vengeance of our God; to comfort all who mourn;..." Jesus promised that he would return. The work of the servant of the Lord is not over. God's love and forgiveness have been the first order of business, but God's justice must still come to pass. The makers of misery who reject the forgiveness of God cannot be allowed to continue forever. Salvation has come, but it is not over yet. Some of Isaiah's prophecies have yet to be fulfilled!

# Day 232
# Isaiah 63-66

ope is one of the seven cardinal virtues. Paul writes
in I Corinthians that it is one of just three things that
remain. Psychologists say that it is the first virtue we
have as infants; the capacity to look out at an
inexplicable world and expect somehow to have it
make some kind of sense. We hope even before we have faith.

Isaiah announced the hope that God's plan extends past this
creation into a new one. "'For behold, I create new heavens and a
new earth; and the former things shall not be remembered or come
into mind.'" 65:17

Some people feel little need for this hope. I am not among
those. I think I have longed for a better world since I was very
young. There are disappointments and sorrows which come even
to those privileged to grow up in a loving family. The pain and
suffering of others only added to the sense that things should not
be this way. My longing for a better world has only increased
since I became a father. Watching the network news is almost
more than I can take. It does not take much for me to imagine the
pain I would be feeling if it were my son or daughter killed by the
drunk driver, or starving in a refugee camp, or dying of an
incurable disease. They are no longer merely someone else's
children, they are mine too; perhaps more distantly related, but I
now know what all parents know, no matter how old they get, they
are still someone's little boy or girl - our little boy or girl.

"'No more shall there be in it an infant that lives but a few
days, or an old man who does not fill out his days...'" 65:20
Death, disease, violence, bigotry, tyranny, are not challenges that
make life better for giving us something to overcome. They are
great evils injected into a beautiful creation; enemies of the
loving, creative, majestic God who made our world. For those
enemies to finally be defeated, for those evils to be completely
removed from existence, is a hope almost too wonderful for
words. I long for the day when I never again have to sit with a
mother whose son was killed in a war, or a father whose
daughter's life was destroyed by drugs, or a son whose parents
died in a hospital room a thousand miles away. If that is "pie in
the sky," then slice me the biggest piece you can. "They shall not
hurt or destroy in all my holy mountain, says the LORD." Amen.

# Day 233
# Jeremiah 1-3

eremiah is the most personal of the major prophets. We will get to know him as a person more than any of the other prophets because we will read more about his own story. It is a sad one most of the time. He had to bring not only a message of doom, but he had to deliver it in competition with false prophets contending for the attention of the king. Worse yet, the false prophets, like Hananiah, were not evil in their intent - they were quite sincere, but sincerely wrong.

Jeremiah also shows us a more personal side to God. We so often feel that what we do is of very little importance one way or the other. Most of us probably think we make little difference, either for good or bad. Jeremiah reminds us that this is not so. God is a person, and very personal. We are His creatures, made in His image, and He is aware of and cares what we do and what we think and what we feel. Our joys and our sorrows, the love we spread and the injury we inflict are felt by God each step of the way. Jeremiah wrote that God felt toward Israel as a man does whose wife has committed adultery; not just with one man, but with anyone who would come along. The metaphor is a very intimate one and we are to understand that God's relationship with us is just that intimate.

We seem to have lost this sense of the intimate presence of God in our lives. In America, this understanding was abused by the Puritans in the early days of our country, to make people feel guilt ridden. Quite understandably, most people finally rejected this idea of a frowning, stern, and angry God looking over their shoulders and probing all their thoughts. But we have thrown out the baby with the bath water. In pushing God away for fear of His judgement, we have also lost touch with the intimate lover of our souls who cares more for our feelings of inadequacy than for all the stars in the Milky Way.

Let us hear this message of Jeremiah to us. God cares very deeply about our love and loyalty. It makes a difference to Him whether or not we love Him and show our gratitude. He misses our worship when we do not give it, He is disappointed when we don't ask Him for His help, and He is crushed, as any lover would be when we give the love He deserves to some dumb idol of money, power, or fame. Tell Him you love Him. He deserves it.

# Day 234
# Jeremiah 4-6

here is an eerie ring of familiarity in chapter five. The streets were searched again as they had been in the day of Sodom and Gomorrah's destruction only this time it was Jerusalem's streets. And again, there was not found any for whose sake the rest could be pardoned.

"They have made their faces harder than rock; they have refused to repent." 5:3 This is a chilling thought, that people can be so hard that they refuse to repent in the face of such clear guilt. It is a frightening capacity that we human beings have to be able to shut ourselves off from reality and refuse to repent. We should not miss the lesson that even God cannot convince some people of their sins. Some are totally lost, and nothing will bring them to their senses that they might repent and be saved.

Malachi Martin wrote an historical novel about the life of David called *King of Kings*. In it, he has the character Raham telling David a very important truth. "Raham continued, 'Remember never to hesitate to say you were wrong. Always be able to say you've erred, you've sinned, you need forgiveness. Always. It is not so much sin but obduracy in sin that angers Adonai.'" I had to look up the word obduracy but I found it to be most appropriate for the subject. Obduracy comes from the latin obduratus meaning, "to harden." It is the hardness of our hearts, our unwillingness to say we are wrong, to ask forgiveness, that cuts us off from God much more than the specific sin itself. God has never (since the fall) expected us to be perfect. Nevertheless, if we will not repent, if we will not turn around and agree that we are wrong, there is no way we can receive the help we need. It is the hardness of heart that turns disobedience into the cold rock hard face of intractable rebellion.

The journey of a thousand miles begins with the first step. That journey can be for ill as well as for good. Judah had begun to harden its heart a long time back and finally there was no turning around. Judgement Day, whatever else it may be, will turn out to be not so much a case of God rejecting people, but people rejecting God. No offer of forgiveness, no sacrifice, however large, will soften the obdurate person resolved to have his own way. Let us soften our hearts that our journey might not take us past the point of no return.

# Day 235
# Jeremiah 7-10

God measures the heart. I know this is a theme I mention often, but it is one of the most critical in the Scriptures, and especially critical to see in the Old Testament. Too many people have the belief that the Old Testament is a story of God's legalism and the New Testament a story of His graciousness. We have seen for ourselves that this is not so.

Jeremiah mentions this several times early in his book. The mark of the people of God, from the time of Abraham, was the sign of circumcision. This mark was to set them apart physically from the other nations. But circumcision and the temple too had become merely religious symbols. God accuses the people of having maintained the *form* of religion without its meaning, and that was (is) simply not good enough. "Behold, the days are coming, says the LORD, when I will punish those who are circumcised but yet uncircumcised ... for all these nations are uncircumcised, and all the house of Israel is uncircumcised in heart." 9:25,26 It is not what we do externally that counts, but what is going on in our hearts.

That does not mean that what we do, doesn't matter. "'Behold, you trust in deceptive words to no avail. Will you steal, murder, commit adultery, swear falsely, burn incense to Baal, and go after other gods that you have not known, and then come and stand before me in this house, which is called by my name, and say, "We are delivered!" - only to go on doing all these abominations?'" 7:8-11 Faith is not something we only feel inside ourselves, it is the basis for our decisions and actions. What we believe and what we do are a unity not a dichotomy. If we steal, it is because we are at heart, a thief. When we are no longer a thief at heart, we will stop stealing. But if we steal and then come to church and tithe, whoever else we may fool, it will not be God.

We need to stop playing religious games with God. He is far too smart to be fooled by them anyway. God calls us to have right hearts and right actions. Without both we play a dangerous game of believing that God is either too busy or to stupid to notice the hollow nature of our ceremonies. We must take the principles of justice and love into our hearts and out to our world or we will have accomplished nothing on our Sunday mornings.

# Day 236
# Jeremiah 11-13

I t has never been easy being a prophet. Aside from the fact that it is hard to get people to believe you, there are those who openly oppose you. The men of Anathoth sought to silence Jeremiah, and if necessary, they were ready to do so by killing him. Religious disagreements have always been (and I suppose always will be) the most bitter. More blood has been shed in the name of religion than any other cause.

But true prophets are not stopped by threats. There is something within them that they fear more than men - being unfaithful to their call from God. That does make them a scary breed because along with true prophets, some false prophets share that conviction. Knowing the true from the false prophets can therefore be tricky because zeal and persecution are not certain indicators of anything other than zeal and persecution.

How do we tell the true from the false? Ultimately, God vindicates His prophets - their prophecies come true. Still, that is often little consolation. Jeremiah loved God and he also loved Israel. He was not happy to have to pronounce doom and found little consolation that his prophecies came true.

One of the other things prophets have in common is the curse of Cassandra. Cassandra was the daughter of King Priam. Apollo had fallen in love with her and conferred on her the gift of prophecy in exchange for her promise to lie with him. When Cassandra went back on her promise, Apollo added to his gift a curse, that her prophecies would never be believed. She lived in a city called Troy, and foretold that Paris' voyage to Sparta would bring doom upon his household, but was ignored. Ten years later, as the Trojan horse was being wheeled into the city, she again tried to warn everyone, but of course, no one would believe her. Even in ancient mythology, the prophets faired poorly. Karl Menninger's book, *Whatever Became of Sin?*, opens with this quote: "A Brief and Biased Review of Moral History: They *hang* prophets, or ignore them, which hurts worse."

So how do we tell the true prophets from the false? That is not something that can be answered in such a short space - if at all. Perhaps the best lesson is that God does send them, and we should be careful about ignoring them all.

# Day 237
# Jeremiah 14-17

"The heart is deceitful above all things, and desperately corrupt; who can understand it?" 17:9 This verse should be posted above the door of every minister's office. It should be footnoted that it applies to the person in the office and everyone reading the sign. It is not cynical, it is simply the truth.

It would not have been true without the fall, but since the fall, it is not wise to trust any person one hundred percent - including yourself. Only God is worthy of our complete trust. Everyone else should be granted only conditional status. If that sounds too harsh, look again at your own motives and ask yourself if they are always pure. Mixed motives are a part of being human after Adam and Eve. We cannot rid ourselves of them, and after a certain point, we cannot be certain we have identified them properly.

I have spoken many times with those sensitive young people who are locked into the search for pure motives. Duplicity is an affront to idealism and youth is a time of idealism. It is a difficult lesson for them to learn that those whom they admire and trust are not the paragons of virtue they had thought. It is still more difficult for them to learn that lesson about themselves. Many have been lost to cynicism or suicide because they could not deal with the deceitfulness of the human heart. But, forewarned is forearmed. If we know to be careful, we can risk being involved with deceitful people - even ourselves.

We must learn that it is unfair to expect that another person will never let you down. They are not God and have flaws that even they can do little about. We must never hand over to another individual, the responsibility for our lives. God has given us that stewardship and we cannot divest ourselves of it no matter how hard we might try.

Then we must learn to accept things which are "mostly" good - especially ourselves. We may not be one hundred percent trustworthy, but neither are we one hundred percent untrustworthy. Let us remember that grace, not law, is the rule in God's kingdom. We must extend grace to others and ourselves, even as God has done so. If God can love us with less than pure hearts, we must learn to do likewise. Just be careful as you do!

# Day 238
# Jeremiah 18-20

There are a fair number of people who understand the doctrine of predestination to mean that people have no free will at all. For them, God is completely sovereign and He chose, even before He created, whom He would save and whom He would condemn. They often quote the example from the psalms where God refers to Himself as the potter and Israel as the clay, and asks the question whether the potter has the right to make the clay anything he wants. Some vessels are made for honor, and some for dishonor, but it is not a matter of justice one way or the other for the potter has the right to make the clay as he sees fit.

I do not subscribe to this interpretation of predestination. God was righteously outraged at Israel's sin. How could this be if He had fore ordained it Himself? God picked up the analogy of the potter again with Jeremiah and says that He can reshape the pot when it has gone bad. There is no suggestion that the potter had changed his mind, but rather that the clay had not done what he wanted, therefore, he was going to recast the entire piece. Whatever we understand of predestination, it should not lead us to the conclusion that we have no say or responsibility in our fate.

This was precisely the error Israel had made from the beginning. They had misunderstood the covenant to mean that God had chosen to bless them regardless of all else. But we have seen, that the covenant was neither based on works, nor did it bind God by promise to a relationship which was against His nature. Covenants do not bind us, they free us to keep our promises. God's promise to Israel would be fulfilled, but that could be (and was) fulfilled in a variety of ways; some much more pleasant than others.

We need to free ourselves on the one hand, from the silly notion that we can earn our relationship with God, and on the other, that grace means we are free to do anything we want without regard for the consequences. God has a plan for our lives - a plan in which we must choose to participate if it is to turn out right. He has more control than we do, but we have our part nonetheless. We can not earn His love, but we can certainly earn His wrath. We are both free and predestined. Living with both those truths is a necessary part of being in proper relationship with God.

# Day 239
# Jeremiah 21-24

 re they dead yet? How many days have we had to read about God's judgement against Judah? It seems like the promised punishment is as long to read about as it was to wait for in its time! Why didn't God hurry up and get it over with?

There does seem to be a rather "plodding" nature to God's purposes. He seems to be in no particular hurry to get things done. Perhaps that is because He has all time and eternity at His disposal, so He has no need to rush things. Or, perhaps it is because of His methodical nature which sees things through to all their logical consequences. Whatever the case, I know that we humans are constantly frustrated by the waiting that goes along with following God. We want instant results, and it seems to us that God wastes a lot of time waiting for people to do things when He could do them Himself much more directly and efficiently.

That might be the most important clue to an answer for our impatience. God could do all of these things directly Himself. Why should He wait for Nebuchadnezzar or us, to act? Why does He choose "human agency" to accomplish things in our world?

I am a computer enthusiast. My personal computer is capable of controlling musical instruments through its MIDI (Musical Instrument Digital Interface) channels. By connecting several synthesizers, I can have my computer play an entire orchestra's worth of instruments and program any song written. The music can even be "sampled" from live instruments and played back, matching their sound precisely. It is an amazing accomplishment to see and hear.

However, no matter how exact and complex, it is not anywhere near the amazing feat accomplished by any live orchestra, because the computer *has* to do what I program it to do. A live orchestra, with one hundred live musicians all playing together in rhythm and harmony, is a much greater feat, because they do not have to do so, but choose to do so. Not only that, but the music is better, richer, and deeper.

God could do anything we can do - and better. Instead, He has chosen not to play every instrument Himself, but to conduct. It is harder that way, but a challenge worthy of Him - and us. But, oh, it does take so much longer!

# Day 240
# Jeremiah 25-27

ebuchadnezzer was to be the instrument of God to judge many nations of his time, including Judah. Jeremiah brought that message to Jerusalem to warn them not to resist the judgement of God or it would be even worse. He also told them that Babylon itself would be judged after that. Babylon was not a favored nation, but an instrument of God's plan.

That raises some interesting questions about history. How often has God intervened in human history in just this way? That is a difficult question to answer, because it requires that we have access to information not available to us. The Scriptures are the history of salvation, and as such, tell us all we need to know to bring us to salvation, but they do not pretend to tell us all there is to know. The judgement against Canaan which Israel was to have carried out, and the judgement against the other nations in Jeremiah's time, infer that God has been more active in human affairs than what is recorded for us in the Bible. However, where the Bible is silent, our conclusions will be highly debatable.

One thing we must be clear about is that God has done nothing in history which would contradict His purpose for salvation history laid out in the Scriptures. He has not brought salvation to the Egyptians or the Chinese through works and offered grace only to the Jews. Whatever He has done in relation to other cultures, it must be consistent with the gracious love and justice so clearly recorded for us. He did not come to the Jews as Yahweh and to the Canaanites as Baal and to the Chinese as Buddha and to the Hindus as Krishna. The cruelty of Baal worship and the loss of individual identity of Buddism and Hinduism, are inconsistent with the love and purpose of Yahweh clearly revealed. God can work through all cultures and nations, but He cannot be inconsistent with Himself. He cannot be loving and gracious to some and bloodthirsty or non-existent to others.

I suppose that human history would read quite a bit differently if we could see God's volume. We may never know this side of heaven, what really happened in so many cases of nations and individuals. Still, we should be certain to hear the message of Jeremiah, not only to his time but our own; this is God's world, and things do not happen by accident.

# Day 241
# Jeremiah 28-31

The new covenant. We read about it in Isaiah and it is given more definition here in Jeremiah. In one sense, all the covenants are alike, they are gracious promises from God that we can depend on. Yet each covenant we have seen so far has had its unique elements. Why have several? Why not the last and simply skip the rest?

There has been a progression of the covenants throughout salvation history. They have served to bring into clearer focus that which was the intention of God from the beginning - a means by which fallen humanity could learn to trust the Creator again. Adam and Eve had failed the test in the garden when they believed God would withhold something good from them. Trusting God has been difficult ever since. He has tried to reveal in many different ways that He can be trusted with our lives, but, while this seems like a straight forward message, it is not an easy one to communicate.

To Adam and Eve, God revealed He would send a savior to do away with the evil in their world. To Abraham, He revealed that through him the nations would be blessed to know that God is loving and gracious, providing substitutionary atonement (the goat instead of Isaac). To Moses, He revealed that He is a God involved in human history, working for justice as well as mercy. To David, He revealed that He would establish a kingdom without end. Finally, to Isaiah and Jeremiah, He revealed that His salvation was not for nations, but individuals. It was a long time in coming into focus, but the promise of the Messiah had come into clear view. His temple would be the human heart.

Still, why wait so long to make it clear that salvation was for the individual? Perhaps we should recall that the value of the individual is a rather recent and western civilization concept based on centuries of Judeo-Christian thinking. As recently as this century, women and children were still considered the property of their fathers or husbands. That is still true in much of our world.

The new covenant is not new, it is the same graciousness as in the other covenants. But the new covenant is for each of us as individuals, and that understanding, on our part, is new. Nineteen centuries later, we are still struggling to grasp it all. Slow learners. Patient God.

# Day 242
# Jeremiah 32-34

Zedekiah was told by Jeremiah that the battle which was going on, would end in victory for Babylon, not Judah. This can not have been an easy message to deliver. It could not have been an easy message to receive. How are we to tell the truth when we know the truth we have to tell will not be welcomed? How are we to react when the truth we hear is not what we consider good news?

The record is silent in terms of *how* Jeremiah delivered this message to Zedekiah. It is obvious that most of the prophets could have benefitted by reading *How to Win Friends and Influence People*. Tact was not necessarily a prerequisite for being a prophet - courage and honesty were. Prophets do not usually have many friends and unhappily, they often do not influence people. But that is not always their purpose either.

God often sent prophets to announce judgement and told them to expect not to be believed. Why would He do so? Perhaps because it is more important than we realize, that the truth be told, whether or not it is believed. In the final analysis, it does not help someone to withhold the truth from them because you can find no nice way to tell it. But we should be very sure that we believe it is the truth, and we must be prepared to suffer the consequences for their not believing it when they hear it.

What about receiving news that is not welcome? Zedekiah offers only a negative example here. The news he received was not good, but it was not wholly bad either. Yet it does not appear that it motivated him to change. He made a covenant to release the slaves and live according to the law of God, and then broke that promise. He could not do anything to stop the victory of the Babylonians, but he could have done much to make the captivity better and the defeat less bitter. He chose to do neither, but went on without regard for the message of punishment.

It is always too soon to stop doing right. It is never too late to repent. It may not change the course of consequences that have been set in motion, but the future is not solely determined by the past, but by the past and the present put together. Failure can be transformed if we can learn from it and not repeat the mistakes. Like it or not, the truth cannot simply be ignored. It can be our teacher or our judge. It is our choice. (Choose teacher!)

# Day 243
# Jeremiah 35-38

The Rechabites make one wonder what causes some people to remain faithful in a world that is so faithless. In a time when the rest of society had given itself over to every carnal pleasure and the worship of many gods, how did the Rechabites keep themselves from strong drink and building houses just because the patriarch of the family commanded them to do so?

Obedience to tradition is not valued highly in our society today. Perhaps it is because we have become suspicious about the motives behind traditions. Perhaps is it because we have become so confident in our own ability to analyze things that we want to know the reasons before we agree to anything. Perhaps that is not all bad - or all good.

The Rechabites did not know why Jonadab had commanded them not to drink of strong drink, nor to build houses or have fields, but to dwell in tents. They were in Jerusalem because they did not really understand why they were to live nomadically, and when Nebuchadnezzar's armies started to threaten them, they did what seemed logical to them; they fled to the safety of the city. Had they known the reason for their nomadic existence, that God was going to destroy Jerusalem, they might have stayed out of the city. Obedience without understanding cannot guarantee safety. Ignorance is blissful only for a while.

On the other hand, their obedience did deliver them. Jeremiah was sent to test them, and to give them the word that they would be preserved because of their obedience. They had already been saved from the debilitating influences of the culture around them. Theirs was a character still intact. They knew the value of life (not merely the pursuit of pleasure) and the fellowship of a community of people who kept their word. The testimony of the parents to the children that there are laws which adults and children alike must obey, should not be underestimated. The faithfulness of one generation had been passed to the next because it was faithfulness of deed, not merely words.

When our children ask why we do certain things in church, we are sometimes embarrassed to admit to them we don't know. Perhaps we should consider that it is not so bad to tell them it is because we believe it is out of obedience to God!

# Day 244
# Jeremiah 39-41

eremiah must have been very frustrated that the people of Judah thought he was saying what was expedient - to go along with the superior force. Had they listened carefully, Jeremiah was saying that they should go along with the superior force, but that superior force was God, not the Chaldeans. God had proven many times that the side He is on is always the superior force. Jerusalem would not be delivered this time because it was God's decision not to do so. It was not lack of patriotism, but truthful prophecy that Jeremiah exhibited.

Betting on God looks like a good bet on paper, but it is a hard one to place in real life. Obviously, when we know that God has willed a thing, betting against it happening is as foolish as betting against water running downhill or the sun rising in the east. Yet we find it hard to do when it comes to less obvious "tests" of our faith.

God wants us, it is His will for us, to be honest in our dealings with others, especially in business. To bet that God will bless us if we are honest, to expect Him to be unhappy with us when we are dishonest, are both more than reasonable. Yet, how often do we give in to the temptation to do what is "expedient." A friend in the insurance industry moved to another state and had to restart her business. In the new state, she discovered that the "standard" practice to help clients get lower rates, was to "reclassify" the vehicles as casual or occasional use rather than as primary or work vehicles. "Everybody" was doing it, and if you didn't, you might not get many clients. They would simply go to an agent who would write up the coverage "more favorably."

The day of decision arrived for her when her first client asked about using this "method" to reduce his rates. Her answer was that she would not do it that way because it was dishonest, and if he went to file a claim and the discrepancy were discovered, he would not get his money. To her surprise he agreed and decided to increase his deductible to give him the lower rate. She told me her decision brought some unexpected benefits. For one, she went home knowing she would not have to worry about any claims down the road. She also said that she felt the decision would be easier next time. She had bet on God. It is a good bet, but is not an easy one to make.

# Day 245
# Jeremiah 42-45

**A** stiff-necked people. That is what Israel had been called back in Exodus and it is still a fair description centuries later. The remnant of Judah was worried about their safety and they went to Jeremiah to ask for guidance swearing that they would do whatever he said God told them to do. When Jeremiah came back with the word not to go to Egypt, it was not what they wanted to hear and so that is exactly what they did - in spite of the warning from Jeremiah that God would punish them if they did. There is an old saying that you should never tell a child not to put beans up his nose. If you do, and leave the room, when you return the child will be crying, either because he has beans up his nose or because he couldn't find the beans!

It wasn't bad enough that they went to Egypt when they were told not to, but they resolved to give sacrifices to the queen of heaven because when they had given sacrifices to the queen of heaven, things had gone well, and since they stopped, things had not gone well. This is the faulty reasoning called, *post hoc ergo proctor hoc*, "after the fact, therefore because of the fact." I sneezed this morning and it rained last night, therefore I must have sneezed because it rained. The argument may or may not be true. There is no way of knowing because the two events have no demonstrable link. But the same could be said about Jeremiah's argument. Judah was being punished by God because of their unfaithfulness. How did they know that the defeat was the result and the sinfulness the cause?

We know from our vantage point in history that Jeremiah was right and the remnant was wrong. But how could they have known? Jeremiah's other prophecies had come true, but those could be written off as chance or good guesses. The only way for them to know was through faith and faith was what they lacked.

Faith is not against reason; faith can go where reason cannot. Reason must have all the information. Faith can move forward with incomplete information; it can fill in, or live with, the blanks that reason leaves open. It is not stupid to believe and we should not believe in things that are stupid, but if we are to avoid the mistake of the remnant, we need to recognize that faith must give us answers when reason no longer can.

# Day 246
# Jeremiah 46-48

I t almost seems unfair that God should judge the nations of Moab and Amon and Philistia. It would almost be like having another God come in and judge them after they had been faithful to their gods. They had played by the rules, and worshipped their idols according to their background and upbringing. How could God come in and judge them by the same standards with which He judged the Israelites who had been given the law?

It almost seems unfair, until you remember that there are no other gods. This is not a case of God coming into another god's territory and usurping its power. Those "gods" were nothing more than stone figures identified with the horrendous lies that people invented to rationalize doing what they wanted to. There was (and is) no Baal who required ritualistic drunkenness or prostitution. There was (and is) no Molech who insisted upon sacrificing children. The twisted minds who invented these hideous rites conveniently forgot that they were the ones who had invented the gods who demanded them. The message of Jeremiah is that there is only one God, and all people, because they are made in His image, are to worship Him. He is not a God of cruelty and licentiousness, but a God of grace and love. He was not coming as a God from some other country or people, but as the only Sovereign Lord of the Universe, whose laws apply to all people.

Still, the Moabites and the Ammonites did not have Moses to bring to them the requirements of God. They may, however, have had their own Moses. We must remember that the Scriptures are not all there is to know, just all we need to know about the Savior who came into our world. God is not limited to working only through Israel. The Scriptures themselves have made it clear that God has been at work in human history doing more than just what is recorded in this book.

Some people are distressed by this. They ask, "What about the other guy?" That may be a very interesting question, but it is quite beside the point. The question for each of us is, "What about me?" How will you respond to God's call? We should first worry how we will respond to the question before we concern ourselves about some else's answer.

Check Here
When Read
❏

# Day 247
# Jeremiah 49-52

The prophecies of the destruction of Babylon are quite extensive and explicit. They also came true. For that reason, many have sought to date the prophecies recorded as having been written after the events. This would, of course, increase one's accuracy (predicting events that have already happened) but it hardly qualifies as prophecy. What are we to believe about these records?

In one sense that is a rather philosophical question. The answer will depend largely on how you view the importance of the question with regard to the Scriptures. Some find the question of the historical accuracy of the Bible to be of little importance. For them it does not matter so much whether or not the events really happened, but instead the "transcendent" message of good and evil to be learned and applied is paramount.

I do not happen to subscribe to that viewpoint. I think that the historicity of the Bible is of great importance. I think it is rather more difficult than what most scholars admit when it comes to determining conclusive evidence about the historical events and the dates of the writings. In an absolute sense, we may only conjecture about who wrote the Scriptures and when they did it. Historical knowledge and scientific knowledge are two different things. In history we do not have the evidence available first hand. Observations are many times removed from the actual events. That means we can either know nothing from history (if we insist on applying scientific criterion of observability and repeatability), or we must accept probabilities to suffice for historical knowledge.

For some, it is improbable that Jeremiah would have been able to foretell the destruction of Babylon with such accuracy. Therefore, for them, a later date, and author, are more probable. For others (myself included), it is quite reasonable to accept that God told Jeremiah, in advance, what He was going to do, and then did it. I find it much less probable that someone would knowingly perpetrate a fraud by writing "prophecy" after the fact, and that anyone at the time of its writings, would be interested in such "late breaking news;" that's a little like forecasting last week's weather. Who cares anymore? Whichever you believe, the fact is that the prophecy has come true - Babylon has never been rebuilt. The implications of that fact are worth considering!

# Day 248
# Lamentations 1-2

hat good does it do to lament? Most all of us have been raised hearing that old saying, "No use crying over spilt milk." The past is past and cannot be changed. We must deal with the present and hope to change the future. Looking back only ties us to the failings of our past. Shouldn't we move ahead rather than wallow in self pity about what we have lost?

There is a danger in looking back at the past and lamenting. We can often use it as an excuse to blame our problems on someone else. William Glasser, in a book called *Reality Therapy*, took the standard Freudian definitions about behavior and stood them on their heads. Rather than define our behavior as a response to what our parents, society or environment did to us, he urged that we forget the past, and focus on the choice before us today. He argued that whatever happened to us in the past did not eliminate our free will to chose right and wrong today. Our past experiences may make choosing more difficult, but not impossible. His therapy was very successful with groups not normally helped by Freudian psychotherapy: criminals. He worked with hardened female inmates at a prison. When they came in and wanted to talk all about what their parents had done to them, he would stop them and simply say, "So, what? What are you going to do today? Are you going to follow the rules or not?" They eventually had to answer that question, and discovered a freedom from their past that had escaped them most of their lives.

On the other hand, not to look back can be to lose two benefits. First, it is to miss learning what went wrong so that you can know clearly, and not repeat the mistake. Until you recognize and agree it was a mistake, you will not repent and change, and you *will* make the mistake again.

Honest lamenting can lead us to a deep recognition of the pain we have caused and the pain we bear. The past *can* be changed. The events cannot be altered, but their effect on the present and future can. To truly learn from our mistakes and be changed people can make the occasion when we began, a good day rather than a bad one. That is no small feat. Do not be too quick to dismiss lamenting the past until it has been transformed into lessons for the future.

# Day 249
# Lamentations 3-5

umility has many benefits, and chief among them is that it gives one such a clear perspective of the world. Jeremiah looked long and hard at the humiliation of Judah and found in it the lessons God intended to teach. Chapter three, in the midst of the lament, shows the clear vision of God that comes only from the perspective of one who has been humbled.

"The steadfast love of the LORD never ceases, his mercies never come to an end; they are new every morning; great is thy faithfulness. 'The LORD is my portion,' says my soul, 'therefore I will hope in him.'" 3:21-24 Hope requires perspective. They were still captives in Babylon, and their captivity was of their own doing, but God had not abandoned them. In Him there was hope. They could learn to look, not to their own failings, but to God's faithfulness. That was no vain hope for them and it is no vain hope for us. No matter what we are facing, God's mercies never end, and they are new every day.

"The LORD is good to those who wait for him, to the soul that seeks him." 3:25 Humility also bring patience. Waiting is not one of the favorite pastimes or diversions for people. Most of us want what we want when we want it. It must look terribly silly to people who used to bake potatoes in an oven for forty-five minutes, to watch our hurried generation stand in front of the microwave oven for five minutes, staring in at the potato and saying, "Come on, come on, what's taking so long!" Just where are we hurrying to? God is with us, and His purposes are not rushed. He never schedules more in a twenty-four day than can be done in a twenty-four hour day, with enough sleep included. Humility learns to accept an agenda other than its own because it has learned that its own agenda may well be flawed.

"...for [the LORD] does not willingly afflict or grieve the sons of men." 3:33 Humility learns to trust in the goodness of God. Humility is not the soul crushed into submission. It is the soul set free to be what it is and to let God be who He is - the loving, compassionate God who would not leave us in our sins. It does not see itself as less, it hardly sees itself at all for the panoramic view of the future God's goodness lays before it; it is the perspective that, on a clear day, *can* see forever.

# Day 250
# Ezekiel 1-3

"**A**m I my brothers keeper?" is a question as old as humanity. Cain uttered it to God when He asked him what had happened to Abel. It is a question never asked with much humor. It always seems to suggest its own answer and a chilling one at that - "No, I am not my brother's keeper." But that was not an acceptable answer from Cain, and it does not appear to have improved any over the centuries.

God warned Ezekiel that he was being called to a special office as prophet. He would have to deliver a message to a "rebellious house." He was under obligation none the less to take that message to them. If he delivered the message and they refused to receive it, then the judgement would be against them; if he did not deliver the message, then he would be at fault. He was his brother's keeper - at least to that degree.

This is an annoying and complex requirement of following God. He expects us to share the truth with others, whether they want to hear it or not. It is not ok to simply enjoy our faith and its benefits without a real struggle to share them with others. This is especially difficult to do in a society that demands the rights of the individual to transcend everything else - even truth. We want to have an orderly society, yet we do not want to impose any kind of demand on the individual that they do not wish. This is, of course, ludicrous and inconsistent. When did you last meet someone who *wanted* to pay his taxes? Societies demand interaction. Part of that interaction is going to have to be sharing your perspective of what is right and wrong, and doing so with the purpose of convincing others to join you in your understanding.

In a desire to provide freedom *of* religion modern society has promoted freedom *from* religion. That is not possible. To believe there is no God is as much a religious conviction as any belief in God. America's freedoms are based on Christian principles, not Buddhist, Moslem, or Hindu. To force others to believe in Christianity is foreign to those principles, but to prevent those principles from being proclaimed because they might offend someone, is likewise foreign. We have truth to proclaim, and woe to us if we fail to do so. That does not mean it will always be welcomed, but truth is not the subject of a popularity contest.

# Day 251
# Ezekiel 4-7

he punishment of the people of God could not have been a secret, and it should not have come as a surprise. God warned Israel repeatedly what He would do if they broke the covenant. They had bet the day would not come, and they lost the bet. Judgement day arrived for the ten tribes of the north, and then for the two tribes of the south.

Ezekiel was given a unique way of showing the judgement. He was told to lie on his left side for three hundred and ninety days and on his right side for forty days to show the judgement against Israel and Judah. Why did God not appear Himself, or make His voice heard from the skies, or something other than having poor Ezekiel spend so long on his sides?

On one hand, that is an impossible question to answer. Why doesn't God do a lot of things? The answer is that He has His reasons, not all of which He cares to tell, or perhaps that we are capable of understanding. We cannot definitively say why He doesn't do some things, only that He doesn't. One of those things is to make "personal" appearances.

We were told back in Exodus, that God in His perfection, could not be seen by sinful people, for we would surely die. But that begs the question somewhat, because most of us would be happy with a few miraculous events, or a voice from on high. Why doesn't God make Himself known more directly?

Perhaps the best answer is to remember the reception He received those times He did. He sent ten plagues on Egypt, led the people with a pillar of fire and smoke, brought them across the Red Sea, and fed them miraculously each day. Still they turned to the worship of idols. After that display, would a voice really have made the difference?

So, the prophets were not necessarily a less effective means of communicating than the miraculous. And God did try to get people's attention. He did not send a card or letter or a person to appear only on special religious occasions. He sent Ezekiel who was strange enough to get their attention if they could be reached at all.

God may not be appearing in your room, but He is trying to contact you nonetheless. Noticed anything different lately?

# Day 252
# Ezekiel 8-10

Cherubim. What fascinating creatures. They sound a bit like the toy transformers children play with, creatures that can be either humanoid looking or transform into cars, trucks, or planes. One wonders what the "wheels" that Ezekiel described really looked like. Why are we told about them in the first place?

There have been several credible stories, mostly from missionaries, about angelic creatures coming to their aid. The interest in angels seems to be a perennial one. Just what do we know about them?

Angels are mentioned infrequently in Scripture. Of the times they are mentioned, especially in the Old Testament, they are always described as powerful and imposing creatures. Their appearance varies, but we must remember they are spiritual creatures, not physical ones, so their physical description is always in terms of "appearance." The implication is that they are not truly "incarnate" - in the flesh. That becomes important when we come to the New Testament and realize the uniqueness of Jesus' incarnation.

As spiritual creatures, they inhabit "heaven" as God does. They stand before His presence, and have direct access and knowledge of God. It is important for us to understand that their primary ministry is to God, not people. In those few instances of angels interacting with people, it is at the specific command of God, and usually for the purpose of bringing about His judgement. The idea of "guardian" angels gets very little support in the Old Testament.

Why do we know so little about angels? I have no doubt that if we could have more interaction with angels we would be worshipping them rather than God. Human beings are incredibly idolatrous, and we constantly turn to anything before we finally humble ourselves and turn to God. Silly of us.

Why then are we told anything at all? Perhaps that we might know that God's creation and purpose is larger than just the universe we inhabit. Perhaps just because it is true and God saw no reason to hide their existence. But we should be careful about seeking their interaction. They do not want our worship and they do not always bring good news!

# Day 253
# Ezekiel 11-14

zekiel wrote of the judgement of God in the most personal terms of any of the prophets. God speaks of the offense of the magic bands and the daubing of the whitewash to strengthen walls that were unsound. God knows all things, the great and the small and all are worthy of His notice and His approval and disapproval.

It is sobering to be reminded that God knows all that we think and do, in secret as well as in public. We so often try to put the best face on things for other people, but God sees through all the sham to the genuine nature of things. This means that He is touched by the good and the bad we think and do. Ezekiel got to see a small sample of what it must be like for God to be constantly aware of the innermost thoughts and desires of people. Far too often it is a dark and negative picture that goes streaming out before the all seeing eyes of God. But there are two sides to every coin, and we should not forget that there is at least as much blessing to the omniscience of God as there is burden.

The idea that God is ever present and ever aware of our thoughts and deeds can almost feel like an unwelcome intrusion. This is in part because we are ashamed ourselves of some of the things we know that go on in our heads. But, imagine for a moment, if what was going on there in your inner self was good and lovely and worthy of praise. Wouldn't that activity be worth the sharing?

God created everything to be connected. When we can look back on this life from the perspective of eternity, I think we will discover that it always was more connected than we realized. But we do know loneliness in this life. Not just being alone, but being lonely. That loneliness is a loss of the connectedness that God intended. We are not islands. God intended for us to enjoy the entire show, the grand movements and the minute details. This is the majestic nature of life, the synergy that makes it more than the sum of its parts.

It must be an ongoing horror show for God to see so much of that intricately woven fabric of life soiled and torn in so many places. Let us be convinced that every day, every moment, what we do and think makes a difference to our audience and divine creator. Be good today. He deserves it.

# Day 254
# Ezekiel 15-17

or the Israelites, there were no greater examples of societies gone bad than Sodom and Samaria. Sodom had been the talk of the ancient world because of the universal public acceptance, even pride in blatant sexual deviance. The ten northern tribes, who founded Samaria to replace Jerusalem as their capital and religious center when the kingdoms divided, mixed the worship of Yahweh with that of old Canaanite gods. If Sodom represented the worst of physical depravity, Samaria represented the worst of spiritual depravity.

When God told Ezekiel that Jerusalem was worse than both Sodom and Samaria, He declared that Jerusalem had hit rock bottom. The city which God had promised Solomon to make His own had surpassed even the worst of the worst in infamy. When the kings of Judah sacrificed their own children in Jerusalem, it was inevitable that God would declare that they were worse than either Sodom or Samaria. They should have known better. They were without excuse and without shame.

Yet in the midst of pronouncing sentence on the people of Judah for their sins, God declares again that He will be faithful to His promise even though they were not. "Yea, thus says the Lord GOD: I will deal with you as you have done, who have despised the oath in breaking the covenant, yet I will remember my covenant with you in the days of your youth, and I will establish with you an everlasting covenant." 16:59,60 God had destroyed Sodom and Samaria, why should He deal differently with Jerusalem, especially when it was worse than the other two?

For one thing, God was being faithful to His covenant promises. If we remember, He had promised not only to bless them if they obeyed, but to punish them if they did not. The covenant was never a "works" relationship, but one of gracious promise that defined their relationship; blessing or punishment, it was established by grace. God was being true to His word.

There is another important message for us here in Israel's sin. There were no greater depths to which they could sink, yet God would not completely abandon them. Can you do something so horrendous that God cannot forgive you if you repent? At least part of the lesson of Judah is to convince us the answer is - NO!

# Day 255
# Ezekiel 18-21

Chapter eighteen of Ezekiel is one of the real gems of the Old Testament. For those who think the Old Testament is a record of an angry and wrathful God, this chapter tells a very different story. For those who think, "Oh no, not again! he's going to tell us how the Old Testament is a covenant of grace and not works!" - you're right!

"Have I any pleasure in the death of the wicked, says the Lord GOD, and not rather that he should turn from his way and live?" 18:23 Repentance and forgiveness are not the sole property of the New Testament. They come into clearer focus in the New Testament, but the message of God to people has been the same throughout all the centuries; repent and be forgiven.

"But if a wicked man turns away from all his sins which he has committed and keeps all my statues and does what is lawful and right, he shall surely live; he shall not die. None of the transgressions which he has committed shall be remembered against him; for the righteousness which he has done he shall live." 18:21 There is no suggestion here that the righteousness has somehow paid for the transgressions. The transgressions are simply "not remembered." Likewise, the "righteous" man who turns from the good and does evil does not have a "positive balance" against which he draws until he overdraws his account. "None of the righteous deeds which he has done shall be remembered; for the treachery of which he is guilty and the sin he has committed, he shall die." 18:24

God is not playing a religious game of keeping accounts or watching for the correct ceremonies. He is not running a sum total which is passed on, positively or negatively, from generation to generation. He judges each person according to their orientation; are they turned toward Him in hope and trust that goodness is not in vain, or are they turned away from Him calculating that He either isn't there, doesn't care, or is grading on a curve whereby their sum total of goodness outweighs their sin. "Cast away from you all the transgressions which you have committed against me, and get yourselves a new heart and a new spirit! Why will you die, O house of Israel? For I have no pleasure in the death of any one, says the Lord GOD; so turn, and live." 18:31,32

# Day 256
# Ezekiel 22-24

ighteous anger. Many people claim to have it. While their claims may be suspect, it is certainly possible, and God showed it in no small measure against the sins of Judah. From the transgressions recorded in these chapters, it is not surprising that this was God's response.

"One commits abomination with his neighbor's wife; another lewdly defiles his daughter-in-law; another in you defiles his sister, his father's daughter. In you men take bribes to shed blood; you take interest and increase and make gain of your neighbors by extortion; and you have forgotten me, says the Lord GOD." 22:11,12  Sins against God are always sins against others. Even those times when we think we are directly insulting Him or "taking His name in vain," it is our selves whom we are hurting, and because God loves us, therefore we hurt Him. But let us not presume so much on our part as to think that we can hit hard enough, or swear loudly enough to truly injure God. If He did not care, we could no more reach Him than scuba dive on the sun.

We are His creatures, beings made in His image, in whom He has taken great care and delight. To see any of us abused, overpowered, tortured, afflicted in any way, even at our own hands, is an injustice that stirs His anger. For it to be any different would be to ask Him to care less than He is capable of doing. It is a rather sad commentary on us that we are capable of the kind of callousness which He is not. Whatever the injury, so long as it is not to ourselves, or our immediate family or friends, we take some solace that it somehow hurts less. This is not the attitude of love. For love, it is always better if the hurt is to itself rather than to the beloved. We most certainly fall short of that vision.

So we should not just pardon God if the sins of the world bring forth His anger. We should rejoice that they do so. It is a rather cynical view of life that makes excuses for suffering. "Well, that's not so bad. After all, what difference does it make? They were ... " (Fill in the blank any way you want - old, sick, weak, slow, dull, poor, "not like us.") We all belong to God and He does not take our pain lightly. We must learn that whatever we do to anyone, even ourselves, God is going to take *very* personally.

# Day 257
# Ezekiel 25-28

elieving prophecy still requires faith. For those who argue that even if what was predicted comes to pass, there is no necessary link between the prophecy and its fulfillment, the prophecy about Tyre is worth considering from an historical standpoint.

Ezekiel predicted the destruction of Tyre would consist of seven elements: that Nebuchadnezzer would conquer it, that other nations would participate in the fulfillment of the prophecy, that the city would be made flat and bare as a rock, that it would be a place for spreading nets, that its stones and timber would be laid in the sea, that other cities would fear greatly at the fall of Tyre, and that the old city would never be rebuilt. Here is the history.

Nebuchadnezzer laid siege to Tyre for thirteen years and when he finally took the city in 573 B.C., he discovered that the Phoenicians had moved everything of value to an island, about a half mile off the coast. Nebuchadnezzer left the city uninhabited, and did not pursue them to the island.

More than two hundred years later, Alexander the Great decided that he did not want the fleets from Tyre opposing him, so he moved to crush the island city. He was unable to do so by sea, so with a stroke of military genius, he built a causeway from the mainland to the island so he could attack it by land. He used all the building materials from the old city of Tyre, and when that was not enough, he had the soil scraped from in and around the old city to complete the causeway. After seven months of siege from land and sea, the city fell to Alexander's forces. Other neighboring cities were so frightened by the fall of Tyre, they simply opened their gates to Alexander's forces.

It became a popular place for fisherman to spread their nets and remains so today. Although there is an excellent water supply that flows through the site, modern Tyre was rebuilt at a new location, and the ancient city has never been rebuilt.

No amount of arguing will convince someone who does not believe, that Ezekiel really prophesied these exact events. It can always be argued that the history was selected which matched a certain interpretation of the prophecy or that it was written after the events. Still, it gives one pause. Just how many cities have been scraped from the face of the earth?

# Day 258
# Ezekiel 29-31

The Egyptian empires were among the greatest in human history. The tombs of the pharaohs, the great pyramids and the sphinx are still among the great wonders of the world today. How is it that so great a society should have fallen from world prominence from the time of Nebuchadnezzar until the present?

Questions like that are subjects for each new generation of historians. Until God writes the definitive work on human history, these kinds of questions will continue to have many more than one answer. There are a couple of factors to consider.

For one thing, the Egyptians, for all of their early advances, did not develop a written language until quite late. Their hieroglyphics which look so interesting to us, were a terrible way to write anything. So much of the ancient arts, including the ways of mummifying bodies, was lost to the world, to their own culture, because there was no way of writing down any formulas. As mundane a thing as the alphabet played a major role in the downfall of the Egyptians. History contains many such ironies.

One of the other things you will not find in many history books about the downfall of the Egyptian empire is right here in Ezekiel. God pronounced a judgement against Egypt. "It shall be the most lowly of the kingdoms, and never again exalt itself above the nations; and I will make them so small that they will never again rule over the nations." 29:15 Historically speaking, from the time of its defeat by Nebuchadnezzar in 572 B.C., Egypt has never again been a dominant world power.

Most historians would dismiss an interpretation which claims that Egypt suffers from the judgement of God. But before we assume too much from our western cultural perspective, let us remember that for all our advances, the closest the world has been to a nuclear confrontation was during the early hours of the war with Iraq in 1991. If Iraq had used chemical weapons against Israel, there is good reason to believe that Israel would have used nuclear weapons against Iraq. History is still His Story, and He regularly plays a part in it whether we recognize it or not.

For all our posturing in the West, that strange little bit of real estate we call the Middle East is still playing a key role in human history. It's something to think about.

# Day 259
# Ezekiel 32-35

zekiel's prophecies were full of metaphors to try to bring the relationship with God and His people into better focus. It is difficult, except through metaphors, to describe the infinite to the finite. God's relationship with people is also so much deeper than anything else we experience, it is hard, if not impossible, to fully define it; in some measure, we can only experience it.

The metaphor of the sheep and the shepherd is one that adds a good deal to our understanding or sense of the intimacy of God's relationship with His people. Jesus later calls himself the good shepherd, no doubt making reference to this part of Ezekiel. The shepherd guarded the sheep, looked after the health of the sheep, guided them to places with the best grass, and kept count of them that none would be lost. It is a twenty-four hour job looking after sheep and a fitting symbol for God's love for us. But the metaphor is more appropriate than just that. Not only is the shepherd a good analogy for God, the sheep are a good analogy for people. I have not known many sheep personally, but what this city boy has read about them convinces me that this is a very appropriate choice.

Sheep are creatures of the flock or herd mentality. They are not very bright and follow along where everyone else goes. If they get separated from the flock, they are easily lost because they will keep their heads down and follow the "sweet" grass into areas where they cannot even turn around. When they are finally lost, they will stand and "bleat" for help announcing to predators their location and situation. They fall into pits and crevices easily because they do not look around enough and seem to have little sense of the danger they can get themselves into. Once the flock is on the move, they will literally follow the leader anywhere, even off a cliff. The phrase "fat, dumb, and happy" could have been created with them in mind.

Not to insult us, but that sounds like a fair description of people, at least part of the time. We need a shepherd. The good news is that God is willing to take on the demanding task of looking after creatures who require so much guidance. Even better news is that while we may be like sheep now, His intention for us is to grow into much nobler creatures!

# Day 260
# Ezekiel 36-38

It is the nature of prophecy to engender differing interpretations. Ezekiel's prophecies are no exception to this rule. Throughout the centuries, the prophecies concerning Gog, Magog, and the rest, have prompted identifications with countries and peoples as diverse as the Goths, the Scythians, and the Russians. The number of different scenarios for the events foretold here near the end of Ezekiel would fill several large books. Given the diversity of opinions, is there anything in general we can conclude from this sea of possible interpretations?

Perhaps the most important is the theme that has drawn so much attention throughout the centuries; the valley of the dry bones. Before any specific prophecies were laid out, Ezekiel was told to prophesy *to* the valley of dry bones, that God would blow His Spirit over and into them, and bring them back to life from the dead. This passage has caught the imagination of people throughout the centuries. The clearest sign of death, the scattered dry bones themselves, are drawn back together by the power of God, and given new flesh and a new spirit to once again make them alive.

This is not a prophecy about individual resurrection, but it is most certainly a prophecy about God's ability to do what is impossible for us; to rebuild life from death. Whether it is an individual, our painful past, a fallen and sinful nation (as in this case), whatever those bones were, God can give them life again. What's more, God *will* give them life again. Human history will not end in a radioactive winter or by the sun expanding and engulfing the earth two hundred and fifty million years from now. God has a plan for history, and it will unfold accordingly, as surely as the sun will rise in the east and set in the west.

Identify Gog and the rest as you will, God will write the last page of history and it will be one of victory over sin and death and triumph for love and justice. This will not be of our doing. Who knows which generation will be the human agents chosen to be the vehicles and the witnesses to the end, but the end will come, and it will be His doing, not ours. Whatever else is unclear, that much is certain. On the whole, that is worth knowing and affirming. The future is securely in His hands. Amen.

# Day 261
# Ezekiel 39-42

zekiel provides yet another blueprint for building the acceptable temple of the Lord. But I wonder why such explicit instruction were given for the rebuilding of the temple. After all, the new covenant was to be written on the hearts of people, so why all these meticulous instructions on the rebuilding of a physical temple?

Perhaps it is because God had promised Solomon that He would honor his request that the temple always be a special place. That may seem like a quaint idea to us, but God keeping His promise is certainly not quaint; it is the foundation of all of our hopes. If God is not good to His word, then we can all put away ours bats and gloves and go home because this game will be called on account of darkness. God takes His vows *very* seriously, and we should be elated that He does.

The temple is also an example of something that many theologians have difficulty with: the physical world. God is a spirit, and as such, the truly enduring and noble things of life are spiritual: love, peace, patience, kindness, justice, faith, hope, etc.. It is easy for theologians to move from this observation that the great things are spiritual, to the thought that physical things are less important, or even inherently inferior. From being inherently inferior, it is but a short step to make the physical world inherently bad or base, which is more a concept of Greek philosophy than a Biblical one. Mercy is indeed more beautiful than a house, but that doesn't make houses ugly. Each possess their own beauty and place in God's creation. So it must also be with the temple.

Having a special place set aside to worship God does not mean that He cannot be worshipped elsewhere. Conversely special places we call sanctuaries are no less special because we can worship elsewhere. The worship we offer in our sanctuaries is not necessarily "more holy" because of the setting. God is to be honored in worship and that honoring should be without limitation but instead, abundant variety.

It is again an example of God's greatness that we do not have to choose between the physical and the spiritual world. He has given us both to enjoy and use. So be merciful *and* build a house wherein you may give thanks for His mercy.

# Day 262
# Ezekiel 43-45

**T**he chapters from forty to forty-eight have posed problems for scholars across the theological spectrum. The rebuilding of the temple does not appear to have been historically fulfilled (at least as described herein) yet its rebuilding also seems to be out of place for the end of things when God has fully established His kingdom in the hearts of His people. If there is to be no sin in the kingdom that is to come, why have the ritual of sacrifice?

Perhaps it was meant for both present *and* future use? Ezekiel was writing during the Exile, when access to the Scriptures was limited and error as to their purpose, layout, and theology would be understandable. These chapters are repetitious of related ones in Leviticus and add no new understanding of the nature or procedure of the temple. Likewise, the instructions for how the priests were to operate were not new, but a repeat of those given centuries before. Why do so?

The message may be that nothing was changed as far as God's forgiveness and salvation were concerned. In spite of Israel's unfaithfulness, God was still not the bloodthirsty one of the pagans. He is a God who requires right living more than right words. The sacrifices were not to change God's attitude, but ours. God had forgiven Judah for their sins, had punished them as He had said He would. He would not hold those sins against them forever, but reestablish the covenant as He promised He would.

Have you ever done something for which you are certain that God cannot or will not forgive you? Many of us carry guilt with us which we are unable to remove. What's more, we are sure that it has changed our relationship with God forever; nothing can set it right again. Perhaps we have even suffered the consequences of our actions and we know there is no going back because the damage done cannot be undone.

As God can make dead bones rise, as He can forgive the Israelites for offering bloody child sacrifices in the very temple dedicated to Himself, He is capable of forgiving and restoring us no matter what we have done - if we will allow Him. If we will turn to Him, we will find He has not changed. We can offer again the sacrifices of our pride and sin and He will accept and forgive us, and we can be changed. Do you believe that? Do.

# Day 263
# Ezekiel 46-48

The vision here in the last chapters of Ezekiel have caused great debate in scholarly circles because they seem to be about the final city of God and yet they differ significantly from the vision of John in the book of Revelation. What does the future hold? Is it a kind of "super" Jerusalem where the temple is the center of the city and all glory will evolve upon the twelve tribes? Or is it like the "new" Jerusalem that John foretells, wherein there is no temple because God Himself is there? And who am I to even venture a guess in only one page?

It is in the area of these "large" questions that small details often hold the clue to greater mysteries. What can get easily overlooked in this lengthy description of the future city of God in Ezekiel, is that it is renamed. It is no longer to be called Jerusalem, but Yahweh-shammah; God is There.

Name changes are always significant in the Scriptures because they are meant to communicate that something substantive in the nature of the thing has changed. From Abram to Abraham, from Jacob to Israel, from Jerusalem to Yahweh-shammah, something very different has come into being. The name Jerusalem meant "city of peace." The new name Yahweh-shammah, God is There, is a giant leap forward. Not only will the city be one of peace, but it will be the place where God dwells. Remember that when we get to the twenty-first and twenty-second chapters of Revelation, because it is the description of the "new" Jerusalem - the city where God dwells.

Israel, and therefore Jerusalem and the temple, were not to have been God's favorites to make the rest of the world second class. They were to have been the showcase people that exemplified God's graciousness to the whole world. For Ezekiel to see them again in their rightful place as beacons shining forth the message that God was again present with his people is completely in line with John's vision of God being in the "new" Jerusalem descended from heaven to reunite heaven and earth. Just as "a rose by any other name would smell as sweet," "God is There" will sound as sweet in any language. Fellowship with God was lost in the garden - it will be restored again in that city, for God is There.

# Day 264
# Daniel 1-4

he book of Daniel is one of my personal favorites. In spite of the difficulties with the interpretations of its prophecies, the lessons in the book from the lives of Daniel, his three friends, and Nebuchadnezzar himself, alone are well worth lengthy consideration. It is one of the great gifts of God that the Scriptures are not all prophecies and propositions about Him, but stories about real people and their relationship with the Almighty.

Some scholars have questioned the historicity of Daniel, but more recent archaeological discoveries have served only to confirm the accuracy of the events recorded. From Isaiah, Jeremiah, and Ezekiel, it is clear that Nebuchadnezzar and the Babylonian Empire were key instruments of both God's purpose in the world of their time and of salvation history. It should not really surprise us to be told more of these people and events.

Daniel, like Joseph before him, stood in stark contrast to the people of their time because they were not only people of vision, they were people of character. Nebuchadnezzar and Pharaoh were great rulers who recognized great men in both Daniel and Joseph. The ability to interpret dreams and manage with wisdom, were qualities valued in both these men and recognized by their respective rulers. Such character is not always recognized and rewarded, at least in this world.

Daniel's friends, who like Daniel refused to eat the rich food of the king and give up their Jewish heritage, were put to the test again at the fiery furnace. They told Nebuchadnezzar he could do what he wanted, God could deliver them or not, they would not turn from Him and worship Nebuchadnezzar's statue. Had they been consumed in the fire, their faith would have been no less valid. They did not trust in God because it was the best way for them to get what they wanted. They trusted in God because they knew there was no other real alternative. Live or die, there is no hope other than God.

Character is not always a guarantee of success, but it is never a bad choice. Our reward may not be immediate, but the One who grants all rewards in the end, values character above any other accomplishments. Daniel and his friends knew that. We should learn from their example.

# Day 265
# Daniel 5-8

ow often have each of us wanted some kind of a clear sign from God like the handwriting on the wall! God doesn't give those kinds of signs very often (just once!), but if that one was any indication of the kind of message it brings, we should all be glad God leaves our walls unmarked!

The interpretation of the word *TEKEL* that Daniel gives is certainly a chilling one to hear - you have been weighed in the balances and found wanting. How can this be if God is a gracious and forgiving God? How can we reconcile all this talk about judgement and punishment with the graciousness of God so clearly revealed on the cross?

This is a difficult question for those whose view of the Old Testament is one of an angry and wrathful God. I would hope that by this point in our course, you would be persuaded that all through the Old Testament, God has revealed Himself as a patient God, slow to anger and quick to pardon. His tolerance of Israel throughout their history speaks more of a patient God than one with a "short fuse" or a "hair trigger." Just how long must God endure the tyranny of the evil against the helpless?

God has never required perfection from His people. The whole sacrificial system existed to make the necessary allowances for sinfulness. But there must come a time when the misery-makers of this world run out of time, or else they will have the final veto power for all of God's goodness. No one who has done evil and not paid immediately for the offense, can complain about the graciousness of God. They have been forgiven and given new chances time and time again. The idea that they deserve "one more chance" misses the point that they (we) did not deserve another chance to begin with. We have been guilty from the outset. Any mercy is more than we have deserved, and God has always poured it out on us in abundance.

Belshazzar was sure that he had not passed the point of no return. He clothed Daniel as he had promised. But he had received all the grace he would get. His reign of excess and tyranny had reached its limit. That God stopped him was not unloving or ungracious, it was justice for his victims. God's justice and mercy were the same then as they are now.

# Day 266
# Daniel 9-12

hese prophecies of Daniel have sparked more debate and disagreement than almost any other passages in the Scriptures. The whole question of "how long before the end" is one we all want the answer to, but one for which a specific interpretation alludes us to this day. What are we to make of the prophecies?

One of the most important tests of any prophet's legitmacy is whether or not their prophecies come true. We should not miss noticing how accurately Daniel's prophecies did predict the events between his time and the coming of Christ. The Babylonian Empire *was* replaced by the Medo-Persian Empire, which *was* replaced by the Greek Empire of Alexander the Great, which *was* divided into four parts (his four generals) and replaced by the Roman Empire. Daniel's track record for correct prophecy is unparalleled.

Of course, we know that now, because we can see how the events unfolded centuries later. The meanings of the events of history we are living through today are seldom as clear as they will appear in tomorrow's history books. Every generation of Christians have thought they were the last (including the first generation of Christians - even the disciples) and, so far, each generation has been wrong. Some argue that we should conclude that there will be no "end times" as described in Daniel. While I may not be able to give an exact interpretation of these prophecies, it seems dangerous to dismiss those which have not yet come true - because most have!

What use can we make of these prophecies? As with all prophecies, these are not meant to provide us with a guide by which we might invest our lives and resources. "Let's wait until just before the end times, and then clean up our act!" The message of prophecy is that God is in control, and history will unfold according to His plan. This does not mean we should fatalistically think there is nothing we can do. It means we should stop putting off living according to the laws of love and justice of a loving and just God. There is no reason to wait to see if being good will make any real difference. The rules are not going to change, and when judgement day arrives, whenever it comes, they will be the standards by which our actions are measured!

# Day 267
# Hosea 1-3

Unconditional love. It is a rare and valuable commodity. To have Hosea marry a prostitute may seem like a strange way to explain it, but the analogy of Hosea's living prophecy may be a much better vehicle than it first appears. Unconditional love is not being a doormat, it is love which is able to endure the worst and prove to be stronger than all else.

Some people have a difficult time understanding that unconditional love does not mean unconditional approval. To love someone is to have their best interest at heart at all times. It does not mean that you want to control them, or remake them according to your likes or desires, but it does not want the beloved to do anything that would hurt themselves or others. Far from being unconditionally accepting, unconditional love is highly ethical. It wants the best for all and does not want to settle for less. It will scream loudest at injustice, no matter who the perpetrator may be because it is sensitive to the good. It can tolerate the bad only for the sake of the good. It can love the unlovely precisely because its love is not based on what the beloved does. But it must hold on to the standard that makes for its very existence - the good above the bad.

For many, this seems like a dichotomy. How can you love someone unconditionally and judge them? Hosea was told to marry the prostitute, and then prophesy against her infidelity. Loving the sinner does not mean you love the sin. If you give up condemning the sin, you will not really have loved the sinner, for you leave them in their sins. It does not do people any good to tell them something that isn't true just because that is what they want to hear at the moment. Conversely, telling them that what they are doing is wrong is not necessarily unloving - uncomfortable maybe, but not unloving.

God's love for His people has never been dependent upon their actions. For good or for evil, God has loved us all. But unconditional love, even God's, does not mean any and all behavior can be condoned, tolerated, or dismissed. We do not hate someone when we disapprove of their actions. That disapproval, combined with the commitment to stick with them, can be the most loving thing we can ever do.

# Day 268
# Hosea 4-7

or I desire steadfast love and not sacrifice, the knowledge of God, rather than burnt offerings." 6:6 For as often as we have read of the judgement of God against Israel, it is important to note the continuing references to God's steadfast love and desire for real justice, not ritual sacrifices. It is important to notice because we need to see that when Jesus comes along in the New Testament, he comes in continuity with the Old Testament - a fulfillment of the law, not a replacement. Sacrifices were never the means of placating an angry God. In Hosea's time the sacrifices were observed strictly, but there was no justice, which meant God was displeased. This is not an interpretation read back into the Old Testament from the New, it is the proper understanding of the Old Testament in and of itself.

"But at [like] Adam they transgressed the covenant; there they dealt faithlessly with me." 6:7 It is noteworthy that Adam's sin is here referred to as a breaking of the covenant. This is another clue to our understanding of this important concept of covenant. Adam, at the time he sinned, had not entered into any explicit "covenant" with God. To what was Hosea referring when he said that they transgressed the covenant like Adam?

Covenant is not merely the specific agreement between two or more parties. Covenant is a statement of the essential relationship between parties. It makes clear the relationship which ought to be lived out between those in the covenant. In creating Adam, God had entered into a covenant relationship with him and all his descendants to be their (our) God; to love us as a parent loves their child, to help us grow, to enjoy our company, to teach, to nurture, and to give purpose. Adam was the gracious recipient of that covenant relationship. All he had to do was to accept what had been given him as a gift. Instead, he chose to believe a lie, that God was not being that loving provider. His failure to trust broke the covenant relationship with God and we have been suffering ever since.

Covenant is not a legalistic set of rules but a dynamic relationship of trust. We must learn to drop our outward religiosity in favor of covenant - the enduring trust that God wants us, not some silly ceremony.

# Day 269
# Hosea 8-10

A relationship with God is a good thing, but it is not an easy thing. Israel discovered the hard way that belonging to God was a privilege that could not be earned, and it came with a responsibility that could not be ignored. We did not ask to be made, yet having come to life, we must learn to live according to the rules of our creator, or else suffer the consequences.

This all sounds more than a bit negative until you consider the alternatives. One alternative would be to live without any rules at all - anarchy. Those who chose to lie and cheat and steal, to rape and pillage and burn, to abuse children, to attack the elderly, to torture or maim others for pleasure, could simply do as they pleased because there would be no right or wrong, only what is. Were God's demands on Israel (on us) really so harsh? They could not treat each other as simply means to an end. They could not offer their children as bloody sacrifices, they could not oppress the poor, they could not neglect the widows or the elderly, they could not worship gods who weren't there, they could not commit adultery or murder or slander or theft. Which of these demands were (are) so unreasonable?

Another alternative would have been to make humans involuntarily obedient; leave out the free will and people become much more reliable. I appreciate my computer, but I will never love it. I don't always appreciate my children, but they are worthy of my love. Need I say more?

"For they sow the wind, and they shall reap the whirlwind." 8:7 Life comes with the responsibility to do good. We have been given free will in order that we might be alive in the most meaningful way. That means our actions have consequences and we must live with those consequences.

"Sow for yourselves righteousness, reap the fruit of steadfast love; break up your fallow ground, for it is the time to seek the LORD, that he may come and rain salvation upon you." 10:12 Obeying God's laws does not obligate Him to do anything for us. Obeying His law's are the rules that come with life itself. But even though we cannot make it rain, we can prepare the ground so that when it does, we make the most of it. God's rain will come too. How prepared is the field of your life?

# Day 270
# Hosea 11-14

osea made it clear that the sins of Israel were not only the injustices perpetrated against the poor and the weak but a rejection of the love of the one true God. God is the lover of Israel. Israel was His bride and He was the loving and faithful husband who had been despised and rejected by His most intimate partner. That is why Hosea was to marry the prostitute. The analogy between Hosea and Gomer and God and His people was precise and accurate. The intimacy of the rejection and the magnitude of the insult was what God was trying to get across. Are we hearing that message?

We think of ourselves often as God's children, but we are more than that to Him. We are His beloved in whom He wants to rejoice. We are His hearts desire and He rejoices in giving us blessings and in seeing us happy. When we turn to other "gods," those of money or sex or power or whatever, He is pained, not only because we will find no love from them, but because He also misses the relationship we should have with Him.

In a small booklet called, *My Heart Christ's Home*, Bob Munger explored the metaphor of God coming to dwell in our hearts. One of the rooms in the house of the heart, was the drawing room. It was a warm and quiet room, filled with volumes that made up the thoughts and ideas one contemplates in solitude. As the main character in Dr. Munger's story was giving Christ a tour of the house of his heart, Jesus stopped and made special note of that room. Jesus made a date to meet with the man there daily, for fellowship and discussion. As the days passed and activities crowded in, the man stopped visiting the study, always meaning to get around to it but never quite making it. On the way out one day, he caught a glimpse of Jesus, sitting patiently waiting for him. He went in and asked forgiveness for being so rude. Jesus told him that his problem was that he saw their time together as only for his benefit. Jesus told him that he loved him and had redeemed him at a great cost. The relationship was important to Jesus too.

It is an astounding thing to consider that we really do make a difference in the Divine happiness. God takes our relationship with Him very personally. Have you talked with Him today? He misses it when you don't!

# Day 271
# Joel

The book of Joel falls into the category of "yet another prophecy of punishment" for Israel's unfaithfulness. As such, it is often overlooked in the Scriptures since it has to compete for our attention with the many other examples of prophecy we have just been reading. Is there anything special in this book?

On the one hand, the answer is no. This is yet another prophecy about God's judgement against Israel. There are some suggestions that it also refers to the times that will come at the end of history, just before God finishes with the world as it is now, and moves on to what comes next. But prophecies about the end times abound in Isaiah, Jeremiah, Ezekiel, and many much clearer than these found in Joel.

There is also the promise of salvation and restoration in Joel, as with the other prophets. God had judged the nation, but He did not abandon it. There was still hope for the future. God will restore the people Himself, and have a new and better relationship with them (us). This is not a new message, but we should not miss the importance of the observation. The message of the Old Testament is not hopelessness, but hope in the loving and forgiving nature of God.

On the other hand there was something very special about this book of Joel - at least in Peter's opinion. On Pentecost, when the Holy Spirit descended upon the apostles and Peter preached his first sermon, he quoted from Joel and said that the prophecy had been fulfilled. "And it shall come to pass afterward, that I will pour out my spirit on all flesh; your sons and your daughters shall prophesy, your old men shall dream dreams, and your young men shall see visions. Even upon the menservants and maidservants in those days, I will pour out my spirit." 2:28,29

It has taken centuries for the church to realize the importance of that prophecy (and some still have not), that God has done a new thing with His people. No longer would there be priests at the temple to mediate between people and God, but God would pour out His Spirit upon them - men and women, slave and free. We all have direct access to God, because He has given us His very Spirit to dwell within us. That was (and is) important news indeed.

# Day 272
# Amos 1-3

Amos was not a prophet of the typical kind. There were always prophets who practiced prophecy as a craft. Amos was not a "professional" prophet and not particularly welcomed by the people of Israel. In addition, his message of judgement, and the rather undiplomatic fashion in which he delivered it, did not exactly endear him to his audience.

Amos was sent to the people of Israel during one of the brief times of relative prosperity for them. He was not from Israel, but from Judah, and he brought word of God's impending judgement of the nations surrounding Israel, as well as Judah. The idea that the "god" of one country could judge another country would have seemed quite presumptuous and foolish to the people of Israel. The chance that he would be believed by the people to whom he was sent was somewhere between slim and none. Yet he delivered his message none the less. Why was he sent?

"Surely the Lord GOD does nothing, without revealing his secret to his servants the prophets." 3:7 Many people feel that God is not there because He does not reveal Himself by personal appearances or miracles when you call on Him. But it is dangerous to conclude that God is not there simply because He does not choose to reveal Himself according to our wishes. He reveals Himself as He chooses, and according to His purpose. We may not understand or like His methods, but as Amos said, He does reveal His secrets. We should be very careful about demanding that God do things in a certain way. His ways are His choosing, and we will be without excuse if we refuse to listen to the truth because it was not told to us the way we wanted.

There is perhaps another reason Amos was sent. There is an old saying that a word to the wise is sufficient. The wise are able to look past the messenger to the message. They may not like the messenger, or even the message, but the only important thing to them is whether or not the message is true. The wise benefit from the message, and that makes it worth the trouble of sending it if for no other reason.

Who are the Amos's in our lives? God does not do things in our lives without trying to notify us first. But He may well send a rather unlikely messenger.

# Day 273
# Amos 4-6

any people say they cannot understand how God could reject anyone. If He is all loving, how could He turn anyone away? After all, we all try our best ... well, at least we all try to be pretty good ... well, ok, we aren't always rotten ... are we?

I think the question of God's attitude toward us as sinners is often misunderstood. He is gracious and loving, slow to anger and quick to forgive. We have read that over and over. In the final analysis, I don't think we will find God rejecting people as much as we will find people rejecting God.

The people of Israel to whom Amos spoke, were very religious people in the sense that they were careful to observe their religious practices - religiously. Unfortunately, ritual sacrifices, originally intended to change the attitude of the sinner, had become understood as instruments to placate an angry God. But God does not want people who are "religious." He wants people who would want to be around Him, in His kingdom, wherein His rules are law.

Would everyone want to live in a place where you cannot cheat anyone, where everyone is honest and generous, where each person has enough because everyone works and shares? Does everyone desire a world where you cannot get privileges that others do not have, or where you cannot prove your superiority to all those insignificant weaklings around you, where you cannot get everything you want when you want it? Could everyone live in a world where being kind, compassionate, unselfish, humble, diligent, and hardworking is the rule? That is what the Kingdom of God is like - and more.

The truth is that we enjoy a good many of the pleasures of our own sinfulness and we are not all that ready to give them up. The power, the greed, the sex, the self-righteousness, that often accompany our sins (for a while) can be a very appealing mixture. Those whose lives have been spent in pursuit of those elixirs can find them very difficult to give up.

If we have not wanted the things of the Kingdom now, what makes us think we will want them then? Those for whom justice and peace without privilege and power is a repellent concept, will reject God, not the other way around.

# Day 274
# Amos 7-9, Obadiah

mos was famous, not only for being a prophet who was called to prophesy against Israel while being a resident of Judah, but for the way in which he spoke out against the moral and ethical laxity of Israel. Israel had sinned against God, not only by worshipping other gods, but by treating the poor unfairly. The true worship of Yahweh was not merely something done in the temple, but in the marketplace and in the home.

"Hear this, you who trample upon the needy, and bring the poor of the land to an end ... that we may make the ephah small and shekel great, and deal deceitfully with false balances... I will turn your feats into mourning, and all your songs into lamentation; ..." 8:4,5,10  The idea of justice for all, not just for the powerful, was not one shared by the nations that surrounded Israel.  Power engenders privilege, but this was not to happen in Israel.  Even the king was not above the law, as David had found out.  God was not interested in sacrifices, but in justice.  They were heirs of God's gracious covenant, but that did not make them free from responsibility, but instead bound them to be righteous.

Some still find this combination of grace and duty to be contradictory.  If God has forgiven us and we cannot earn our salvation, then how can we be required to perform "good works"?  J.S Whale once wrote, "Faith without ethical consequences is a lie.  Good works must necessarily follow faith.  God does not need our sacrifices but he has, nevertheless, appointed a representative to receive them, namely our neighbor.  The neighbor always represents the invisible Christ."  It is not a matter of grace or works, but rather an order of priority.  If we seek to justify ourselves, to earn grace, then we will never succeed.  But if we receive grace, we cannot help but be bound, by gratitude, to share the love and forgiveness and graciousness that has been shown to us.  Faith necessarily comes before works, as works necessarily follow true faith.

God does not love the poor more than He does the rich, but He certainly loves them no less.  Power does not mean privilege in the Kingdom of God, but it does mean responsibility.  Faith calls us to use whatever power we possess for justice's sake, not to earn God's love, but because we have experienced it ourselves.

# Day 275
# Jonah

Although the book of Jonah is only four chapters long, it has sparked more heated debate than others many times its length. Some have a hard time "swallowing" the story about a big fish eating Jonah and regurgitating him three days later, still alive. Others argue that if God can create the universe, He could make a fish with carpeting and air conditioning if He chose. Whether or not Jonah is historically accurate is a question we may never be able to resolve, but we should not be distracted from seeing the message of the book by the debate over its credibility.

Still others have used Jonah as a warning not to ignore the callings of God. Many a sermon has been preached to convince people that if you don't do what God tells you, some kind of disaster will befall you until you are obedient. They then infer that if something bad is going on in your life, you must be ignoring some calling of God, say perhaps, sending their ministry some of your money. But the fact is that this is not the message of Jonah. Many have refused to answer God's call, while few have been eaten by big fish, be they literal or figurative.

What was, and is, the truly shocking message in Jonah, is that God is not only the God of Israel, but of all peoples. He holds everyone accountable to Himself and He is "...a gracious God and merciful, slow to anger, and abounding in steadfast love, and repentest of evil." 4:2 We have read that statement in relation to Israel many times, but here, in the heart of the Old Testament, is the same message about people who were, at the time, Israel's greatest enemies - the very Assyrians who later carried them off into a captivity from which they never returned. "Love thine enemy" is not just a New Testament message, it has always been the methodology of God.

Loving our enemies has not gotten any easier over the centuries. We do not want our enemies saved, we want them utterly defeated. We want pity to be reserved for us, not them. Israel was not to have carried the message that God loved them more, but that God loves all. That is the message which God has given to the Church to take to the world. We should still be reading the book of Jonah and learning its lessons. Who are your enemies? Have you tried praying for them?

# Day 276
# Micah 1-3

hen does a society or a people pass the point of no return? When does a nation become so corrupt that God can no longer tolerate it and pronounces His judgement, and saves a remnant out of it ? It may be impossible for us to know where to draw that line, but the line does exist. Israel and Judah had crossed it, and God passed His judgement and sent the word through His prophets. Those prophets, including Micah, did not want to deliver the message, but it was the truth, and God had called them to tell it.

Throughout history, parallels have existed between the corrupt society of Israel and Judah and many other societies, some of which have long since crumbled or are now in the process. We can find many uncomfortably close parallels between American society today and those of Israel and Judah.

Of all the sins of societies, there are a few things that are particularly heinous to God. The sacrificing of children is one of them. We no longer sacrifice our children on an altar, but I wonder how many of our children today have been sacrificed to the "gods" of convenience and materialism. If you had told Americans thirty years ago that the State would be taking over raising their children in State run institutions, they would have branded you a communist and run you out of town on a rail. Now, there is a cry for the "inalienable rights" of national "day care" centers to allow both parents their "rights" to pursue a career. Who will raise our children? It seems that we do not want the job.

There is probably no need for a litany of the woes of our society; divorce, adultery, pornography, homosexuality, violent crime, white collar crime, drug abuse, murders, child molesting, racism, political corruption, not to mention destroying the environment. The question is how close are we as a society to passing that point of no return? Most would agree that we are closer than we have ever been before.

"Repent!" is not a popular message, but it is a necessary one. God will always make sure there is a remnant, but the Scriptures are filled with calls to stop before it has to go that far. Are we willing to listen to the message of Micah? If not, those who will not learn from history are doomed to repeat it.

# Day 277
# Micah 4-7

As with all of the prophets of judgement, Micah does end with a note of hope. After all is said and done, with Israel and all the nations, God will act decisively to bring about a new era of peace and harmony to His creation it has not known since the days of the Garden of Eden. "He shall judge between many peoples, and shall decide for strong nations afar off; and they shall beat their swords into plowshares, and their spears into pruning hooks; nation shall not lift up sword against nation, neither shall they learn war any more..." 4:3

This will not come about as a result of a vast educational process by which all people learn to live at peace with one another. It shall not be brought about by each person finding "the divine spark" within them or discovering that love is more fulfilling than hate. God will do this Himself. "But you, O Bethlehem Ephrathah, who are little to be among the clans of Judah, from you shall come forth for me one who is to be ruler in Israel, whose origin is from of old, from ancient days." The Messiah was to come from Bethlehem to deliver his people.

This is not an interpretation we place on this Scripture passage from a New Testament perspective. The Pharisees, who were no fans of Jesus, knew this prophecy well. Not knowing of Jesus' birth in Bethlehem, they used it to argue against the person they knew of as Jesus of Nazareth. The promise of God was that the Messiah would come from that small town, among the least of the kingdom of Judah.

It is reassuring to know that from the perspective of both the Old and New Testaments, the salvation of the world will not depend on people, but on God Himself. No matter how bleak things became for the Jews, that promise held out hope that could not be extinguished. It holds the same promise of hope for us too.

Micah did not know that the promised Messiah would still be more than half a century ahead of him, nor that two millennia (at least) would transpire before the fulfillment of the promise of peace. It does not really matter though, whether that promise is delayed another two weeks or two more millennia, it is still the promise of the loving God who has never broken a promise. That promise can give us hope until the promise is fulfilled.

# Day 278
# Nahum

e met Nineveh earlier in the book of Jonah. There they were warned of God's impending judgement and that time, they repented and were saved. Nahum pronounced the judgement from which there would be no heeding of the warning, and no salvation from the judgement.

There are probably at least two important lessons we can learn from Nineveh's experience. One is that as far as faith is concerned, God has no grandchildren. The Ninevites who repented and had been forgiven could not automatically pass on to their children their faith in their experience of the grace and forgiveness of God. They could tell the story, they could recount the circumstances, they could give praises to the God who had forgiven them, but their children would have to trust in God's forgiveness for themselves, or not. You cannot inherit faith; it is a commodity that we must each pick up for ourselves or it will never be ours.

Another lesson is that we are all God's people. The individuals who made up the city of Nineveh and the nation of Assyria, were all God's people. They were descendants of Adam and Eve as are we all. Regardless of whether or not they worshipped other gods, Yahweh is the only God, and they all belonged to Him. They had transgressed His law and were guilty of the same kinds of sins as Judah and Israel. The difference is that the people of Nineveh, as a "people" were not His. Individuals in all times and places belong to God, but the claim to be God's "people" is a very special status. Israel had been chosen as a "people" - a showcase "people" - and therefore, preserving them as a "people" has always been part of God's revelation of Himself to all His individuals.

The Assyrians as a "people" had clearly not been any worse than the "people" of Judah and Israel. The difference was that the Assyrians as a "people" were not part of the covenant which God was using to reveal His salvation. This meant that as a culture, they were not guaranteed a remnant. But we should not mistake our culture for ourselves. God is not a racist or bigot. We all belong to Him and we will all have to receive or refuse His forgiveness as individuals. Our nationality will be of no help.

# Day 279
# Habakkuk

Habakkuk in one of those books used frequently in Bible trivia quizzes. Most people would be hard pressed to tell anything about what was in this "minor prophet." But as my mother used to tell me, good things come in small packages, and Habakkuk is a real little powerhouse of a book.

"Behold, he whose soul is not upright in him shall fail, but the righteous shall live by his faith." 4:4 This verse is quoted three times in the New Testament (in Romans, Galatians, and Hebrews) as summing up the understanding of the key place faith plays in our lives. Even the Pharisees who wrote the Talmud (a "commentary" on the Old Testament) felt that Habakkuk had summed up all the commandments in this one sentence. The understanding that worshipping God was not a matter of righteousness by works goes back to the earliest of the Scriptures. God has consistently revealed Himself to be loving and gracious; to require of His people, not impossible perfection, but righteousness through faith. Just as Abraham's faith had been reckoned to him *as* righteousness when it was not, the righteous in all times and places are those who live by faith in God, not in their own works.

It is so important for us to see that this has always been the teaching of the Scriptures - faith, not works - precisely because it has been so misunderstood for so many centuries. Whenever we try to do right, we begin to want some kind of credit for it. Habakkuk did not understand how God could punish Judah by using the Chaldeans (Babylon) when the Chaldeans were so much worse than the people of Judah. God reminded Habakkuk that regardless of the sins of the Chaldeans, the people of Judah had sinned and deserved punishment. We have all failed to make the grade. After that, arguing about whether we deserve a "high F" or a "low F" is to have missed the point.

In whom will you put your trust? Who will be able to save your life? Who will be able to pardon your sins and make atonement for your iniquities? That the answer is God and not ourselves is not a new message that Jesus brought with him, but the truth that God has been revealing from the beginning. The message of the Scriptures has never been any different.

# Day 280
# Zephaniah

**W**here is God most of the time? A lot of people struggle with this question. If God is so interested in us that even the hairs on our heads are numbered, why is He so hard to communicate with? Why doesn't He help the good people more often and stop the bad people more often? Just what is He doing?

These are difficult questions. God certainly does seem to operate on His own set of priorities. He does not do things the way most of *us* would, given His power. Most of us would use the ability to be present everywhere (omnipresence) and the power to do anything (omnipotence) to fix the mess the world is in constantly. Of course, when you consider the sheer number of interruptions that it would require (with the over five billion people in the current world population) it seems more reasonable for Him not to interfere. However, He is God, and it should certainly not be impossible. So why does He not take a more active role?

It is part of the arrogance of human beings that we feel everything should be made known to us and anything that is not known must not be important. Why should God reveal His plans to us? Why must we be aware of all of the things which impact our lives and know them now? For centuries, the ozone layer protected us without our knowledge, but that does not mean it wasn't there. Now that we may be destroying it, it is important for us to know, but why until now? Should we really be surprised if we discover that God has been far more active in our lives than we ever imagined?

Zephaniah warns, "At that time I will search Jerusalem with lamps, and I will punish the men who are thickening upon their lees, those who say in their hearts, 'The LORD will not do good, nor will he do ill.'" 1:12 We cannot explain all of God's actions, but we had better be careful about assuming He is a neutral force in our world. He has chosen to act differently than we would, but act He has and act He will. Those actions have never been and never will be neutral. He alone is the force of good which will finally defeat every evil, maybe not in the way we expect, but in the way He knows is best. In that day, those who have counted on His neutrality are in for a rude awakening.

# Day 281
# Haggai

"If you will just send in your seed faith, love gift, trust promise pledge offering, to the JoeBillyBob Apostolic Faith Community Ministry of the Airwaves, Gawd will bless you with a tenfold return - yes, brothers and sisters, I said tenfold!" We hear this message from many sources and you could almost argue Haggai is making the same claim. The remnant that had returned to Jerusalem had not fared well, and Haggai announced it was because they had not rebuilt the temple. Put God first. Isn't that the message?

Put God first. That is the message of Haggai and of the Scriptures. But the questions of how one puts God first, and why one puts God first are equally important.

Putting God first in your life does not mean sending money to the church before you feed your family. Each year there seems to be some sad story about a family who did precisely that and had a child starve to death. There are even more stories of people sending in large sums of money they could not afford, in order to receive the "tenfold blessing" that gets promised. That is not putting God first, that is trying to manipulate God for your own purposes.

Putting God first means placing the value of the spiritual ahead of the physical. In material terms means knowing that whatever car you drive, it will eventually end up in the junk yard. It also means knowing that every person you meet will live on for an eternity in one place or another and that those people are more important than the car. God does not need our money, but we need to give of our time, treasure and talent *first*, to Him. The tenfold blessing is not often in cash, it is in being free from the delusion that any amount of money will bring you happiness. It is possible to be possessed by the desire for money whether you have a lot or a little.

It is equally important to remember that putting God first does not mean putting God "only." God has given us beautiful things in life to enjoy. If we put Him first, the rest of our priorities will fall into place and we can appreciate all those gifts in proper balance. But if we try to put Him first in order to get the rest we will find He is not easily manipulated. Put God first. Let JoeBillyBob make his own money.

# Day 282
# Zechariah 1-4

o much of the Scriptures are written as history that the few parts which are apocalyptic can be difficult to interpret. Added to that, our western scientific mindset lends itself easily to history but it is not comfortable with allegory. We want the plain truth, the bottom line, the straight scoop. Say what you mean, and for Pete's sake, don't use "word pictures"!!!

Zechariah does not give us what we want at this point. His prophecies come in typical apocalyptic language - colorful yet obscure, passionate but not precise, full of feeling but difficult to analyze. Perhaps that is as it should be. Perhaps what we are meant to learn from these visions are not roadmaps for the future but a foretaste which tells us the quality of the banquet yet to be.

We value critics highly in our society. The abundance of reviews in newspapers, magazines, and television, would make you think we are starved for informed opinions. So, what do we want from these critics? It is not their detailed description of the plot or their analysis of the acting, but their opinions. Was it good or wasn't it? That's what we really want to know.

Zechariah, and the other apocalyptic prophets, are in a sense more critic than prophet. If we are to believe that God actually allowed them to see things which were yet to happen in history, then much of what they saw would be impossible to relate in terms their generation could understand (how would you describe a helicopter to someone from 500 BC?), save for their impressions of it all. And perhaps that is all they need tell us anyway. Is it going to be good, or bad? Go on, tell us, we can take it!

Zechariah's prophecies have that rich, colorful quality, that imparts a clear message: "For thus said the LORD of hosts, after his glory sent me to the nations who plundered you, for he who touches you touches the apple of his eye:..." 2:8 The details are not as important as the message - God has not forgotten His people, and He will be their defender even unto the end.

Betsy ten Boom, who died in a German concentration camp because she had helped Jews escape the Nazis, told her sister Corrie, "I pity them, Corrie. They have touched the apple of God's eye." Betsy had gotten the message. She had not missed the forest for the trees. We should do no less.

# Day 283
# Zechariah 5-8

Flying scrolls and lead covered ephahs with women named "Wickedness" in them! Apocalyptic writing is so - unusual. I suppose that I am typically modern in my dislike for this kind of revelation. I am not at all sure just what it is revealing. It is almost enough to make one nostalgic for the passages describing the ornamentation of the ark! Almost.

If you have been reading in an annotated Bible, you will have noticed the large number of Scriptural cross references in the book of Zechariah. While it may not hold much attraction for us, it most certainly did in its time and through the time of the New Testament. It is essentially the antithesis of what modern people want - short on facts but long on meaning. We prefer our history to be long on facts and allow us to draw our own interpretations of the meaning. How did this shift come about?

The answer to that question could well be a doctoral dissertation, but it must be in some part the development of the "body of understanding" we have amassed. We have more books, scrolls, articles, artifacts, available to us than ever before. We have the ability to look more deeply into the heavens, the oceans, even the atoms that make us up, than ever before. Surely, we must be long past any old fashioned superstitions that have need for flying scrolls and long haired, wild eyed, prophets.

Still, for all our knowledge, just what do we know? We know where are brains are, but where are our minds? We can define symmetry and perspective, but what exactly is beauty? When a young child is beaten and abused and its soul cries out in anguish, do we really know what impact that has on the spiritual world around us? "These are the things that you shall do: Speak the truth to one another, render in your gates judgments that are true and make for peace, do not devise evil in your hearts against one another, and love no false oath, for all these things I hate, says the LORD." 8:16,17

We want to know the times and seasons of judgment; that is our desire from prophecy. But when we seek those answers, we have missed the point. The point is that it is always the time for truth, and always the season for justice. Whatever the historical facts of the future, that is the meaning. Thus saith the LORD!

# Day 284
# Zechariah 9-11

Progressive revelation. That is the belief that God has revealed Himself and His will progressively across the centuries. We do not know for certain what Zechariah's original audience made out of these strange foretellings. These were clearly messianic prophecies, however, and the people of Zechariah's day understood that much as clearly as we do.

"Rejoice greatly, O daughter of Zion! Shout aloud, O daughter of Jerusalem! Lo, your king comes to you; triumphant and victorious is he, humble and riding on an ass, on a colt the foal of an ass." 9:9 When Jesus rode into Jerusalem on Palm Sunday, he fulfilled this prophecy, as he did all the other prophecies about his coming. What a strange King he was, who came not in pomp and circumstance, but in humility. No wonder he was not well understood, in spite of his coming being foretold. Kings should be great, not lowly, but this king revealed his greatness in his grace not his power.

As with so many prophecies, they only become clear once they have been fulfilled. The thirty shekels of silver become the payment to Judas for betraying the Good Shepherd, who laid down his life for his sheep. It gives one a rather eerie feeling to think this was foretold more than five hundred years before it happened. Some might argue that the Pharisees who paid off Judas would have known this prophecy of Zechariah's well, but there is a thread running through history that belies coincidence - if one has the eyes to see it.

What good are all these things to us now? Perhaps of little importance in our daily life. Most people never read Zechariah and many who do find little of any real interest. But that is one of the fallacies of our culture, that day-to-day living is nothing more than ordinary. By all measures, life of any kind on this planet is here only by the narrowest set of "fortunate" circumstances. Any closer or further from the sun and the temperatures would be wrong. Any slower rotation and the earth would be alternately too hot and too cold, any faster and the winds would be cataclysmic, and we could go on. There is really nothing ordinary about us. And Zechariah's prophecies should remind us that there is nothing accidental either.

# Day 285
# Zechariah 12-14

I suppose never having had the experience of seeing my nation conquered and its people carried off into captivity, I have a hard time feeling the emotions that Zechariah and his generation did. The desire to see one's enemies utterly destroyed with no mercy shown comes from witnessing atrocities at a closer range than the television set. I do not think all people who want revenge are barbaric. To witness, first hand, the slaughter and torture of your loved ones and not feel the desire for revenge would be abnormal and unhealthy. But that does not mean it is right. There is nothing really final about revenge. It is always a hollow victory.

Justice itself is not a destination but a process. It is part of the process that leads to the real destination, which is the Kingdom of God wherein love is the law. For Zechariah and his people who had watched the unspeakable happen to Jerusalem, it is understandable they would envision that destination as Jerusalem restored, her enemies crushed, and God vindicated. This is why we have more than just Zechariah to guide our understanding. Defeating all who choose to cling to evil will be part of the process by which God's Kingdom is restored, but the Kingdom itself will be beyond justice because love is always at least just.

Nationalism must give way to the reality that we are all sons and daughters of Adam and Eve, creatures made in the image of God. Justice must give way to the law of love, which goes beyond mere equality to the self-giving quality which looks to the good of the beloved ahead of its own interests.

As you watch the evening news with its successive stories of the injustice and inhumanity in this world, ask yourself if it is important to know that God will not let it continue forever. That is the message of Zechariah, whatever specifics he saw. We must remember that apocalyptic literature cannot be interpreted the same as history, whether it is referring to the past or the future. But the future itself will be historical. The Kingdom of God will not be merely a state of mind, it will be heaven and earth once again joined together. That vision is revealed more clearly in John's Revelation, but the message is still the same. The Kingdom will come, and it will wipe everything else away. Praise God!

# Day 286
# Malachi

**M**alachi closes out the books of our Old Testament. This book was written after the Babylonian captivity, after the Jews had returned to Jerusalem, and after they had rebuilt the temple. They had been back in the promised land for a hundred years and the Messiah had not come. Israel's fortunes were not getting better and the people had gotten to the place where they questioned if it was all worth it. Was God ever going to act? If so, why wait so long?

It would yet be four hundred years after Malachi before God would send the Messiah. Why God waits so long to do things is a question that has always been with us. Why is He so slow to move? Why doesn't He get this over with? Why doesn't He act?

Malachi provides some clues for these questions of God's activity in our lives. On the one hand, we have no answer as to why God doesn't act in the way we think He should - He simply chooses not to. If we believe that He is all knowing and all loving, it would be reasonable for us to conclude that when He doesn't act the way we think He should it is because He knows better. "For I the LORD do not change; therefore you, O sons of Jacob, are not consumed." 3:6 God will act decisively as He knows is best - not sooner, and not later.

On the other hand, Malachi points out that we play a fundamental part in this process. "Bring the full tithes into the storehouse, that there may be food in my house; and thereby put me to the test, says the LORD of hosts, if I will not open the windows of heaven for you and pour down for you an overflowing blessing." 3:10 This is not just about money (although it includes money) but about trusting in God and making His values our own. If we feel He has not acted in our lives, we need to ask if we have left Him any room to do so? If we will not trust Him with our heart's desires, how can He be expected to bless us with them? (Remember Psalm 34:4!)

The Old Testament closes with a challenge to be vigilant and patient (not two of our stronger traits). God will act in His own time, and in the mean time, if we want Him to act now, we must do our part and trust Him. That means putting our money (and time and talent) where our mouths are.

# Day 287
# Matthew 1-4

s much as Ruth was a refreshment to read after the dark and confusing time of the Judges, so Matthew's account of the birth of Jesus comes as the spring after a long cold winter. Here now is the promised one of Israel who has come to fulfill the covenant given back in Genesis chapter three - the "seed of woman" who would defeat the enemy of all people!

For many who have never read through the Old Testament (Congratulations! You are no longer in that catagory.) the first chapter of Matthew seems pointless. I hope you enjoyed recognizing so many more names on that list - and knowing which were the important ones!

In these first four chapters, Matthew directs our focus to five Old Testament prophecies fulfilled by Jesus. As Jesus said himself, he had come, not to abolish the law, but to fulfill it. Matthew took great pains to make sure that his readers knew that Jesus was the Messiah whom the Scriptures had promised. There was no lack of continuity between the Old Testament and the New Testament in his mind. Jesus was (and is) the bearer of the same Grace which had been offered from the beginning, but he brought with him a new, fuller, revelation of the Covenant between God and His people. The chosen people had misunderstood Moses, they had ignored the prophets, and so God had finally sent His own Son.

As we start to read the gospels it is important to remember that like all Scripture, they do not contain all there *is* to know about the life of Jesus, just all we *need* to know for our salvation. Almost nothing is told of his early life or preparation for ministry. But notice that even in these first four chapters, we find the character of the God we have seen in the thirty-nine books of the Old Testament: a patient, loving, and methodical God at work. No arriving via the Concorde with twenty hours of meetings scheduled the first day. He came as a baby, grew up like everyone else, submitted to baptism, was anointed and tested, all in proper time and sequence; busy, but never rushed, open to the situations as they unfolded, but never without a purpose. Lesson one: there is always enough time to do God's will. After that, how significant is the rest?

# Day 288
# Matthew 5-7

These chapters are generally referred to as the "Sermon on the Mount." In addition to being famous for the beatitudes, these passages are among the most quoted by non-Christian sources throughout the centuries. Even those who do not accept the claims of Jesus concerning his divinity, regard these teachings on the nature of the way life should be lived, to have been the high water mark for human ethics. Not only in deed, but in thought and intention, God made us to live with the highest respect for all of His creation; anything short of that goal is sin. And you thought the Ten Commandments were tough! "...and whoever says, 'You fool!' shall be liable to the hell of fire." 5:22 Which of us could pass that test?

This is one of the things that is so important to see about the message of God's grace. So many people labor under the mistaken idea that God was legalistic in the Old Testament and forgiving to the point of senility in the New Testament. Jesus did not teach that forgiveness becomes license to do anything we choose. He came to proclaim God's graciousness that gives us the liberty to obey out of gratitude. This is the same message God gave to Abraham and Moses and all the prophets. "You, therefore, must be perfect as your heavenly Father is perfect." 5:48 If we are to earn our salvation we will never be able to pay the price. If we will accept God's forgiveness by faith, our faith will be counted "as righteousness" just as it was for Abraham. "...but the righteous will live by his faith." Habakkuk 2:4 Grace and the law are not opponents but are each part of God's love for the creation He made and the people in it.

"And when Jesus finished these sayings, the crowds were astonished at his teaching, for he taught them as one who had authority, and not as their scribes." 7:28,29 I hope that the Sermon on the Mount will be one of those sections of Scripture that you return to many times. It is so full of practical as well as profound counsel that it warrants our continuing reflection. It also shows what a quintessential teacher our Savior was and is. May God grant that our lives would be able to reflect even a small part of the ideal of the Kingdom which Jesus taught us about in these chapters.

# Day 289
# Matthew 8-11

esus was not an easy person to understand (and many find that true even today). He was not the kind of messiah that they had expected. Even John the Baptist was confused by Jesus. John had continued to preach against Herod's immorality of divorcing his wife and marrying his brother's wife, for which Herod had him imprisoned. John did not understand why he should be locked up in prison if Jesus were the messiah. John even sent word to ask Jesus if he were indeed the messiah or if they should wait for another.

Jesus' response seems indirect to us, but it spoke volumes to John. "...Go and tell John what you hear and see: the blind receive their sight and the lame walk, lepers are cleansed and the deaf hear, and the dead are raised up, and the poor have good news preached to them. And blessed is he who takes no offense at me." 11:4-6 These were the signs of the Kingdom of God. All the enemies of God and humanity, sin, evil, and even death, were being defeated. Jesus was (and is) the messiah, and the messiah of promise who would deliver his people, but not in the way they expected.

"He who finds his life will lose it, and he who loses his life for my sake will find it." 10:39 This is one of the affirmations we still have difficulty understanding. What is Jesus doing in our lives? Following him has never been a guarantee of success or privilege (look at John). But why should this be so? Why shouldn't being a Christian guarantee that we win all the lotteries, get the best jobs and have perfect health?

It comes down to the fact that God's priorities are not like our own. He has different values than we do, and we have need of re-examining ours. If we were to win all the lotteries and never be sick a day in our lives, we would still die. In the end, no matter how many blessings we may receive in this life, our lives will be "spent." The real question is what will we have purchased with them? If our lives now are to have meaning, it must be in relation to our eternal lives which are yet to come. Quite frankly, God is more concerned with what we are going to be like a million years from now than He is with how life is going today - and so should we! We will lose our lives. If we are to find them again, it will only be by finding the one who can give them back to us.

# Day 290
# Matthew 12-14

hy speak to them in parables? It was a valid question on the part of the disciples. Why tell these rather quaint little stories to people instead of just coming right out and saying what he meant? Didn't he want them to understand what he was saying?

Jesus' answer was to quote from Isaiah about people seeing but not seeing, and hearing but not hearing, lest they see and hear and understand, and turn and be healed. This sounds strangely as if Jesus did not want them to understand. Can that be true?

Robert L. Short in his book *The Parables of Peanuts*, examines this same question - why talk in parables? He suggests that parables, like all art, have a way of disarming people, of getting around their first line of defenses. Like most good comedy, the message sneaks in while we are laughing or looking at the pictures they conjure up in our minds. Short suggests that Jesus was using parables to get past the initial resistance people have regarding religious matters - to see truth not in some dogmatic doctrinal fashion, but as part of real life. Short argues that Charles Schultz in his *Peanuts* comic strips has written many of the gospel's truths in the same fashion as the parables which allowed them to be printed even in Communist Russia.

I think Short is right about the parables being disarming, but I think there is another aspect to them - they require the eyes and ears of faith to understand them. In that respect they provide both opportunity and judgement. They are the opportunity to see the truth, if not now, then perhaps later. If the story is not understood it can come back to memory later when understanding is possible. They are a judgement because if the lesson is not learned, there can be no excuse of not having been told. The truth is there for all to see. Failure to understand parables, those simple little stories, is not a matter of the head, but of the heart.

Like all good teachers, Jesus wanted to teach when people were ready to learn. That time of readiness varies from person to person. We should be glad he chose a way that allows us to understand when we are ready and not be repelled (although perhaps confused) until we are able to comprehend. They are lesson and test wrapped together. Pretty clever, Lord!

# Day 291
# Matthew 15-18

I t is sometimes difficult for us to accept the gospels as they are written. We want them to be biographies rather than the unique genre they are. Where did Jesus go to school? What kind of music did he like? What was the strategic plan for his ministry? At first glance, Matthew writes as if Jesus wandered around rather aimlessly, randomly healing and teaching, until the crucifixion. But if God is so deliberate, how could this be true of Jesus' life?

Perhaps to Matthew their travels together did seem rather random. But when we see the testimony of all the gospels, we can see the purpose behind Jesus' journeys. A case in point is the encounter with the Canaanite woman in chapter fifteen.

Jesus had gone to preach his message that the Kingdom of God was at hand, first to the Jews. The gift he had to bring was for all people, but, as promised, it was first shared with the house of Israel. When was it time to open the message to the rest of the world? The Canaanite woman's faith was the turning point.

Matthew records the feeding of the five thousand (who were Jews) just prior to this. After the encounter with the Canaanite woman, Jesus went to the region of Galilee, to teach and heal. Galilee was a region filled with "gentiles" and his feeding of the four thousand there was the message that the gospel was now for *all* people to hear and to respond. The seven extra baskets were the symbol that this ministry would also come to its completion (seven being the number of completion).

Matthew still leaves some with the uncomfortable impression that Jesus was not very nice to this Canaanite woman. It is difficult for us to accept that God, and his son, are not the warm fuzzy kind that always want to make everything easy for us, like an Aunt Martha who pinches our cheeks. They are more like the coach who seems rather gruff and makes us run the extra laps we are sure are unnecessary. But the laps are necessary and we would hardly run them if we were asked "nicely." God would rather be good than nice. The Canaanite woman was not merely an historical event, she was a child of God who needed to exercise her faith before it was any use to her. The exercise was not for her to qualify for God's grace, but to prepare for it. There is a world of difference there. Jesus knows exactly what he is doing. Amen!

# Day 292
# Matthew 19-21

**T**here were many things about Jesus that were offensive to the Pharisees and Sadducees of his day. They did not like the idea that he would associate with sinners and tax collectors and women. They did not like the fact that he did not observe the "laws" which they had built up around the Scriptures during the four hundred years when there was no prophet; laws like not healing on the Sabbath because it was "work." They most certainly did not like it when he told them that they were blind guides and the Kingdom would be taken away from them and given to another nation that would produce the fruits thereof. 21:43

But before we look down our noses too far at the Pharisees and Sadducees, we should ask just how offensive Jesus is to us today. Jesus told us that we are to love our enemies and to be good to those who persecute us. We are to forgive those who have wronged us, even if they do not want our forgiveness. And there is that parable about the householder who paid the same wages to those who only worked one hour as to those who had worked the whole day. What kind of justice is that?

Grace, unmerited favor, is not an easy thing to give or to receive. We much prefer wages to grace, getting what is due to us rather than what is not deserved or earned. Even those saints who have long ago accepted the gift of God's love can be rankled by the idea that some people enjoy the "fun" of a thoroughly hedonistic lifestyle all their lives, and finally, on their deathbeds, accept God's forgiveness and get all of the blessings of the Kingdom as well. It just isn't fair! (We would have liked to try of few of those things ourselves!)

Of course, it doesn't have anything to do with fairness. It is grace. Whether we receive that gift early or late, it is still grace. Whether we live a lifetime or only a few minutes with it, it is still grace. If we are offended, we had better be careful that we have not slipped too far into believing we deserved it after all.

Out of His generosity He has chosen to forgive us. The good news is that if He is willing to forgive those who repent in their final hour, He can keep forgiving those of us who have accepted His grace long ago but kept on sinning. If that's offensive, insult me some more!

# Day 293
# Matthew 22-25

"But of that day and hour no one knows, not even the angels of heaven, nor the Son, but the Father only." 24:36 The belief in the second coming of Christ has engendered more bitter disputes within Christian circles than almost any other doctrine. It has spawned radical interpretations ranging from Jesus returning, "as a matter of fact, in the next five minutes," to "Jesus is never coming back in the flesh, he has always been with us in his courageous conquering of the fear of death."

It is impossible to solve this debate in these pages and is beyond the scope of what we are trying to do here. What I hope we do not miss is the continuity of the mission and message of Jesus with the mission and message of the Old Testament. Not only was grace the theme in the Old Testament and New Testament (as we have seen) but justice and judgement are the themes in both Testaments as well. Grace and justice were not opponents in the Old Testament and they are likewise companions in the New Testament. Jesus did not come to do away with the law, but to fulfill it. His sacrifice does not do away with the need for justice and judgement, it provides a means by which we can receive forgiveness and have our penalty paid for us, since we could not "afford" the cost ourselves.

The idea that God will just forgive everyone and forget the whole mess makes Jesus' death on the cross a cruel and meaningless waste. The idea that he did not rise again from the dead makes death the final victor in all our lives. The idea that there is no punishment for sin and no Kingdom of God to come makes the whole idea of salvation history ludicrous. Saved from what? History for what purpose?

The message of the whole of Scripture is that God created the world, mankind fell, and God promised to send a savior to redeem His creation. Take that message out and what you have left isn't worth reading and would make no difference anyway. We cannot know when Jesus will return to complete this mission (24:36) but we should understand clearly that the Old and New Testaments declare that he will return to judge, to save, and to move history to its next phase. When that will happen is for none to know; that it will happen is what faith is all about.

# Day 294
# Matthew 26-28

he crucifixion and the resurrection are the two most important events in all of human history. These two things stand out above all others as the consummation of the covenant promise made in Genesis chapter three and embody all the hopes of all the other covenants in the Scriptures. Why then are both these events so frequently misunderstood?

Many people do not understand the necessity of the crucifixion. Isn't this another example of the bloodthirsty mentality of the Old Testament and its sacrifices? If God was going to forgive, why not just forgive? Why demand blood?

Those who struggle with this question have misunderstood the sacrificial system of both Testaments. We have seen ourselves that the sacrificial system of the Old Testament was not like those of the pagan religions. The sacrifice was never to change the mind of God, but rather the minds of those who offered the sacrifice. God's graciousness was shown in allowing a substitute to take the place of the sinner - substitutionary atonement. Jesus' death was the ultimate sacrifice. His death was the ultimate substitutionary atonement which is meant to change, not God's mind, but our minds forever. What greater proof of the love of God than that He gave up the life of His own Son for you and me? If that sacrifice does not drive home the seriousness of our sin and the length, depth and breadth of God's love then *nothing* will. God loves us and has forgiven us. Jesus' sacrifice was meant to communicate that and change our minds toward God, not the other way around.

Jesus' resurrection is the hope of our own salvation realized. God intends to save us, not by remembering us forever, or allowing us to "live on through our children," but to have new bodies and new life in a new creation, just as Jesus rose again and is alive today! No antiseptic absorption of our selves into the great cosmic consciousness, but ourselves as we are now, individuals, but given new life and able to eat the bread from His hand and drink the cup He gives us. That is the message of the gospel and of all of salvation history from the Old through the New Testament. It is also the best news possible. May God grant that we share it as often and in every way we can!

# Day 295
# Mark 1-4

I t is such a marvelous gift that we have more than one account of the life and ministry of Jesus. To see the works and understand the teachings of Christ from only one perspective would indeed be a great disadvantage. In the four gospels we get to see things that might have escaped the attention or the interest of just one person.

Mark's gospel has Jesus on the go. "He immediately" is Mark's favorite phrase for everything that happened to and through the Lord. You almost get the feeling that Jesus came through our world and barely slowed down to sixty miles per hour his whole life! Mark's gospel is good for those who don't like to read all that "extra stuff" like long sermons or lessons. "Just the facts, Ma'am."

And the facts are important for us to know. Jesus was not just a lot of talk, he was also a lot of action. He did not just speak of healing, he brought healing. He did not just talk about solutions to life's problems, he was the solution to those problems. His greatness was not merely in his ideas, his greatness was in real power: power to heal, power to defeat evil, power even to raise the dead. If we are to place our hope in him to solve the problem of our own death, it is vital for us to know that he, in fact, not theory, displayed that kind of power.

For some, this raises disturbing questions. Why does God not still exercise His power that way every day? Why does God not clear out the hospitals all the time? Why did Jesus not heal everyone?

The miracles of Jesus bear witness to his power, but the power to change the physical world is not the most important aspect of his authority. "Which is easier, to say to the paralytic, 'Your sins are forgiven,' or to say, 'Rise, take up your pallet and walk'? But that you may know that the Son of man has authority on earth to forgive sins" - he said to the paralytic - "I say to you, rise, take up your pallet and go home." 2:9-11 Jesus' greatest power was not to heal bodies (doctors can do that) but to heal souls. We are impressed with the former, we should be more impressed with the latter.

Mark wanted to make sure we knew the extent of the power of Jesus. Are we hearing that testimony?

# Day 296
# Mark 5-7

Two things made the early church stand out in rather stark contrast to the religious practices of the old covenant. The most obvious was that with the perfect sacrifice of Jesus, the lamb of God, the sacrificial system was brought to an end. That is why we no longer bring animal sacrifices to church. The final sacrifice has been made. No other blood could be as precious, no other example as convincing, so there was no further need for any sacrifices to change our minds.

The other practice was the eating of "unclean" foods. The Levitical laws which were to set Israel apart were no longer needed to set the church apart in the world. This was not practiced immediately throughout the church, but Mark makes it clear that the change was instituted by Jesus himself. "'Do you not see that whatever goes into a man from outside cannot defile him, since it enters, not his heart but his stomach, and so passes on?' (Thus he declared all foods clean.) And he said, 'What comes out of a man is what defiles a man. For from within, out of the heart of man, come evil thoughts, fornication, theft, murder, adultery, coveting, wickedness, deceit, licentiousness, envy, slander, pride, foolishness. All these evil things come from within, and they defile a man.'" 7:18-23

The Levitical laws had been given in order for Israel to be set apart, a showcase people, for the rest of the world to notice. So quickly the Israelites had misunderstood the purpose of those laws and mistaken righteousness to be a matter of ceremony and not a matter of the heart. Jesus brought them back to the real issue of righteousness - it is a matter of the heart, not the outward actions. We are *not* what we do; we do what we are. We sin because we are sinners at heart; we are not sinners at heart because we sin. What we do comes from the "abundance" of the heart; our actions are the results of our inner beings.

"Cleanliness is next to Godliness" is an old adage, but not a Biblical one. A clean heart, not clean hands, is what matters. God measures the heart. It was true for Abraham and David and it is true for us. Jesus clarified again what had been revealed from the beginning; righteousness is a matter of the heart, not outward ceremony. He has come to change our hearts. Will we let him?

# Day 297
# Mark 8-10

A nd some people say that there is no humor in the Bible! Reread Mark 9:7 and try to imagine yourself being there. Jesus has taken his three closest apostles with him up on a mountain (remind you of Mt. Sinai?) and in an instant, Jesus is transformed into a being of glowing nature in pure white and flanked by two of the greatest figures from the Old Testament: Moses and Elijah.

This is the moment you have been waiting for! You have seen Jesus heal the sick and raise the dead. You have left everything you have to follow him and now he has revealed himself fully. "Let's build some booths!" as military people would to prepare for battle. "We are really going to stomp those Romans now! Just wait until they see our army! Everyone they kill, Jesus can raise up from the dead, and we can travel anywhere with just five loaves and two fish! And if Jesus can heal at a word, just think how many he could kill with a growl! This is going to be great!" Or so they must have thought.

As if that were not enough, you suddenly hear a voice. It is so deep that the earth itself seems to shake at the sound. "This is my beloved Son; *listen to him*!!!" 9:7 [emphasis mine]. And then everything is gone and Jesus is left standing as he was.

I am reminded of Moses' final address to the people of Israel in Deuteronomy 30: 19 when he said, "... I have set before you life and death, blessing and curse; therefore *choose life* ..." [emphasis mine]. When all is said and done, what else is there to say! Cutting through all the complications of what we want and what we think and what we would do if we were God or if only He would listen to us and do what we want, "This is my beloved Son; *listen to him*!!!" If I may be so impolite, perhaps it should read, "Shut up and listen to him!"

Even the apostles had hoped for a different Jesus than the one who confronted them. God had given them a glimpse that what they had hoped for in a messiah was in fact there, but he had something else in mind for his plan of salvation. They did not need to give up their hope, only to listen for God's better idea.

Is your life not going the way you want? Has being a Christian disappointed you? Perhaps it is time to listen and trust that God has a better plan!

# Day 298
# Mark 11-13

he scribes asked Jesus which of the commandments was the greatest. It should not escape our notice that his answer (which even the scribes had to agree with) was not one of the Ten Commandments. "The first is, 'Hear, O Israel: The Lord our God, the Lord is one; and you shall love the Lord your God with all your heart, and with all your soul, and with all your mind, and with all your strength.'" 12:29,20 This was known as the Shema and it came from Deuteronomy 6:4. The commandments of God, the definitions of the covenant, were not restricted to the ten on the tablets that Moses brought down from the mountain.

Jesus volunteered a second answer to their question. "The second is this, 'You shall love your neighbor as yourself.' There is no other commandment greater than these." 12:31 This was quoted from Leviticus 19:18. How can this be one when it is two, and why quote something other than the Ten Commandments?

Jesus came to make clear the understanding which had been lost throughout the centuries, but it was the same truth as revealed to Moses. Relationship with God and others is not dependent on law, but on love. Love is the fulfillment of all the law. Justice is always the least that love would attempt or accomplish. Love is self-sacrificing and looks to the good of the beloved. Love does not treat the beloved equally, it puts the beloved ahead of itself. Love not only fulfills the law, it goes far beyond it to the needs and the good of the beloved.

That may sound self-evident, but in our day and age, we have mistaken equality as being the highest good. We want men and women to be equal and all races and religions and children and animals, too. But equality is not enough for relationship. If my wife and I simply divided all of the chores fifty-fifty we would be roommates, not lovers. Equality keeps accounts; love does not. If love is not at least equal then it is most certainly not love, but if it is not more than equal it will not be alive.

The fulfillment of all the law and the prophets is to love. The "movements" of our era have fallen short of that goal. They want equality, but equality will never be enough. We must love God and each other. Anything less will turn out to be an insufficient tie to bind our lives together.

# Day 299
# Mark 14-16

he crucifixion of Jesus was symbolized in the Passover events of Moses' time. Jesus is the flawless lamb of God, led to slaughter, whose blood marked those whom death is to pass over. He even chose to make his sacrifice at the celebration of the Passover that had given the nation of Israel its identity. He is the lamb of God who takes away the sins of the world.

So much of that sacrifice fits the pattern of the Old Testament sacrifices, but some does not. Jesus reinterpreted some of that symbolism in his last passover meal with his disciples.

In all of the animal sacrifices of Israel, they were never to eat or drink any of the blood. Blood symbolized life, and life was only for God to give. The blood was always poured on the altar and let run into the earth, never consumed. Jesus poured out the wine (which was used as a symbol of blood) and gave it to his disciples and told them to drink it. That sounds normal to us, but to the apostles, this was a whole new message.

Wine symbolized blood and blood symbolized life. Jesus was giving himself as the sacrifice for their sins (his body broken for them) but he was also telling them that they were to partake of his blood - his life.

What does that mean exactly? That is a very difficult question to answer. We aren't sure all that it means, but it does at least mean that being a Christian is more than just living a "pretty good life" - or even an "extremely good life" for that matter. Being a Christian is more than just following, to the best of our ability, the teachings of Jesus about loving others and loving God. In short, it is not just something we do, it is something we are - it is becoming children of God with Jesus' life in us.

This may not seem to be a very helpful description, but in some respects, it is the best we can do, and it is good enough. We do not merely have a new better set of laws, rules, or doctrines to take to our hurting world - we have new life. We do not simply have new ideas to share with a sinful world, but a power to heal, renew, and restore. The Passover spoke of God's gracious forgiveness; the Lord's Supper goes a step further to tell us not only of saving our old lives, but giving us new life. No longer do we just live for God, we may live with Him. Thank you, Jesus!

# Day 300
# Luke 1-4

uke was the church's first historian and we could hardly have asked for a better one. He intended to compile a careful narrative and write an orderly account from the eyewitnesses and he succeeded marvelously. He even addressed his account to "Theophilus" whose name means "lover of God."

Luke describes many events in Jesus' life, ministry, death, and resurrection, in either greater detail or not included in the other synoptic gospels; e.g., the birth of John the Baptist, the angel's visit to Mary and Joseph, the genealogy from Joseph's line, and much more. One of those more detailed accounts is of the temptation of Christ in the wilderness.

Jesus came as God in the flesh, and as such, he accepted the limitations of being human. The temptations Satan offered were all things aimed at getting him to reject that limitation and to rely on his divine nature to handle the difficulties of life. It is the same temptation which confronts us - the desire to be more than human - to be "gods."

"... command this stone to become bread." 4:3 This is the kind of power which we are constantly asking for in our prayers. We want to be able to turn the stone into bread at a word. The fact is that we can turn the stone into bread already. We would have to plant the wheat, mill the flower, and bake the loaf, but God has already provided us with the means to meet our needs in this life. What we want is the short cut, not the work. We want to be more than human because we are too lazy to use the gifts we already have.

"If you, then, will worship me, it shall all be yours." 4:7 Sell your soul for comfort today. It is the same pathetic pottage Esau bought from Jacob - buying the present pleasure at the cost of future glories. A bad bargain every time.

"... throw yourself down from here;" 4:9 This is trying to manipulate God for our own purposes rather than serving Him for His. "But Lord, I prayed/attended church/tithed... why didn't You bless me?" God is not ours to command or control. He has made us to love Him and worship Him and enjoy the blessings of being human. If that was good enough for Jesus, it should be good enough for us.

# Day 301
# Luke 5-7

ne of the true mysteries of the gospels is the calling of the disciples. It is not so much the way in which they were called, but the question of why Jesus chose those twelve men? I hope I am not insulting anyone's favorite apostle, but this was a motley crew if ever there were one.

. Matthew was a tax collector which meant he had turned traitor to his people and was helping the Romans collect tribute from the Jews. Peter was a mixed bag who mostly could be counted on to do the wrong thing at the right time, or the right thing at the wrong time. James and John were brothers who had their mother asking for their promotions. Thomas was a skeptic. The rest were rather nondescript, at least as far as the gospels are concerned. None were well educated or particularly talented. Why choose this group?

Then again, God has a rather long history of picking the unlikely to accomplish His will. If we remember, the Jews were likewise chosen to be God's people, not because they were especially bright or obedient or courageous - they were certainly not any of those - but in some sense, to prove that if God could love them, and work with them, He could do so with anybody. The encouraging news about the twelve rather ordinary people that Jesus chose is that if he could work through the twelve of them, he can work through rather ordinary people like us.

The Scriptures do not tell us much about what happened to all of these men after the resurrection. But tradition has it that they all met a martyr's death after establishing churches throughout the known world. Certainly the testimony of the changes in Peter alone tell us that what is really important is not where we start out when God touches our lives, but where we end up after He has been at work in us.

There is at least one other message for us from this strange crew of twelve who followed Jesus. They followed him. They did not always understand him, but they followed. They listened with their hearts and voted with their feet. That is a powerful combination in the hands of God. What is really important is not *who* we are, but *whose* we are. What a wonderful message for him to send through motley disciples like us.

# Day 302
# Luke 8-11

he parable of the good Samaritan is one of the best
known of all of Jesus' parables. It has been used
throughout the centuries to argue against prejudice
and racism which has inflicted the world in every
culture and country the gospel has reached.

While racism and prejudice are clearly unbiblical and
against the whole understanding of people being sons and
daughters of Adam and Eve and creatures created in the image of
God, that is not really the message of the parable and the real
message is often missed.

It is a lawyer who posed the question that Jesus was
answering with this parable. Not to malign an entire profession,
but it is a lawyer's standard tactic. Lawyers specialize in finding
loopholes that obey the letter of the law but not the spirit. Yet we
all succumb to the temptation. If you doubt, consider some of the
ways in which even children can devise a means of doing what
they were told, without doing what they were told. "You said,
'Get in the tub', you never said anything about soap and water!"
The lawyer knew that the commandment was to love his neighbor,
and he wanted a definition of "neighbor."

However, the original question had been "...what shall I do
to inherit eternal life?" The question is at the heart of how one
relates to God. Are there some ceremonies or duties to be done in
order to be saved? Jesus' answer could be reduced to "Be real."
This is the real message of the parable.

What made the Samaritan the true neighbor? He did what a
real neighbor does. God is not interested in our ideas about life
save for the impact they have on our living of it. The search for
truth can never be simply an academic exercise that provides us
with reliable data; it is the activity of the will that is trying to live
in the world of reality, not fantasy. When we talk about loving
but do not do it, we have not yet entered into the real world where
love is not an abstract concept, but real living itself.

We must stop talking so much about loving God and our
neighbor and get to doing it. "Go and do likewise." Eternal life is
a gift; it cannot earned. If we want assurance that we will be
"going to heaven" it will be shown in seeing some of "heaven"
come out of us into our world.

# Day 303
# Luke 12-14

"So therefore, whoever of you does not renounce all that he has cannot be my disciple." 14:33 So much for the "gentle Jesus meek and mild." When we actually consider what Jesus had to teach about the Kingdom of God and following him, we will find that Os Guinness was correct when he wrote, "Too often Christianity has not been tried and found wanting; it has been found demanding and not tried."

What of this "renouncing everything"? Throughout the centuries there have been some who have taken this quite literally and given everything they have to the poor and entered into a life of service and poverty. Jesus warned that it was easier for a camel to get through the eye of a needle than for a rich person to enter the Kingdom. Are we all to be like Francis of Assisi who gave away all his possessions?

There is a certain freedom that comes with going to an extreme. Decisions are difficult to make because there seems to be a never-ending procession of them. If we can once settle some of the basic ones, the others become easier because they have been determined by former decisions. You will never have to worry about whether to wash the car or clean the house if you never have a car or a house.

The problem is that when we give up all these things, we still have to use someone else's possessions. If we do not sleep in our own house, we must sleep in someone's building, wear someone's clothes, cook in someone's kitchen. We cannot all be free of possessions - or can we?

We can take Jesus' command to renounce everything no less literally than St. Francis, but with a different interpretation. We can renounce our *ownership* of all our things and recognize that they are gifts from God over which we are to be *stewards*.

Stewardship carries with it the same freedom of possessions but adds the responsibility to use those resources wisely. Following Jesus does not mean giving everything away, it means recognizing that everything we have - even our very lives - belongs to God anyway. We are called to give up the illusion of ownership in favor of the gifts of stewardship. It is surprising how hard an illusion that is to give up! Help us, Lord!

# Day 304
# Luke 15-18

r. George Eldon Ladd was the professor of New Testament Theology at Fuller Seminary when I attended there. He had the reputation of being rather, shall we say, "demanding," of his students. He would require that we read out of our Greek New Testaments in class, translating "on the fly;" an ability few of us possessed with any measure of expertise. To put it simply, he had us all scared to death that he would call on us!

One particular day, he asked what we were all sure was a loaded question. "How do you *know* that you will enter the Kingdom of God; that you will be going to heaven?" Our silence irritated him, but we were all afraid to answer what seemed so obvious a question. Finally, one poor soul offered tentatively, "Because Jesus rose from the dead?" "No!" was the thundering reply from Dr. Ladd. "That is how anyone will go! My question is how do *you* know you will enter the Kingdom?" After a long silence, and another tirade wherein Dr. Ladd questioned just what the church teaches young people these days, he answered his own question - an answer I shall never forget. "You can *know* you will enter the Kingdom of God, because the Kingdom of God has already entered *you!*"

"The kingdom of God is not coming with signs to be observed; nor will they say, 'Lo, here it is!' or 'There!' for behold, the kingdom of God is in the midst of you." 17:21 Jesus also spoke of his second coming in this same chapter. How can both be true?

The problem is solved when we realize what the Kingdom of God really is. We think of kingdoms as marked territories, but the Kingdom of God is anywhere (and everywhere) that God reigns as King. The Kingdom is therefore present (in our hearts) and future (yet to be fully established). We can know we will be in the Kingdom, because the Kingdom is already in us.

Dr. Ladd was correct, the church has not done a very good job of teaching Jesus' primary subject matter - the Kingdom of God. If God reigns as King in your heart, you have already entered into the Kingdom. There can be no greater assurance for us than this; our life with God has begun and it will never come to an end. Praise God!

# Day 305
# Luke 19-21

he encounter with Zacchaeus on the road through Jericho has captured the imagination of people throughout the centuries. We have all stood in a crowd trying to see a celebrity and hoped that suddenly the celebrity would see us and call out our names in recognition. It happened for Zacchaeus and at the most opportune time.

As we have seen, tax collectors were hated because they had turned traitor to their own people. The Romans hired and protected local officials to collect the apportioned tribute for a given area. Obviously, these officials would know who and how much to tax. Revenue over and above their quotas was kept by the tax collector. The more unprincipled tax collectors became very rich and further gained the people's hatred by hiring others to help in this injustice.

The idea that Jesus would eat with such a man was totally disgusting to everyone. Then to declare that salvation had come to Zacchaeus and his household was unbelievable. Yet it is a marvelous example of what Jesus came to earth to do.

Zacchaeus had every reason to believe that he was lost beyond hope. He had betrayed his people and his God. Why he even climbed the tree is a question we can never fully answer. But in some deep part of himself, he must not have given up hope - hope that somehow, someone great enough, could help him undo the years of sin and betrayal. Probably not enough hope to even put that into words, but enough to get him up that tree.

Someone great enough did come along. In fact, the important thing for us to see in this whole encounter is not that Zacchaeus sought out Jesus, but that Jesus sought out Zacchaeus. "For the Son of man came to seek and to save the lost." 19:10 What good news! When we are finally done with our feeble efforts to reach God, we find that He has been trying to reach us all along! He will use any opportunity we will provide.

Do you feel that you have lost touch with God? Is there something you have done, or not done, that makes you feel sure He doesn't want to hear from you? Take a page from Zacchaeus' book, and climb any tree. You will find that God has been reaching out to you all along with His saving grace.

# Day 306
# Luke 22-24

Crucifixion and resurrection. These are the two things that Jesus' first coming was all about. The lessons, the parables, the miracles, the healings, are all secondary to these two crucial events. Take these two out and all you have left is a lovely bunch of platitudes that do not come close to touching the real needs of fallen humanity.

That is a strong statement, but I believe it with all my heart and clearly the disciples believed it, too. The power of Jesus' sacrifice and his resurrection is written all over the lives of the apostles and all his disciples since then. It is the power to overcome all obstacles and persevere to the end of life with the belief and hope that death has been overcome and life eternal in the Kingdom of God is ours through Christ.

Amazingly, some people accept the crucifixion but not the resurrection. There is a Biblical example of the difference between those who see one and not the other. Both Peter and Judas had something in common. Each betrayed Christ; Judas by turning him over to the Pharisees, and Peter by denying him after swearing he would die with him rather than desert him.

Some scholars have suggested that Judas actually thought he was forcing Jesus' hand by turning him over to the Pharisees; that Jesus would finally have to reveal himself and unleash the power he had shown in his miracles. Whatever Judas' motive, the sad fact is that he despaired and committed suicide.

There was only one thing that could have washed away the guilt from both Peter and Judas and that was not suicide, it was the resurrection. No amount of talking about the frailty of the human soul or how every one else deserted him nor good intentions behind bad choices would have made any difference. Without the resurrection there is no triumph in the cross, only tragedy. Judas knew that. His great tragedy was that he was not around on Easter Sunday to know the transforming power of the resurrection; Peter was, and that made all the difference.

Whatever other great truths about salvation history we may miss in the New Testament, let us not miss these, for they are the only ones that count. Christ died for us, Christ was raised for us, Christ lives for us. He lives, he lives, he lives! Amen!

# Day 307
# John 1-4

ohn's gospel is so different from the synoptics. He is more concerned that we understand the meaning of the events of Jesus' life than the details of it. He does not start even with Jesus' birth, but with his divine nature as an eternal member of the Godhead and his divine purpose as the savior of the world.

John also wants us to be clear about our place in life. "But to all who received him, who believed in his name, he gave power to become children of God; who were born, not of blood nor of the will of the flesh nor of the will of man, but of God." 1:12 We are all creatures created in the image of God. That is what it means to be sons and daughters of Adam and Eve. But we are not all children of God by birth. When I make something, it is my creation, but in order to be my child, it must have my life in it. In order to be God's children we must have His life in us. In Jesus' words, "... unless one is born anew, he cannot see the kingdom of God." 3:3

What is this new birth? It is the same fundamental change that has been necessary for people since the fall - the willingness to trust in God for our salvation, not in our own power or in our own righteousness - in a word, grace. Believing in Jesus is believing that "For God so loved the world that he gave his only Son, that whoever believes in him should not perish but have eternal life. For God sent the Son into the world, not to condemn the world, but that the world might be saved through him." 3:16,17 It is the same thing as Abraham's faith being reckoned as righteousness. It is finally accepting that God does not hate us for our sins, but will forgive us and remake us.

The day my daughter was born I understood what John 3:16 meant in a whole new way. As I looked down into that innocent face of my first child, I realized that the very last thing I would ever do would be to give her life up for someone. I would gladly die myself before making that sacrifice. If God did not spare even His own son, we may believe that He loves us full measure.

Learning to trust God, accepting your salvation as a gift which cannot be earned, unmerited favor, grace - these are the gospel, the covenant, the love of God manifest. Believe it. That's why he came, that we might be more than his creation, we might become his children.

# Day 308
# John 5-7

"But Jesus answered them, 'My Father is working still, and I am working.' This was why the Jews sought all the more to kill him, because he not only broke the sabbath but also called God his own Father, making himself equal with God." 5:17

Surprisingly, many Christians could not say where Jesus ever claimed to be God. It is important to know that the claims of deity came from Jesus himself; he claimed to be able to forgive sins, raise the dead, and give eternal life. "For as the Father raises the dead and gives them life, so also the Son gives life to whom he will. The Father judges no one, but has given all judgment to the Son, that all may honor the Son, even as they honor the Father. He who does not honor the Son does not honor the Father who sent him. Truly, truly, I say to you, he who hears my word and believes him who sent me, has eternal life; he does not come into judgment, but has passed from death to life." 5:21-24

In the New Testament, the question of the nature of Jesus is the central issue. He embodies the New Covenant completely. His life, death, and resurrection fulfill the twin laws of justice and love. Accepting him, not a set of rules or ethics, is what Christianity is all about. We must not merely accept his teachings, we must accept *him*. C.S. Lewis said it in *Mere Christianity* better than I ever could.

I am trying here to prevent anyone saying the really foolish thing that people often say about Him: "I'm ready to accept Jesus as a great moral teacher, but I don't accept His claim to be God." That is the one thing we must not say. A man who was merely a man and said the sort of things Jesus said would not be a great moral teacher. He would either be a lunatic - on a level with the man who says he is a poached egg - or else he would be the Devil of Hell. You must make your choice. Either this man was, and is, the Son of God: or else a madman or something worse. You can shut Him up for a fool, you can spit at Him and kill Him as a demon; or you can fall at His feet and call Him Lord and God. But let us not come with any patronizing nonsense about His being a great human teacher. He has not left that open to us. He did not intend to.

# Day 309
# John 8-11

ohn uses a good deal of space in his gospel retelling the story of the man born blind. What was so important about this incident? Why were the Pharisees so interested in discrediting this man? What does this say about our understanding of sin?

The Pharisees were horrified at Jesus' claim to be the Son of God. They knew he was not claiming to be a godly man, or a son of God as you or I might be, but claiming a unique relationship with the Father. Jesus had claimed to be able to forgive sins, give eternal life, and even raise the dead. To prove these claims, he had healed the sick, pronounced forgiveness for sins, and even raised the dead. No mere mortal could do such things or make such claims. Why did the Pharisees not accept his proof as the blind man had?

The answer is they did not want the truth Jesus had to offer - that salvation, right relationship with God, was not a matter of works, but grace. They wanted what they thought they deserved for all of their hard work at trying to be righteous. That is why they believed the man born blind had been punished for the sins of his parents. God must reward and punish according to one's works; that way they would get the best rewards because they had worked the hardest.

Jesus came proclaiming again the message of the Old Testament - right relationship (righteousness) by grace through faith, not works. God is worshipped in spirit and in truth (John chapter four) - He measures the heart, and counts faith *as if* it were righteousness. You cannot earn salvation, you must accept it as a gift you don't deserve.

Sickness and disability are not punishments for sins; some may be consequences of our sins, but certainly not all. Our real sin is in trying to live our lives as if there were no God, or as if He could be as easily controlled as doing our "religious duties."

In healing this man and declaring that his disability was not a result of sin, Jesus undercut the whole understanding of salvation by works that the Pharisees so much wanted to protect. Their lives had been built on a lie they could no longer reject. Theirs were the eyes that could not be opened. May God grant that we see the truth which will make us free indeed!

# Day 310
# John 12-14

**I**t must have been very difficult for the disciples during those last few days before the crucifixion. Jesus was such a commanding presence and yet he was always doing unexpected things. He returned to Jerusalem against sound advice, but delayed when he was told about Lazarus. After he raised Lazarus, he refused to enter Jerusalem as a powerful king but washed the feet of his disciples - the work of a slave. He could raise people from the dead, yet he spoke increasingly of his own death.

It must have been difficult for Jesus during those days, too. He knew what he must do, and how confusing it would be for his disciples. It pained him to see them so confused and struggling to understand him. That was why he wept with Mary even though he knew he would be raising Lazarus. He has suffered with us.

It must have been difficult for him to decide what so say before his sacrifice. These apostles had been with him two or three years, had heard him teach, witnessed his miracles, and yet were so far from having any idea of what was to occur. That last night in the upper room must have been agonizing for him.

He knew that the Holy Spirit would come and bring back to their memory all that they needed to understand, but just because you know the outcome of something does not make it easy to accomplish. There would be much pain from the cross for everyone before Easter morning would transform it. How to summarize all he wanted them to know?

He issued a commandment. "A new commandment I give to you, that you love one another; even as I have loved you, that you also love one another. By this all men will know that you are my disciples, if you have love for one another." 13:34 It is a witness, a service, and a calling. We are to love, not just as we have understood love, but as he understood love and showed it with his willing sacrifice.

If you have wondered what it means to be a Christian, this is it. Christianity has never been just words, it has always existed in the living and the loving. If we claim to be his followers, then we must love as he did. No higher standard could be set, no clearer example given. May God grant us the grace to obey this one commandment from our Lord.

# Day 311
# John 15-18

"I am the vine, you are the branches. He who abides in me, and I in him, he it is that bears much fruit, for apart from me you can do nothing." 15:5 This is a familiar passage to most of us, but that does not make it an easy one to understand. Most of us are constantly trying to live our lives for God rather than live our lives with God.

There have been many devotional books written throughout the centuries trying to explain this very concept of "abiding" in Christ. We live our lives of devotion, trying to do the right thing, and most of the time, our efforts are feeble, even by our own accounts. Yet some of the saints throughout the centuries have been able to achieve that sense of peace and joy that alludes so many Christians. What is their secret? Abiding.

Alexandr Solzhenityzn wrote that, "Pride grows on the human heart like lard on a pig." The tendency to take ourselves too seriously is so deep in the human heart that it is almost impossible to get rid of it. No matter how often we tell ourselves that it is the Lord's work, we are quite certain that without our contribution, the job would suffer substantially.

This is a passage and a message that as a pastor, I need to come back to with great regularity. The messianic complex infects many more than just clergy, but we are particularly prone to it. Without us, where would the Church be? I must go to *this* meeting, or teach *this* lesson, or give *this* sermon, or make *this* hospital call. And so we rush around from place to place until we are ready to drop, working for God rather than working with Him. Jesus' public ministry was only about three years long, and there is no indication that he was ever in a hurry.

So how do we goal oriented types do this "abiding"? We start by remembering that God loves us, He does not want us for what we can do for Him. If you never accomplished a single "good work" for God, He would love you no less. From that standpoint, anything good you can do becomes a "bonus" of sorts. God will accomplish His work in His own way, and somehow, beyond all sense and reason, be able to work in your contribution and mine. We can stop worrying about doing something important, and just try to do something right. And try to be patient; God isn't finished with us yet!

# Day 312
# John 19-21

oubts. We all have them. They are not the opposite of belief - that is disbelief. Doubts are the area between belief and disbelief; that place where we are not sure what is true. That may make them uncomfortable, but that does not make them sinful - necessarily.

Sadly, for all the wonderful things he did as an apostle, Thomas will forever be known as the doubter. Still, he provides us with a marvelous model of how and how not to handle our own doubts.

Why did Thomas doubt? John tells us that he was not there when Jesus first appeared to the other apostles. Doubters often make that critical mistake - they withdraw from the fellowship of the group. It is hard to be around people who seem certain when you are not, but doubt is uncomfortable even by itself. It is a mistake to cut oneself off from the help of the community that can provide support in times of doubt. How many times have we heard people say, "He wouldn't show up if God himself were to make a personal appearance!" In Thomas' case, he did, and Thomas missed it! In fact, we believe He still does today. He's hard to see in many churches, but we believe He is there. He promised he would be.

There are also at least two types of doubt; honest doubt, and dishonest doubt. Dishonest doubts are those which come from some source other than a real reason for being uncertain. Many people doubt because they are afraid of what would happen to them if they were to believe. Honest inquiry is necessary for honest doubt. We must not be afraid of the truth if we really intend to find it. Otherwise, we will have decided in advance what our conclusions will be before we go looking for evidence.

What makes doubts honest is knowing what it would take to convince you of the truth. Thomas knew what it would take. This does not mean that we will always get all the proof we ask for, but we will get the evidence we need to know. Do we all need to see the nail marks? The answer is that we don't. Just how much evidence do we need in order to have faith? Remember, faith is not knowing all, just knowing enough.

Have doubts? Are they honest? Then ask away. God will provide enough evidence. He wants us to believe.

# Day 313
# Acts 1-4

Pentecost. This was one of the most unexpected events in the Bible. The idea that God would send His Holy Spirit on people was not particularly new. He had done so with the great prophets of the Old Testament. But the idea that He would give it to "common" people, even though it had been promised in the Old Testament, was shocking to those who received it. The change that it made was quite unexpected.

Some have questioned the accuracy of the account of Pentecost. Others have used it to support the idea of a "baptism of the Holy Spirit" being necessary and "speaking in tongues" being the sign. While these are larger questions than we have space for here, it is important to notice that the birth of the Church was the action of God (therefore why rule out the miraculous?) and that the "tongues" were languages the people who spoke them understood.

The task of the Holy Spirit is not an easy one. On the one hand, His responsibility is to comfort and guide us as we try to go about the task of being stewards of these lives we have turned over to Christ. He is to empower us without taking us over. He must direct us without removing our free will. In that sense, His is the same dilemma it has always been - how to work with these strange little creatures He created. Perhaps that is why the Holy Spirit is so difficult for most Christians to understand - He is God's Spirit in us, but not the God we expected.

Most of us would love to have the kind of experience that Peter and the other apostles had at Pentecost. We would love to stand up and have words simply flow out, without any preparation by us, and have it understood even by those with which we cannot otherwise communicate. We want the miraculous. But we should remember that this did not happen again even for Peter or the apostles. God is with us, even in us, but not in the way we think or will probably ever really understand.

It would be nice (we think) to have the Holy Spirit empower us to do the miraculous, never make mistakes, and have trouble free lives, but that was not what He came to do - for the apostles or us. Whatever else Pentecost means, it was the arrival in our world and lives of the God who cannot be controlled, only trusted. That is a little frightening; it is also the best possible news!

# Day 314
# Acts 5-7

tephen was the first Christian martyr. What is less recognized but no less true, is that he was also the first theologian of the Church. In spite of the fact that the apostles had been with Jesus as his "inner circle," it took Stephen to realize that following Christ was going to be different from the "business as usual" of first century Judaism.

One of the most wonderful things about the Scriptures is that they tell the truth about people. That means that they are not always too complimentary to the people in them, but Scripture lets us see the truth - that God uses people like you and me, not larger-than-life characters.

Jesus' great commission to his disciples was to go unto all the world making disciples. The last thing he told them before he ascended was to be his witnesses even to the ends of the earth. So what did they do? They settled into Jerusalem, continued going to the synagogue and the temple, and waited for the world to come to them. The most enduring debate in the book of Acts was whether or not a person had to become a Jew before they became a Christian. The apostles had missed the point.

Still, God always gets His work accomplished. From the ranks of those the Church set aside to handle the menial tasks of serving tables (is there a message here?) God used Stephen to make it clear that it was the Jews, not Jesus, who had gotten the true faith confused. God did not live in a temple. The temple had been a foolish idea to begin with, the well-meaning but silly gift David wanted to give to God. It was Stephen who interpreted salvation history correctly, albeit with a noticeable lack of tact. Jesus' sacrifice had made the sacrificial system obsolete and salvation had always been meant for all people.

God got the gospel out of Jerusalem. He had to persecute it out after the death of Stephen, but it got out. Throughout the rest of Acts we will find that the gospel arrived through unrecorded people, long before Peter or Paul visited. That has always been God's methodology - He works through those of whom the world takes little notice.

So take heart. The world may not notice, but He changes it through people like you and me!

# Day 315
# Acts 8-11

The conversion of Saul has been written about at great length, especially in our century. Many have used it as evidence of the truth of the claims of the gospel. What would cause a man who was zealously persecuting a group suddenly to become one of its principal leaders? Personally, I think Ananias' obedience is more of an argument for the gospel than Saul's conversion.

Imagine yourself in Ananias' position. You have recently heard that a person named Saul was coming to your city with papers that would allow him to kill Christians. You have also heard that this great enemy of the faith has been struck blind by God! Then, as you pray, God tells you to go to a street and a home and lay your hands on this very man to restore his sight. At this point I would be banging my "prayer telephone" on the table a few times because I'd be sure we had a bad connection! God can't mean him! He is a murderer - the enemy! Yet Ananias did as he was told and restored Saul's sight.

Some people have argued that Saul became a convert because of the guilt he felt about holding the coats of the people who had stoned Stephen. While that may have been a part of what was going on for Saul, what possible explanation can there be for Ananias' actions except obedience to God? Changing one's beliefs about God must be easier than doing so toward a flesh and blood person who was persecuting you.

Corrie tenBoom survived a Nazi concentration camp but her sister did not. After the war was over, she travelled around Europe trying to heal the hatred the war had caused. After speaking to a group one night, a man came up to her and asked for her forgiveness. She immediately recognized him as one of the guards from the concentration camp. She prayed quickly because she discovered she could not bring herself to forgive this man who had been so cruel to her and her sister. She admitted to God that she could not forgive him. God spoke to her and told her He could. In the name of Christ, she reached out and forgave her former captor.

Love your enemy. Jesus meant it when he said it. That he has the power to give us to make good on that commandment is one of the surest signs I know that he is risen indeed!

# Day 316
# Acts 12-14

There is a rather popular belief in our time that what really matters in religion is not so much what you believe, but how well you believe it. In America we are fond of saying, "Well, if it works for you, that's fine, but don't try to impose your beliefs on me!" That sounds like a very "democratic" idea, but it does not apply very well to reality.

Paul and Barnabas on their first missionary journey were careful in communicating the gospel. In Lystra, when Paul healed the man who had been born crippled, the people hailed Barnabas and Paul as gods. This upset the two so much that they tore their clothes and went running to straighten out the confusion. If the content of the people's faith was not important, but only their believing, why bother?

The problem is that reality is not very "democratic" at all. Cigarettes don't ask you whether or not you believe them to be bad for your lungs, they just are. If you eat spoiled food, it does not ask if you desire food poisoning, it just makes you sick. If there is radon present in your home, it doesn't consult you as to whether you want to get cancer, it just kills you. We simply do not get to vote on the nature of the universe. What makes us think that our opinions about the existence and nature of God will make any difference to His reality? He is either there, or He is not. What we believe about it does not change the reality one way or the other.

It does, of course, make a difference to us. People speak of "breaking God's laws," but in reality, we are really breaking ourselves on God's laws. When you jump off a ten story building, you have not broken the law of gravity, but you will break yourself on it. Deny the reality for as long as you can (the first nine floors) but eventually, the ground will show up and it will not ask for your opinion as to whether or not it should be hard.

Paul and Barnabas were not Hermes and Zeus. *God* had healed the man, not Paul. Jesus rose from the dead and is alive today. These statements are either true or false. We must decide what we are going to believe about them, but let us not operate under the delusion that our beliefs will change the reality no matter how strongly we hold to them.

# Day 317
# Acts 15-17

ontroversy and the Church have never been strangers. From the very beginning, Jesus' followers have found questions which were not specifically addressed by our Lord while he was with us. What must you do in order to be saved? Do you have to become a Jew before you become a Christian? Why didn't Jesus write all this down, or establish a clear hierarchy of command for the Church?

These are difficult questions. From the very first century Christians have been struggling with how to make decisions. The first Council at Jerusalem is an example of how the Church has struggled from the beginning. However conflicts are resolved, one thing seems clear; God intended for us to struggle with each other.

One of my friends in high school was a "rock hound" and would go with his family into different desert areas collecting rocks. I always marveled at how they recognized the valuable ones from the ones you toss into a stream. When they first brought them back, they looked ugly. They were rough and dirty. Then they put them into the noisiest machine I have ever met - a rock polisher. The rock polisher was simply a metal drum that you put the rocks and some water and some sand into and then it turned around and around for several weeks. The noise was tremendous and irritating, but when they stopped it and took out the rocks, they were smooth and beautiful. In the tumbling into each other, they had knocked off all the rough edges and brought out the beauty beneath. This is perhaps the best metaphor I know of for the Church. God takes some really dirty and rough people, throws them together to bang into each other and bring out the best in us all. The process is long and noisy and uncomfortable, but it works.

Too many people in churches do not understand the nature of the process they have entered into. They think that Church should be the place where everyone always smiles and agrees with one another. But the church will not always be happy and sweet. The rougher we are when we go in, the more noise and pain we cause, but we belong together. Growth is seldom, if ever, a neat and easy process. As difficult as it often is, we should not withdraw from Christian fellowship, for in truth, we may be the ones whose edges need the treatment.

# Day 318
# Acts 18-21

aul. This man reminds me of Moses more than any other figure in the Bible. His was a special mission that would run against the grain of the whole of society, Jewish, Roman, and Greek. He would war with everyone (including the other apostles) and be beaten, derided, shipwrecked, and even abandoned by friends, but he could not be stopped. He was as subtle as manure at a banquet and as harsh to friends as he was to enemies. He was also chosen by God.

We know quite a bit about Paul, not just from Acts, but from his own writings which make up so much of the New Testament. Yet you cannot miss the feeling that no one (except Jesus) has ever really known Paul. We have more insight into his psyche than almost any other ancient person and what we discover is that people are more complex and profound than we realize. He was truly a man of God in the Old Testament sense - a force to be reckoned with and not a little bit scary.

One of my favorite stories about Paul is in the twentieth chapter. For all Paul's gifts and all the power in his ministry, he was not a very good speaker. At times when I begin to feel discontented with preaching or teaching, it is a comfort to remember that at least I've never "preached" somebody to death! Poor Euthychus! But then again, I've never raised anyone from the dead either!

Like so many of the great figures of the Scriptures, we should learn from them that God is not in search of perfect people. What is so impressive about Paul was not his talent or his training or his credentials, but his Lord. God has chosen to work through what looks to us like the most unlikely people. Paul was too fanatical and disagreeable to get a job in most modern churches. He did not share his toys and play well with others. But he had a heart fully given over to the Lord and God used him; sometimes because of himself and sometimes in spite of himself.

God is not looking for polish as much as persistence. He is not as concerned with talent as He is with tenacity. And He is most definitely more interested in character than charisma. Paul offers us the same lesson that Israel did in the Old Testament - if God could work with them, He can certainly work with us!

# Day 319
# Acts 22-24

An old bumper sticker from the 70's read, "If being a Christian were illegal, would there be enough evidence to convict you?" There most certainly was enough to convict Paul and he was "tried" several times for just that offense. The questions the bumper sticker raises are a little different though. Just what would constitute "proof" and of what would your "testimony" consist?

There is no small amount of guilt attached to and intended by that bumper sticker. The author wanted us to question the "level" of our commitment. Sadly, throughout the centuries, Christians have done this to one another. Paul even did this in relation to John Mark which occasioned his going separate directions from his friend Barnabas. There remains a strong element of judgmentalism which sets a certain minimum level of commitment as being necessary for salvation.

During the persecution of the Church in the first and third centuries, that level was very difficult to set. For those whose relatives had martyred themselves rather than recant their faith, anyone who had done less, even those who had simply fled, were not worthy to be counted among "the saints". When the persecutions were over and Christianity became legal, the first serious division of the Church was over that very issue. But only God can know and measure our hearts. Who are we to judge the servant of another? God's is the only court in which we will finally have to "prove" our faith, and in His court, faith, not works at any level, will be the deciding factor.

What then will our testimony be? In God's court it will be nothing more than our own hearts. Before then, may I suggest that it will be no more than what we can give witness to. Paul's testimony was of his encounter with Jesus on the Damascus road. Paul did not testify with theological arguments in support of the trinity, he told what is really the only acceptable testimony in a court - that to which he had himself been an eyewitness.

Most of us have never had an encounter with Jesus like Paul's on the Damascus road. Does that mean we have no "testimony" to give? I think not. I do think it means that we need to consider how we ourselves have experienced God's presence in our lives. That is our testimony. How would you tell yours?

# Day 320
# Acts 25-28

ower. The hearing before Festus and Agrippa was the classic confrontation of the power of the kingdoms of this world and the power of the kingdom of God. Luke notes the majesty with which Agrippa comes to this encounter and the lowliness of Paul, yet the servant of the Lord was not in any way overwhelmed, but met his adversary with the dignity inherent in his position.

How ironic that Agrippa and Festus should have exhibited such self importance as they stood in the presence of a man who was greater than they were by any measure. Paul was more than their equal in learning and influence. Arguably, he has had more impact on people and cultures than any other single individual in history (except Jesus), while Agrippa's and Festus' claim to fame is only that they once examined him as a common prisoner.

What was the source of Paul's power which would eventually so overshadow Rome and all the other nations? God, or course, but more specifically, the truth of God. Paul could stand before the "powerful" of his time because he knew there is nothing more powerful than God's truth. What God has ordained and spoken can never be changed. Paul knew that Jesus was the Christ and he had come to fulfill the promise of God given all through the prophets, to bring salvation and eternal life to all people. Nothing could change that. Jesus had also called Paul to proclaim that truth. It did not really matter whether Festus or Agrippa believed it, it was true nonetheless. And Paul was not responsible for how they responded to the truth, only that he told them. The source of Paul's confidence was in knowing what he was called to do, and doing it.

This should be our confidence too in sharing the good news of forgiveness and eternal life. Power is not something conferred by councils; it is rooted in reality. If we will tell the truth, we need not worry about always having to "prove it," because no false theory will ever be able to stand against the truth. I hear many people who are afraid to share the gospel because they can't answer everyone's questions. No one can except God, and He's not telling everything yet! We are called to trust in the truth and to tell what we do know, not what we don't. If we do, like Paul, we will find our testimony will stand the test of time.

# Day 321
# Romans 1-3

in is separation from God. Being a real Jew, one of the people of God, is not a matter of the flesh but a matter of the heart. We are justified not by our works, but by grace through faith which we receive not as our due but as a gift from God. Romans is absolutely packed with important theology.

Saul had been a Pharisee. He had been trained in the current understanding of Judaism of his time. He had read the Scriptures and understood the place of the Jews - they were God's chosen people. God had given them the law and through the law the promise of eternal life belonged to those who zealously followed the law. Then he met Jesus on the Damascus road.

Paul emerged from his encounter with Jesus with a new understanding of the Scriptures. Now the Jews were not a people preferred, but a people priestly. God's love of Jew and Gentile had been there all along and the law was not the means of grace for the Jews but a means of witness to the Gentiles. Sacrifices had never purchased God's forgiveness, they had been signs of God's grace and now were no longer needed since Jesus had come and made the perfect sacrifice. Jew and Gentile both, like Abraham, were not justified by the law but by faith in the gracious character of God.

This is why most Christian scholars say that in order to understand the Old Testament properly, you must read it from a New Testament perspective, and in order to appreciate the New Testament, you must understand the testimony of the Old Testament. Saul had read the Old Testament and missed the message. When Paul's eyes were opened he understood what he had missed before. Romans touches on the most critical of those understandings. Here we will find the fundamental principles of salvation history laid out.

For those who have wondered where the idea came from that the Old Testament is a message of grace, the answer is here. Paul had seen the continuity of the message of salvation - all have sinned and we are justified by faith. It had been so for Abraham and Moses and no less for us. If it seems that the Scriptures are repeating themselves on these issues, they are! Let us not miss the message - grace through faith. It has always been so.

# Day 322
# Romans 4-7

"More than that, we rejoice in our sufferings, knowing that suffering produces endurance, and endurance produces character, and character produces hope, and hope does not disappoint us, because God's love has been poured into our hearts through the Holy Spirit which had been given to us." 5:3-5

Lest I give the impression that the New Testament has no new insights to offer, we should make special note of the way in which understanding the gospel can transform our outlook on even the most difficult things in life.

So much of the Old Testament had to do with the Israelites complaining about their suffering. The Psalms were filled with it, the prophets were devoted to explaining it, and the book of Job is consumed by it. Yet nowhere was this insight offered - rejoice in your sufferings. It almost seems masochistic.

We should recall what Paul wrote just before this. "Therefore, since we are justified by faith, we have peace with God through our Lord Jesus Christ." How can we be at peace when we are suffering, especially when we are suffering unjustly as happened to the early Church? It comes from having a promise and a purpose.

Ecclesiastes argued that all was vanity because we would eventually die. Paul argues that even suffering can be redeemed because we will be raised. Our suffering can build endurance, our endurance character, and our character hope as we wait for our salvation which is guaranteed, not by ourselves, but by Christ! We have a hope worth holding on to, a promise (covenant!) based not on ourselves, but on the gracious love of God. One day there will be an end to all suffering. That is no mean promise!

There is also a purpose in our suffering. We may die never understanding it, but Paul argues that nothing arbitrary happens to us. Life has a purpose; to trust God and spread the good news of eternal life! It does not fully explain suffering, nor does it make it good. Suffering is still evil and God has promised to do away with it. But it does make suffering tolerable. We can get something good out of it - a stubbornness that, like Job, will not curse God and die. That takes character, and character is the greatest witness to God's transforming power I know.

# Day 323
# Romans 8-10

"hat then shall we say to this? If God is for us, who is against us? He who did not spare his own Son but gave him up for us all, will he not also give us all things with him?...No, in all these things we are more than conquerors through him who loved us. For I am sure that neither death, nor life, nor angels, nor principalities, nor things present, nor things to come, nor powers, nor height, nor depth, nor anything else in all creation, will be able to separate us from the love of God in Christ Jesus our Lord." 8:31,32,37-39

What more is there to say than that? This is the hope of every person; to come to understand that it is God who has forgiven us so there can be no one to condemn. No amount of doubt or denial or persecution from within us or without, can separate us from that love. Even if we are unfaithful, God is not. Even when we turn our backs, God will not. Even when we lose hope, God does not abandon us. If we will trust Him even a little, God will do the rest.

That is the saving grace of having faith in the truth. The truth does not depend on our shifting loyalties or the fortunes of life. The truth stands all on its own and the truth is that God has forgiven us. That is the gospel. Why do so many people still reject it?

Perhaps we have been inundated with false gospel messages which are really some form of legalism. But that should not discourage us from trying to share the good news whenever and wherever we can. People need to hear the real gospel, especially if they have been subjected to some false legalism which has been called the gospel.

God does not hate us. He never has. Whatever other questions we have about predestination or justification or the atoning work of the cross or angels or devils or suffering, let us not miss the most important fact of all - God is for us, not against us. He proved that conclusively when He gave up His Son to die for us. If we never understand any more than this, it will be enough. If we never communicate anything else to people about God, this will be sufficient. If we carry no other confidence with us, this will see us through. God loves you. Believe it!

# Day 324
# Romans 11-13

Paul was such a consumate theologian that it is difficult to go past so many of his insights without comment. All of the Scriptures are inspired, but not all of them are equally inspiring. Paul's insights are so rich and varied that they are worth reading over and over again. Mark these sections for they are worthy of much more contemplation than three or four chapters a day allow!

"Let love be geniune; hate what is evil, hold fast to what is good; love one another with brotherly affection; outdo one another in showing honor. ... Do not be overcome by evil, but overcome evil with good." 12:9,10,21 What a different tone from that of the Old Testament. "Love your neighbor" was from the Old Testament, but it seems like that was quickly interpreted to mean, "Don't cheat your neighbor." So much of the focus of the Jews was in not doing the wrong thing that the commandments to do the right thing got lost along the way. The difference may seem subtle, but it is replacing a positive statement with a negative one. The New Testament finds a new reason to focus again on the positive - Jesus.

Jesus came not as a conquering King, but as a lowly servant. He did not confront the world with the might of his power, but with the strength of his love. He was not overcome by evil, but overcame evil with good. There is a power and a peace to be found in following his example that the world cannot offer. Paul found it and wrote about it to the other believers, including us.

Once we have it fixed in our minds that our salvation is secure, not through anything we could do, but through what God has done for us, we are finally freed from trying to satisfy our own needs to serve the needs of others. Our cries for justice for ourselves are transformed into shouts of love and forgiveness for both our enemies and our friends. We do not have to return evil for evil, but can offer the same grace we have received, and do good, even in return for evil and thus prove ourselves children of God.

"Let love be genuine." It is not so much the evil that we don't do that transforms our world, but the love we share with it from the one who overcame the world and all the evil in it. This is the mark of the Christian - to love as he loved us.

# Day 325
# Romans 14-16

"How in the world does God expect us to work with people so block-headed they think that _____ colored carpeting belongs in a sanctuary!" "Pastor, can you believe those people who want to have the church picnic in _____?! Why, we have always had the picnic in _____! Just who do they think they are!" (Fill in the blanks any way you want, it makes no difference!)

Disputes in the Church are as old as the Church itself. How do we get along with those who cannot see the "obvious" truth that is so clear to us? Certainly we can tolerate a certain amount of diversity, but enough is enough! We must draw the line somewhere!

The fact is that there are lines that must be drawn. But the Scriptures are given to be our guide in most of the matters of great importance. What happens though when they say nothing or we differ strongly on their interpretation?

Paul offers an answer, at least in terms of an approach to these matters. "Let every one be fully convinced in his own mind. he who observes the day, observes it in honor of the Lord. He also who eats, eats in honor of the Lord, since he gives thanks to God; while he who abstains, abstains in honor of the Lord and gives thanks to God." 14:5,6 We must learn to trust and respect each other's motives.

I have witnessed far too many meetings where people who would otherwise be embracing each other, are accusing one another of being the most despicable people alive, because they disagree about something. We need to learn to look past one another's opinions to the motives behind them. We may still conclude that those who disagree with us are perhaps the most stupid people we have ever met, but that does not make them evil, only dumb. We should be happy if they were to conclude the same about us.

Stupidity needs our love and understanding. Evil deserves our contempt. We need to realize that for the most part, people are much more stupid than evil, and that includes us. Why we do things is finally more important than what we do. Remember, God measures the heart! Perhaps if we could learn to trust that, our disputes would be less bitter, and considerably less divisive.

# Day 326
# I Corinthians 1-3

The church at Corinth was very gifted, but also very troubled. There were many signs and wonders that went on in that first century church, but it was also rife with division and misconduct. It appears that Paul, as the "founding pastor" had been written to and told of a number of problems facing his old congregation which he felt compelled to try to help them correct.

The Corinthian church is a marvelous example of the impact the culture can have on the institutional church and its individual members. Corinth had always seen itself as an "also ran" in relation to Athens. Athens had the reputation for learning, culture, and the Olympics. Corinthians had long tried to compete in every area. They even had the Isthmian games to compete with the Olympics. For Corinthians, it was important to keep up with the Joneses, and that meant having the lastest style in everything, even religion.

That is not to say that the Christians of Corinth had converted in order to be in vogue - far from it. Christianity was still a long way from being in fashion. Yet the desire to be in vogue came along with them and they applied it to their faith as easily and unknowingly as they had to the rest of their lives. Hence, they argued over who was the best person to follow. Some said Paul, some said Cephas (Peter), some said Apollos, and some (no doubt raising their noses the highest) said, Christ. One must get in the "right" camp. Being out of step would simply not do.

How easy it is for us to miss the forest for the trees. The one prayer of Jesus for his followers was that we should be one, even as He and the Father were one. Instead, we are able to split the narrowest of hairs and make ourselves foolish in the process.

It is difficult to see the bias of our culture on the gospel, but it is an important exercise. Before we laugh too long at the mistake of the Corinthians, perhaps we should ask where we have mistaken our culture for the gospel. We value individuality and independence almost above all else. Is that really the gospel? How many pastors, fathers, mothers, children, try to handle their guilt, sins, responsibilities alone without asking for help?

Perhaps we are not as much wiser than the Corinthians as we would like to think.

# Day 327
# I Corinthians 4-7

If salvation is a free gift which cannot be earned, and God is able to forgive us for anything, why not just do what we want, and ask for forgiveness later? That is a reasonable question. It gains even more weight when you add the understanding that no matter how good any of us are, we must still be forgiven - none are righteous, no not one. If you can't win the race, why run it?

Paul had done such a good job in declaring that faith, not the law, was what makes us righteous, that many in his Corinthian congregation had decided they could do anything that seemed good to them, including adultery and visiting the temple prostitutes. After all, if God in fact measures the heart, then what we do with our bodies doesn't make any difference. If then, it doesn't make any difference, we can do what we want with our bodies, knowing our souls are safe. Right? Not exactly.

Being free from the necessity of earning our salvation does not make us free from the laws of God. God's love for us is not dependent upon how well we obey the rules He put into the world. His love for us, however, does not mean He has changed those rules to suit us. If we overeat and do not exercise, we will have all the problems that go with being overweight and out of shape. If we cheat on our spouses, we will find they no longer trust us, and probably won't like us much anymore either (at least!). If we lie to people and use them for our own purposes, we will find they do not want to associate with us any more. If we are unreliable, untrustworthy and selfish we may be no less loved by God, but He may be the only one left who can stand us.

The truth is that we are always free to do right, but no one is ever really free to do wrong. Sin enslaves. No one who acts selfishly ever really gets ahead. Acting selfishly only confirms the fiction that we must fend for ourselves and not trust others. Pride, greed and self-indulgence are their own reward and they always leave us more needy, not less.

Salvation by grace is not the opportunity to sin without consequences. We cannot cheat reality. Love and the law are not enemies, for love fulfills the law and goes far beyond. The law then is our guide not our judge. We are truly free to do all the good we can devise. Not because we have to, but because we can!

# Day 328
# I Corinthians 8-10

ating meat offered to idols is a practice quite foreign to most of us today, but the problem and principles still apply. How do we get along with all of the diversity of the Church? Shouldn't we all really be doing the same kinds of things if we all believe in the same Lord?

The problem is that we confuse objective and subjective reality. Objective reality describes those things whose existence is not dependent on our knowledge or belief. Germs existed even before the microscope was invented. The world was not flat even though ancient peoples thought it was. Those elements of creation whose existence belong to themselves, are what make up objective reality.

Subjective reality describes those things whose existence is dependent on our knowledge or belief. The monster under my son's bed has no objective reality, but it has plenty of subjective reality at 3:00 a.m. when he wakes up crying. In fact, until he can believe otherwise, it is as good as objective reality for him. He will behave as if the monster were there until I can convince him it is not.

Paul knew that the idol, as a rock, had no objective reality as a god. He also knew that for those who were not convinced of that, it could have the same effect as if it were a god. To further complicate matters, God measures our hearts, and therefore is usually more concerned with why we do things than with what we do. Those who abstained from eating meat offered to idols could be worshipping Him as well as those who ate the meat offered to idols which they knew were only rocks.

How then do you solve the dilemma? "So, whether you eat or drink, or whatever you do, do all to the glory of God." 10:31 Our common ground may never be our understanding of the objective reality, but it might be on the subjective reality of serving God.

Why did God make things so? Why not just make it so that everyone's understanding of objective reality had to be the same? Variety. In a world where no two snowflakes are exactly alike, why should everyone's views of music, art, or even worship be the same? How boring! God had a better idea; more complicated, but infinitely more interesting!

# Day 329
# I Corinthians 11-13

Using the metaphor of the body to describe the relationship of members of the church was a stroke of absolute - inspiration! How thoroughly appropriate for what we are and what we are supposed to do in the world. Sadly, it has lost a good deal of it power because of a poor translation into the english.

The word Paul used which is translated "member" would be more precisely translated "organ." He made that clear in calling some parts eyes, and others ears and others noses. The trouble is that when we think of "members," we generally don't think along the same lines as "organs."

Membership in most organizations usually implies sameness. In most clubs or organizations, those who are members are more like one another than different; not so in a body, or the Church. The heart and the foot are not alike at all, yet both are part of the same body. Membership in the Church should not mean that we all look, sound, and think alike on everything, but that we belong together and work together for a common purpose.

In addition, our true source of individuality will be found when we learn to be the organ, that part of the body of Christ, God made us to be. There is another popular misconception that God has made our personalities like beautiful flowers waiting to unfold. The church must therefore make some place for us and our gifts, such as they are. The truth is that our personalities are like lumps of clay that need to be molded. God has given us a place and a function within the body. We have a job to do. We will find our true selves when we try to do the best job we can at what He has given us to do.

And we must all do our part. No organ in the body is unimportant - no member of the Church is unimportant. The healthiest bodies and the healthiest churches are those in which all organs and members are active.

Finally, we need to remember it is only a metaphor. Paul tells us to desire earnestly the higher gifts, but he would show us a still more excellent way - love. Whether you have figured out if you are an eye, ear, or nose in the body, don't fail to love whenever and wherever the opportunity arises. That's what this body is all about anyway!

# Day 330
# I Corinthians 14-16

"Eat, drink and be merry, for tomorrow we die." Most people would not have guessed this was from the Bible. Of course, it *is* taken out of context. The proper context is that *if* there is no resurrection from the dead, we should eat, drink, and be merry for tomorrow we die. That is the fundamental message of salvation history, that there will be a resurrection from the dead, through God's grace.

It surprises me that so many people want to be followers of Christ but do not believe in the resurrection. It probably *shouldn't* surprise me because even in Paul's time there were members of the church at Corinth who were doing the same thing and they were historically much closer to the event of Jesus' resurrection. But whatever distance from the event, the argument Paul raised is still valid. If there is no resurrection, if we die and are just dead and gone, then none of this life makes any sense. We might as well enjoy what we can now, for good or bad, right or wrong, we just disappear into dust and that is the end. But the Bible knows nothing of that kind of meaningless existence. While it may be much clearer after Jesus' resurrection than it was in the Old Testament, the message has always been there and even the Pharisees had seen it. Life after death; death, were is thy victory, death, were is thy sting. That is the name of the hope of the gospel - eternal life. Nothing less fills the bill.

Some would still argue that our spirits go on, but of course, our atoms cannot be regathered into our old bodies. That is true, but the resurrection has never been about bringing back the old, but being given the new. We will have new bodies, "spiritual bodies," but bodies nonetheless. Jesus was not Casper the Friendly Ghost. He ate, he drank, he could be touched. Our future as human beings is not to be disembodied spirits, but ourselves with new bodies. Personally, I'm hoping mine will be taller. I will be satisfied though with one that doesn't grow old.

When I visit a family in the hospital whose son, daughter, brother, sister, mother or father has died, I know of no other hope worth sharing. We will hold them again and they will hold us. That is the promise and the hope of the gospel. Anything less is unworthy of being called paradise.

# Day 331
# II Corinthians 1-4

Success. How is it measured? For the apostle Paul that was a difficult question. The church at Corinth could not agree on their definition. Paul had been their founding pastor, yet for many of them he did not embody the ideal of what they thought a Christian leader ought to be. Apollos was more eloquent, Peter was more traditional, and Paul was always under arrest or being beaten up. What kind of role model was that for discipleship?

Before we think the Corinthians too shallow, we should admit that there is a legitimate problem represented by Paul's version of success. Why is it that some of God's most faithful workers have to suffer so much? Why does God not protect His "best people" better than that? Why does obeying God not guarantee success?

I don't know if we can ever answer that question in this life. Perhaps, though, the most intelligible response was given by Paul here in II Corinthians. God's strength is not given to us in order that we might avoid all difficulties, pains, and conflicts in this world, like some kind of protective armor. Instead, it is the strength to endure through all those things with a sense of purpose for our lives. It is the ability to claim, even in the face of disaster, that our suffering is not without purpose, even if we cannot see the purpose ourselves.

What is so outstanding about Christianity is not that it makes all its members rich, thin, beautiful, and healthy, but that even when we are not any of those, we can still find joy and peace. Most early Christians were slaves, yet they had been set free at heart. Even their lives could no longer be taken because they had already given them away.

Has the "prosperity gospel" dulled our thinking so much that we only whine when we face adversity? In the Kingdom of God, success is not measured by comfort, but by strength to do God's will and the ability to endure hardship with grace and peace. "For this slight momentary affliction is preparing for us an eternal weight of glory beyond all comparison, because we look not to the things that are seen but to the things that are unseen; for the things that are seen are transient, but the things that are unseen are eternal." 4:17,18

# Day 332
# II Corinthians 5-7

"Therefore, if any one is in Christ, he is a new creation; the old has passed away, behold, the new has come." 5:17 Just what does it mean to be a "new creation"? In what way are we new and how can we, or anyone else, tell the difference?

This idea that as Christians we are qualitatively different, a "new creation," has sparked much controversy and many opinions. Perhaps that is because it is a characteristic of "newness" that it is difficult to define using old modes of thinking or language. In other words, we should not find it so surprising that explaining the "new" part of being a Christian is difficult precisely because it is new. Once again, our experience of life turns out to be more profound than our understanding of it. However, our failure in being able to describe it fully should not make us reject the truth. We are new creatures, qualitatively different than we were before. What then is the qualitative difference?

I would suggest that the difference is faith - the capacity to trust in God. Way back in the Garden of Eden at the beginning of this unusual experiment of God's we call our universe, there was a choice to be made. The choice was either to trust God or not. Our ancestors chose not to trust and we have lived with the consequences ever since. We are all born with that inbred fear that our needs will not be met and that we must look out for our own good or no one else will. We write our own rules to life because we do not trust that God's rules will adequately meet our desires.

To trust that God loves us and would not withhold any good thing from us may not seem like much of a qualitative difference, but the change becomes more noticeable as we grow. Think of those people who you know that face life's injustices and pains with a vibrant faith that God has not abandoned them as compared to those for whom no security is sufficient. The peace of the one and the paranoia of the other are just hints of the difference that will eventually show them to be whole different species. The heart of the one grows greater each day while the heart of the other shrinks into a vain attempt to hold on to a life which will slip inevitably through its fingers.

We are new creatures to be sure. And we have only begun to see how much faith will transform us!

# Day 333
# II Corinthians 8-10

**M**oney. It always seems to come back to this topic - or so some people think. They sit in church or around dinner tables during the discussion of religion and wait like panthers ready to pounce. "See, I knew it would get around to this eventually, all they really want is my money!"

There is a certain amount of truth to that charge. Eventually, bills must be paid. No work on this earth proceeds without being supported somehow, and that inevitably means money. But those who are angered by that reality miss seeing two very important aspects about giving to the work of the Lord.

"Each one must do as he has made up his mind, not reluctantly or under compulsion, *for God loves a cheerful giver*." 9:7 [Italics mine] God's work does not need our money. If God wanted to, He could provide His followers with the winning ticket in the lottery as often as necessary. But *we* need to give our money to the work of God - cheerfully! Until we have learned to do so we will never have rid ourselves of the mistaken notion that it is ours in the first place. There is a story that Rockefeller's accountant was asked how much money the financier had left after he died. The accountant is reported to have said, "All of it!" To rejoice in being able to give to do some good, is to recognize the double blessing God has offered us. God loves a cheerful giver, and cheerful givers love God! That is not mercenary or manipulative, but magnificent planning on God's part.

Then again, why do we think that this principle of giving only applies to money? We are told to tithe not only of our treasure, but our time and talent as well. How much different would the church be if each member gave cheerfully, a tenth of their time and talent each week? Assuming fourteen waking hours a day (we'll be liberal), six days a week (take the Sabbath off - rest is not equal to religious activity), amounts to eighty-four hours. A church that could count on eight hours of cheerful volunteer labor a week from each member would field an army of grinning servants that would be down right scary!

But I mentioned tithe, and many are not ready to cheerfully give that much yet. So give only freely whatever the amount. The smiles on that army are finally more important than its size.

# Day 334
# II Corinthians 11-13

trength. Our society reveres it. Weakness. Our society fears it. No small number of people have been kept out of the Kingdom of God because of these two attitudes. Survival of the fittest and might makes right - the law of the jungle, and it certainly is a jungle out there - right?

Perhaps our world has turned into a jungle, but that was not what it was intended to be, nor is it the destiny of human life, if we are going to believe the testimony of these Scriptures. The relationship of the strong and the weak must certainly be something different than the victor and the vanquished in the ideal order of things. In God's Kingdom, the great cannot stand without the small, nor the mighty without the humble. All things fit together and work for the common good in God's economy.

But this is not the ideal world. Power, not weakness, is needed to confront the strongholds of evil in our world. Gandhi could lie down in front of British tanks and expect them to stop. Had he tried that in front of Nazi tanks he would have gotten quite a different response. So what of Paul's statement, "For the sake of Christ, then, I am content with weaknesses, insults, hardships, persecutions, and calamities; for when I am weak, then I am strong." ?12:10

The answer is obvious. The power that is significant is not Paul's, but God's. Paul may have been weak, but God was not. God's power shows forth all the more in our weaknesses, but that is only because of our severe myopia. Do we really think that even at our best and our strongest, that it is our power which shapes the events of our world? Human history moves according to God's design, not the other way around.

This is why those who have tried to turn Paul's argument into a formula have failed. Sad to say, I have even heard it used as a "reason" for a sermon being poorly prepared, "...for when I am weak, then I am strong." God cannot be manipulated. God has chosen to work through us and it is His power that makes the difference, not ours. But that is not an excuse for laziness.

Whether we are "weak" or whether we are "strong", we are to seek God's grace, which will always be sufficient regardless of the task.

# Day 335
# Galatians 1-3

"There is neither Jew nor Greek, there is neither slave nor free, there is neither male nor female; for you are all one in Christ Jesus. And if you are Christ's, then you are Abraham's offspring, heirs according to promise." 3:28, 29

This has been called the *Magna Charta* of Christian liberty. Paul argues against all the foolish and vain attempts to divide the grace of God toward people; race, gender, social status, even religious background. God's grace has been poured out on the whole of humankind and it was always so.

"Judaizers," Christians who taught that in order to be a Christian you must first become a Jew, had led the Galatians astray. The freedom of salvation by grace, through faith, had been supplanted by the bondage of laws which had originally been signs of grace. Circumcision was the mark of gracious inclusion into the covenant with Abraham; a covenant of faith and grace. Paul himself had argued that true circumcision is a matter of the heart, not the body.

Paul wanted the Galatians to regain the freedom they had in Christ. Salvation comes as the free gift of God which cannot be earned, only accepted. Grace knows no distinction between men and women, slave or free, rich or poor, smart or dumb, Jew or Gentile; all are creatures created in the image of God whom He loves and wishes to redeem. That is the freedom of the gospel.

The legalism of the "Judaizers" might seem remote from our modern day, but is it? How often do we hear that God loves us when we _____ (the blank is filled in a thousand different ways). The truth is that God loves us before we do anything, and whether or not we do anything. His love is not based on us, but on Himself. That means we are free to be good because we no longer need to be good in order to save ourselves.

We have "Judaizers" of our own. They would have you believe that God expects you to behave in a certain way or He will not love you. They are wrong. He loves you, and when you let that sink in, you will behave in a certain way. Grace does not leave us without morals, it gives us a new motivation for our good works. We should be good, not because we have to, but because we want to. Anything less is bondage, not freedom.

# Day 336
# Galatians 4-6

piritual power. Most people associate it with miracles and healings. If you could pray and have a steak dinner miraculously appear on the table, even the atheists would be in awe of your great spiritual power. Certainly, if you could walk into a hospital and heal the sick, you would be greeted with messianic worship. But is that really spiritual power?

The fact is that I can make a steak dinner appear on the table. It will take me a little while to cook it, but I can make it appear nonetheless. I can also walk into any hospital and heal the sick by giving them the medicine they need (under a doctor's supervision). Far too often we mistakenly want spiritual power to be power over the physical universe. For the most part, God has already given that to us. When we pray, asking for healing, we think God has not answered when we don't rise up immediately all well. But what if we need to exercise, or we need to rest to allow the body's own system (which God provided) go about the task of getting well, or we need to go to see a doctor who can make use of the advances in modern medicine. God has not failed to answer, He may simply have given a different response than we were prepared to hear.

Spiritual power is not really seen in the miraculous or in healings. Eventually, we will all die. Healings are only temporary and miracles only last for a moment. Real spiritual power is seen not in the physical world, but in the spiritual world. "But the fruit of the Spirit is love, joy, peace, patience, kindness, goodness, faithfulness, gentleness, self-control; against such things there is no law." 5:22,23 What should impress us is not the ability to walk into sick people's rooms and heal their bodies (which will one day die anyway) but the ability to go in and bring to them a sense of peace and joy even in the midst of their suffering. It should impress us that anyone would even want to try. A hospice sees more miracles than a hospital.

Truly spiritual people are not those whose prayers move mountains, but whose compassion melts the hardened hearts of people. That may seem less flashy, but after the mountains have melted away, those changed people will still be around. Now that's powerful!

Check Here
When Read
❏

# Day 337
# Ephesians 1-3

"For by grace you have been saved through faith; and this is not your own doing, it is the gift of God - not because of works, lest any man should boast. For we are his workmanship, created in Christ Jesus for good works, which God prepared beforehand, that we should walk in them." 2:9,10

Some people have told me that I talk too much about salvation by grace. I tell them I don't think that is possible. I do not think that we ever comprehend this truth deeply enough. The longer I am a Christian, the more I discover the subtle ways my heart invents to feel proud of itself and sure that God at least "ought" to forgive me because of all the good I have done. My wife frequently helps me when my head gets that swollen. My kids are learning how to help, too!

But God forgives us even for that! What good news! I cannot imagine how one could proclaim it too well or too often. We are saved by grace through faith! There can be no better news for weak and failing creatures such as we. Commit Ephesians 2:9 to memory. It combats both pride and despair.

While you are at it though, don't forget to memorize verse ten. Too often the doctrine of salvation by grace has been used as an excuse for loose morals. The liberty of the gospel is not license to sin. Once grace has touched our lives, gratitude will do the good works that are its joy. Good works are not payment, they are descriptions of the activities of the heart and soul set free. When we continue to sin, we show that we do not understand sufficiently the love which has been given to us. We need not despair about our failings, but we should take notice. Good works are not the prerequisite for God's love, but they are the sure sign of its presence.

All this has been determined before the foundations of the world. Paul brings us back to the message of salvation history. God's purpose to love and to bless His creation has never been an accident. Through all the different twists and turns of our fallen world, God's purpose has been fulfilled - to save His people. Through that purpose we will live to know His grace and love a thousand fold more than we do now. We are such terrible young creatures! What incredibly good news! Share it!

# Day 338
# Ephesians 4-6

**E**phesians is referred to in theological circles as the "queen" of the epistles. The scope of its content and the eloquence of its language have made it one of the richest letters of Paul which we have to study. So much here is worth considering that it is difficult to focus on just one aspect.

One passage in particular has been rather badly interpreted in more recent times. Paul has received a bad reputation for having a "low" view of women. "Be subject to one another out of reverence for Christ. Wives, be subject to your husbands, as to the Lord." 5:21,22 This does not exactly sound very "liberated" to our modern ears. Oddly enough, though, it would have been considered a virtual feminist manifesto when Paul wrote it.

By ignoring Paul's statement that we are to be subject to one another out of reverence to Christ, many, on both sides of the issue, exploit the statement that wives should be subject to their husbands. This verse literally jumps off the page for conservatives and liberals alike. It would not have done so in the first century. To tell a woman of the first century Roman world to be subject to her husband would have been akin to telling her to get dressed in the morning. However, "Husbands, love your wives, as Christ loved the church and gave himself up for her ... Even so husbands should love their wives as their own bodies," would have had men of the first century leaping to their feet! Wives were property and sources of legitimate heirs. As such, one might take reasonable care of them, but love them? Why? That's what mistresses were for.

The two shall become one. That is the description of marriage from the Old Testament as well as the New. Love is by its very nature, submissive. It puts the good of the beloved ahead of its own good. Love cares nothing for equality, but considers the needs of the beloved ahead of its own. In Paul's day, that was assumed to be the attitude of women. He wanted to remind them that this should also be the attitude of men, because that is the attitude of love.

Be subject to one another; that's what love does. If we would do this, there would be a lot less arguing and a lot more happy marriages.

# Day 339
# Philippians

hilippians. What a beautiful letter between a pastor and his people who loved him. Of all of the churches that Paul founded, the Church at Philippi was closest to his heart, for it was the one which always supported him and did not question his call to apostolic ministry. The depth of teaching and the practicality of advice have made this letter a gem for the Church throughout the centuries.

Paul wanted his friends at Philippi to know that in spite of the troubles he had experienced in his ministry, he was all the more convinced that God was in control and would bring everything to its proper conclusion. Salvation history was not out of control but proceeding according to God's divine plan and so in spite of all difficulties, they could rejoice.

This was not mere "positive thinking" on Paul's part nor that of the Church at Philippi. Both were experiencing persecution. Yet Paul wrote to encourage them to bear the true mark of the believer - joy. "Rejoice in the Lord always; again I will say, Rejoice. Let all men know your forbearance. The Lord is at hand. Have no anxiety about anything, but in everything by prayer and supplication with thanksgiving let your requests be made known to God. And the peace of God, which passes all understanding, will keep your hearts and your minds in Christ Jesus." 4:4-7

Rejoice. Why? Because if you are doomed you might as well be happily doomed? Absolutely not! There is not an iota of fatalism in Paul's advice. We may rejoice because of what Jesus Christ has done for us. "Therefore God has highly exalted him and bestowed on him the name which is above every name, that at the name of Jesus every knee should bow, in heaven and on earth and under the earth, and every tongue confess that Jesus Christ is Lord, to the glory of God the Father." 2:9-11

Rejoice - God has won! The battles are not yet all over, but the outcome is certain. No matter what hardships may befall us still in this life, God will raise us up to a new time and a heaven and a new earth. Paul wanted those whom he loved the most to enjoy even now the promise of what is to come - the love of God. May we too hear his message - Rejoice! God has won and nothing can change that! Praise God!

# Day 340
# Colossians

aul had never visited the Church at Colossae when he
wrote his letter.  But he had received word of the
difficulties they were having and wrote to help settle
the disputes.  It must have been difficult for those who
had grown up in pagan religions to understand the
message and the meaning of the gospel.  As apostle to
the Gentiles, Paul most certainly had his work cut out for him.

The particular problem the Colossians were struggling with
had to do with Jesus' divine nature, but it raises a larger question
for us.  How does God expect to reach people of quite diverse
backgrounds, both religiously and culturally?  How will they ever
be able to discern the truth from the multiplicites of partial truths
and outright lies?

This seems like an inexplicable problem until we remember
the roots of the human race.  We are all creatures created in the
image of God.  Our different cultures and religions are inventions
*we* have constructed.  If the Bible is correct, there is only one God
and people are all much more alike than different.  Regardless of
what our culture teaches, we are born knowing that lying, stealing,
hatred, injustice are wrong - especially when we are the objects of
the injustice!  Our culture may teach us to believe the lie that it is
all right to do these things to some other race or religion, but it is a
thinly veiled lie.  The fact that we object when evil is done to us
testifies that we know at heart it is wrong.

Likewise, regardless of what our cultures or religions teach
us, we inherently know the value of love, patience, kindness,
gentleness; again, especially when we are the recipients of these
blessings.  The gospel does not go out into wholly foreign
territory for it speaks the language of love, which is the native
language of human hearts, regardless of the language of the lips.

There are certainly things which we cannot know about God
without His revelation.  That has been the purpose of God's
people and His word through the centuries; to tell us what we
otherwise would not be able to know. But when that revelation is
given, it finds familiar ground in the human heart, for there are
also things which we know about God without having to be told.
Paul's job with the Colossians was as much reminding as it was
revealing.  So is ours.

# Day 341
# I Thessalonians 1-3

iplomacy. Along with patience it is one of my least favorite words in the church. There is a real desire amongst ministers (not too far under the surface), to go crashing into the pulpit or a committee meeting like the action adventure movie hero, demolishing the opposition left and right. Or at least to be able to state the truth simply without having to carefully "acknowledge the sincere intent" of the otherwise ludicrous suggestions you sometimes hear; "No, Jill, we can't move Christmas to a warmer time of year!"

As if that were not enough, diplomacy requires that we carefully consider the unintended slights and insults that we *might* commit that *could* send our audience off on yet another tangent to the point we are trying to make. We must try to bow or not bow at the right time, shake hands or not shake hands with the proper people, laugh or not laugh at the appropriate comment, and a thousand other requirements of communication barriers. Paul spent fully half his letter doing what might be called in less complimentary terms, "shmoozing" the Thessalonians. Why?

Knowing the truth is perhaps no more than ten percent of the battle of communicating the truth. The other ninety percent is made up of getting around the roadblocks, both conscious and unconscious, which people erect to protect themselves. So why worry about those? Why not just state the truth and if some won't listen, that is their problem?

Love. If we love the people we are trying to reach, we will do whatever it takes to get through to them; we will at least keep trying. We must remember that the ones we are trying to reach are not those who already agree with us, but those who do not. They will be harder to reach, but they are the ones that need reaching. Love will be patient and diplomatic or whatever else it needs to be to get through - except to be phony.

That is what makes the diplomacy of love something other than "shmoozing." Love cannot lie to convey the truth, but it can be patient, respectful, deferential, and even apologetic; in short, agonizingly diplomatic.

For the love of the Thessalonians, Paul was trying to get them to listen, even if it took more than half of his letter to do so. Perhaps there is a lesson for us in that approach.

# Day 342
# I Thessalonians 4-6

As believers, what happens to us when we die? That was the question on the minds of the Thessalonians, and it is one still asked of pastors today. Very little is said in answer to this in the Scriptures, but let us remember that the Bible is not all there is to know, just all that is necessary to know for our salvation. As much as we might feel to the contrary, it appears that we don't really need to know much about that question.

Paul was concerned that the Thessalonians be reassured that whatever happens, we will be in the hands of God, ..."that you may not grieve as others do who have no hope." He uses the euphemism of "falling asleep" to refer to those who have died. The accuracy of the analogy cannot be determined. It is important to some people I counsel that they believe they will be with Jesus immediately - no delay. But even if the analogy of sleep is correct, it will seem like being transformed immediately since we have no sensation of the passage of time while we sleep, so I am not sure what difference it makes.

What is clear is that when we die we do not come back to assist our loved ones. Theologians have argued throughout the centuries about whether people are dichotomous (body and soul) or trichotomous (body, soul, and spirit). Whichever the case, we are only human and alive when we are together, the whole being greater than the sum of the parts. The promise of the resurrection is that we will be given new bodies, because without them, we are not really human or alive.

A woman whose father had died came to speak to me because she was sure that he could not be resting peacefully knowing he had left his daughter and grandchildren behind (he had been their sole support). Reading Thessalonians was of no comfort to her so I tried a different approach. I asked her if she believed that God loves her family even more than her father did. She agreed that was true. I then pointed out that if her father was awake in God's presence, he would know as present reality what we can still only affirm on faith; that God really does love her family more than anyone else could. Her father would not be worried and neither should she. We may not know everything, but it happens that we know enough after all.

# Day 343
# II Thessalonians

he second coming of Christ has generated more useless speculation than almost any other doctrine in the whole of Scripture. Considering the fact that Jesus himself said that he did not know the day and the hour, and that we won't know until it happens, it is bewildering that determining the time has been a preoccupation, even an obsession for many in the church throughout its history. We can't know, so why do we keep trying?

I suppose it is akin to the desire to know of our death a month before the event. We assume that if we could know, we would live that last month differently because of the knowledge. In the case of the Thessalonians, some of them thought the second coming was so near that they stopped working and were living off the graciousness of others. Like those who think they will die soon, they chose to live their last days differently.

The problem with that kind of reasoning is of course that if your premise is wrong, your conclusions are also wrong. The Thessalonians missed guessing the date of the second coming by at least two thousand years. A significant error! It is popular to say instead, that we should live each day as if Jesus were returning today. But that notion is as unpromising as the old bromide, "Live each day as if it were your last day on earth." Human beings are just not made like that.

Perhaps a better attitude would be to live each day not as creatures whose days are numbered, but as people who know they will be living forever. Whether today or tomorrow is my last day on earth, it will not be my last day alive. That is what the hope of the gospel is all about. Death is not the final victor. Whether Jesus returns tomorrow or not for another thousand years, his return will not be the end, but the beginning. Whenever God decides to do that is fine with me (as if my opinion made any difference anyway!).

This much is clear. The Scriptures tell us that we will die and Jesus will come again to complete salvation history. Ten million years from now, neither of these events may be all that outstanding in our memories. What God will have us doing then may be so engaging that we rarely, if ever, mention this life at all. Don't live each day like your last, live each day like your first!

# Day 344
# I Timothy 1-3

aul's first letter to Timothy has been one of the most useful to the Church throughout the centuries. In this letter, Paul outlines the kind of structure he tried to institute in the churches he founded and gives us an insight into the principles behind the offices of bishop and deacon.

Jesus himself wrote no book, nor did he establish an organization with a clear structure. Instead, he trusted in leaving his message written on the hearts of his followers - and the gift of the Holy Spirit to teach and guide them. As a result, *how* the Church organizes itself is less important than *why* it chooses a given structure. That does not mean there are no guidelines, but it does mean there is no single dogmatic style for going about being the Church. Instead, Paul provides us with the key principle to any kind of organization for the church.

"For there is one God, and there is one mediator between God and men, the man Christ Jesus, who gave himself as a ransom for all, the testimony to which was borne at the proper time." 2:5,6   This is the principle behind our relationship with God and others of which we must not lose sight. Neither bishop, deacon, priest, man, or woman can stand between us and direct access to God. There is only one mediator, and that is Jesus Christ. As believers, we are all priests, that is mediators between people and Jesus, to introduce them to their savior. This should be the guiding principle in all our relationships with other believers. Relationship with God is not a hierarchy, either of men or women or dead saints or angels, but through the Holy Spirit we are all one in Christ. The Church has only one head, Jesus. After that, there are no other levels to be considered, just different functions we perform.

Why didn't Jesus establish the offices of the church himself? Perhaps it is because he wanted each of us to turn to him, and he knew that we would be all too willing to turn instead to priests, husbands, mothers, fathers, or anyone else whom we supposed had divine authority. Taking responsibility for one's own spiritual life sounds a good deal easier than it turns out to be. But no one should think that Christianity ever promised to be easy - just great!

# Day 345
# I Timothy 4-6

here is a great deal of wisdom and sound counsel in this first letter to Timothy. After all the theology has been argued, a good deal of what goes on in life and in ministry comes back to some fairly basic things. Treat people with honor, be honest, just, and faithful, and live life in light of the fact that you belong to an eternal kingdom where love, not lust, is the law. One would almost think that this would all not even need to be said.

Yet in our day, as in Paul's, it bears repeating that "There is great gain in godliness with contentment; for we brought nothing into the world, and we cannot take anything out of the world..." 6:6,7  Recent surveys of college and university students reveal that the majority of students cheat on their exams and feel that it is wrong only when they are caught.  If surveys of this kind were done on business men and women in regard to taxes or finances in general we might well find that those students have learned from their elders after all.  There is no substitute in a society for simple honesty and integrity.

The problem is that it is much easier to talk about honesty and integrity than it is to be honest and incorruptible.  How do we resist the temptation to compete in this world by cheating when "everyone else" is doing it?

For one thing, we are to remember that our lives are much longer than they appear.  The eighty, ninety, or one hundred years we may live now are but a very small fraction of what our lives really will be.  "...take hold of the eternal life to which you were called..." 6:12  This does not imply that this life is unimportant, it means remembering that long after the car and house have turned to dust, the neighbor we are tempted to cheat will still be around.  People, and how we treat them, will have much more significance than anything we can possess.

We must also become convinced that Christianity is not a bunch of "don'ts" but a lot of "do's".  The point is not to be "not rich" or "not dishonest" or "not greedy," but to *be* generous, honest, and charitable. Human beings are not idle creatures; we will do something.  As a society we must learn again that it is never a waste to be good and to do the right thing.  No great revelation, but it needs to be said.

# Day 346
# II Timothy

aul's second letter to Timothy is full of the kind of pathos that comes from a heart and soul striving for those things which truly matter in life. Paul was in prison, facing death, and this letter to his beloved friend Timothy is a testimony to the true strength of the Christian faith.

One of the privileges of being a pastor is to be with people as they face their final hours. Many people would not consider that a privilege, but most people have never been at the side of a dying person. It is a solemn time, but it need not be a depressing one. The way some people face their own deaths can be as inspiring a witness to the resurrection as any sermon ever preached.

"I have fought the good fight, I have finished the race, I have kept the faith. Henceforth there is laid up for me the crown of righteousness, which the Lord, the righteous judge, will award to me on that Day, and not only to me but also *to all who have loved his appearing.*" [emphasis mine] 4:7,8  What a beautiful way of understanding our faith.  To have loved his appearing is the essence of the gospel.  It is to rejoice that Jesus did *not* come to make everything easy for his followers or to set one nation above another or to establish some religious system by which we could work at earning God's favor, but that he came with open arms and open heart to embrace us and heal our souls.  To have held on to that hope all through life, even as one faces his own death is truly a victory.  What a marvelous epitaph for a person's life.

I have been privileged to be with some of God's great saints as they faced their final hour with the confidence of Paul.  They are moments which I will never forget.  I have had a strong desire at those times to ask them to pray for me rather than the other way around.  They have exhibited a peace and a clarity of vision that sees death as the real enemy that it is, but knows it to be a defeated enemy.  It does not matter then whether or not they have achieved the fame of a Paul, they have shared in the same faith, they have loved the Lord's appearing, they have finished the race, they have kept the faith, and they will receive their reward.  There is no greater success in this life.

# Day 347
# Titus, Philemon

**T**he letter to Philemon has to be one of the most carefully crafted works in the Bible. Onesimus was Philemon's slave who had run away from him and ended up meeting Paul, and subsequently, the Lord. Paul was sending Onesimus back to Philemon with only this letter as guarantee that Philemon would not have his runaway slave killed. It was a bold move on Paul's part as well as Onesimus' part for going.

Paul wanted to remind Philemon (who had also come to know the Lord through Paul) that Philemon may have had the legal right to have Onesimus killed, but not the moral right. Onesimus (whose name meant *useful*) was now a brother in Christ and Philemon was bound by love to accept him back as such. Paul was certainly bold enough to command Philemon, but phrased his message as a request, so that Philemon could do the right thing for the right reason. The whole interplay of rights, responsibilities, and accountabilities, make this situation an excellent example of the way Christianity transforms society.

Some have wondered why slavery was not attacked directly as an institution, either by Jesus or his early followers. The fact is that the New Testament was more concerned about slavery to sin than about slavery to another person. Slavery to sin meant eternal death. No amount of money or freedom (or lack of same) could make up for that deficit. If Christ has set us free from sin, there is no other freedom which can be granted or denied that can compare with that freedom.

But slavery itself is a sin and one which holds the master more surely than the slave, for there is only one master and He is the Lord. Paul makes it clear to Philemon that God will be everyone's judge and we must act accordingly. This is the unique nature of the gospel, that it is as concerned for the victimizer as it is the victim. Paul sent Onesimus back to Philemon that he too might be freed from his bondage.

Slavery was officially ended in the United States more than a century ago, yet bigotry still enslaves the hearts of many people. While it is progress that slavery is now illegal it can never really be ended until we recognize that we are all sons and daughters of Adam and Eve and treat each other accordingly.

# Day 348
# Hebrews 1-4

The book of Hebrews sets forth the gospel of Jesus Christ for us in a way in which none of the other letters attempts to do. This was a new understanding of God's grace, and yet it was also the same message of salvation that was promised from the very beginning. Making this fact clear was the burden of this letter and it is still the struggle for the Church today.

To understand this new covenant to be the fulfillment of the old covenants, it is important to understand the central figure of salvation history - Jesus Christ. The writer of Hebrews makes it clear that Jesus is superior in every way to every other revelation of God's salvation. Jesus is greater than the angels, greater than Moses and Joshua, greater than the law, greater than the temple, greater than anything else. He is the Christ, the promised Messiah, whose sacrifice on the cross paid the penalty for our sins and whose resurrection sealed our hope for life eternal. He is truly the author and finisher of our faith.

But the writer of Hebrews also wanted to make it clear that he is not just the Christ, but also Jesus. Too many people today still think that Christ is Jesus' last name instead of his title or office. Jesus is the Christ, but he is also a human being. "For because he himself has suffered and been tempted, he is able to help those who are tempted." 2:18 Having faith in Jesus as the Christ is not merely trusting that the "legal" matters of our salvation have been taken care of, it is believing that we are loved and understood by our savior, our high priest, our Lord.

Sadly, many people want to settle for having Jesus be the savior of their eternal lives and but not the lover of their souls. No one understands our weaknesses and failings better. No one has more compassion for our pains and our fears. No one cares as much about our joys and our sorrows. Faith is not a cold-blooded understanding of some kind of spiritual jurisprudence that applies only to our life after death, it is the warmest of personal relationships with the Son of God who knows us better than we know ourselves and loves us more than we will ever love ourselves - even now. Jesus' salvation is not just about a great historical moment, it is about you and me and our hearts. Talk to him today. He cares, and he wants to hear from your heart.

# Day 349
# Hebrews 5-7

The priesthood of Christ is a difficult concept for Protestants to comprehend or appreciate. However, in early religions, priests, were a very important part of their understanding of God and their relationship with God. Priests were there to take your sacrifice to the God and offer it in an acceptable way. They were to pray for you since they carried more weight with the deity, and you could trust telling them anything because they were not there to judge you, but to represent you to the judge.

These were the functions of the Aaronic priesthood, and most priests of other religions. The whole idea presumes a distance which exists and must be maintained between the worshipper and the deity. For the Jews, it was understood that even the priests had to maintain a certain "distance" since they were sinful too, but the common, ordinary religious follower was certainly further away from the righteous deity. That distance was not always seen as a disadvantage, but was often quite a comfortable divide that separated one's religious life from one's secular life.

The writer of Hebrews argues that Christ's priesthood was superior to Aaron's because Christ was sinless, so he did not have to make atonement for himself, and since he had been the perfect sacrifice, no other sacrifices were necessary. That is quite a benefit (I am grateful I do not to have to bring an animal to Church to sacrifice!), but the greater implication is that the "distance" between ourselves and God has been cut to nothing! Jesus is our high priest. He is also God himself!

The trinity is certainly a mystery in some ways, but in this instance, it is the kind of understanding that enriches our experience with God. Jesus is our high priest. He has offered to God his sacrifice on our behalf and secured forgiveness for us. He prays for us because he does carry more weight with God the Father who is also the Judge and we can be confident of telling him everything because, as high priest, he is our advocate.

This great news does come at a cost. We can no longer "enjoy" that comfortable distance between ourselves and God. But take heart, our high priest knows what its like to be human - and he loves us anyway!

# Day 350
# Hebrews 8-10

ebrews makes it clear that salvation is not through any kind of work on our part, but through Christ's sacrifice alone. "For if the sprinkling of defiled persons with the blood of goats and bulls and with the ashes of a heifer sanctifies for the purification of the flesh, how much more shall the blood of Christ, who through the eternal Spirit offered himself without blemish to God, purify your conscience from dead works to serve the living God." 9:13,14 Works are dead; grace alone can bring us righteousness.

If that is true, if salvation comes to us through Jesus Christ alone and not from any work we do, then why come together as a Church and why struggle to do good works?

That is a question many people ask who are frustrated with the Church. They don't like all of the hypocrites who attend church. They don't like being "preached at." They don't like feeling that they are doing some things they shouldn't or not doing some things they should. They just want to believe in Jesus and avoid contact with all those "religious do gooders who think they're better than they are, when they're not!"

Aside from the fact that God has told us specifically that we should not neglect gathering together, ignoring for the moment our responsibility to share this wonderful gospel with the world, and overlooking the need for compassion for the sick and needy, Christian education at all levels, the sacraments, worship, comfort for the grieving and fellowship, there really is no good reason for us to come together as Christians. God does not love us more if we attend Church, but we will find more of the love of God if we do, because God chooses to love us, in part, through one another.

The writer of Hebrews gave a wonderful description of what churches should be like. "...and let us consider how to stir up one another to love and good works, not neglecting to meet together, as is the habit of some..." 10:24,25 Church should not be a place where we come to perform our religious duties, it should be a place where we "stir up one another to love and good works." We do not have to do anything in order for God to love us, but since He has loved us, how else could we respond except to love one another and do good things? Stirred up to love and good works; that is a Church worth joining!

# Day 351
# Hebrews 11-13

Faith. It is the essential quality for making any decision. It is the quality that God could not put into human beings in the garden. It is the quality which they had to choose freely for themselves, and failing to do so, it is the quality with which we all struggle. Without faith, no decision can be made and no action taken.

Some people think faith is simply a religious crutch for those not strong enough to face reality. They are wrong. Every person operates on faith. The belief that there is no God is as much a statement of faith as the belief that there is a God. We use faith in every aspect of life, depending upon the laws of the universe to operate consistently and not arbitrarily. Even believing that there are such laws is an act of faith. Faith is not a religious concept, but an everyday element of being human.

Faith does not have to be "blind" that quality which allows us to trust those things we cannot prove. "Now faith is the assurance of things hoped for, the conviction of things not seen." 11:1 The scary part of faith is that it can be disappointed. We can have faith in something and have that thing let us down. That element of risk and the sting of having our faith disappointed has led many people to want to abandon faith. But that is not possible for creatures. God knows things as fact in a way which we cannot. Faith is an inescapable part of not being God.

There is an old story about a man who wanted to prove he was the greatest tightrope walker in history, so he had a tightrope stretched across Niagara Falls. He walked across and back successfully and gathered a large crowd in doing so. Next, he pushed a wheelbarrow across and back to cheering crowds. Then, he put two hundred pounds of bricks into the whellbarrow and successfully pushed it across and back. Finally, he said to the crowd, "Do you believe I can carry a man across and back?" The crowd shouted, "Yes!" He responded, "Who will get in the wheelbarrow?"

Faith gets into the wheelbarrow. Belief can only talk, faith acts. Ultimately, those who refused to get in the wheelbarrow had faith that the man could *not* do it. If we refuse to have faith that God exists, we have faith that He does not. My advice - get in God's wheelbarrow!

# Day 352
# James 1-3

I t is a shame that many people miss the wonderful counsel of this letter because they, like Martin Luther, get stuck on James' use of the word "faith." James was dealing with those who thought that you could be justified by your beliefs apart from your actions. Faith itself cannot be faith without action. Until it acts, faith is merely belief, and as James pointed out, even the demons believe - and shudder.

The practical nature of this letter is what makes it valuable. James wanted to bring us back to the reality that the liberty of the gospel was not license to do as we please without consequence. True religion, like true faith, has measurable results, and those results must be in line with the character and nature of God. To be "hearers" of the word and act contrary to that word, is not to have faith. Whatever else you want to call that kind of hypocrisy, it is not faith. You cannot deceive God and you cannot cheat reality.

Dr. M. Scott Peck wrote a book called, *People of the Lie: The Hope for Healing Human Evil*, which looked deeply at the effects of the kind of self deception to which James referred. A practicing psychiatrist, Dr. Peck observed the devastation caused to themselves and others by people who could no longer tell or hear the truth about themselves. When we lie to ourselves we not only hurt others, but we damage our own ability to face the truth. In lying to ourselves we make it so "expensive" for anyone to try to tell us or for us to admit that we have been not only wrong but conspiratory in covering it up, that no one can pay the price. Perhaps it is that level of self deception that keeps the demons, who know of God's existence, from being able to have faith in His love. Martin Luther is reported to have said that if Satan himself were to ask for forgiveness, God would forgive him. It is chilling to think that sentient beings could be so self-imprisoned as to be unable to reach out for help - but so it is. Satan would never ask or even believe the offer.

Faith without works is dead. Faith without works is also dangerous, not only to those around us, but to ourselves. Faith that shows itself in action, gives us reason to trust that we have truly received grace; without the action, we have reason to wonder whether we have or not.

# Day 353
# James 4-5

How do the faithful live in a world so full of anger, hatred, deception, and evil? For James, the answer was to live not in compromise to the world and its passions but to live the life of faith that recognizes the presence and power of God in our lives.

"You do not have, because you do not ask. You ask and do not receive, because you ask wrongly, to spend it on your passions." 4:2,3 This is a difficult balance to achieve in asking God for things. On the one hand, we want to ask for what we want. Frequently, we know that what we want is not something we should be asking for, and so we do not bother to ask, which tends to develop the habit of never asking for anything. That in turn puts us in the position of trusting in our own devises to get what we want. Once we have gone that far, we are on the same ground as those who have no faith in God; we are all trying to get what we want, any way we can.

It is hard work to ask God for what we want. We must risk that God will simply say "No." We risk that He will say, "Later," and that we won't be able to distinguish between "Later" and "No." We even risk that we will begin to lose our faith in Him because it is hard to distinguish "Later" or "No" from "no response." And finally, we risk discovering that even we know that what we want is not the right thing and that we must give up wanting it. With all that risk it is a wonder we ever ask God for anything!

But what a cost there is in not asking. When we refuse to take the risk of bringing our requests to God, we put ourselves in the position of people who do not know God. We also cut ourselves off from the God who loves us so much that He sent His son to die for us. We further isolate ourselves from the loving mirror that can help us see our lives and passions for what they really are, and find those deeply rooted desires to be loved and accepted which are beneath most of our passions anyway.

Can you take the risk? Are there things that you have wanted, for which you have been afraid to ask God? Consider asking anyway. It may take many prayers, but our confidence must be that He never gives "no response" and His answer will be precisely what we need to hear.

# Day 354
# I Peter 1-3

"But you are a chosen race, a royal priesthood, a holy nation, God's own people, that you may declare the wonderful deeds of him who called you out of darkness into his marvelous light." 2:9 The doctrine of the priesthood of all believers has been a fundamental understanding of the Protestant Church since the Reformation. It has at least two very important implications.

The first is that the distinction between clergy and laity, the leaders and the members of the church, cannot be as it was for the old covenant. For Israel, the priests acted as intermediaries between the people and God, offering prayers and sacrifices on their behalf. For the Christian, there is only one intermediary between God and people and that is Jesus Christ. Individuals may be set aside for a particular function within the life of the church, but there are no levels of hierarchy that set people apart as having a special status with God.

The Church is still in need of learning this lesson. Far too many people are still too willing to let someone else be close to God for them. They give clergy not only too much authority in their lives, but too much responsibility. Not surprisingly, many clergy succumb to the temptation to take advantage of that submission, or burn out under the pressure of that responsibility.

Secondly, and perhaps more importantly, the Church still struggles to live out the implications of its priestly office. We are all priests; that is, intermediaries or ambassadors to those who do not yet know God. Most people have never wanted to be priests and yet that is the calling which comes to us as believers. How well do we see our neighbors or co-workers or friends who do not know Christ, as our parishioners? Have we considered praying for them regularly, whether they asked us to or not? Do we pray that God would forgive them and bless them? Can we conceive of ways to show them God's love in a tangible form before we try to tell them about it in words?

Before the idea overwhelms us, let us remember that God has called us to this priesthood, not to do His job from Him, but that He might do His job through us. Trusting that God can work, even through you, is "lesson one" for any priest. It is humbling, but also empowering. Welcome to the priesthood!

# Day 355
# I Peter 4-5

Simon Peter knew a great deal about change. Perhaps more than any other disciple, he had gone through a personal transformation as a result of his contact with Jesus. Not only had his life become different when he ceased being a fisher of fish to become a fisher of men, but his very personality had changed. Jesus had even given him a new name to mark that change.

Before he met Jesus he was Simon bar Jonah; Simon son of John. One of the meanings of the name John was dove, so his name could be read as Simon, son of the dove. When Jesus first met him, he gave him the name Peter, which means rock. Jesus saw in Simon, a Peter, a strength that needed to be drawn out - a rock that could be used as a solid foundation. The Apostle John perhaps saw him as being in transition, because throughout his gospel he always referred to him as Simon Peter; somewhere between the dove and the rock.

Simon Peter wanted to be the best of the best. Anything worth doing was worth overdoing. He was the first disciple to recognize Jesus as the messiah, yet he was first to reject the idea of Jesus sacrificing himself. He walked on the water, but he lost faith and had to be saved from drowning. He received the revelation of salvation to the Gentiles in a dream, witnessed Cornelius' whole household receive the Holy Spirit, and yet left when Jewish friends came because he did not want to be caught defiling himself by eating with Gentiles. One could argue that God had to raise up Paul because Peter had refused to take the gospel to the Gentiles, although he and Paul later agreed that the gospel was for everyone and Paul would take it to the Gentiles, and he would take it to the Jews.

From Peter's up and down life we hear the wisdom that came from surviving so much change of personality, career, and expectations; "Above all, hold unfailing your love for one another, for love covers a multitude of sins." 4:8 From the man who had wanted to be the rock upon which the church was built but had discovered that Jesus alone was that cornerstone, this advice is especially noteworthy. What a difference it would make in our churches if we could apply this principle, for we certainly have a multitude of sins which need covering!

# Day 356
# II Peter

ime. It has an objective side and a subjective side. On the objective side it goes along at the same unalterably measured pace it always has; it neither speeds up nor slows down; it waits for no one. On the subjective side, it moves as an almost constantly varying pace. For the young mother giving birth or the small child waiting for Christmas morning, it moves so slowly as to almost stand still. For the birthday boy at Disneyland or the parents watching their children get married it seems to have moved so fast as to have past in the wink of an eye.

The second coming of Christ will happen in this same kind of objective/subjective time. It will come on the day and date set by God Himself; not a day sooner or a day later. How long the world will have to wait objectively for that coming is unknown. For those whose hearts have been broken by the deaths of loved ones and the tragedies of this life, it will seem like an eternity if it comes tomorrow.

This problem was what Peter was addressing when he wrote, "But do not ignore this one fact, beloved, that with the Lord one day is as a thousand years, and a thousand years as one day. The Lord is not slow about his promise as some count slowness, but is forbearing toward you, not wishing that any should perish, but that all should reach repentance." 3:8,9 It is probably impossible for us not to think of our lives as being very long. For the disciples to have felt that Jesus would return in their lifetimes meant they knew the pain of waiting that infinitely long subjective time. But they also realized in their old age, that God's purpose was moving on a different time line that intended to include people who had not yet been born - even us.

Certainly our lifetimes represent only a moment in the eternal movement of time - but what important moments they are. Peter wanted to assure us that Jesus' second coming was still in the future, but not because time doesn't mean the same thing to God as it does to us. Subjectively speaking, the passage of time that God endures as He watches the killing and the hatred on earth, must make history agonizingly long for Him too. Instead, we are so important to Him we have been worth the wait. Given that, He should take all the time He wants! He will anyway!

# Day 357
# I John 1-3

"If we confess our sins, he is faithful and just, and will forgive our sins and cleanse us from all unrighteousness." 1:9 If God is all knowing and He has forgiven us for all our sins through the atoning work of Jesus on the cross, why do we still need to confess our sins to Him? And what happens with those sins which we never confess, either through ignorance or dying before we get the opportunity?

Why indeed do we need to confess our sins to an all knowing God? The word John uses which is translated "confess" is also used in places to mean "agreeing," as in publicly proclaiming our agreement. When used with that understanding, confession becomes a much different concept. When we confess our sins to God, we are not telling Him something He did not already know, we are agreeing with Him that what we have done is wrong. As a parent, I understand the necessity of that part of the process of repentance much more clearly than I did as a child. "Now you see that putting your toy in the oven was the wrong thing to do" we prompt our crying child as he watches us scrape melted plastic from the porcelain surface. Without his agreement, we know that a change in behavior will not occur, and greater tragedies are still possible.

As with the Old Testament sacrifices, it is not God's mind that needs to be changed, but ours. If we are to repent, to turn around and go a different direction, it must start with confession, agreeing that we are going the wrong direction. If we will not agree, then we will never accept the forgiveness offered. Why would we need it, we didn't do anything wrong!

As a young child I hit a parked car with my bike. I went to my mother in tears, not because I was physically hurt, but because I felt that I had nearly killed myself, and I was worried that if I *had* died and not confessed my sins from earlier in the day I would die without forgiveness and be lost. My mother held me and assured me that God had forgiven my sins, past, present, and future. Love does not keep accounts. Confessing our sins is not a legalistic game we must play to win our salvation; it is agreeing with God that we might repent and be changed. Our salvation is secure in His love. Our confessions only bring us closer to the God who can heal us even now.

# Day 358
# I John 4-5

"Beloved, let us love one another; for love is of God, and he who loves is born of God and knows God. He who does not love does not know God; for God is love." 4:7,8 This is one of the most profound statements ever written about love. Love is not merely an invention of God's, like time and space, but it is a description of the very character and nature of God Himself - that thing which is most fundamentally true about Him and His actions.

Love is the primary motivation for all that God does. He created because He loves to love. He is just, because love cannot be anything less than just. He is forgiving because love chooses to be no less and is willing to pay the price itself. He is gracious because love looks not to itself, but the needs of the beloved. Solomon said that the fear of God is the beginning of knowledge, but John makes it clear that the end of the knowledge of God is to know that He is love, and perfect love casts out all fear. We may truly, wholeheartedly, give ourselves, without reservation, to the loving nature of God.

But saying God is love is not the same as saying love is God. God is a being (The Being), not a force of nature or a character trait of life. God is the source of beings. We can be individuals only because God Himself is not some disembodied force, but the one true person in all there is or ever will be. We reflect a part of His greatness as individual souls, but He has chosen to share with us the greatest gift of all in allowing us to experience a part of that which is the essence of His nature - love. Yet, as great as love is, it is not God, but part of God's nature.

This distinction seems to have become blurred in western culture. We have thought love a sufficient force to exist on its own. That is ridiculous. Love is not a force like gravity, it is character trait, a force of the will. It cannot exist outside the beings who choose to do it.

Just because we love, does not mean that we are God, or any part of Him. Our love will never translate us past the grave, it can only point us to the source of love, who can. "In this the love of God was made manifest among us, that God sent his only Son into the world, so that we might live through him." 4:9 In the statement, "God is love," God is still the most important word!

# Day 359
# II John, II John, Jude

The apostle John was described in the gospels as the disciple whom Jesus loved. Jesus loves us all, but there must have been a special kind of relationship of understanding and support between John and our savior. It is John whom Jesus told to take care of his mother, Mary. He was the only apostle at the crucifixion.

John understood Jesus on a different level from the other apostles. He is the one who understood the deity of Jesus and its implications better than any of his contemporaries. He understood the universal nature of Jesus' claims, powers, and teaching. "In the beginning was the Word..." "God is love..." John's writings teach us of the nature of God and His Son across all barriers of time, culture, and experience. And yet he was also among the most practical of the apostles. His theology could not have been loftier, and at the same time, more down to earth.

"And now I beg you, lady, not as though I were writing you a new commandment, but the one we have had from the beginning, that we love one another. And this is love, that we follow his commandments; this is the commandment, as you have heard from the beginning, that you follow love." II John 1:4-7 From beginning to end, love shows us the way. It is the loftiest of principles, and yet the most practical advice for living for us all. To love is to obey all the commandments, not out of an obligation to earn some kind of reward, but from a sincere desire to give good things to the beloved. The commandments were never a way to *earn* love, they were always the way to *express* love. If we need a measuring stick to evaluate our choices, if we need a compass to guide us, if we need a scale upon which to judge the rightness of things, we have certainly found it in love.

This is not new. It has been the message of God from the very beginning. In every covenant, in every commandment, in every parable and story and lesson, the message has been love. From the very beginning of the book of Genesis, through the end of the book of Revelation, and on into eternity, this is not a story of law, but of love. If we understand no more theology than this, love will be a sufficient guide to lead us into obedience and freedom. To love is to know the very heart of God. That has always been the message of the whole Bible. Thank God!

# Day 360
# Revelation 1-3

nterpreting apocalyptic literature is difficult work. There are probably as many interpretations of the book of Revelation as there are people who have read it. But the first task in interpreting anything, is to read it through once in its entirety. One must first get a look at the whole forest before studying the individual trees.

That principle is indispensable in understanding the book of Revelation because the large picture is certainly clearer than the details. What the white stone means or the lampstands or the bowls, must be understood in light of the general message; that God is in control of history and intends to write the final page, before closing the book on salvation history and moving on to what is next.

There are some other "large" concepts that can be seen clearly. In these first chapters, Jesus addressed the seven churches. These seven churches represented the church throughout the world, and he had praise and critique for each. Many have found that whole idea frightening, but it is the same message we have seen throughout the Scriptures - God's grace does not negate His justice or judgement.

The Church, like ancient Israel is predisposed to a mistaken idea that there is special status in grace that allows any action. But Christian liberty is not license. For a church to act that way is to invite, and receive, judgement. The law of love requires no less.

Unfortunately, some people fail to understand that these judgements were applied to the corporate church - the people as a community, not as individuals. Judgement for individuals comes after death. Judgements on nations, and churches, as collective groups, has always come in this life. We need not fear that Jesus will "spew" us out of his mouth. However, the nation, or church, of which we are a part, may very well come to an end, and some should. Salvation is not for groups, but for individuals. We will outlive the civilizations of which we have been a part.

There will be an accounting for what has been done in human history; that is the message of Revelation. One day this will all end, and God will do something new with us; not our nations or even our churches, but us. That is good news indeed!

# Day 361
# Revelation 4-7

The beautiful world which God created has become badly corrupted. That has been true from early on in human history. The first sin was rejecting God and choosing to write our own rules. The second sin was murdering a brother out of jealousy. Sin developed rapidly. If the world is more sinful now, it is in part because there are more people alive now than ever before. We have not invented new levels of infamy, there are just more of us doing it.

Still, to say that it is not worse to have millions of murders rather than one is to have no sense of justice at all. Each sin adds to the total evil, not just arithmetically, but by some greater factor. It is not just the sins of murder or rape or torture, but the sins of the heart; jealousy, hatred, lust, pride, that add to the accumulated total. And who are we to judge those who have committed these offenses, when we are guilty of them ourselves, in our hearts if not in our actions? Let him who is without sin, cast the first stone.

Who then is worthy to open the seal of judgement against the sins of the world? "Worthy art thou to take the scroll and to open its seals, for thou wast slain and by thy blood didst ransom men for God from every tribe and tongue and people and nation..." 5:9 Jesus, the sinless man, the sacrificial lamb who was slain for the sins of the world, he alone is worthy to open the seal of judgement. He faced the temptations but did not give in to them; he knew the hatred of others, but loved them still; he was lied about, betrayed, and executed unjustly. He can judge us, because he has walked in our shoes.

It is interesting that John cried when he thought there was no one to open the seal of judgement. If forgiveness is so desireable, why not want it to continue forever? The answer is in the weight of that accumulated sin. Anyone who has seen sin close up, knows that it should stop. The hatred, the killing, the disease, the dying, the torture, should not be allowed to go on forever. The day that death, disease, and destruction is ended on every level, will be a good day indeed. There must come a day when the purveyors of pain and hate are no longer permitted to inflict suffering on others, or else Hell will have vetoed Heaven. Having known the pain and the persecution, it is understandable why John looked forward to the day when God will say, "Enough!" We should, too.

# Day 362
# Revelation 8-11

There is an old joke, with many versions, about a messenger coming to the chief religious official of a church announcing both good news and bad news. The good news is that Jesus has returned. The bad news is that he called from _____; and you fill in whatever place represents the headquarters of some enemy. How will Jesus return, and what will it all be like?

The descriptions in Revelation are certainly specific and graphic. They invite interpretation in the most literal of terms. That is perhaps why so many people have, throughout the centuries, tried to identify the people and events which will mark the end times. The attempts have been so numerous, and all wrong up to this point, that the idea itself has become discredited in some circles. There is a story about a college professor who wanted to drive home this point and asked his students to read the book of Revelation and write their own scenario of how things would all turn out, to show just how arbitrary these interpretations can be. One student is supposed to have raised his hand and asked whether they got extra credit if they turned out to be right!

While it may be impossible to know with much certainty, exactly how things will all unfold in the end, we should not miss the point that God works in human history quite physically and openly. There was nothing subtle or overly spiritual about the ten plagues on Egypt, the parting of the Red Sea, the destruction of Jericho, or the birth of Jesus. The idea that God would become flesh, as a small child no less, was so disgustingly common and "down to earth" that many of the intellectual elite did, and still do, reject it. But God does not deal with us in mere abstracts. Our physical existence is just as real as our spiritual existence, and there is no reason, from the Scriptures, to believe that God is going to suddenly stop meeting us on the grounds of our existence - both physical and spiritual. When we read that He will one day bring about an end to this world and make a new one, we should be confident that it will not be merely in concept, but in fact.

What exactly that will look like is not clear - at least to me. But that those present will be able to look and see it with their eyes, I have little doubt. But I won't mind at all if I am not one of them!

# Day 363
# Revelation 12-14

"This calls for wisdom: let him who has understanding reckon the number of the beast, for it is a human number, its number is six hundred and sixty-six." 13:18 This verse has touched of a veritable phobia for the poor number between six hundred and sixty-five and six hundred and sixty-seven! Just what does it mean?

The meaning of the number is not made clear; John only says that it calls for wisdom and understanding. The Greeks and Hebrews did not have separate number symbols, but instead, assigned numerical values to some of their letters. As with old phone numbers, many words could be constructed, or inferred, from the same number, and likewise, several numbers could be made out of words.

Many theories have been suggested as to the name represented by the number 666. One of the most interesting that comes from John's time, involved taking the name Neron Caesar (the Caesar Nero) and transliterating the Greek letters into Hebrew. The Hebrew letters then, when added together, result in 666. Considering the persecution of Christians under Nero, and his claim to be a living deity (before he was killed), he looks like a good candidate to represent the forces of evil. However, it should also be noted that using similarly carefully selected numerical assignments, the names of Hitler, the Pope, and Ronald Reagan have been calculated to total 666. Given enough time, I'm sure yours and mine could be made to do the same.

Perhaps the best method for understanding all of this is to focus on what was symbolized rather than the symbol itself. Evil is not a force, but a character trait, which means that there is always an embodiment of evil. Given the blatant character of that kind of evil, the open persecution, the cruelty, the violence, it hardly seems necessary for us to know the person's "number" in order to identify them. If we find ourselves unable to differentiate between the character of our leaders other than to add up the number equivalents of their names, we will already be beyond hope. John could not have written accusing Nero of being a beast, but no one who lived then had any question that he had been. We too have reason to fear someone like a Nero, but we can recognize them by their actions, not their number!

# Day 364
# Revelation 15-19

nother bad day for planet earth! After seven seals and seven trumpets it hardly seems like there would be anything left for the seven bowls to destroy! It seems unfair that the good earth should suffer for the sins of mankind, but the descriptions suggest a thoroughly devastated planet.

Yet we betray our egocentric attitude when we are surprised that the earth will share in judgement. The trees and the rivers and the birds and the fish are all innocent victims, but they cannot escape their connection with people any more than we can escape our connection with them. All creation was intended to fit together like the interlocking pieces of a vast puzzle. When disaster happens to even one part, it has effected the whole, and will eventually be felt by every other part.

Still as bad as things will get, God promised Noah that He would never again destroy all life on the planet. He has a different end in mind and a purpose to be served before He brings all these things to an end. The same methodical God who did not stop this human experiment in the Garden, intends to see it through to the end and nothing will stay that purpose.

Why all the concern for the destruction and humiliation of "Babylon"? That is certainly hard to say, but the answer would seem to lie again in that propensity of God to take human history seriously. Much less a talker than a doer, God has consistently *shown* his grace and justice. The actions, whether keeping His promise to a hundred-year-old Abraham, or delivering His people out of Egypt, or sending His son to die, or raising him from the dead, have all been the last word to those who witnessed them. No more room for debate; watch and know the will of God.

"If Jesus is alive, why doesn't he show himself?" He will, and when he does the politics and the posturing will be over. The arrogance of "Babylon," the pride that thought it could live by its own rules as if there were no God, will be utterly shattered.

History has always been His Story and He will act it out. We only play parts in the drama; His is the starring role. But we must not forget that the plot of this story is about the main character's love for all the other members of the cast. And in the end, love, not hate, will be victorious. Praise God!

# Day 365
# Revelation 20-22

What more is there to say to this hope? What better end to salvation history? What was divided at the fall, has been restored at the end. Heaven and earth were torn apart in the Garden, they will come together again in the Heavenly City. God once walked with His people and spoke to them face to face in Eden; He will again in the new Jerusalem. There will be no temple, for the Lord will be with us. Death, disease, hatred, will be no more.

The sequence of events leading up to this great new day have always caused debate. Personally, it seems to me to fit into the character of the rest of salvation history that Jesus would return and reign for a thousand years, just to prove that it always could have been done correctly. Not cheating in business or family, not polluting the environment or mistreating our bodies, not greedily hoarding riches or committing violent crimes, was always a possibility, even in this life. The problem of this world has always been one of the heart. It seems to me, quite in keeping with God's character to want to prove that historically, before moving on to what is next.

Some have a very difficult time with the idea of judgement and the pit. But evil is never separate from the being which possesses it; it is a character trait, not a force. Some diseases can only be surgically removed. Whoever will not let go of sin, will be removed before the new creation, so that it can have a clean start. In the end we will get our heart's desire.

But, as someone said, "I am on the welcoming committee, not the planning committee." Whatever the sequence of events, the culmination of salvation history is the end of these sufferings and a new beginning - new bodies, a new heaven, a new earth, and as Paul said, to "... understand fully, even as I have been fully understood." I Corinthians 13:12

I once feared that an eternity of "goodness" would be boring. I now know that there could never be too much time to enjoy the smiles on friends faces or the thrill of making beautiful music or any of the thousand other things that make life a joy. I am already making plans for what I want to accomplish for my first millennium - perfecting skiing is an early favorite. And maybe, by then, I'll even be ready to write another book!